THE CLASSICS
OF WESTERN
SPIRITUALITY

THE CLASSICS OF WESTERN SPIRITUALITY
A Library of the Great Spiritual Masters

President and Publisher
Kevin A. Lynch, C.S.P.

EDITORIAL BOARD

SYMEON THE NEW THEOLOGIAN
THE DISCOURSES

TRANSLATION
BY
C.J. deCATANZARO

INTRODUCTION
BY
GEORGE MALONEY S.J.

PREFACE
BY
BASILE KRIVOCHEINE

PAULIST PRESS
NEW YORK • RAMSEY • TORONTO

Cover Art
A graduate of The Pennsylvania Academy of the Fine Arts in Philadelphia, cover artist ANDRIJ MADAY has won numerous awards for his graphic designs and prints. He has exhibited his paintings and woodcuts in approximately eighty shows in the United States and has permanent collections at universities in Italy, Canada, and the United States. Mr. Maday's art, based on simple rectangular and circular designs, is inspired by ancient Ukranian icons and conveys Mr. Maday's own deep mystical experience and rich Ukranian Eastern Orthodox heritage.

Design: Barbini, Pesce & Noble, Inc.

Library of Congress
Catalog Card Number: 80-82414

ISBN: 0-8091-0292-7 (cloth)
0-8091-2230-8 (paper)

Published by Paulist Press
Editorial office: 1865 Broadway, New York, N.Y. 10023
Business office: 545 Island Road, Ramsey, N.J. 07446

Printed and bound in the
United States of America

CONTENTS

Author of the Preface

ARCHBISHOP BASILE KRIVOCHÉINE was born in St. Petersburg on July 30, 1900. His father, Alexandre Krivochéine, was minister in the imperial government and, after the Revolution, Prime Minister to General Wrangel (1920). The future archbishop terminated his middle studies in his hometown and entered the historical faculty at the University of Petrograd, but his studies were interrupted by revolutionary events. In 1919 he joined up as a volunteer in the white armies, and in 1920, after the defeat, he left Russia on an English vessel. After a brief stay in Egypt and Constantinople, he settled in Paris where he studied at the Sorbonne and received the degree of *licence es lettres* (equivalent of the Master of Arts). For a time he studied philosophy at the University of Munich. In 1925 he left for Mount Athos and became a monk in the Russian monastery of St. Panteleimon, where he stayed for twenty-two years. He served as the secretary of his monastery and as its representative in the monastic government of the Holy Mountain. In 1936 he published in the review *Seminarium Kondakovianum* (Prague), a study on the ascetical and dogmatic theology of St. Gregory Palamas (translated into English and German).

In 1951 he moved to Oxford, England where he became a priest at St. Nicholas Orthodox parish and also collaborated with Professor G. W. H. Lampe on the edition of *A Patristic Greek Lexicon.* He has published in *Sources chrétiennes* a three-volume critical edition of *The Catechetical Discourses* of Symeon, the New Theologian (including unpublished Greek text, with introduction and notes, 1963–1965).

In 1959 Basile Krivochéine was consecrated Auxiliary Bishop of the Exarchate of the Moscow Patriarchate in Western Europe, and in 1960 became Archbishop and was appointed to Brussels where he now resides as Archbishop of the Russian Orthodox Church in Belgium (Moscow Patriarchate). A book entitled *St. Symeon, the New Theologian: Life, Spirituality, Doctrine* will soon appear, a result of his studies (published in French by the Editions de Chevetogne, in Russian by YMCA Press). For his edition of the *Catecheses,* Archbishop Basile received the degree of Doctor of Theology from the Academy of Leningrad (1964).

Author of the Introduction

REV. GEORGE A. MALONEY, S.J., was ordained in Rome as a priest of the Russian Byzantine Rite, April 18, 1957. He earned a doctorate in Oriental Theology June 21, 1962, summa cum laude from the Pontifical Oriental Institute.

In 1965, he launched an ecumenical journal, *Diakonia*, to promote dialogue between Orthodox Christians and Roman Catholics. He served as editor of all the Eastern Rite articles for the *New Catholic Encyclopedia*.

He is fluent in several languages, including Russian and Greek. He has made extensive travels in Russia, Greece, Egypt, Lebanon, Jordan, Israel, and Turkey in an attempt to meet the Eastern Christian groups and to understand their religious background, especially spending two summers on Mt. Athos.

Fr. Maloney is the founder and director of the John XXIII Institute for Eastern Christian Studies at Fordham University. He teaches Oriental theology and spirituality on the master and doctoral levels.

Fr. Maloney has established himself as an outstanding author on works on prayer and Eastern Christian Spirituality as applied to the daily life of Western Christians. Some of his books include *The Cosmic Christ; Inward Stillness; Bright Darkness; Listen, Prophets; Nesting In The Rock; Jesus, Set Me Free!; Theology Of Uncreated Energies;* and *Inscape—God At The Heart Of Matter.*

The Translator of the Volume

REV. C. J. DE CATANZARO was born in 1916 in New York. After an early education in Copenhagen, Denmark, he came to Canada in 1930 and subsequently took his degree in classics at King's College and Dalhousie University Halifax, N.S. in 1937, completing there a master's degree in Greek in 1938. After a year at Keble College, Oxford, he completed theology at Trinity College, Toronto, in 1941. With five years of parish work completed, he returned to the faculty of divinity at Trinity College and obtained his Ph.D. in Semitics from the University of Toronto in 1957. After occupying the chair of Old Testament for six years at Seabury-Western Theological Seminary, Evanston, he returned to Canada in 1965 and to parish work. Following the Church Congress at St. Louis, Missouri, in 1977 he joined the Anglican Catholic Church and is now bishop-elect of the Canadian diocese.

His other writings include translations of Richard of St. Victor's *De Sacramentis* for the Library of Christian Classics and *The Gospel according to Philip* (1962), and he was a participant in the project of translating the Nag Hammadi coptic texts. He also translated *The Life in Christ* by Nicholas Cabasilas (1974).

PREFACE

The Catechetical Discourses of Symeon, the New Theologian, published for the first time in English by Paulist Press, constitute only a part of the total literary work of this saint; they give us a lively and impressive picture of his personality as a monastic head and spiritual director, as well as of his doctrine in general. As sermons directed by the young superior Symeon to the monks of St. Mamas, the cenobite monastery of Constantinople, their content and spirituality are conditioned naturally by the monastic milieu to which they were destined, but this only enhances their interest for us by giving them their concrete character. One finds therein fewer abstract theological arguments, less theoretical spirituality, less complex biblical typology than in the *Theological and Ethical Discourses*, which, although directed to a wider and perhaps more learned public, yield to the *Catecheses* in freshness and literary spontaneity. One finds there, in comparison, fewer sublime mystical visions, fewer unheard-of confessions of the divine revelations about which Symeon speaks with such strength and with so many details in his *Hymns*. But the foundation of Symeon's spirituality remains the same in all his writings: mysticism of light, conscious experience of the Spirit and of the vision of God during this very life, Christ as the center of all. This mysticism of experience is also considered to be the necessary sign of an authentic Christian life.

Symeon's *Catecheses* are, in great part, the product of the first period of his life and are characterized by a youthful vivacity and simplicity not always present in his *Theological and Ethical Discourses* or in his *Hymns*. However, all these ecstatic effusions and confessions in the *Catecheses* generally bear the character of

witness before his monastic brothers to the love of God for man
and are spoken to urge them to follow the narrow way that leads
to conscious union with Christ. They are also appropriate to a
community setting of liturgical life with an emphasis on penitence, obedience, humility, and ascesis as the only means to attain high spiritual states. Symeon is careful never to separate
these virtues from the contemplation and vision of God which
gives them their meaning. The love of Christ and its experience
here on earth remain in the *Catecheses*, as in Symeon's other writings, the essence of the Christian life, even when he speaks in
detail of the daily life of the monastery. It is this spiritual witness, simple, realistic, and at the same time so authentic and pa-
thos-filled, that Symeon gives us in his *Catecheses*. Symeon also
gives us his assurance that everyone is called to participate in
and can attain life with Christ through the narrow way of the
Lord's commandments and participation in His sufferings. Symeon's witness is of particular importance in our time, a time so
poor in spiritual experience and so deprived of authenticity that
it has forgotten the goal of the Christian life.

It is important to note that this spirituality, which may
seem strange in its boldness and its confidence in man, is
integrated within the framework of a strictly orthodox faith and
of a patristic and conciliar theology, always richly nourished by
Holy Scripture, St. John the Theologian, the Apostle Paul, and
in particular the Psalms. It is a spirituality essentially monastic
and traditional, but at the same time it is creative and always set
forth with an inimitable personal stamp. It is, no doubt, in this
sense that Symeon was called the New Theologian, a baffling
appellation in the Byzantine world.

As well as being spiritually alive, the *Catecheses* are psycho-
logically perceptive in their observations of Byzantium's monastic life with all its routine, exterior ascesis, laxness and intrigues,
as well as with its positive traits. A unique literary beauty also
characterizes the work; for example, young Symeon's sermon on
charity as the only way to the kingdom of heaven is filled with
enthusiastic inspiration and bold metaphors. Symeon's tales of
his first visions of light are written with an immediacy and
freshness scarcely equalled in early Christian literature. The story of the aching penitence of the sinner, suddenly transformed
by divine mercy into a state of ecstatic joy, is characteristic of

PREFACE

Symeon's spirituality. He always insists on God's mercy and assures us that God answers quickly the call of the person in distress, if only one cries to God without hesitation and in all the confidence of one's heart.

Symeon's *Catecheses* keep their attraction and importance for the modern reader, for they tell in a lively and simple manner the mystical experiences of Symeon the superior in the midst of his monastery. They can, by their striking authenticity, stimulate the efforts of those who now seek spiritual renewal, putting them at the same time on their guard against the all-too-easy ways of a mysticism without ascesis and not founded on the faith of the Church.

FOREWORD

The Discourses of S. Symeon the New Theologian comprise "Catecheses" or addresses on spiritual topics delivered by the great tenth century abbot of S. Mamas in Constantinople on various occasions to his monks and others interested in the spiritual life. They are marked by the saint's burning conviction that the Christian life must be more than a routine observance of a rule, however strict that rule and exact its observance. To be at all meaningful there must be the personal experience of the presence and the power of the living Christ. To reinforce his argument Symeon is not afraid to use his own personal experience of conversion and illumination.

In his own day his challenge to religious conventionality and formalism raised a storm of controversy. This did not prevent the Orthodox Church from canonizing him and applying to him the title "the New Theologian," thus assigning to him a position of special pre-eminence together with S. John the Divine (the Theologian) and S. Gregory of Nazianzus, the great fourth century patriarch of Constantinople, also surnamed "the Theologian."

It is only within recent years that an unabridged printed text of his works has become available. This is the first English translation of any of his prose works, apart from excerpts.

INTRODUCTION

The times in which Saint Symeon the New Theologian lived (949–1022) are in some respects similar to our own present religious situation. In the West, Saint Bernard (1091–1153) was strenuously fighting Peter Abelard and the other nominalist philosophers who sought to separate mystical theology from positive or speculative theology. Abelard was victorious and theology, the "queen of all sciences," became *scholasticism* in the West.

Saint Symeon saw a similar thing happening within the Byzantine Christian world. Earlier thinkers, such as Photius, Michael Psellos, and John Italos, used Aristotelean categories to give more autonomy to reason in order to articulate in rational terms the mysteries of revelation. A Byzantine scholasticism was taking over and theology was being divorced from authentic religious experience or mysticism.

After the monastic reform by Saint Theodore Studite in the ninth century, the monastic Office was imposed on the parishes. Christian worship and prayer had become formalized and so complex that the individual Byzantine Christian found it difficult to meet the living God of Abraham, Isaac, and Jacob. Symeon felt a special vocation to call, not only monks, but also laity in the Byzantine world back to a living experience of God. He called himself the "enthusiatic zealot" who burned with a holy zeal to call Christians back to an authentic mysticism, which he considered available to all baptized Christians.

Concretely, the battle of two opposing views of theology centered around Saint Symeon and his mystical, apophatic approach of the experiencing of God immanently present to the individual as opposed to the "head-trip" scholastic theology as

1

INTRODUCTION

represented by Archbishop Stephen of Nicomedia, the official theologian at the court of Constantinople. Stephen represented the abstract, philosophical type of theologizing while Symeon strove to restore theology to its pristine mystical tendency as a wisdom infused by the Holy Spirit into the Christian after he had been thoroughly purified through a rigorous asceticism and a state of constant repentance.

The main writings that we have of Symeon were directed more particularly to monks. Monasticism had become ossified, not only in its extrinsic and impersonalized formalism, but also in its worldly sycophancy toward the emperor. The Byzantine emperor had favored monasticism and used it as a means to maintain a unity within his empire between the civil administration and the masses of Christians. Monks had acquired through such favor vast holdings in property, libraries, and art objects. This caused most monks living within an urban setting, as Symeon would live most of his monastic life, to lose much of their spirit of poverty and detachment, to say nothing of their interest in deeper prayer.

Symeon, therefore, zealously wanted to bring back monasticism to a radical living of the Gospel as the perfect form of Christianity and to call monks back to their prophetic, charismatic role within the Church. Prayer in most monasteries had become a liturgical spectacle with very exacting rules for the performers. Symeon would rail against such religious "magic" and idolatry by calling monks back to a state of constant brokenness, austere asceticism, purity of heart, and constant prayer.

A SPECIAL CALLING

Apparently Symeon's own monks as well as Stephen and others, who bristled under the fiery attacks of Symeon against the tepidity of the times, protested Symeon's right to set himself up as one-man crusader for reform. Especially did they resent his appeal to his own personal, mystical experiences as a norm for all true Christians. This is clear from the many times in Symeon's writings that he seeks to offer a justification for his approach since he represents the first Byzantine mystic who speaks so freely about his own mystical experiences. He shared them precisely because he felt that God was asking him to do so.

INTRODUCTION

... why are you suspicious of the instructions that we have so often given you in different words? What judgment have you passed within yourselves against him who has so frankly spoken such things? Have you suspected us of saying something that is beyond the Scriptures? Have you secretly found fault with us and accused us of speaking with presumption? Have you condemned us for being boastful? If this is your attitude toward what I have spoken, may Christ pardon you! As for me, I entreat your charity that no one persist in this judgment. We have not written these things for the sake of exhibitionism—may God who has had mercy on us and led us this far not allow it! We have written them because we are mindful of God's gifts, which He has bestowed on our unworthy self from the beginning of life until the present moment ... and in gratitude we show to all of you the talent He has entrusted to us. How can we be silent before such an abundance of blessings, or out of ingratitude bury the talent that has been given to us (Mt. 25:18), like ungrateful and evil servants? ... By our oral teaching we encourage you too to strive that you may have part in His gifts and enjoy them, the gifts of which we, though unworthy, have been partakers through His unutterable goodness.[1]

Symeon calls himself a poor man who loves his brothers. He has asked an alms from a wealthy person and now runs to his brothers and tells them that they too can go to the same person and receive a similar alms.[2] He insists that he is not boasting but humbly wishes to share what the Lord has done in life that they too may have a similar share. "Brethren, my boasting, as some regard it, consists in this, that the love of God moves me (2 Co. 5:14) to reveal to you, my fathers and brethren, God's ineffable goodness and love toward us."[3] Basically his argument is

---

1. Discourse XXXIV, 7–33. I shall avail myself of this present translation whenever I cite from Symeon's *Discourses*.
2. Ibid., 37–67.
3. Ibid., 98–101.

that they err who insist that no one living at that time can truly experience God mystically, directly, and intensely, habitually living in the consciousness of God's immanent indwelling, since he himself has reached this. And this should not be an exceptional case but Holy Scripture and early Fathers constantly exhort Christians to obtain such a treasure. This, for Symeon, is the end of the Christian life, an obligation on all who call themselves Christians.

AN ORIGINAL SYNTHESIS

Symeon's ultimate witness to his "orthodox" teaching is not merely his own experience but that he presents to his monks a view of Christianity that he is persuaded is completely rooted in Holy Scripture and the tradition of the best of the Greek Fathers, the true "theologians," who theologized out of their living experience of what is given in Scripture, namely, a consciousness of the indwelling Trinity. Symeon, therefore, wants to be faithful to the Gospel message (and we are overwhelmed by his knowledge and frequent citations of Scripture) and to the leading spiritual Fathers of Byzantine spirituality. The result is a synthesis that is fresh and new in the annals of Byzantine mysticism and yet is very solidly rooted in the best of the scriptural and patristic traditions.

Symeon very successfully brings together the two main lines of authentic Byzantine spirituality: that of the intellectualism of the school of the Alexandrians, represented by Clement of Alexandria, Origen, Evagrius and the Cappadocian Fathers, Basil, Gregory of Nazianzus, and Gregory of Nyssa; and that of the "affective" school of the heart, represented by the writings of Pseudo-Macarius, Mark the Hermit, Diadochus of Photike, John Climacus, Nilus, Hesychius, and Philotheus.

It is because Symeon was so rooted in the tradition of the great mystical theologians of the East, the true theologians who were taught by God ("theodidact") through prayerful experience, that down through the centuries he has been called "the New Theologian." Some authors claim that he is called "new" to distinguish him from the other two eminent theologians, Saint John the Evangelist and Saint Gregory of Nazianzus, both of whom discoursed so eloquently about true theology in the

Eastern Christian sense, that is, about the experience of the indwelling Trinity.[4] Other authors do not stress the *theologian* as much as the *new* to distinguish him from his spiritual director, Symeon the Studite. However posterity bequeathed to Symeon his title as the new theologian, we can trust that his readers who came after him believed that he exemplified the best in true Eastern Christian theology, which could never be separated from an infused mystical knowledge about the mystery of God in His loving condescension to share His trinitarian life with human beings.

HIS LIFE

If we are to understand this volume of Symeon's writings, his *Discourses*, we must know something about his life, since he wrote out of his life situation as abbot and spiritual director of monks and the laity that visited him. His writings grew out of his preaching and giving spiritual direction to those under his charge. Therefore, if we are to understand, especially his discourses, we must know the setting in which they were written. Also, as Symeon is a writer sharing his intimate experiences in prayer, we must see how those experiences developed to shape his personality and his thinking.

We gain much information about Symeon's life from his very own writings, especially concerning his mystical experiences. The other main source of information about his life can be drawn from the *Life* of Symeon that one of his disciples, Nicetas Stethatos, wrote after Symeon's death. Drawing from Nicetas's *Life*, one must be cautious since he follows the usual hagiographical style of placing his hero into a conventional pattern of approved sanctity. This not only renders Symeon a bit artificial and unreal but it also serves to highlight his subject in a polemical attack against Symeon's enemies, especially Stephen of Nicomedia. We must, therefore, go to Symeon's writings to seek a corrective of what Nicetas offers us as biographical data.

Symeon was born in Galatia in Paphlagonia (Asia Minor) in

---

4. On this point of Symeon's title as theologian, cf. I. Hausherr, S.J., "La Methode d'Oraison Heyschaste," in *Orientalia Christiana*, vol. 9–2, no. 36 (Rome, 1927), p. 102.

INTRODUCTION

949. His parents, Basil and Theophana, belonged to the Byzantine provincial nobility that sided with the Macedonian Dynasty, which had given the Byzantine Empire one of its greatest periods of peace and expanding prosperity.[5] Apparently, Symeon received only the basics of a primary Greek school education until he was about eleven years old. His uncle Basil saw in him one, in the words of Nicetas, "distinguished by a beauty and elegance not common."[6]

The uncle wished to present him to the court of the two brother emperors, Basil and Constantine Porphyrogenetes. It is in this court that Symeon finished his secondary education but refused to continue to pursue higher studies. The reason lies in his meeting at the age of fourteen the holy monk of the famous monastery of Constantinople, the Stoudion, Symeon the Studite. This Symeon became the spiritual father of Symeon the younger and led his disciple into the ascetical and prayer life. Although Symeon wanted to enter the Stoudion even at the early age of fourteen, his spiritual father had him wait until he reached twenty-seven years of age. During this time of preparation Saint Symeon occupied himself with management of the household of a patrician and possibly even entered the service of his emperor as a diplomat and a senator. At any rate Symeon strove to combine a busy life in the world with living an interior life of a monk in the evenings, which were spent in night vigils, living out what he had read in the spiritual writings of Mark the Hermit and Diadochus of Photike, the two preferred authors given him to read by his spiritual father.[7]

Symeon in his discourses describes himself in the third person as "George." He describes himself as a man of twenty, "handsome in appearance and who possessed a showy exterior, manners, and gait, so that some people even had bad suspicions

5. Cf. J. M. Hussey, *Church and Learning in the Byzantine Empire* (867–1185) (Oxford, 1937), pp. 22–36.

6. The citations from the *Life* by Nicetas Stethatos are taken from the translation by I. Hausherr, S.J., *Un grand mystique Byzantine, Vie de Symeon le Nouveau Theologien* par Nicetas Stethatos, in *Orientalia Christiana*, vol. 12, no. 45 (Rome, 1928), hereafter cited as *Vie*. This citation is on p. 4.

7. *Vie*, p. 6; Discourse XXII, 35.

on his account."[8] He shares with his listeners how each evening he prostrated himself in prayer, pouring out tears abundantly as he begged God to have mercy on him and grant sight to the eyes of his soul.[9] It was at this time that Symeon received his first vision of God as light, a grace that he attributed to the prayers of his spriritual father, Symeon the Studite.

> One day, as he stood and recited, "God, have mercy upon me, a sinner" (Lk. 18:13), uttering it with his mind rather than his mouth, suddenly a flood of divine radiance appeared from above and filled all the room. As this happened the young man lost all awareness of his surroundings and forgot that he was in a house or that he was under a roof. He saw nothing but light all around him and did not know whether he was standing on the ground. . . . Instead, he was wholly in the presence of immaterial light and seemed to himself to have turned into light. Oblivious of all the world he was filled with tears and with ineffable joy and gladness. His mind then ascended to heaven and behold yet another light, which was clearer than that which was close at hand. In a wonderful manner there appeared to him, standing close to that light, the saint of whom we have spoken, the old man equal to angels who had given him the commandment and the book (Symeon the Studite).[10]

In spite of the great mystical graces that Symeon was receiving at this period of his life, he complains that he was not living a moral life in keeping with such graces. Still, even though he fell back to his wordly ways, he continued to visit his spiritual father. Through his prayers Symeon received the grace of another overwhelming conversion and entered the Monastery of Stoudion at the age of twenty-seven.

---

8. Discourse XXII, 22–27.
9. Ibid., 74–81.
10. Ibid., 89–105.

INTRODUCTION

ABBOT OF MAMAS

Symeon put himself completely under the spiritual guidance of his mentor, Symeon the Studite, a simple lay monk and not an ordained priest. In Symeon's *Hymn 4*, he exhorts other monks to a total obedience to each one's spiritual father:

Listen only to the advice of your spiritual father,
answer him with humility
and, as to God, tell Him your thoughts,
even to a simple temptation, without hiding anything,
do nothing without his advice.[11]

It is easy to imagine that Symeon strove to lead such a life at the Stoudion. Such a zealot within their midst did not sit too well with the abbot and the other monks, as Nicetas reports.[12] The Abbot Peter insisted that Symeon leave the community after only a few months there. His spiritual father led him to the neighboring monastery of Saint Mamas, which was falling apart through both physical and spiritual decadence. Even though Symeon the Studite remained in the Stoudion, Symeon the younger advanced rapidly in the monastic life at Saint Mamas under his tutelage. Within three years of his entrance, Symeon was tonsured a monk, ordained a priest, and elected abbot over the monks of Saint Mamas. He was thirty-one years of age and was faced with a monastery that Nicetas describes as a refuge of worldly monks, a cemetery for a great number of dead. Here Symeon would spend twenty-five years laboring as abbot to make Saint Mamas an outstanding monastery modeled on the teachings of the early Fathers and the commandments of Jesus Christ given in the Gospel. He acquired a reputation in Constantinople for his sanctity and learning that drew to him other monks and influential members of the clergy as well as members of the nobility.

Symeon's life as abbot and reformer was not spared the cross. As the reader of these discourses will note from the con-

---

11. St. Symeon. *Hymns of Divine Love*, tr. George A. Maloney, S.J. (Denville, N.J.: Dimension Books, 1975), p. 22. Hereafter cited as H.
12. *Vie*, pp. 24–26.

tent, Symeon never ceased to exhort his monks to the highest degree of sanctity and contemplation. Over half of these exhortations to his fellow monks touch on repentance and conversion of heart. He exhorts them to a constant spirit of interior weeping for sins and a Baptism in the Holy Spirit shown by the gift of tears. Not only is Symeon's doctrine the solid, unanimous teaching of the Fathers of the desert, but he goes a step farther and uses his own personal mystical experiences as the sign that the Holy Spirit is speaking through him to his monks. Before such an assured and strong personality who made demands on his monks, the same that he made on himself, the account given by Nicetas of a rebellion of a group of over thirty monks seems completely plausible.

One morning during matins when Symeon usually preached his discourses to his monks, this group rose up against him "like enraged dogs"[13] and tried to lay hands on their abbot. Nicetas describes the scene in a parallel to that of Christ in the Garden of Olives: "But they were impeded by a force from on high from putting their criminal hands on him. The grace that indwelled in Symeon held them at a distance and repelled them."[14] The monks ran out of the church, breaking the glass windows as they headed for the palace of the Patriarch Sisinnios. The patriarch sided with Symeon and the rebels were sent into exile.

Besides such opposition from within his own household, Symeon had much to bear from the attacks of Archbishop Stephen, who was the chief theologian at the emperor's court. No doubt there was much jealousy on the part of Stephen toward the successful preacher and spiritual director of so many illustrious people of Constantinople. But the main source of Stephen's attacks against Symeon lay in two areas: Stephen found fault with the charismatic approach of Symeon that at times seemed to denigrate hierarchical authority in favor of a mystic's feeling that he was in grace and empowered by God directly with authority to preach and absolve sins, even without ordination to the priesthood; and Stephen approached theology in a speculative manner rather than the mystical approach of Symeon. Thus

13. *Vie*, p. 52.
14. Ibid.

INTRODUCTION

Stephen challenged the learning of Symeon to a formal disputa-
tion in the patriarch's palace concerning the distinction between the Father and the Son in the Trinity. *Hymn 21* was
composed by Symeon as his answer to Stephen[15] and gives us
the main reason behind the forced exile of Symeon in 1009.

IN EXILE

We can legitimately suspect that the main reason Stephen
obtained the condemnation of Symeon into exile concerned Stephen's fear that Symeon and his followers were introducing
into Byzantine Christianity a new form of "enthusiasm." Such a
charismatic approach stressed the necessity of consciousness of
grace. Stephen feared that Symeon, was denying the authority
and jurisdiction of the official hierarchy. Several of Symeon's
statements do seem exaggerated and skirt very close to heresy or
at least very dangerous doctrine. Because Symeon is writing for
a specialized audience of monks who should be leading a special
type of contemplative life, his writings reveal a wide spectrum
of emphasis and often apparent contradictions. He often is at-
tempting to share his most intimate, mystical experiences of the
Trinity with his fellow monks. His theology is a mysticism as an
experience of the mystery of God that employs the dogmas defined by the Church but goes far beyond them in his experiential kowledge of God.

Basically the theology of Symeon cannot be faulted as even
approaching any erroneous or heretical teaching. He is solidly
rooted in Holy Scripture and the teachings of the first seven ecumenical councils, which defined the basic truths that Symeon
constantly is preaching, namely, the two distinct but not separated natures of Jesus Christ, the divinity of the Holy Spirit, the
triune God and the indwelling of that same Trinity within the
heart of the purified Christian. Over and over we find the basic
themes of the great Fathers of the early Church stressed and correctly presented by Symeon, such as the Trinity, the *homoousion*
(of the same nature as the Father) of Jesus, man's divinization by
grace (*theosis*), and the importance of the sacraments, especially
Baptism, Eucharist, and Penance.

---

15. H. 21, pp. 95–106.

But his mystical theology goes far beyond anything that *cataphatic* or positive theology could express in terms of dogmas and doctrines. He constantly falls back on the apophatic language of Saints Gregory of Nyssa and Gregory of Nazianzus. He knows human language cannot express what he has personally experienced and he knows he is not deluded. He strongly believes that the Holy Spirit wants him to speak of such to show people in his day that they too can reach such intimacy and transformation in Christ if they follow the same teachings of Holy Scripture and the Fathers as he has.

Thus the thought of Symeon cannot be put into a neat systematization. His language does at times seem fuzzy, vague, indefinite, and even skirting the edges of heresy, at least if we were to push his words to their logical conclusions. This no doubt is the area of contention that brought a sentence of exile to Symeon in 1009. His teaching about the consciousness of grace brought him into difficulty with the institutional Church of his day since he seemed to be saying much that the heretical Messalians said in their belief that unless you experienced grace within yourself, you were not in grace.

But the reader of Symeon must keep in mind the zeal of Symeon to bring his monks to a greater sensitivity to the indwelling Trinity and to bring the hierarchy and clergy to a reformation of life. With what fire Symeon attacks the priests and bishops of his time! He puts into the mouth of Christ these strong words:

> They (the bishops) unworthily handle My Body
> and seek avidly to dominate the masses . . .
> They are seen to appear as brilliant and pure,
> but their souls are worse than mud and dirt,
> worse even than any kind of deadly poison,
> these evil and perverse men![16]

But it is his doctrine of the primacy of personal experience of God over the hierarchical authority that gave Symeon his greatest difficulty with Stephen and the hierarchy of his day and brought on his exile. Symeon constantly resorts to such

---

16. H. 58, p. 288.

11

words as seeing, feeling, knowing, experiencing, to convey his idea of a growth in conscious awareness that lies beyond a mental concept and that affects the whole person.[17] Grace or the indwelling of the Trinity, for Symeon, was meant, in the teaching of Jesus Christ as recorded in the New Testament, to be directly and immediately experienced by all Christians. The important question that Symeon poses to his listeners is not whether the Holy Spirit lives within them but whether they are *consciously* aware of this presence within them through a continued penitential conversion.

Symeon's teaching about a charismatic, nonordained monk able to forgive sins brought him into a great deal of conflict with the hierarchy. But this teaching and practice were consistent with a long patristic tradition that continued in the East until the fourteenth century.[18] Symeon insists that his teaching on this subject of conferring jurisdiction to nonordained monks to hear confession is based primarily on the writings of the Holy Fathers. Jesus Christ gave this authority first to the Spirit-filled Apostles, who through consecration of other bishops passed on this same Holy Spirit as well as the authority over sin to succeeding generations. But when the bishops became sinful and ambitious, selling out to the emperor, this authority was passed on to the parish priests so that people could receive forgiveness of their sins. But when priests became worldly and sinful, the power was given to simple monks, whether priests or unordained.[19]

---

17. On this question of consciousness of grace in Symeon's writings, cf. P. Miquel, "La Conscience de la grace selon Symeon le Nouveau Theologien," in *Irenikon*, vol. XLII, no. 3 (1969), pp. 314–342.

18. On this practice cf. K. Holl, *Enthusiasmus und Bussgewalt beim Griechischen Mönchtum: Eine Studie zu Symeon dem Neuen Theologen* (Leipzig, 1898) pp. 138–233.

19. Much of this teaching is found in a writing entitled *De Confessione*, found in Migne: *PG* XCV. This letter is falsely attributed to St. John Damascene. P. Michael LeQuien, O.P., who prepared this Vol. 95 of Migne, asserts in his foreword that it could not belong to John Damascene since in many of his writings, especially against the Messalians, he clearly rejects the basic teaching given in this letter, namely, that unordained monks have power to absolve sins. From the content of this letter, the style, words used, and reference to his nonordained spiritual father, it is clear that it is a work of Symeon the New Theologian. K. Holl goes into great detail to prove this from the theology of Symeon and the content found in this letter. Cf. K. Holl: *Enthusiasmus und Bussgewalt*, esp. pp. 106–107.

INTRODUCTION

At any rate, we find Symeon in exile near Chrysopolis on the Asiatic shore of the Bosphorus in a small town called Paloukiton. There he found a small chapel in ruins, dedicated to Saint Marina. With the help of one of his disciples who was also a patrician, Symeon was able to build a small monastery around this chapel and there he lived out his life in relative solitude, surrounded by a few of his monk-disciples who followed him into exile. The Patriarch Sergios lifted the exile and even offered to Symeon the archbishopric by way of reparation but the latter refused and continued to live out his life in guiding others and in writing until he finally died in 1022.[20]

WRITINGS

Those facts constitute the main lines of Symeon's life. But his writings, due to their personal, experiential character, reveal to us much more of the person Symeon and his ideas. Other authors before him, such as Saint Augustine in the West, Pseudo-Macarius, Evagrius, Saint Gregory of Nyssa, and Saint Gregory of Nazianzus, along with the "hesychastic" Fathers, such as Mark the Hermit, Diadochus of Photike, John Climacus, Elias Ecdicos, Philotheus of Sinai, and the Syrian writers Saint Ephrem and Isaac of Nineveh, all wrote somewhat in the same style, developing similar themes, full of personal love for Jesus Christ. But Symeon's writings constitute a new genre of spiritual writing, at least among the Eastern Christian writers. No Christian writer before Symeon, not even Saint Augustine, opened his own interior experience of Jesus Christ and the indwelling Trinity to a reading audience as does Symeon. Thus his writings become a mirror of the man in a greater sense than do most spiritual writings.

If we are the recipients of the rich writings of Symeon on the spiritual life, we owe this boon to Symeon's disciple, Nicetas Stethatos. Not only was he the biographer of Symeon but he was "editor-in-chief" of his works. Symeon had published, even during his lifetime, most of his works, distributed to his disciples and friends for their spiritual edification. But as we pointed out before in regard to the burning zeal that Symeon exercised

---

20. *Vie,* pp. 130ff.

to preach his message and share his mystical gifts with others so that they too might grow in greater perfection, Symeon felt an equal call and burning impulsion that he attributes to the Holy Spirit to write and to have his writings edited by Nicetas, whom he met at Saint Marina in the last years of his life. Nicetas indicates Symeon's attitude in regard to his writings:

> While the blessed (Symeon) was still living, he was writing, even in spite of himself, night and day, the mysteries that the Divine Spirit was confiding to his intelligence. The Spirit that was stirring and leaping within him was not allowing him any repose until he had put into writing His words and interior operations. He was giving me these improvisations and I was transcribing them with the other hymns into notebooks of parchment. When I had finished copying them I would return them to him.[21]

Nicetas, therefore, met Symeon at Saint Marina and became his disciple without entering the monastic life. There he helped Symeon edit his works from rough copies before he entered the Stoudion Monastery in Constantinople. Symeon continued to send him the rough copies so that Nicetas might recopy and edit them in more fluent form on parchment. Symeon writes to Nicetas, ". . . it is the same reason why I am asking you to make these copies in the notebooks in order that you may bequeath all my writings to posterity."[22] However, Nicetas must have slackened in his dedication as editor of Symeon's works, probably leaving the monastery. After sixteen years he reentered Stoudion and while in prayer received a vision of Symeon and an outpouring of the Holy Spirit that encouraged him from that date of 1035 to finish the editing and publication of all of Symeon's writings.

THE DISCOURSES

Symeon was abbot at Saint Mamas for nearly twenty of the most productive years of his life, between the ages of thirty and

---

21. *Vie*, pp. 188–190.
22. Ibid., p. 190.

fifty (980–998). During this time he worked on his two most important works: his *Discourses* (*Cathecheses*) and many of his fifty-eight *Hymns of Divine Love*. Without a doubt his *Discourses* forms the central work of his life, for it is in these thirty-four discourses, given mainly to his monks at Saint Mamas, plus two works of thanksgiving that we find the main ideas he developed in his hymns and other writings. This work was probably edited by Symeon himself and had been read already by many in Constantinople before Symeon's exile.

These discourses, as has been already pointed out, were delivered originally as teachings and exhortations to his monks, preached to a live audience during the matins service. Hence we can expect a unique type of writing that captures somewhat the liveliness and ardent language of Symeon as he dialogues with his live audience. His language is sincere, simple, yet full of fire and persuasion. The personality of Symeon leaps forth from every line as he humbly shares his own "heart" with his monks. In no other writing of Symeon do we capture his personality as in his *Discourses*. And nowhere else does his doctrine, which is so much a part of his very own life, come through in clear lines as in this work. Later we shall present the main lines of Symeon's mystical theology, which are basically found in these discourses, but let us examine specifically the main themes treated in this work.

We see immediately on examining the content of these thirty-four discourses and the two works on thanksgiving that there is no logical sequence or order holding them together. Symeon may have delivered each day such a discourse, but what we have here is material edited from a large selection of topics chosen as instructions according to the liturgical period or feast of a given saint or whatever matter Symeon as abbot felt he ought to call to the attention of his monks.

Still we find in reading these discourses two main characteristics that keep recurring throughout the entire work. The first is the accent on the same traditional themes that the hesychastic Fathers or the mystical theologians of the Christian East wrote about. These would touch on the two areas of praxis or the ascesis necessary in order that a Christian might reach the state of true contemplation, *theoria*. The specific themes that dominate the discourses recur throughout all of Symeon's writings and these can be generally summarized as: repentance, detachment, renunciation, the works of mercy and other virtues, charity, impassibility (*apatheia*), remembrance of death, sorrow for sins (*penthos*), the practice of God's commandments, faith, and contemplation. Such themes are found in all of the classical works of Byzantine spiritual writers from Evagrius, John Climacus, Macarius, Mark the Hermit, and Diadochus directly down to Symeon, even though the latter rarely quotes directly from such writers. Symeon is sure that he is in good company, the best of the mystical theologians, who were so completely rooted in Holy Scripture.

The other main characteristic that shines forth on each page of this present work is the new and insistent accent on the operations of the Holy Spirit, who effects the end of the spiritual life and all Christian ascesis and contemplation, namely, greater mystical union with the indwelling Trinity. Symeon is one of the great charismatic figures in Christian spirituality. He felt that the Christian religion of his day had degraded into a static formalism that had stifled, for the masses of Christians, including monks, the real message of Jesus Christ and His Gospel. The two great writers who formulated the basic teaching of the Church on the Holy Spirit were Saint Athanasius and Saint Basil, both of whom had fought in their writings the heresy of the *Pneumatomachoi*, who denied the divinity of the Holy Spirit, hence denied the Holy Trinity. Other writers such as Mark the Hermit, Diadochus of Photike, Philoxenos of Mabboug, Gregory of Nazianzus, and John Damascene wrote on the Holy Spirit but only to maintain the orthodox teaching concerning demonic possession, the efficacy of Baptism, the need of the ascetical life along with prayer, and the problem of impassibility and grace against the doctrine of the heretical Messalians.[23]

But Symeon adds a great difference. He is solidly rooted in the traditional teaching of the Fathers about the Holy Spirit but he accentuates with great originality the need of a stage in the Christian life beyond the mere Baptism of water, which Symeon calls the Baptism in the Holy Spirit. This second Baptism gives

---

23. Cf. I. Hausherr, S.J., "L'erreur fondamentale et la logique du Messalianisme," in *Orientalia Christiana Periodica*, vol. 1 (Rome, 1935), pp. 328–360.

to the individual Christian, who seeks by repentance a deeper conversion to Jesus Christ, a greater conscious awareness of Jesus Christ as Lord and Savior. It is interesting to see how Symeon quotes from Holy Scripture the same texts that modern charismatic Christians use to highlight the need for the Baptism in the Holy Spirit. Symeon appeals to the example of the early Jerusalem community's sending Peter and John to Samaria to pray for those who had already been "baptized in the name of the Lord Jesus" (Acts 10:6), that they "might receive the Holy Spirit, for He had not yet descended on any of them."[24]

The great blasphemy against the Holy Spirit, as Symeon argues in Discourse XXXIII, is to deny that the Holy Spirit can be experienced today and divinize Christians as He did in the early Church. But this Baptism in the Holy Spirit is accomplished through repentance received by the penitent that cries out in sorrow to be reborn by the Spirit.

> Display a worthy penitence by means of all sorts of deeds and words, that you may draw yourselves the grace of the all-holy Spirit. For this Spirit, when He descends on you, becomes like a pool of light to you, which encompasses you completely in an unutterable manner. As it regenerates you, it changes you from corruptible to incorruptible, from mortal to immortal, from sons of men into Sons of God and gods by adoption and grace—that is, if you desire to appear as kinsmen and follow-heirs of the saints and enter with all of them into the kingdom of Heaven.[25]

In Discourse XXXIV Symeon appeals to Holy Scripture to show that the individual Christian must grow into a greater conscious awareness of grace operating within his life since the Son of God had such a conscious knowledge of the Father. A conscious union such as that Jesus had with His Father is what He wishes to bring to all who desire to receive His Holy Spirit.

---

24. From Symeon's work *The Ethical Treatises,* ed. Jean Darrouzes, A.A., in *Sources Chrétiennes* vol. 129, p. 282 (Paris: Cerf, 1967), hereafter cited as *TE.*
25. Discourse XXXIII, 78–86.

INTRODUCTION

This conscious union with the indwelling Trinity is possible in this life and should be sought after as the goal of the Christian life. This depends very much on one's desire and efforts to seek purity of heart through a state of constant repentance and faithful observance of God's commandments. Symeon argues that if the Son were consciously aware of the Father, and the Father truly knows the Son and the Son knows the Father (Jn. 17:21), then we also are one with the Trinity and should be aware of that union.[26]

Thus Symeon continually exhorts his listeners and readers in the discourses to bend every effort to reach this consciousness of knowing through mystical contemplation the indwelling God that is united with them:

> May I entreat you, let us endeavor to see Him and contemplate Him even in this life. For if we are found worthy sensibly (*aisthitos*) to see Him here, we shall not die, "death will have no dominion over us" (Rm. 6:9). Let us not wait to see Him in the future, but strive to contemplate Him now, since John the Theologian tells us, "We know that we have God in our hearts, from the Spirit which we have received from Him" (1 John 3:24, 2:27).[27]

Out of the thirty-four discourses, Symeon devotes seven to the Holy Spirit.[28] But the chief work of the Holy Spirit, the beginning, foundational stone for the building of contemplation, is the stirring of the Christian to true repentance. On this most important and solid link between the Holy Spirit's operations and man's cooperation in keeping alive a constant state of penitence, Symeon lays stress in six main discourses.[29] This accent on repentance and the gift of tears becomes a main characteris-

---

26. Ibid., XXXIV, 102–118.
27. Discourse II, 422, 429.
28. Cf. Discourses VI, X, XVI, XXIV, XXIX, XXXII, XXXIII.
29. Discourses II, IX, V, XIV, XXIII, XXX.

tic of Symeon's other writings as well, and in this regard he again is in perfect accord with the writings of the early Fathers.

OTHER WRITINGS

Symeon continued to write after the revolt of the thirty monks (around 995–998) up to his resignation from his office as abbot of Saint Mamas in 1005 and his exile in 1009. He continued to write his hymns, which he completed only in exile, along with numerous letters and many polemical works that have been lost to us. This period gives us another genre of his writing: the polemical works that came out of controversy with the official theologians of the court. These are his theological and ethical treatises.[30]

Different in style from the discourses, these treatises were not delivered verbally before live audiences but were thought-out positions on key issues of controversy engaged in by Symeon and his adversary Stephen and other official "scholastic" theologians. Here Symeon is no longer the abbot exhorting his monks to ascetical practices in order through detachment to reach true contemplation, but he takes on the role of the guardian of the patristic teaching on mystical theology. He feels a very special zeal and mission to combat the faulty, scholastic theology that sought to destroy the apophatic, mystical approach, so characteristic of the best of the earlier Byzantine mystical theologians.

The basic question at issue remained: "What is true theology?" Symeon mounts his charge by insisting on the key doctrines of revelation found in Scripture that can be comprehended only through an apophaticism or a knowing by not knowing with man's rational powers alone, but from the gift of infused contemplation that the Holy Spirit gives to the humble and pure of heart.

The first series of *Theological Treatises* deals with the subject of the unity within the Trinity. No doubt these were written in defense against Stephen's attacks on Symeon's doctrine

---

30. These have been edited in two volumes by Jean Darrouzes, A.A.: *Traités Théologiques et Ethiques*; tome 1: Theol. 1–111; Eth. 1–111; vol. 122 (1966) in *Sources Chrétiennes* hereafter cited as *TT*; and Tome 11: Eth. IV–XV; vol. 129 (1967) (*TE*).

about the Trinity. These three treatises show us Symeon as a most capable theologian in the best sense of the word. He handles the unity of Trinity that cannot admit a distinction of reason that Stephen was insisting upon. Symeon appeals to Scripture and fashions his exegesis and analogical application of oneness in multiplicity, drawn from the tripartite distinction found in man's soul and the example of light. The mystics have "true" knowledge and are the true theologians since they have no knowledge revealed in experience.

The fifteen ethical treatises present us with a variety of subject matter. Numbers three through eleven form a fairly unified whole, giving us Symeon's doctrine on mysticism. In the first two treatises we find similar themes already touched on in the discourses such as creation, sin, restoration of man through Christ, the question of predestination, and the necessity of responding to God's invitation through faith. Symeon shows himself as an original theologian through syntheses in which he employs many scriptural typologies and Pauline themes.

We see also many of the same themes dealt with in the discourses redeveloped in treatises three through eleven. Symeon evidently is battling the speculative theologians of Constantinople as he presents such themes as the necessity of faith, *apatheia* or impassibility, the possibility in this life of "seeing" God and experiencing His presence through a conscious knowledge, the need of the ascetical life and penitence in order to enter into this conscious knowledge, the possession of the Holy Spirit as attained only through practice of God's commandments and humility, the Baptism of the Holy Spirit, and living the death of Christ through the different stages of Christian virtues.

The last four treatises, twelve through fifteen, are short compositions written after 1005 when Symeon was no longer abbot. They deal with a variety of general topics such as the need for Christians to be like merchants at a market, using earthly time well to gain eternal goods; salvation as realized only by faith and good works, especially through confession and penitence; external rites and their interior effects produced to lead us to the divinity of Christ; and, lastly, the need for solitude if one is to become a channel of grace to others.

Nicetas informs us that Symeon, after his resignation and

before he was sent into exile, also wrote his *Practical and Theological Chapters.*[31] He describes this work in the *Life:*

> Having arrived at this degree of union with the Spirit, he published his ascetical chapters on the virtues and vices which oppose them. This was the fruit of his own "practical philosophy" and of his divine knowledge, his teachings on perfection for those who lead the life of philosophers (lovers of wisdom) and through this he has become for the people of Israel, the monks, a river of God, filled with the waters of the Spirit.[32]

In this work, which probably grew out of notes Symeon had used on various occasions to instruct monks or other persons on the ascetical and contemplative life of Christians, he gives us a collection of ideas about several unrelated subjects. He employs the traditional form of instruction used by the Eastern Fathers who wrote on asceticism and contemplation called the "Century." This is a collection of ideas that center around one theme, such as prayer or asceticism, that divides into one hundred (hence the name *Century*) paragraphs that are usually quite short.

Here Symeon gives us in the first and third Centuries ideas on a number of generally related topics dealing with the ascetical life. His aim is to lead the reader to the heights of contemplating God and thus to make each person into a perfect human being, a living book. In the middle Century of twenty-five chapters, we find a greater unity, revolving around what Symeon terms the gnostic and theological chapters. Symeon shows himself the inheritor of what his predecessors, such as Evagrius, Gregory of Nyssa, Gregory of Nazianzus, and Maximus the Confessor, had written in their various teachings about the praxis or practical life of the Christian.

This refers to all of the practices or areas of activity that an

---

31. Jean Darrouzes, A.A. has also edited these in his work *Chapitres Théologiques, Gnostiques et Practiques,* in *Sources Chrétiennes,* vol. 51 (Paris: Cerf); hereafter cited as *TGP.*

32. *Vie,* p. 96.

individual must engage in, in order to render himself open to receive God's pure infusion of *theoria* or contemplation. Such praxis involves any and all attempts to eradicate sin from one's life. This is the negative side of praxis or the ascetical life and has as its aim purification from vices and inordinate passions. The positive aspect of praxis focuses on the development of Christian virtues, especially those of faith, hope, and love. Love of neighbor and prayer are the two most important positive means of reaching that state of *apatheia*, or impassionability, where the individual Christian is capable of total listening to God's Word. We could call it the reintegration of the human being into the fully alive person that God in His Logos always called him to be. *Apatheia* is the door that leads into true contemplation, for when the turbulence of self-love, *philautia*, is silenced, then God can speak His Word and man can respond totally to that Word.

In this middle section, Symeon describes *theoria*, the fruit of contemplation, that follows praxis. This is a gnosis, an infused knowlege or contemplation, not derived at by man's individual efforts, but as a sheer gift from God, given when man has disposed himself through purity of heart to see God. Thus the individual Christian now is able to see throughout all of God's creation and intuit the divine plan of God as he contemplates the Logos of God within the created logos of each creature. Such gnosis, developed with continued praxis, especially through purification and greater infusion of faith, hope and charity, leads the contemplative to a permanent state of experiencing the one and the many, the Trinity living within himself and the same triune God as a loving community of one and many working out of love within all creatures outside the contemplative. This is what Evagrius and Maximus the Confessor called *theoria theologica*, true theology for Symeon.[33]

Much of this work is quite impersonal writing and lacking in depth of treatment and conciseness. Symeon refrains from appealing to his own personal, mystical experiences as he so often does in his discourses and in his two thanksgivings. This work is undoubtedly intended by Symeon to reach a greater au-

---

33. Cf. the article by J. Le Maitre, "Contemplation," in *Dictionnaire de Spiritualité d'Ascese et de Mystique*, vol. 1, col. 1779, 1786–7.

dience, including laity, and thus he refrains from projecting his own experiences as a model of what can be attained by other Christians. He gives the classical descriptions of the ascetical life along with the degrees of contemplation, but what goes beyond these descriptions is his insistence as always that the ordinary Christian should tend toward such for of such is every Christian life necessarily made up. He continually comes back to the theme that the divine life, the indwelling of the Trinity, is what Jesus Christ merited for all of us and that this is an experience that should become a living, conscious experience within man's soul, made known through the outpouring of the Holy Spirit.

Symeon's teaching in this work is succinctly given in the following quotation:

> If the Holy Spirit is in you, you will comprehend well enough His action within you as the Apostle says about Him: "There where the Spirit of the Lord is, there is liberty." . . . All those who have been baptized in the Holy Spirit have put on Christ completely; they are children of light and walk in the light which has no decline.[34]

THE HYMNS

Next to the discourses, the most important work of Symeon is his *Hymns of Divine Love*.[35] One could almost say that the hymns are basically Symeon's discourses written in poetic form with poetic meter and rhyme. These were composed at the time of the composition and editing of the discourses, but Symeon finished writing and editing them in the small monastery of Saint Marina from 1009 until his death in 1022. Like the discourses, there is no one single unifying theme running through the hymns, but themes similar to those in the discourses dealing with the traditional, ascetical themes of repentance; death; exhortation to practice virtues, especially charity toward neighbor; detachment from the things of this world, and so forth.

---

34. *TGP* 111, 43, 14–22, p. 92.
35. These can be found in an English translation, G. A. Maloney, S.J., *Hymns of Divine Love* (Denville, N.J.: Dimension Books, 1975).

INTRODUCTION

Some of the hymns pick up the theological polemics already discussed in his *Theological Treatises.* This is seen in *Hymn 21,* where we find the same material that Symeon used against Stephen in dealing with the unity within the Trinity and the sublime mysteries of the interaction of the three persons or hypostases.

But the greatest power and beauty in the hymns come in the hymns that deal with Symeon's own mystical experiences and personal love toward Jesus Christ. Not even Saint John of the Cross rivals the lyricism of Symeon as he opens the reader up to share his burning love for Jesus Christ and the ecstatic happiness of living in the unity of the Trinity. We see this in his descriptions of his visions of Christ as light, already described in the third person of George, in his discourses; but now it is Symeon sharing with us directly in ardent language that allows us to enter somewhat into his experience as though it were happening at the moment of our reading about it.

His *Hymn 25* can best serve to illustrate both his style of ecstatic writing and his mystical content that becomes very personal, both to Symeon and to the reader:

—But, Oh, what intoxication of light, Oh, what
    movements of fire!
Oh, what swirlings of the flame in me, miserable one
    that I am,
coming from You and Your glory!
The glory I know it and I say it is Your Holy Spirit,
who has the same nature with You and the same
    honor, O Word;
He is of the same race, of the same glory,
of the same essence, He alone with Your Father
and with You, O Christ, O God of the universe!
I fall down in adoration before You.
I thank You that You have made me worthy to know,
    however little it may be,
the power of Your divinity.
I thank You that You, even when I was sitting in
    darkness,
revealed Yourself to me, You enlightened me,
You granted me to see the light of Your countenance
that is unbearable to all.

INTRODUCTION

I remained seated in the middle of the darkness, I
    know,
but, while I was there surrounded by darkness,
You appeared as light, illuminating me completely
    from Your total light.
And I became light in the night, I who was found in
    the midst of darkness.
Neither the darkness extinguished Your light
    completely,
nor did the light dissipate the visible darkness,
but they were together, yet completely separate,
without confusion, far from each other, surely not at
    all mixed,
except in the same spot where they filled everything.
So I am in the light, yet I am found in the middle of
    the darkness.
So I am in the darkness, yet still I am in the middle
    of the light.
—How can darkness receive within itself a light
and, without being dissipated by the light,
        it still remains in the middle of the light?
O awesome wonder which I see doubly,
with my two sets of eyes, of the body and of the
    soul![36]

The work of the hymns is not a treatise one sits down to
read. It is a launching of the reader into an orbit of mystical
prayer, into an inner world filled with beauty and mystery. Yet
the hymns do not merely speak in ecstatic language of Symeon's
mystical experiences. He also gives hard teachings on repentance using the material similar to that found in his discourses,
but now presented in a dramatic manner that is doubly convincing. We cannot, therefore, expect any systematic plan in the
hymns. They were often experiences put down in elementary
form and later on enhanced and polished. We find no new teaching or new material that was not already written in his earlier
works. But we find here in the hymns Symeon's best writing

---

36. *H.* 25, pp. 135–136.

and a gift of classic proportions to the history of Christian mysticism.

J. Koder, who edited the Greek text,[37] gives a detailed treatment of Symeon's poetics, showing us his genius in writing poetry according to the metric conventions known in his day of eight, twelve, and fifteen syllables to a line.[38] In a way Symeon needed the discipline of metrics to harness his rampaging spirit, but in the process his rapturous love for God is intimately communicated and shared with the reader.

Symeon's ardent love for Jesus Christ bursts out frequently in the form of a dialogue between the author and Jesus Christ.[39] This form of mystical dialogue was not original to Symeon, for Romanos the Melodus had made it famous. But, as Koder points out, for Symeon the visions and words are not fictitious but events and conversations that really took place.[40]

Symeon wrote many letters and other works, especially hymns and an office in honor of his former spiritual father, Symeon the Studite, but these have been lost to us. In the *Discourses* and the *Hymns* we have the substance of Symeon's thought and the most intimate insights he shared of himself as a mystic. We can be grateful that he did not hold back in any false humility but that he cooperated with the inspiration given him by God to edit through his disciple, Nicetas, and publish his main works.

One last work that is included as a part of this present volume is Symeon's two *Thanksgivings*, which form Discourse XXXV and Discourse XXXVI of the present work. The style is a personal prayer of gratitude poured out to God for His great blessings given personally to Symeon over his lifetime. He thanks God especially for the mystical experiences and the ability to share these with others, for the gift of his holy spiritual father, Symeon the Studite, for his great mystical visions for the manifestations of the Spirit in the lives of the saints, and even for the trials and sufferings that came his way. He gives a final,

---

37. J. Koder, *Hymnes,* in *Sources Chrétiennes,* vol. 156 (1–15, 1969), vol. 174 (16–40, 1971), vol. 196 (41–58, 1973) (Paris: Cerf).
38. Ibid., pp. 82–93.
39. Cf. *H.* 15, 17, 18, 22, 23, 53, 58.
40. Koder, vol. 156, p. 79.

humble prayer that God may continue to bless him and grant him perseverance.

He could have written these thanksgivings at different times of his life. It would be proper to suspect that he wrote them toward the end of his life as a rapid review of how God has worked through him during his lifetime. The second repeats his gratitude for his spiritual father that he expressed in his first thanksgiving but seems to be a point of challenge in his life, at having lost his spiritual guide. Thus the second thanksgiving could have been written shortly after the death of his spiritual director about the year 986 or 987.

JESUS CHRIST AS LIGHT

It remains for us to review some of the main themes that are found in the writings of Symeon, especially in his discourses as presented in this volume. Saint Gregory of Nyssa often expressed the Christian contemplative life in terms of a triadic dialectic that moved from light to shadow or cloud to darkness. One can never say which triple movement is the more important for without darkness there could never be light. Saint Symeon, however, both in his personal visions and in his writings, accentuates the symbol of light. He continually presents God as light, applying light equally to each person. "You say, for example, 'light.' At the same time, each of them (the Divine Persons) is on His own account light and all three are only one light."[41]

But Symeon's habitual way of presenting Jesus Christ is the Johannine symbol of Him as light (Jn. 8:12, 9:5). The light that is Christ shines within the Christian mystic and he lives in that light. In Discourse XXVIII Symeon describes this light within:

> It shines on us without evening, without change, without alteration, without form. It speaks, works, lives, gives life, and changes into light those whom it illuminates. We bear witness that "God is light," and those to whom it has been granted to see Him have all beheld Him as light. Those who have seen Him have received

---

41. Discourse XXXIII, 194–195.

27

Him as light, because the light of His glory goes before
Him, and it is impossible for Him to appear without
light. Those who have not seen His light have not seen
Him, for He is the light, and those who have not received the light have not yet received grace. Those who
have received grace have received the light of God and
have received God, even as Christ Himself, who is the
Light, has said, "I will live in them and move among
them" (2 Cor. 6:16).[42]

The light is different from the knowledge that is received
since it brings such knowledge about.[43] This light of Christ is
given only to those who seek Him through purification. Symeon
distinguishes between an actual physical, sensible light whereby
Christ appeared to him in several, unforgettable visions and the
spiritual light that becomes synonymous with an infused contemplation of the constant unity with the indwelling Jesus
Christ.

VISIONS

The first type of sensible light was seen by Symeon several
times, as he shared with his listening and reading audience in
his discourses and hymns. This experience of seeing Jesus Christ
as light was so powerful that Symeon confesses that he did not
know "whether he is in the body or out of the body" (2 Cor.
12:2). He seemingly went out of his habitual "in the body" local-
ization or orientation and was transported "out of himself" to a
higher plane of spiritual existence.

The first vision that Symeon had was when he was twenty
years old and still had not entered the monastic life. Using the
third person narrative, Symeon describes this ecstatic experience:

One day, as he stood and recited, "God, have mercy
upon me, a sinner" (Lk. 18:13), uttering it with his

---

42. Discourse XXVIII, 106–119.
43. Ibid., 230.

mind rather than his mouth, suddenly a flood of divine radiance appeared from above and filled all the room. As this happened the young man lost all awareness (of his surroundings) and forgot that he was in a house or that he was under a roof. He saw nothing but light all around him and did not know whether he was standing on the ground. He was not afraid of falling; he was not concerned with the world, nor did anything pertaining to men and corporeal beings enter into his mind. Instead, he was wholly in the presence of immaterial light and seemed to himself to have turned into light. Oblivious of all the world he was filled with tears and with ineffable joy and gladness. His mind then ascended to heaven and beheld yet another light, which was clearer than that which was close at hand. In a wonderful manner there appeared to him, standing close to that light, the saint of whom we have spoken, the old man equal to angels, who had given him the commandment and the book (Symeon the Studite).[44]

His second great vision of God as light occurred when he was a novice at Stoudion. As he stood praying the *Trisagion* (Holy God, Holy Mighty One, Holy Immortal One, have mercy on us), he was suddenly overwhelmed by the presence of God, which lifted him outside of himself. The light took away from him "all material denseness and bodily heaviness that made my members to be sluggish and numb."[45] In this ecstasy he received great spiritual joy and sweetness, which brought a newfound sense of freedom and transcendence and an understanding of the manner in which one enters into eternal life through physical death.

But in one particular vision Symeon seemed to have reached a breakthrough to a new consciousness of Jesus Christ, ever dwelling within him as a light, a "formless form" that never left Symeon: ". . . and then I knew that I had Thee consciously within me. From then onwards, I loved Thee, not by recollection of Thee and that which surrounds Thee, nor for the

---

44. Discourse XXII, 89–105.
45. Discourse XVI, 80–108.

memory of such things, but I in very truth believed that I had Thee, substantial love, within me."[46]

TEARS

Symeon's spirituality could hardly be attractive to dilettantes. There are many who might be moved to desire a share in the ecstasies of Symeon. But Symeon, true to the Gospel message of death-resurrection, mourning in true repentance and rejoicing in greater surrendering love to God, as well as being faithful to the best spiritual writers of the Christian East, insists with even greater emphasis on repentance than on ecstasies. The spiritual warfare never ceases.[47] This is realistic because man harbors within himself sin and the roots of his own spiritual destruction. "It is incorporeal enemies that we face, they are constantly facing us even though we do not see them. . . . No one may escape the alternatives of either winning and staying alive or of being overcome and dying."[48] This is nothing but the constant message of the Eastern Fathers concerning *nepsis*, or that state of constant vigilance and discernment of the spirits of light and darkness.

When the individual Christian is faithful in doing the spiritual battle, the Holy Spirit gradually brings about the purification of the heart. The sign of this state of purification and reintegration into the "new man" in Christ is the continued state of *penthos* or an abiding sorrow for sin.[49] *Penthos* reaches its peak of intensity when the Holy Spirit pours out tears in great effusion and abundance. This is what Symeon constantly refers to as the Baptism in the Holy Spirit.

Next to Isaac the Syrian, no other patristic writer stressed more than Symeon the necessity of receiving this gift of tears from the Holy Spirit. Little attention is given to this teaching today, yet Symeon knew that he was merely repeating what was

---

46. Discourse XXXVI, 269–273.
47. Discourse III, no. 9.
48. Ibid., 335–346.
49. On this subject of *penthos*, cf. I. Hausher, S.J., *Penthos*, in *Orientalia Christiana Analecta*, no. 132 (Rome, 1944). This is the classic work on this topic, drawing especially from the Fathers of the desert and the heyschastic writers.

consistently taught by the early Eastern Christian Fathers.[50] Evagrius in the fourth century gave this basic insight when he wrote:

> Before all else, pray to be given tears, that weeping may soften the savage hardness which is in your soul and, having acknowledged your sin unto the Lord (Ps 31:5), you may receive from Him the remission of sins.[51]

Symeon saw the gift of tears not as a rare gift given to a few chosen persons, but as something that could be experienced by all sincere persons who seriously enter into the spiritual battle of weeping for their sins. The importance of this gift is stressed by Symeon:

> Without tears our dried heart could never be softened, nor our soul acquire spiritual humility, and we would not have the force to become humble. For he who has not such dispositions cannot be united to the Holy Spirit and without such union with the Holy Spirit after purification one can no longer expect knowledge and contemplation of God nor merit to be instructed in the hidden virtues of humility.[52]

FASTING

Symeon stresses the importance of fasting in the spiritual life of each Christian. In doing so, he again was being consistent with his desire to present a spirituality that was traditional and rooted in the constant teaching of the early Fathers. For Symeon there could be no serious prayer life without fasting. Each

---

50. On this subject cf. L. Gillet: "The Gift of Tears," in *Sobornost* (1937), pp. 5ff.; M. Lot-Borodine: "Le Mystere du 'don des larmes' dans l'Orient chrétien," in *Vie Spirituelle*, vol. 18, *Supplement* (1936) pp. 65–110; B. Steidle, O.S.B., "Die Tranen, ein mystiches problem im alten Monchtum," in *Benediktinische Monastschrift*, vol. 20 (1938) pp. 181–187.
51. Evagrius, *De Oratione; PG* 79, 1168D.
52. *TGP* 3, 23; p. 87.

person was to fast habitually, but according to each one's needs, abilities, and attractions given by the Holy Spirit. Fasting brings about a healing of the unspiritual parts of us. "For this healer of our souls is effective, in the case of one to quieten the fevers and impulses of the flesh, in another to assuage bad temper, in yet another to drive away sleep, in another to stir up zeal, and in yet another to restore purity of mind and to set him free from evil thoughts. In one it will control his unbridled tongue and, as it were, by a bit (Jas. 3:3). In another it will invisibly guard his eyes and fix them on high instead of allowing them to roam hither and thither.... Fasting gradually disperses and drives away spiritual darkness and the veil of sin that lies upon the soul, just as the sun dispels the mist."[53]

Fasting through a basic moderation of one's appetite for food and drink not only leads the Christian to a well-regulated discipline over his passions and other appetites, but helps him to grow in deep humility and charity toward God and fellowman. When this attitude of fasting enters into the spiritual realm, then the Christian can be called a true ascetic who is constantly alert, living the sobriety (*nepsis*) that allows him to be alert and attentive to God as He speaks His Word in the life of the individual.

CHARITY

Symeon's "inaugural" discourse on being elected abbot of Saint Mamas dealt with charity, and this became his constant theme. For he saw charity toward the neighbor as the true index of holiness and the degree of attained contemplation. Without such charity there can be no true Christian.[54] This is because charity is not a virtue acquired by man's own doing but is a theological virtue along with faith and hope that is infused into the Christian by the Holy Spirit.

> For love is not a name, but the divine essence,
> both participable and yet incomprehensible, but
>   totally divine.

---

53. Discourse XI, 50–63.
54. Discourse VIII, 100–110.

That which communicates itself is comprehensible,
but that which is more than the former cannot be so.
This is therefore why I have told you that love is
    comprehensible
and it is personalized insofar as it is communicable
    and understandable.[55]

Symeon naturally aims his teaching on charity, especially
in his discourses, to monks. He seeks first to show them that
their neighbor, the one closest to them needing charity, must be
themselves for if one were to show charity to everyone else and
neglect oneself this would be to neglect the Body of Christ.

As His brother and His member you may honor all
others, give them hospitality and care for them. Yet if
you ignore yourself and, instead of striving by every
means to attain to the summit of that life and honor
which is pleasing to God, leave your soul in the famine
of laziness or the thirst of indifference or imprisoned in
the dungeon of this filthy body through gluttony or
love of pleasure . . . have you not treated Christ's brother with contempt? Have you not abandoned Him to
hunger and thirst? Have you not failed to visit Him
when He was in prison? (Mt. 25:42ff.)[56]

True charity begins with seeking in a healthy way to be
perfect as God wants all of His children to be. Thus before one
can exercise true charity toward the neighbor, one must learn to
be freed from all self-attachment by showing a love toward the
real *ego*, the person God knows us as in His Logos. Then a monk
can exercise true charity according to his state of life. There
should be nothing he can share with his neighbor on a material
level if he has already given up all to follow Christ's poor. But
the sharing is by one's Christian *presence*.[57]

---

55. *H.* 52, p. 263.
56. Discourse IX, 163–169.
57. Symeon is consistent with the common, patristic teaching of a monk's
true apostolate of presence. Cf. I. Hausherr, S.J., "La Théologie du monachisme
chez S. Jean Climaque," in *Theologie de la vie monastique* (Paris, 1961), pp. 405ff.
Also L. Bouyer, *Le Sens de la vie monastique* (Paris, 1950), p. 211.

Others, especially within the monastic community, will be most helped eternally by an individual monk's recollection, holiness, detachment, and spirit of prayer. This presence may develop, as in the case of Symeon, with a responsibility to many to feed the sheep by word and teaching.

In a most moving text, Symeon describes the burning zeal that a Christian should have for all of his neighbors, even to the extent that he would plead to God to allow him to suffer in their place for their punishment.

> He often implored God, who loves man, with all his soul and with warm tears, that either they might be saved or else that he be condemned with them. His attitude was like that of Moses (Ex. 32:32; Num. 14:10) and indeed of God Himself in that he did not in any way wish to be saved alone. Because he was spiritually bound to them by holy love in the Holy Spirit he did not want to enter into the kingdom of heaven itself if it meant that he would be separated from them. O sacred bond! O unutterable power! O soul of heavenly thoughts, or rather, soul borne by God and greatly perfected in love of God and of neighbor![58]

KEEPING THE COMMANDMENTS

Throughout the discourses and Symeon's other writings, keeping the commandments is a vital part of his spirituality as it was the standard phrase used by all of the earlier Eastern Fathers to summarize in the concrete one's test of true love toward God and neighbor, namely, obedience to the will of God as expressed in the commands given by Jesus Christ in the Gospel. True love is proved by the exact observance of all the commandments of God and this goes much beyond the mere Decalogue. In the discourses Symeon several times gives his monks an examination on the Beatitudes, those large precepts that can never be totally fulfilled but are ideals to be striven toward at each moment. A sensitive love of God's will, wish, command and delicate inspiration, as received from the indwelling presence of Jesus

---

58. Discourse IX, 58–68.

Christ and His Holy Spirit, comes as a result of *apatheia*, a passionless passion to do whatever at the moment corresponds to God's good pleasure as manifested by Jesus Christ through His Spirit, in accord with Gospel values.

This is the goal of praxis and the true test of contemplation. To the degree that one has died to selfishness and is in union with the indwelling Trinity, to that same degree one will seek at every moment to do whatsoever God may command or wish. In short, for Symeon this phrase, to do the commandments of Jesus Christ, is almost a hendiadys for fulfilling the teachings of the holy Fathers.[59]

TRINITARIAN MYSTICISM

These are some of the main themes developed in this volume of Symeon's *Discourses*. They are consistently found also in his other writings. But every theme that Symeon presents to his readers is only a part of a whole. The ascetical practices that he develops and the constant stress on purification and repentance have meaning only in the light of the goal, the divinization of the individual Christian into a loving child of God, more and more consciously aware of the transforming love of the indwelling Trinity that makes him "a god by adoption and grace," a phrase repeated continually by Symeon. Symeon seeks to share his own experiences, which he feels are in harmony with the solid, traditional teachings of the Eastern Fathers that preceded him, but only because he is motivated to lead his readers into that very delicate process of interior growth. He wishes to move Christians away from any superficial, externally motivated relationship with God into a deeper person-to-person relationship. This means one has to destroy idols, go beyond words and ideas, and live in the awesome darkness of mystery that becomes a light to those who have become purified.

The inner presence of the Trinity, like a magnet, draws man's "conscious attention" away from old mental concepts that have become clichéd and lifeless into a new manner of intuitively experiencing or knowing God. As the Trinity becomes that center of inner direction, the individual loses the conscious con-

---

59. Discourse I, 37.

trol he had developed earlier over his instinctive impulses and drives, repressed fears, and anxieties, which pour out in an avalanche of new, unheard-of experiences of sin. Yet Jesus Christ as Light, along with the other two indwelling Divine Persons as Light, unites Himself with the Christian, making him "light from Light, true god from true God." This union defies description.

Symeon does share his experiences but always ends up with the traditional Eastern apophatic language to keep the experience dynamic and in a process of growth in mystery, uncontrolled by man's rational powers. Symeon still has tremendous relevance for modern man as he continues to share his mystical experiences with us, as he challenges us to heed Saint Paul's exhortation: "Awake, thou that sleepest and arise from the dead, and Christ shall give thee light" (Eph. 5:14). The question that Symeon asks us who read his works, especially this volume of his *Discourses,* is:

And how is it that one made god by grace and by adoption will not be god in awareness and knowledge and contemplation, he who has put on the Son of God?[60]

---

60. *H.* 50, p. 254.

TRANSLATOR'S NOTE

Despite the fact that Saint Symeon the abbot has been so highly regarded in the Orthodox Church that he has been called "the New Theologian," second only to Saint Gregory of Nazianzus, "the Theologian" par excellence, only a small portion of his writings has been accessible in print until quite recently. This was remedied only by the publication of the critical text edited by Archbishop Basil (Krivochéine) of Brussels in the series Sources Chrétiennes (Paris, 1963), accompanied by the French version by Joseph Paramelle, S.J.

It is from this Greek text that the present translation has been made. The accompanying French translation has often proved helpful, though it has by no means been slavishly followed. From it, for the most part, have been derived the various headings, whether of the several discourses or their subsections, as are not found in the original text. All such have been enclosed in square brackets [ ]. Similarly, the footnotes are based on those by Archbishop Basil, though generally considerably abridged. At times square brackets have been used as well to indicate words added in the English translation to preserve the sense. Lines in the text have been numbered for easy reference.

Biblical quotations in general follow the Revised Standard Version, except in the case of the Psalter, in which the version of the [Anglican] Book of Common Prayer, which is closer to the Septuagint text used by Symeon, has been followed. Where Symeon, as he often does, quotes loosely, or where his biblical text differs from that which is the basis of the English versions in question, the translation has been adjusted accordingly. In the latter case the abbreviation "LXX" after the reference indicates that the divergence is due to the Septuagint version from which Symeon quotes. In a few cases his use of a biblical text reflects a notably different nuance of the Greek original from that represented in the English version. Here too the quotation has been adjusted.

Unlike the edition of Sources Chrétiennes, the biblical references in this translation are limited to the more obvious reminiscences of Scriptural phraseology, for the sake of greater convenience to the reader. Regrettably, this fails to do justice to a writer whose thought is so steeped in Holy Writ.

The translator is grateful to Orthodox friends who have instigated and encouraged this effort, in particular Father John Meyendorff, who first made the suggestion, and Professor C. B. Ashanin, for his continued interest. He thanks Mr. Andrew Morbey of the Department of English of Carleton University, Ottawa, for his invaluable help in improving the English style. The progress of the work was materially aided by the help of Miss Rosemary de Catanzaro and the late Mrs. Enid Scott with parts of the typescript. The latter, shortly after finishing her portion, was called to her eternal reward. "Grant rest, O Lord, to Thy servant with Thy Saints."

May this translation, with its imperfections, be used by God to spur on souls to the same spiritual endeavor of which Saint Symeon was so eminent an example and exponent.

Τῆς παναγίας ἀχράντου ὑπερευλογημένης ἐνδόξου δεσποίνης ἡμῶν θεοτόκον καὶ ἀειπαρθένου Μαρίας μετὰ πάντων τῶν ἁγίων μνημονεύσαντες ἑαυτούς καί ἀλλήλους καί πᾶσαν τὴν ζωὴν ἡμῶν Χριστῷ τῷ Θεῷ παραθώμεθα

Commemorating our most holy, pure, blessed, and glorified Lady, the Mother of God and Ever-Virgin Mary, together with all the Saints, let us commend ourselves and one another and our whole life to Christ our God.

Liturgy of S. John Chrysostom

SYMEON THE NEW THEOLOGIAN
THE DISCOURSES

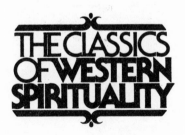

THE CLASSICS OF WESTERN SPIRITUALITY

I

OF CHARITY

The ways and practices of spiritual men. A beatitude addressed to those who have charity in their hearts.

[§ 1. SYMEON'S UNWORTHINESS.]

Brethren and fathers,

It is my intention to speak to you of the things that pertain to the benefit of the soul. Yet, as Christ who is the truth bears witness, I feel shame before your charity, because I know my unworthiness. For this reason I would rather be silent forever, as the Lord knows, without even lifting up my eyes to look at any man's face, since my conscience condemns me. I was appointed to be the superior of all of you, though I am wholly unworthy, as though I understood the way who do not even know where I am going and have not at all come to the path that leads to God. Thus it is no small and ordinary grief that possesses me for having been chosen, lowly as I am, to lead you who are most worthy. It is you, rather, who should have been my guides, since I am the last of all both in seniority and in age[1]. My life contains neither the practice nor the testimony with which I may exhort you and remind you of that which pertains to God's laws or His will. Of that which I wish to make my subject, I know that I have put nothing into practice. I am well aware that it is not he who merely speaks whom our Lord and God calls blessed, but rather he who first puts into practice and then speaks, for He says, "Blessed is he who does and teaches them, he shall be called great in the kingdom of heaven" *(cf. Mt. 5:19)*. When the disciples hear such a teacher they become eager to imitate him.

10

20

---

1. At the time of his election Symeon had spent but three years at S. Mamas and was about thirty-one years of age.

41

30   The profit they derive from his words is not as great as that from being stirred up by his good works and compelled to do likewise. I know that this does not apply to me, for I realize that "there is nothing good in me" *(Rom. 7:18).* But I beg you all, I entreat you, my dear brothers, do not look at my slackness of life, but consider the Lord's precepts and the teachings of our holy fathers. Those shining lights wrote nothing they had not first practiced, and by practicing it succeeded in it.

[§ 2. LET US FOLLOW ON THE WAY
OF CHRIST'S PRECEPTS.]

40   Let us therefore follow one and the same path, Christ's commandments, which lead us up to heaven and to God. Even though the word describes to us different paths, their intrinsic nature is the same; they are spoken of as though branching off into several paths according to each person's ability and disposition. We begin from many and varied works and actions, just as travelers depart from different places and many cities; the destination we are anxious to reach is one, the kingdom of heaven. The actions and ways of godly men must be understood as spiritual virtues. Those who begin to walk in them must run toward
50   one goal, just as those who come from various countries and places come together, as we have said, to one city, the kingdom of heaven. There together they become worthy to reign with Christ and become subjects of one King [our] God and Father. By this city, which is one, not many, you will understand the holy and undivided trinity of virtues. Above all it is that virtue which comes before the others but is also mentioned as the last of them, since it is the goal of all good things and greater than them all—charity. All faith comes from it and is built on its foundation; on it hope is based. Apart from love nothing what-
60   ever has existed, nor ever will. Its names and actions are many. More numerous still are its distinctive marks; divine and innumerable are its properties. Yet it is one in nature, wholly beyond utterance whether on the part of angels or men or any other creatures, even such as are unknown to us. Reason cannot comprehend it; its glory is inaccessible, its counsels unsearchable. It is eternal because it is beyond time, invisible because thought cannot comprehend it, though it may perceive it. Many are the beauties of this holy Sion not made with hands! He who has be-

gun to see it no longer delights in sensible objects; he ceases to be attached to the glory of this world.

[§ 3. CHARITY IS ALTOGETHER DESIRABLE.]

After this preamble let me then briefly deal with the subject and address myself to it and consecrate to it all that I have of desire. My dear fathers and brethren, as soon as I called to mind the beauty of undefiled love, its light suddenly appeared in my heart. I have been ravished with its delight and have ceased to perceive outward things; I have lost all sense of this life and have forgotten the things that are at hand. Yet again—I am at a loss how to say it—it has removed far from me and left me to lament my own weakness. O all-desirable love, how happy is he who has embraced you, for he will no longer have a passionate desire to embrace any earthly beauty! Happy is he who is moved by divine love to cling to you! He will deny the whole world, yet as he associates with all men he will be wholly untainted. Happy is he who caresses your beauty and with infinite desire delights therein, for he will be spiritually sanctified by the water and blood *(cf. Jn. 19:34)* that in all purity issue from you! Happy is he who passionately embraces you, for he will be wondrously changed! In spirit and in soul he will rejoice, because you are the ineffable joy. Happy is he who gains possession of you, for he will count the treasures of the world as nothing, for you are indeed the truly inexhaustible riches. Happy and triply happy is he whom you accept, for though he be without any visible glory he will be more glorious than all that is glorious, more honored and august than all that is honored. Worthy of praise is he who pursues you; even more praiseworthy is he who has found you; more blessed he who is loved by you, received by you, taught by you, he who dwells in you and is fed by you with Christ, the immortal food, Christ our God!

[§ 4. DIVINE LOVE.]

O love divine, where are you holding Christ? Where are you hiding Him? Why have you taken the Savior of the world and removed yourself far from us? Open but a small door even to us unworthy ones, that we too may see Christ who has suffered for us, that by His mercy we may have confidence that we will die no more once we have seen Him. Be opened to us, for you have become His door so that He might be manifested by His flesh. You who have constrained the generous and unforced compassions of our Master to "bear the sins" and "infirmities" of all men *(Jn. 1:29, Mt. 8:17)*, reject us not by saying, "I do not know you" *(Mt. 25:12)*. Be with us that you may know us, for we are not known to you. Dwell in us, that for your sake the Master may visit even us lowly ones, as you go before to meet Him, for we are wholly unworthy. So He will stop briefly on the way to converse with you, and will thus permit even us sinners to fall at His spotless feet. You will intercede on our behalf and plead that our debt of evil deeds be forgiven, so that through you we may again be found worthy to serve Him, our Master, and be sustained and nourished by Him. For even if we owed no debts but were perishing with the hunger of destitution, it would be almost as great a punishment and chastisement.

May you then pardon us, O holy love, and through you may we enter into the enjoyment of the benefits of our Master. Of their sweetness no one will taste except through you! He who does not love you as he ought and is not, as he must be, the object of your love, may well run, yet not attain the prize *(1 Cor. 9:24)*, and whoever runs is doubtful until he has completed the race. But he who has laid hold on you or on whom you have laid hold *(Phil. 3:12)* is certain [of victory], since you are the end of the Law *(Rom. 10:4)*. It is you who surround me and inflame me, you who by the labor of my heart enkindle me with boundless desire for God and for my brethren and fathers. You are the teacher of the prophets, the companion of the apostles, the power of the martyrs, the inspiration of the fathers and teachers, the perfection of all the saints, and now my commission for the service that lies before me.[2]

[§ 5. LOVE AS THE CRITERION OF THE TRUE FOLLOWERS OF CHRIST.]

Forgive me, brethren, for digressing a bit from the teaching of my discourse because of my longing for charity. For as I was mindful of it "my heart rejoiced" *(Ps. 16:9)*, as holy David says,

---

2. Symeon here refers to his priestly ordination and appointment as abbot.

and I was moved to sing the praises of its marvels. I therefore 140
entreat your love to pursue it with all your strength and to run
after it with faith so that you may lay hold on it. You will by no
means be disappointed of your hopes! However great your zeal
and many the efforts of your asceticism, they are all in vain and
without useful result unless they attain to love in a broken spirit
(Ps. 51:19). By no other virtue, by no other fulfillment of the
Lord's commandment, can anyone be known as a disciple of
Christ, for He says, "By this will all men know that you are My
disciples, if you have love for one another" *(Jn. 13:55)*. It is for
this reason that "the Word became flesh and dwelt among us"
(Jn. 1:14). For this reason He was incarnate; He willingly en- 150
dured His life-giving sufferings, in order that He might deliver
man, His own creature, from the bonds of hell, and restore him
and lead him up to heaven. Moved by love the apostles ran that
unceasing race and cast on the whole world the fishhook and net
of the word to drag it up from the deep of idolatry and bring it
safe into the port of the kingdom of heaven. Moved by love the
martyrs shed their blood that they might not lose Christ. Moved
by it our God-bearing Fathers and teachers of the world eagerly 160
laid down their own lives for the Catholic and apostolic Church.
We, though worthless, have entered on the leadership of you,
our most worthy fathers and brethren, so that we may imitate
them in every way as much as in us lies and suffer and endure
for your sake and do all for your edification and profit, that we
might present you as perfect sacrifices, reasonable burnt offer-
ings *(cf. Rom. 12:1)* on the table of God. For you are God's children, "whom God has given to me" *(Is. 8:18)* as sons, "my very
heart" *(Philem. 12)*, my eyes. In the words of the apostle, you are
"my pride" *(2 Cor. 1:14)* and the seal of my teaching office *(1* 170
Cor. 9:2).

My dear brethren in Christ, let us then be eager to employ
all means, including mutual love, to serve God. Have as your
pattern him whom you have chosen as your spiritual father,
even though I fall far short of being worthy thereof, so that God
may rejoice over your harmony and perfection. Thus I too in
my lowliness may rejoice as I see your continual progress in the
life that is in accordance with God, as you increase in faith, in
purity, in the fear of God, in reverence, in compunction and

180   tears. By these the inward man is purified and is filled with divine light, and wholly becomes the possession of the Holy Spirit in a contrite soul and a downcast mind. My joy will be a blessing for you and an increase of imperishable and blessed life in Christ Jesus our Lord, to whom be glory forever. Amen.

II

[TO CHRIST THROUGH THE BEATITUDES]

Of the need to avoid pestilential and corrupting persons, and to reject their words and to stand up to practice virtue. Further, that we must examine whether we have in ourselves the characteristics of Christ's beatitudes. Of tears and compunction.

[§ 1. REJECTING THE FALSE REASONINGS OF MEN.]

Brethren and fathers,

Whoever desires to find God, "let him deny himself" (*Mt. 16:24; Mk. 8:34*). Let him not spare his own soul, but let him "set enmity" (*cf. Gen. 3:14; Rom. 8:4*) between himself and all those who walk according to the flesh. Let him not turn back, misled by any of their so-called comforting words, nor let him "sit in their seat" (*Ps. 1:1*). Let him not cultivate bad associations (*1 Cor. 15:33*), which poison the soul and constrain it to be occupied with its former evil reasonings and thoughts. Be afraid, O man, of the bait that accompanies the hook; listen to me, and keep far from them! Do not lead your own soul down again into hell (*cf. Ps. 30:4*). Decide in your mind, and permit it not to err by listening to vain things! Do not turn back (*cf. Lk. 9:62*), do not delay or be weighed down by sloth! "Give not sleep to your eyes" (*Ps. 132:4*) nor "let your taste be sweet" (*Prov. 24:13*) with the pleasant savor of any food, until you see that by which and for which you have been called and the goal you are striving to reach. Reject the thought that suggests to you—"Why must you endure so much trouble, such untimely wretchedness? You have already spent a year, two, or three, at it, and have found no profit in it." My brother, be not trapped by this snare, nor betray

30 your own salvation! Rather, press on with greater zeal and courage in the practice of virtues, and be not faithless toward the
words and teachings of your fathers in God. Determine in your
mind to die rather than depart from this life-giving pursuit; for
had you done this without hesitation from the very beginning
God would not, in His goodness, have disregarded you, but
would have granted you to enjoy what you long for.

[§ 2. RENOUNCING EVERYTHING IN ORDER
TO FIND CHRIST.]

Therefore, my brother, if you wish to attain that which you
strive for and long after, that is, the good things of God, and
from among men become an angel on earth, you must love bodily affliction and embrace suffering. As for trials, love them as
40 the means of obtaining every blessing. Tell me, what is more
beautiful than a soul undergoing tribulation, which knows that
by enduring it will inherit joy in all things? What is more courageous than "a humble and contrite heart" *(Ps. 51:19)*? Without
difficulty it routs the massed troops of devils and pursues them
to their end. What is more glorious than spiritual poverty,
which is the means of obtaining the kingdom of heaven *(cf. Mt.
5:3)*? Can anything equal it either now or in the world to come?
To have no care for any earthly thing for oneself *(cf. Mt. 6:25ff.)*
but to have one's mind wholly set on Christ, how great
50 are the eternal benefits that you think this will procure, how
great an angelic state? To despise all temporal things alike, including even the urgent needs of the body, yet without any rivalry with anyone on this account, so that peace and love may
be preserved undiminished in a tranquil state of mind, what rewards will this not deserve, what crowns and prizes? In truth
the commandment is beyond nature and its rewards beyond
words. For such, Christ will become all and take the place of all
things. Christ—as you hear this do not heed the simplicity of the
word or the brevity of the expression. Rather, join with me in
thinking of the glory of the Godhead, which is beyond thought
60 and understanding. Think of God's unutterable power, His im-
measurable mercy, His inconceivable riches, which He generously and bountifully gives to men. These will suffice them in
place of all [other] things, as they receive into themselves Him
who is the Cause and the Bestower of all blessing. He who has

been found worthy to see Him and contemplate Him has no desire for anything else, nor can he who has been filled with the love of God have more love for anyone on earth.

[§ 3. THE ATTRACTIVENESS OF CHRIST.]

Let us therefore, my beloved brethren, be eager to find Christ and see Him as He is, in His beauty and attractiveness. We see many men who are moved by the desire of transitory things to endure many toils and labors. They will travel great distance and even disregard wife and children and every other glory and enjoyment, and prefer nothing to their purpose in order that they may secure the attainment of their goal. If, then, there are some who make every effort to attain transitory and temporal ends even to the point of laying down their very lives, shall we not deliver our souls and bodies to death for the sake of the King of kings and Lord of lords *(1 Tim. 6:15)*, the Creator and Sovereign of all things? Whither shall we go, brethren, "whither shall we flee from His face? If we go up to heaven, there we shall find Him; if we go down to hell, there He is present. If we go to the uttermost part of the sea, we shall not escape His hand, but His right hand will encompass" our souls and bodies *(Ps. 139:7–10)*. Since then, brethren, we cannot withstand the Lord or flee from His face, come, let us give ourselves as slaves to Him, our Lord and God, who for our sakes "took on Himself the form of a slave" and died for us. Come, let us be humbled under His mighty hand *(1. Pet. 5:6)*, which makes eternal life to spring forth for all, and imparts it abundantly through the Spirit to those who seek [it].

[§ 4. GREATNESS AND CONDESCENSION OF GOD.]

O my dear brethren, with what pain and sorrow my heart is filled when I want to proclaim the wondrous deeds of God's hand and its ineffable beauty, so that you may know and learn its greatness and seek to receive Him within yourselves! Yet I see that some of you lack the desire of fervor to heed what I say and strive for the enjoyment of such glory! This is the reason why I remain altogether tongue-tied; I am quite unable to tell or explain to anyone the glory of Christ our God, which He bestows on those who seek Him with all their soul. How it fills me with amazement! How great are God's gifts! He has left behind the wisdom, the power, and the wealth of the world, and has chosen its weakness, foolishness, and poverty *(1 Cor. 1:27)*, out of His great and ineffable goodness. For this alone who is capable of giving Him worthy thanks? Nearly all men reject the

110 weak and the poor as objects of disgust; an earthly king cannot bear the sight of them, rulers turn away from them, while the rich ignore them and pass them by when they meet them as though they did not exist; nobody thinks it desirable to associate with them. But God, who is served by myriads of powers without number, who "sustains all things by the word of His power" *(Heb. 1:3)*, whose majesty is beyond anyone's endurance, has not disdained to become the father, the friend, the brother of those rejected ones. He willed to become incarnate so that He might become "like unto us in all things except for sin" *(Heb. 4:15)* and

120 make us to share in His glory and His kingdom. What stupendous riches of His great goodness! What an ineffable condescenscion on the part of our Master and our God!

[§ 5. THE SEAL OF CHRIST.]

Why then, brethren, do we not run toward the merciful God who has so loved us? Why do we not give up our souls to death for Christ our God who has died for us? Why are we fearful and why do we dread our departure from the body? Surely hell is not about to receive or take possession of the souls of those who have hoped in Christ. Can death have any power over the souls that have been sealed by the grace of the all-Holy Spir-

130 it and the Blood of Christ? Dare the spiritual wolf look straight at the seal of Christ "the Chief Shepherd" *(1. Pet. 5:4)*, which He places on His own sheep? By no means, faithful brethren of godly mind! Therefore, as many as lack the seal, run to Him! All who have not been signed, hasten to be marked with the sign of the Spirit! But who is he who lacks the seal? He who is frightened of death. Who lacks the sign? He who does not know for sure the form of the sign. For he who has learned of the divine imprint is bold in faith and has acquired hope that cannot be put to shame. Wherefore let us seek Christ, with whom we have

140 been clothed through Holy Baptism *(Gal. 3:27)*. Yet we have been stripped of Him by evil deeds, for though we were sanctified without knowing it while we were yet infants in mind and age, yet we have defiled ourselves in our youth—not to mention

that we defile our souls and bodies every day by the transgression of His commandments! Acordingly let us recall ourselves by salutary repentance, and do and perform all the things that are well pleasing to Christ, so that we may be marked with His seal and from henceforth live without fear. Further, let us receive mercy from His hand so that He may count us worthy to receive "the knowledge of the mysteries of Christ" *(cf. Mt. 13:11; Lk. 8:10)*—that knowledge, I mean, which is not imparted by mere word and sound, but by contemplation in deed and practice.

[§ 6. CHRIST IS OUR WEALTH.]

How then does one contemplate by deed and practice the knowledge of the mysteries of Christ within us? Listen!

Day by day Christ our God explicitly proclaims in His Gospel, "Blessed are the poor in spirit, for theirs is the kingdom of heaven" *(Mt. 5:3)*. When we hear this we ought to look at ourselves and examine ourselves carefully, whether we are such as are truly poor, so that the kingdom of heaven belongs to us in such a way that we may be sure of its possession in the perception of our souls and have such a hold on its riches that we may perceive without doubt that we are within it and that we may enjoy and find pleasure in the blessings that are in it. That it is "within us" *(Lk. 17:21)* the same Lord made known to us. As for the signs and the proof that it is within anyone, they consist in not desiring anything that is visible and subject to corruption, by which I mean the affairs and pleasures of this world, wealth, fame, pleasure, or any other worldly or bodily enjoyment, but that one so abstains from all these things that one takes displeasure at them in soul and in will. It is like the revulsion of those who are in authority and who enjoy royal dignity toward such as spend their lives in surroundings of vice, and as great as the abhorrence of those who wear clean garments and are anointed with perfumed herbs toward evil odors and filth. He who turns to any one of the things that are visible has neither seen that kingdom of heaven nor perceived or tasted its joy and pleasantness.

[§ 7. OF MOURNING AND AFFLICTION.]

Again He says, "Blessed are those who mourn, for they shall be comforted" *(Mt. 5:4)*. Again let us look and examine

ourselves, whether we have that sorrow in ourselves, and what is the comfort He tells us will follow on that sorrow. First, He has pronounced the poor in spirit to be blessed, since the kingdom of heaven is theirs. As has been said, the poor in spirit have no attachment to the things that are present, nor are they even in thought passionately involved with them, not even to the extent of simple enjoyment. How and why, then, will he mourn who has contempt for the whole world and, in addition, so re-
190 moved himself from it in his attitude of mind that he is not close to it in body? He who has no desire for anything that is visible, what cause will he have for grief or joy? How will he mourn who possesses the kingdom of heaven and daily finds his joy in it? For it is to those who mourn that He has promised that they will receive comfort. So I entreat you to listen to what I say, and you will know the sense and the meaning of what I tell you.

When the faithful man, who always pays strict attention to the commandments of God, performs all that the divine commandments enjoin and directs his mind toward their sublimity, that is, to a conduct and purity that are above reproach, he will
200 discover his own limitations. He will find that he is weak and lacks the power to attain to the height of the commandments, indeed that he is very poor, that is, unworthy to receive God and give Him thanks and glory, since he has as yet failed to attain any good of his own. One who thus reasons with himself in the perception of his soul will indeed mourn with that sorrow which is truly most blessed, which will receive comfort and make the soul meek *(cf. Mt. 5:5)*.

[§ 8. THE COMFORT THAT FOLLOWS ON SORROW.]

The pledge of the kingdom of heaven is the comfort that
210 springs from sorrow. According to the apostle, "Faith is the assurance of things hoped for," and the comfort that comes to the souls that mourn from the enlightenment of the Spirit is a visitation of God. On them He bestows the reward of a humble mind, which is called "the seed" *(Lk. 8:5)* and "the talent" *(Mt. 25:15ff.)*, for when it grows and multiplies in the souls of those who struggle it bears fruit for God "thirtyfold and sixtyfold and a hundredfold" *(Mk. 4:20)*, the holy fruit of the gifts of the Spirit. Where there is unfeigned humiliation there is also the depth

of humility, and where there is humility there is also the enlightenment of the Spirit. Where there is the enlightenment of the Spirit there is the outpouring of the light of God, there is God in the wisdom and knowledge of His mysteries. Where these mysteries are to be found, there is the kingdom of heaven and the experience of the kingdom and the hidden treasures of the knowledge of God *(cf. Col. 2:3)*, which include the manifestation of poverty of spirit. Where poverty of spirit is perceived, there is also the sorrow that is full of joy. There are the everflowing tears that purify the soul that loves these things and cause it to be completely filled with light.

By these means the soul looks upward and recognizes its Master. It begins eagerly to bring forth the fruit of the other virtues for Christ and for itself. And naturally, for when it is always being watered and made fruitful by tears and wholly extinguishes its temper it becomes meek *(Mt. 5:5)* and incapable of being moved to anger. On the other hand, it will desire and yearn with both "hunger and thirst" *(Mt. 5:6)* to learn God's judgments. Further, the soul will become "merciful" *(Mt. 5:7)* and compassionate, and by all these things its heart will become pure and, as has been promised, thus attain to the vision of God and clearly see His glory *(Mt. 5:8)*. Those whose souls have become such are in truth "peacemakers" and will be called the sons of the Most High *(Mt. 5:9; Lk. 6:35)*. They clearly recognize their own Father and Master and love Him with all their souls. For His sake they endure every labor and every tribulation; they are insulted, reproached, and in dire straits because of His righteous commandment, which He has enjoined on us as well! They are objects of abuse and persecution; for His name's sake every evil word is falsely spoken against them, yet they gladly endure it and exult *(Mt. 5:11–12)* because they were actually found worthy of suffering dishonor on the part of men for the sake of His love.

Learn then, brethren, what is the true imprint of the seal of Christ. You faithful ones, recognize the features of His mark! Indeed, there is but one seal, the illumination of the Spirit, although the forms of its energies are numerous and the tokens of its virtues are manifold. The first and most necessary of these is humiliation, for it is their beginning and foundation, as of it He says, "On whom will I look, but on him who is humble and con-

trite in spirit, and trembles at My word?" *(cf. Is. 66:2)*. Second is
sorrow and the fountain of tears. Of this I would speak at
260   length, but I am at a loss for the words I would choose to deal
with this topic.

[§ 9. CONCERNING TEARS.]

It is indeed a marvelous thing how that which flows from
eyes, which are the objects of the senses, spiritually washes the
soul of the mire of sins. As they fall to the ground they burn and
crush the devils and set the soul free from the invisible bonds of
sin. O tears, which flow from divine enlightenment and open
heaven itself and assure me of divine consolation! Again and
many times over I utter the same words out of delight and long-
270   ing. Where there is abundance of tears, brethren, accompanied
by true knowledge, there also shines the divine Light. Where
the light shines, there also all good gifts are bestowed and the
seal of the Holy Spirit, from whom spring all the fruits of life, is
implanted in the heart. Here also the fruit of gentleness is borne
for Christ, as well as "peace, mercy, compassion, kindness, goodness, faith, and self-control" *(Gal. 5:22–23)*. It is the source of the
virtue of loving one's enemies and praying for them *(Mt. 5:44)*,
of rejoicing in trials, of glorying in tribulations *(Rom 5:3)*, of
looking on the faults of others as if they were one's own and lamenting them, and of laying down one's life for the brethren
280   with eagerness even unto death.

[§ 10. THE TOKENS OF THE SEAL OF CHRIST.]

Brethren, let us then look and see whether this seal is in us,
and so accurately examine ourselves and carefully observe our
souls. From the aforesaid signs let us recognize whether Christ
is in us. I pray you, Christian brethren, listen and come to your
senses and examine whether "the light has shone in your hearts"
(2 Pet. 1:19), whether you "have seen the great light" *(Is. 9:2)* of
knowledge, whether "the Dayspring from on high has visited
us, shining to those who sit in darkness and the shadow of
290   death" *(Lk. 1:78–79)*. Let us continually give glory and thanks to
the good Master who has granted this gift, and let us strive to
feed and increase the divine fire within us by practicing the
commandments, that fire which makes the divine light shine
more brightly and brilliantly. If, however, we have not yet re-

ceived Christ or His seal and do not recognize these signs in ourselves, but instead see that the deceitful world lives in us and
that we are so unhappy as to live in it, and attach great importance to transitory things and succumb to tribulations; if we are
vexed by injuries and delight in pleasure and riches, what a loss!
What ignorance, what darkness! By what misery and obtuse-   300
ness we are swayed and dragged down to things of earth! In
truth we are objects of pity, totally wretched, alien to eternal
life itself and to the kingdom of heaven! Such are we when we
no longer possess Christ in ourselves, but have the world alive
in us just as we are living in it, and have "our minds set on
earthly things" *(Phil. 3:19; Col. 3:2)*. He who is in this state is an
enemy and opponent of God, for attachment to the world is "enmity toward God" *(Jas. 4:4)*. As God's apostle states: "Do not
love the world or the things in the word" *(1 John 2:15)*. No one   310
is able to serve God and live in accordance with man, since all
the things of the world are obstacles to the love of God and [pre-
vent us from being] well pleasing to Him.

[§ 11. MERCY AND LOVE OF PEACE.]

Is there anyone who loves the glory and the honor that
come from man *(Jn. 5:41, 12:43)* who will ever regard himself as
the last and the most worthless of all? Will he ever become humble in spirit, contrite in heart? Will he ever mourn even if he is
at all able to do so? Does anyone who loves riches and is con-
trolled by love of money and by covetousness become merciful
(Mt. 5:7) and compassionate, instead of being more savage and
cruel than any wild beast? Who ever rids himself of envy or mal-   320
ice if he is dominated by vainglory and possessed by self-con-
ceit? As for him who yields himself to the passions of the flesh
and wallows in the mire of sensual pleasures, does he ever become pure of heart? How will he ever see God who has created
him *(Mt. 5:8)*? How shall one become a peacemaker *(Mt. 5:9)*
who has estranged himself from God? He does not listen to him
who says, "As ambassadors for Christ, God making His appeal
through us, we beseech you, be reconciled to God" *(cf. 2 Cor.
5:20)*. For everyone who stands against God and is at war with   330
Him is an enemy of God, even if he makes all men to be at peace
with each other, for even as he makes them to be at peace with
each other he does it in a way that is not pleasing to God. Since

he is his own first enemy as well as God's, even those whom such make to be at peace become enemies of God *(cf. Jas. 4:4)*. When one is at enmity toward another he in no way understands how to counsel others aright of that which the other approves and which pleases him, nor to instruct them what he desires. The very fact that he is living at variance with him

340 causes him to be ignorant of what he wishes. Moreover, with his antipathy and hostility toward him he is constantly concerned with going contrary to his wishes, so that it becomes a habit. Even should he wish to speak to others in his favor he cannot readily do so, and with good reason. The soul that has no light and is ruled by passions, especially by envy, and thinks with envy of someone, cannot bear that anyone else should speak favorably of the object of its envy, let alone do or even speak anything in his interest. An inveterate passion and a long-standing evil habit in the soul acquire the strength of a [second] nature, so

350 that one may never be able to be cured of it. Such persons are changed from light into darkness; since they have fallen from goodness into wickedness, their sickness is incurable.

[§ 12. SEEING THE LIGHT AND LIVING IN IT.]

He, however, who is united to God by faith and recognizes Him by action is indeed enabled to see Him by contemplation. He sees things of which I am not able to write. His mind sees strange visions and is wholly illuminated and becomes like light, yet he is unable to conceive of them or describe them. His mind is itself light and sees all things as light, and the light has life and imparts light to him who sees it. He sees himself wholly united

360 to the light, and as he sees he concentrates on the vision and is as he was. He perceives the light in his soul and is in ecstasy. In his ecstasy he sees it from afar, but as he returns to himself he finds himself again in the midst of the light. He is thus altogether at a loss for words and concepts to describe what he has perceived in his vision.

[§ 13. POVERTY, HUMILITY, AND GENTLENESS.]

On hearing of these mysteries, who can fail to marvel and as he marvels run to Christ? Who will not long to see God's wondrous works and love Him who freely bestows these gifts and extraordinary graces? Indeed, brethren, there is nothing better in the world than to have nothing that belongs to the world and to desire nothing beyond the bare needs of the body. What these needs are the word [of Scripture] knows—bread and water, clothing and shelter, as God's apostle says, "If we have food and clothing, with these we shall be content" *(1 Tim. 6:8).* Should we have need of anything more than these, He will without fail supply them to us if we trust in Him and believe in Him, since He gives things yet greater and "fills every living thing with plenteousness" *(Ps. 145:16).* Let us but forsake all the other things that belong to this transitory life, such as vainglory, envy, mutual strife, deceit, complaining, intrigue, all the things that turn us away from God and imperil the soul. Let us long with all our soul for the things God commands us to embrace: spiritual poverty, which the word calls humiliation; constant mourning by night and by day, from which there wells forth the joy of the soul and the hourly consolation for those who love God *(Rom. 8:28).* By this means all who strive in truth succeed in attaining meekness. Those who hunger and thirst for righteousness and seek it at all times will obtain the kingdom of God, which "surpasses all human understanding" *(Phil. 4:7).* Further, one becomes merciful, pure in heart, full of peace, a peacemaker, and courageous in the face of trials *(cf. Mt. 5:3–11).* All this is the result of mourning day by day. It also brings it to pass that we hate evil; it kindles in the soul that divine zeal which does not allow it to be ever at ease or to incline to evil deeds with evil men, but fills it with courage and strength to endure to the end against adversities.

[§ 14. WE MUST FLEE THE TRANSITORY WORLD.]

Let us then, dear brethren, flee from the world and "the things that are in the world" *(1 John 2:15).* For what have we in common with the world and the men who are in the world? Let us run, let us pursue, until we have laid hold of something that is permanent and does not flow away, for all things perish and pass away like a dream, and nothing is lasting or certain among things that are seen. The sun, the stars, heaven and earth, all things pass away; of all things man alone abides. What, then, among visible things can profit us at the time when we must needs die, when we depart from hence to the rest that is in the world beyond, when we leave all these things behind? If visible things pass away, what do they avail us when we depart and abandon this body as dead? When the soul abandons its own body it can neither see by means of it nor be seen by any other. From that time on it deals only with the things that are invisible and has no concern for the things that are here. Before it lies a twofold life and destiny, either that of the kingdom heaven and eternal glory, or else the opposite, that of hell and the fiery punishment. It is one of these that it receives from God as its eternal inheritance, as it deserves for its deeds in this life.

[§ 15. BECOMING WORTHY OF THE VISION OF CHRIST.]

For these reasons, then, I urge that we must flee the world. Let us flee from the deceit of life and its supposed happiness and run to Christ alone, who is the Savior of souls. Him let us endeavor to find who is present everywhere, and when we have found Him let us hold Him fast and fall at His feet *(cf. Mt. 28:9)* and embrace them in the fervor of our souls. Nay, I entreat you, let us endeavor to see Him and contemplate Him even in this life. For if we are found worthy sensibly to see Him here we shall not die, "death will have no dominion over us" *(Rom. 6:9)*. Let us not wait to see Him in the future, but strive to contemplate Him now, since John the Theologian tells us, "We know that we have God in our hearts, from the Spirit which we have received from Him" *(1 John 3:24, 2:27)*. If any of you, then, have shown by your works that your faith in Him is unbreakable and solid, and have well and truly examined what we have said before, see that you do not deceive yourselves! Do not imagine that you have Christ in you when you have nothing, and so depart this life with empty hands and hear this word (I pray that He may preserve you from it!): "Take away that which that wicked one thinks he has, and give to him who has more" *(Mt. 25:28f.; Lk. 19:24ff.)*. Then you will weep and lament, and you will have infinite grief forevermore.

Far be it from us, who have denied the whole world and the things in the world and have run to Christ, that we should hear such a voice and suffer such a fate! Rather, when we have kept God's commandments may our hearts be cleansed by tears and penitence, so that from henceforth we may see the divine Light,

410

420

430

440

THE DISCOURSES

Christ Himself, and possess Him abiding in us. Through His most Holy Spirit may He feed our souls and keep them alive by making us taste the pleasant sweetness of those benefits of His kingdom, of which may we all be found worthy in Christ Jesus our Lord, to whom be glory forever and ever. Amen.

III

[FAITHFULNESS TO MONASTIC VOWS]

On the need for proper submission and of mindfulness of the vows we have made to God. That we must not complain about watching all night at Lauds.

[§ 1. RISING AT NIGHT TIME.]

Brethren and fathers,

Keep in mind God's precept that states, "Judge not, and you will not be judged" *(Lk. 6:37)*, and in no way meddle in the lives of others. Rather, do as the priests tell us, but, as you have heard, "do not what they do" *(Mt. 23:3)*. Therefore obey me as servants of Christ, unworthy though I am. Without heeding my faintness of heart and my carelessness consider, I beg you, your own souls and hasten resolutely to perform the commandments. Nor complain against me, wretch as I am, as if it were but once a year that you were roused at midnight, but be mindful of him who said, "At midnight I will rise to give thanks unto Thee because of Thy righteous judgments" *(Ps. 119:62)*. So rather give God thanks, and thank him who has roused you from sleep to glorify God. Rejoice and leap for joy that you have been found worthy to join the holy angels in singing praise to God! For if one is annoyed with the usual Office and complains of the length of the hymns that are sung and is wearied thereby, he really does not know how the oracles of God are sweet in the throat of those who love Him, and "sweeter even than the honey and the honeycomb" *(Ps. 119:103)* in the mouth of those who know Him. He is nothing but flesh, his mind is carnal *(cf. Rom. 8:6f.)* and his perception more carnal still. He is unable spiritually to taste what God, as our Benefactor, has given us. Rather,

60

the things of God all seem bitter to him, and he does not understand the saying, "taste and see how gracious the Lord is" *(Ps.* 30
34:8). He who does not clearly understand this is alien to the
love and the sweetness of Christ. He who has not tasted the
things of God and is a stranger to them—woe is me, how unfor-
tunate am I, for I must make my own what is alien to me!—is an
enemy of God and an alien to the kingdom of heaven. Tell me,
what other hope will he have, to what other love will he cling,
what other comfort will he find, either here or after death? But
he who contradicts and complains and curses those who rouse
him for the divine praise and the glorifying of God, what de- 40
fense will he find on the day of judgment, when both for himself
and for others he has become an offense to cause perdition?

[§ 2. SYMEON'S SADNESS AT THE TEPIDITY OF HIS MONKS.]

Believe me, my spiritual fathers and brethren, whenever I
hear these things or even find any of you suffering because of
them, I am oppressed by such affliction and my heart is so
vexed that it seems as if I were delivered to such punishment. I
feel no more joy in the world and even would rather not live. I
weep and lament as though I were already condemned, since I
plead with you without being heard, I rebuke you and am ignored. I reprove you and become the object of hatred, I correct 50
you and am in turn chastised, and suffer persecution as though I
were an enemy, and as I do these things I cannot find rest. I
wish I could stop and look only on my own faults, but whenever
I want to make this decision, then my heart is kindled like a
flame *(cf. Jer. 20:9)* and I, wretched man, am at it again! I am
constrained and suffer pain for your wounds no less than every
one [else] suffers for his own stripes. It is for you that I burn and
find life unlivable. I am seized by amazement—how have we
sunk down to such a darkening [of mind] that we do everything
against our own souls, murder ourselves, kick ourselves as 60
though we still were alive, joyfully chain ourselves with our
sins, and devour those who remove such bonds? If someone prevents us from doing what is harmful to our souls we bark at him
like mad dogs and reproach him and do not cease until we have
done the action and have destroyed our souls. Then, when the
habit of these unlawful acts has grown on us, we, as it were, be-

come evil by nature and are no longer willing to reconsider. We
have professed to be monks and have become worse than the
70 worldly! We have agreed to suffer hunger and thirst and mortification, yet we are not ashamed of arguing and cursing over a
single crust of bread—even, perhaps, one that we want outside
the set time for meals. We have come to renounce all who are in
the world, that is, parents, brothers, and friends, yet cease not to
feed them even better with the bread of the monastery. Though
we have fled from the world as from an enemy, we love the persons and things that belong to the world more than we love
Christ Himself!

[§ 3. THE PURPOSE OF MONASTIC PROFESSION.]

Please tell me, brother, when you entered the monastery
did you believe that there is a judgment and resurrection and a
80 recompense for what we have done in this life? Did you confess
that there is a God who "will repay every man for what he has
done" *(Mt. 16:27)*? Or did you ponder none of these things in
your heart? Have you come in order to keep the vows to which
you have assented, which you promised to Christ "in the presence of many witnesses" *(1 Tim. 6:12)*? Or did you deceitfully
pretend this in order to associate yourself with the community
and grasp at becoming a member of the Church with no other
purpose in mind than that of receiving without fail enough food
to satisfy your gluttony and of living a life without anxiety or
toil? If, however, you have come in order to become a servant of
Christ and our brother, I beg you, keep His commandments!
90 Display eagerness to serve Him with fervor, that by your deeds
you may appear to be a true Christian and bear the name of our
brother who loves God and become like us in all things. "Take
your share in suffering as a good soldier" *(2 Tim. 2:3)*, so that
you may receive the crown and "be glorified with Him" *(Rom.
8:17)* and delight in eternal glory. If, however, it was in pure
pretense that you came to be tonsured and to become a monk,
and you thought only of eating and drinking with them and
finding everything as it were ready of itself, listen, and I will tell
you what things will happen to you. First and most important,
know that you will not be reconciled to God or accepted as His
100 friend, but you will be accounted His enemy and a traitor to
Him. How can you avoid being a traitor when you meditate one

thing in your heart and profess something else before all men? Do you think that you are deceiving God who cannot be deceived? He explicitly commands all, "Be not anxious concerning the morrow, what you shall eat or what you shall drink or what you shall wear" *(Mt. 6:34, 35)*. But you have received the tonsure solely in order to be a brother and share in possessions and money you perhaps might not have owned if you had been in the world. The apostle exhorts us, saying, "If we have food and clothing, with these we shall be content" *(1 Tim. 6:8)*. But you are not content with what is strictly necessary and even steal and purloin things that belong to the monastery! In all the things that pertain to bodily pleasure and care you wish to be the brother of all, without special effort, and even to be equal to those who toil hard in the work of the Lord. But when it comes to fasting and vigil and bodily mortification, let alone mourning and ceaseless prayer, standing all night, psalmodies, and spiritual songs, if you see some of the brethren eagerly practicing this and running with all their soul and all their purpose, you claim that you are an outsider and unable to do these things. Not only that, but when you go into hiding and are not present at the Office you think that you gain something for yourself! O what exceeding blindness and ignorance and delusion in your thoughts! What is yet more dangerous, when you are put to a very slight test by your superior appearing before you and trying you out by causing you some slight distress, you even deny your very habit and say (as I have often heard said), "Have I come here to become somebody's slave, am I here to be insulted?" O what madness!

[§ 4. THE STRUGGLE TO KEEP ONE'S VOWS.]

Have you not come to fight against invisible foes? Did you not come here to take up the warfare against your passions? For what reason did you wish to be enlisted and take your place in the ranks of Christ's soldiers? Was it to receive rations and pay on the same terms as they, and to sit at their table like those who on the stage eat their fill and get drunk? If that is what you think, woe is you on the day of judgment, when Christ comes "to repay every man for what he has done" *(Mt. 16:27)*. Then He will require of His monks, who have pledged themselves to Him "in the presence of many witnesses," the vows they have

110

120

130

140 promised to perform and observe before the holy altar and His
holy angels. What are the questions to which we must reply? Is
this not why we have approached the holy altar and this holy as-
sembly? Is it with a desire for embracing the monastic life and
the angelic way of living? And what do we answer to this question? "Yes, reverend father." The priest then says to us, "You
know, brethren, that inasmuch as you have come to be numbered with the servants of Christ the King you have prepared
yourselves for trials. Know well, then, that from now on especially the enemy will set in motion every device against you.
You must therefore be hungry and thirsty and cold, be dishon-
150 ored and spat upon, be slapped in the face and be mocked, and
endure all painful things that are in accordance with God."
What do we reply to these words? Do we not promise to suffer
and endure all things, and pronounce the answer "Yes, reverend
father" to every question about the endurance of afflictions? Do
we not before God and the angels agree to observe self-control,
vigils, and prayers, and obedience till death to our superior and
the whole community? And now our disposition is such as if
there were no one who will require an account from us of the
160 vows we have made. We pass our time without fear of God and
in contempt of His commandments. We are arrogant not only
toward the rest of the community, but even toward our superiors. We complain, contradict, curse, and are lazy; we do all the
things God hates, and which lead our souls to destruction in the
fire of hell.

[§ 5. FERVOR AS THE ANTIDOTE AGAINST PASSIONS.]

Where from all eternity has one heard of so great a work of
deceit? What devil will invent a means of destruction against
our souls that is greater than this? Or, rather, what more will
the devils plan or plot against us? Since the devils see us domi-
170 nated by the will of the flesh, they see that we carry our death
with us. For what other reason do they wage war against us?
The whole warfare of the demons against us is waged with the
one purpose of alienating those who obey them from the glory
of God and the grace of the Holy Spirit. But, as I see it, we have
already deprived ourselves of such a gift before they even attack
us, because we have forsaken the commandments of God and
have not been eager to seek Him with all our soul. Had we

sought Him we should not have lived so idly and carelessly! Had   180
we been concerned for the things of heaven we should not have
shown such great eagerness for the things of earth. Had our
thoughts been on things incorruptible we should not have gaped
greedily after the things that are transitory and corruptible.
Had we striven for things eternal we should not thus have pursued things temporal. Had we loved God we should not thus
have turned away from those who guide us to Him. Had we
sought to acquire virtues we would not have abhorred the teachers of virtues. Had we gladly embraced fasting we should not
have complained of the lack of food and drink. Had we fought to   190
gain control over our passions we should not have given ourselves unrestrainedly to pleasures. Had we a right and firm faith
we should not have performed the works of the faithless. Had
we the fear of God in our hearts, we should not have opposed
those who are His true servants in every virtue pleasing to God.
Had we acquired humility we should not have been arrogant toward God's servants. Had we been found worthy to attain true
love we should have known God. We should have been eager
not only for discipline, but even to suffer dishonor and blows,
injustice, curses, every trial and every affliction, for Christ's   200
sake.

[§ 6. HOW INDIFFERENCE MAKES LIGHT OF FAULTS.]

Now, however, we are so enslaved by passions and find
ourselves in such blindness and ignorance that we do not even
perceive our condition nor realize that we are doing badly.
Therefore, even when we are reminded by someone of some sin
we reply as though we had never heard the Christian Scriptures.
[We ask,] "But is this action a sin? For what reason or what
cause is it considered a sin? It is unreasonable that some people
should call it a sin! As long as we take care of the more important matters God will not at all be strict about these details."   210
Who are they that say these things? Monks, of all people! Those
who have renewed their profession and their vow with God,
those who wear the habit as [a sign of] virtue and bear the name
as [a title of] holiness. They have covenanted with Christ to cast
away "the world and the things in the world," and have professed renunciation of parents and friends; they have covenanted to be subject to their spiritual father as to God, and have

committed themselves to rigorous asceticism extending even to looks and careless words *(Mt. 12:36)*. By such monks, envying, reviling, complaining, contradicting, lying, living in one's own way, swearing, purloining what belongs to the monastery or giving it to someone without the superior's consent, are not regarded as sins! Moreover, they do not consider it at all sinful to mismanage affairs that have been entrusted to them, such as acting in any matter with passionate attachment or with personal interest, with deceit, envy, unscrupulousness, or with cunning!

Do you not tremble, O man, when you hear God day by day saying to you through the whole of sacred Scripture, "Let no evil talk come out of your mouths" *(Eph. 4:29)*? In truth I tell you, "You will render account for every careless word" *(Mt. 12:36)*, and receive a reward even for the gift of a drink of cold water *(cf. Mt. 10:42; Mk. 9:41)*. Have you not heard that God is Judge "of the thoughts and intentions of the heart" *(Heb. 4:12)*? What does He say? "He who looks at a woman lustfully has already committed adultery with her in his heart" *(Mt. 5:28)*. Do you see how he who looks at someone's face with lust is judged as an adulterer? Know then for sure, O man, that he who is ruled by lust of money is judged covetous, even though he possesses nothing at all. He who lusts after many and costly dishes is a glutton, even though he on account of poverty feeds on nothing but bread and water. He is a whoremonger who attaches himself to his imaginations and so is defiled, even though he has never seen the face of anyone. So too he who says in his heart, "This has been badly done, and has not turned out right," and "Why has this and that happened?" "Why did that not happen?"—let him not deceive himself. He is a slanderer and will be judged as one who condemns, even though he utters not a word with his tongue and no one hears his voice.

[§ 7. NO SIN IS TRIFLING.]

Be not deceived, my brethren. God loves mankind, He is merciful and compassionate. Of this I bear witness and this I confess, for it is by His compassion that I am confident that I will be saved. But know this, that it will be of no avail for those who are impenitent and do not keep His commandments with all exactitude and with much fear; they will be punished far more severely than the unbelieving and unbaptized heathen. Be not deceived, brethren; let not any of your offenses appear insignificant to you, nor dismiss them with contempt as though they do not greatly damage your souls. Servants who are grateful do not recognize any difference between a small offense and a great one. Even if their offense consists merely in a glance or a thought or a word, they feel about it as though they have fallen from the love of God, which I believe is true. He who even 260 thinks the least thought that is at variance with the divine will and does not at once, when he has repulsed the assault of that thought, become penitent, but instead accepts the thought and dwells on it, is considered to have committed a sin. Even if he is ignorant of the evil it is so accounted. For once the Law came, that is, the teaching of the Holy Scriptures, the evil that was restrained in ignorance revived *(cf. Rom. 7:9)* and sin was found dwelling in me *(Rom. 7:17, 20)* and I became dead *(Rom. 7:10)* and alien to goodness.

[§ 8. DISCERNMENT OF THOUGHTS.]

We must therefore carefully discern the thoughts that come on us and set against them the testimonies from the divinely in- 270 spired Scriptures and from the teaching of the spiritual [teachers], the holy Fathers, so that if we find them to agree with these witnesses and correspond to them we may with all our might hold fast these thoughts and boldly act on them. But if they are not in harmony with "the word of truth" *(Eph. 1:13; Col. 1:5)* we must expel them from us with much anger, as it is written, "Be ye angry, and sin not" *(Ps. 4:5)*. As from something defiling and from the sting of death, so must we flee from the interior assault of passionate thoughts. Accordingly we need great soberness, great zeal, much searching of the divine Scriptures. The Savior 280 has shown us their usefulness by saying, "Search the Scriptures" *(Jn. 5:39)*. Search them and hold fast to what they say with great exactitude and faith, in order that you may know God's will clearly from the divine Scriptures and be able infallibly to distinguish good from evil *(Heb. 5:14)* and not obey every spirit *(1 John 4:1)* nor be carried away with harmful thoughts *(cf. Eph. 4:14)*. Be assured, my brethren, that nothing is so conducive for saving us as the following of the divine precepts of the Savior. Nevertheless we shall need many tears, much fear, much patience and persistent prayer, if the full meaning of even one 290

single saying of the Master is to be revealed to us, in order that
we may know the great mystery hidden in small words, and lay
down our lives unto death even for a single dot of God's commandments. For the word of God is "like a two-edged sword"
(Heb. 4:12), which cuts off and separates the soul from every
bodily lust and feeling. Even more, it becomes like a burning fire
(Jer. 20:9, 23:29) in that it kindles the zeal of the soul. It causes us
to despise all life's painful experiences and to count as joy every
300   trial that assails *(Jas. 1:2)*, and to desire and embrace death,
which is so frightening to other men, as life and the cause of life.

[§ 9. HOW THE SPIRITUAL WARFARE NEVER CEASES.]

I entreat you therefore, my brethren, let us come to our
senses. As we stir up one another by the encouragement of the
word to zeal and to imitation of that which is good, let us run
with zeal and hasten with eagerness and fervent will. By means
of detachment let us separate ourselves from the world, by humility let us be united to the saints who have been from of old.
Let us "put off the old man" *(Col. 3:9)* by cutting off the earthly
310   will and by the mortification of the mind of clay. Let us put on
"the new Adam," Jesus Christ *(cf. 1 Cor. 15:45)* through pure
and immaterial prayer and wipe ourselves clean with constant
tears. Hour by hour, day by day, let us by penitence work at being renewed, so that we may learn to fight and wrestle with the
devils, our enemies who are always at war with us. He who has
not obtained the weapons of which we have spoken will not be
able to stand in the day of battle *(cf. Eph. 6:11ff.)* but will be
wounded again and again. Since he lacks those weapons he can-
320   not live in peace and freedom, for the warfare within ourselves
is not like the wars and weapons that are outside, but is far more
terrible. When men fight against other men they at times fight
with weapons, but at other times they withdraw and stop fighting and lay down their arms and in all security enjoy sleep and
food. Often they surround themselves with fortifications and
take turns to be on guard duty. Thus he who takes to flight sur-
vives; if he is taken prisoner he may perhaps escape being slain,
but having exchanged his freedom for honorable servitude he
330   may even rise to greater fame and fortune. Here it is different;
warfare goes on constantly, and the soldiers of Christ must at all
times be armed with their weapons. Neither by night nor by

day nor for a single instant is this warfare interrupted, but even when we eat or drink or do anything else *(cf. 1 Cor. 10:31)* we find ourselves in the thick of battle. It is incorporeal enemies that we face; they are constantly facing us even though we do not see them. They are watching us closely to see whether they can find some member of ours unprotected so that they may be able to stab it with their weapons and slay us. No one can seek 340 protection for himself behind visible walls and ramparts and even for a single hour hide himself and briefly catch his breath, nor can anyone flee and be saved thereby, nor yet may we engage in the battle by relays. On all men there lies the inescapable necessity of joining in this conflict. No one may escape the alternatives of either winning and staying alive or of being overcome and dying.

[§ 10. THE NEED FOR REPENTANCE.]

The deadly wound consists of every sin that is not repented and confessed, and of falling into despair. This depends on our choice and will. If we do not yield ourselves to the pit of care- 350 lessness and despair the devils cannot at all prevail over us. Even when we have been wounded, if we so wish we may through fervent penitence become more courageous and skillful fighters. To rise again and fight after being wounded and slain belongs to the noblest and bravest—it is worthy of great praise and most admirable. It does not depend on us whether we should be preserved from suffering wounds. To become either mortal or immortal depends on us, for if we do not despair we shall not die, "death will have no dominion over us" *(Rom. 6:9)*, but we shall 360 always be strong if we flee in penitence to our all-powerful and gracious God.

Therefore I encourage myself and us all to display all eagerness, all patient courage and endurance by means of good deeds. Thus may we make our way through all the commandments and precepts of Christ, so that in readiness of soul we may attain to the eternal habitations by the guidance of the Spirit. So shall we be found worthy to stand before the one and indivisible Trinity and in Him worship Christ our God, to whom be the glory and the power forever and ever. Amen. 370

IV

[ON TEARS OF PENITENCE]

Of penitence and compunction, and by what kind of
deeds it is possible to achieve it. How it is impossible
for anyone without tears to achieve purity and freedom
from passion.

[§ 1. COMMUNICATING WITH TEARS.]

Fathers and brethren,

You read the inspired writings of our holy father Symeon
the Studite on his sublime actions, which he, being moved by
the Spirit of God, composed for the benefit of many. Among his
many extraordinary practices there was this in particular,
10   which he observed without fail throughout his life and in teaching and writing summed up as follows: "Brother, never communicate without tears." At this his hearers—and they were many,
both laymen and also monks who were well known and renowned for virtue—were amazed. As they looked at one another
they would say, gently smiling, with one accord and with one
voice, "Well then, we shall never again communicate, but we
shall all go without communion." When I miserable and wretched man had heard them speak and privately remembered those
20   who had said these things and what they had said I was greatly
distressed and wept bitterly. In anguish of heart I spoke thus
within myself: "Is this really their attitude toward this matter?
Did they say what they said because they thought in their soul
that this is impossible? Or did they not rather mock his statement because they thought it a trifling thing to weep at the time
of communion?" In every way, unless one takes the trouble every day and night to weep before Christ [our] God, even when
he wishes to partake of the divine Mysteries he will be unable in
any way to mourn or weep or shed tears in a godly manner.

How could he, unless it were to come upon him by some ineffa-   30
ble divine dispensation or some rare chance? To me it does not
seem strange, since many at the very moment of the departure
of their souls have wept and shed tears. (They were not many, I
think, but very few and easy to count.) But if they think it wholly impossible day by day to partake of the awesome Mysteries
with tears, what ignorance on their part, what lack of feeling!
Alas for the folly, the indifference, the hardness of heart of those
who say these things! For if they judged themselves, they would   40
not be judged by their own words *(cf. 1 Cor. 11:31)*. If they paid
attention to repentance they would not have uttered the words
"it is impossible." Had they pursued fruitful activity, they
would not have been entirely without experience of so great a
benefit, such a gift of God. Had they acquired the fear of God in
their hearts they would have borne witness that it is possible to
mourn and to weep, not only at the time of the receiving of the
divine Mysteries, but at any time, so to speak.

[§ 2. COMPUNCTION—THE FRUIT OF THE WILL.]

Therefore, it is with the desire to satisfy your charity about
this matter that I should wish to pose this question, as if I were
addressing those who speak in this way: "Tell me, most excel-   50
lent brethren, why is this impossible?" They say, "It is because
some are readily and easily brought to compunction, while others are hard-hearted and have hearts of stone so that even when
they are beaten they are without compunction. How are those
who are so disposed able to mourn and weep, and how can they
always communicate with tears? Even the very priests who celebrate the divine and bloodless liturgy, how are they able to
weep?" "As for the fact that they are hard and difficult to move
to compunction, tell us, if you know, how this happened to
them? If you do not know, be not ashamed to come down a little   60
from your high perch and listen kindly to me, and do not disdain to learn from me, who am the last of all. For it is written,
"If a revelation is made to the last, let the first be silent" *(cf. 1.
Cor. 14:30)*.

You say, "What is the cause that one is hardened, and another readily moved to compunction?" Listen! It springs from
the will, in the latter case a good will, in the former an evil one.
It springs also from the thoughts, in the former case evil

thoughts, in the latter from the opposite; and similarly from actions, in the former case actions contrary to God, in the latter godly ones. Examine, if you wish, all who have ever lived and you will find that it is from these three causes only that many who were good became evil, and many who were evil became good. To recount them from the beginning, why did Lucifer fall *(cf. Is. 14:12)*? Was it not by consenting to evil in will and thought? Why did Cain become a fratricide *(Gen. 4:8)*? Was it not by his evil will? He preferred himself to his Creator and followed after evil thoughts and so became abandoned to envy and committed murder. Why did Saul seek to apprehend and kill David whom he had formerly honored as himself and greatly loved as a benefactor *(cf. 1 Sam. 18:24ff.)*? Was it by nature or out of an evil will? Obviously it was out of ill will. No one is born evil by nature, since God did not create evil works but things that were very good *(Gen. 1:31)*. Or, rather, He did so since He is good, and that not by disposition and choice, but in nature and in truth. Further, why did the one bandit who was crucified with the Master Jesus Christ say, "If you are the Son of God, save yourself and us," while the other replied to him, "Do you not fear God? For we indeed [suffer] justly, for we are receiving the due reward of our deeds, but this man has done nothing wrong" *(Lk. 23:39ff.)*? Tell me, why did the one utter the former speech, and the other the latter? Why was the one justified, and the other condemned? Was it not because of each man's will and thoughts, good in the case of the one, evil in the case of the other? It was by these that the one came to unbelief, while the other acquired faith as he said, "Remember me, Lord, in Thy kingdom" *(Lk. 23:42)*.

[§ 3. THE CHOICE OF THE WILL.]

I will pass over the other examples because they are so many. But learn and be instructed by the examples I shall mention that it is by the free choice of the will that every person either attains compunction and humility, or else becomes hardhearted and proud. It stands to reason. Suppose two men renounce the world, men of the same occupation, the same family, the same age, two brothers of the same mind and habits. They are both wicked and hard, without mercy, very cruel, licentious and avaricious, and pass from all kinds of evil and wickedness to enter simultaneously on the career of asceticism. The one succeeds in attaining to all virtues together; by a fervent faith and will he makes a total break with all vices, while the other becomes worse than he was before he made his renunciation. Why did not they not both equally succeed in virtue just as they both became champions of wickedness? Is it not because the one endured all afflictions according to God's will by the set purpose of a good soul, and in addition that he from his first entry into religion and his renunciation attentively applied himself to the divine Scriptures? And that he spontaneously, on his own, chose to do good by imitating the lives of the most godly men and clung to them in fastings and prayers *(cf. Lk. 2:37)*, in supplications *(cf. 1 Tim. 2:1)*, in the silence of his lips, in compunction and tears, in abstinence from pleasant foods and from untimely conversations, by restraint of temper and anger and complaining? Did he not patiently endure insults, tribulations, and distress *(cf. 2 Cor. 6:4, 12:10)* and choose the meanest and lowliest tasks without contradicting or murmuring when he was commanded, but eagerly fulfilled them all? He always sought for the lowest place *(cf. Lk. 14:10)* and considered himself more worthless than all [others]; in short, he did with knowledge all things that the divine Scriptures clearly teach us, in order to obtain mercy and pardon for his past vices and find assurance before God. The other, as he did the opposite of all these things out of the will of a wicked soul, remained the wicked man that he was before he made his renunciation, if I should not say even worse than he was before.

[§ 4. HOW SOME MONKS HAVE NO COMPUNCTION.]

Thus it is not, as some think, by nature but by will that every man becomes either humble and apt for compunction, or hard-hearted, hardened, and insensitive. When, tell me, will he be contrite in soul and shed a tear from his eyes who passes almost all the day aimlessly without paying heed either to silence of lips, or prayer, or reading, or recollection, but at times talks to his neighbors at the Offices (thus depriving of profit both himself and those to whom he talks), at other times disparages and reproaches the devout brethren and sometimes even the superior himself? When will he acquire compunction who meddles in all the affairs of the monastery, and not of the monastery

140   alone, but of everyone's life? One who at times says to some of the brethren, "Yesterday I heard such and such," and again, "Do you know what happened to poor so-and-so?" and, "Did you hear of such a one's misfortune?" Will such a person ever be mindful of his own vices and be so distressed that he will shed a tear from his eyes? One who leaves the Office at the time of reading of the divine Scriptures to sit somewhere near some and converse with some of the others, one after the other, as they re-tail unprofitable events in such terms as these, "Have you heard

150   how the abbot treated brother so-and-so?" and the other, "But what will you say if I tell you how he treated that poor fel-low?"—he who occupies himself and others with such conversa-tions and worse than these, and with such nonsense, when will he attain to the perception of his own faults and bewail himself?

[§ 5. ATTENDANCE AT THE OFFICES IS NOT ENOUGH.]

     What of a man who does not heed the inspired oracles and does not "set a watch about his lips" *(Ps. 141:3)*, nor turn away his ear from hearing vanity *(Ps. 119:37)*? One who is not mindful of the final defense before Christ and His awesome judgment seat, where we must all stand before Him naked and exposed to view *(Heb. 4:13)* and give account of the lives that we have lived?

160   Even if he has lived more than a hundred years in the monastic habit, how will he find a tear that he may fervently mourn over himself? How will he who seeks for the front place in the church and the first seat at table and is always fighting and grieved for such things ever grieve for his own soul and weep bitterly *(Lk. 22:62)* before God? He who "makes excuses for his sins" *(Ps. 141:4 LXX)* pleads his weakness even though he is strong and vigorous and young? One who stands in the church

170   and compares himself with the more devout brethren who have labored much and spent a long time in asceticism and says, "Surely I am not inferior to this man or that man? He has a place where he can lean at prayer and stands there when he comes back." If he puts himself on a level with them (though he may be unworthy of even the lowest place!), will he ever become conscious of his own weakness, so that he may groan in his soul, be contrite of heart, and weep with his eyes? The vainglory that enslaves him to *accidie* will never permit him to persevere in

180   anything with patience. Anyone who is in this state will from

thenceforth waste his time in idleness and carelessness at every Office as he constantly tells vain and silly stories to those of his neighbors who endure listening to him. So when he joins with spiritual and God-fearing men for the divine Offices he does so without feeling, or, rather, without pain. He goes out from thence without any benefit and perceives no change whatever for the better coming on him. Such a change is given by God to those who strive through compunction. He thinks that it is enough for him that he merely does not miss the compulsory Offices, that is, lauds [Orthros] and vespers and the hours that are sung in common,[1] and that by simply doing this he will at- 190
tain to perfect virtue and to the perfection of those who have achieved it, to "the full stature of Christ" *(Eph. 4:13)*. I have known some who were under such a delusion and who most zealously avoided any fall into carnal sin, in the sense of union with the bodies of others, and who were yet not at all concerned to avoid sins committed in secret or meditated in the hidden depth of the heart. They thought that they would be saved without any further effort, without prayer, silence, vigil, abstinence, poverty of spirit *(Mt. 5:3)*, humility, or love, but merely by at- 200
tending the Offices in the way mentioned above. But this is not so! God does not look on the appearance *(1 Sam. 16:7)* nor on the mere sobriety of conduct, nor on our cries, brethren! He looks on the "contrite and humbled heart" *(Ps. 51:19)*, the heart that is quiet and clothed with the fear of God. "On whom," says He, "will I look, but on the man that is humble and quiet, and who trembles at My word?" *(Is. 66:2 LXX)*.

[§ 6. CARELESS BEHAVIOR IN THE CHURCH.]

But what shall I say of those who approach their superiors without just cause and make demands on them? There are some 210
who are concerned with a merely external devotion, or, rather, who seek only for personal advantage and glory and for things present. They say, "Reverend Father, are we not also worthy to serve the monastery and the brethren? Or is it only this one or that one who is worthy to render the one service or the other? Does he know better than us how to administer things? If you

---

1. I.e., as distinct from the prayers that each monk had to say individually, and from the midnight Office.

wish, try us out, and you will find that we are more suitable for carrying on and administering the affairs of the monastery."

220 Others since their very renunciation have given themselves over to carelessness and laxity on the pretext of bodily weakness. Some have come from the world but yesterday or the day before and are full of a myriad of vices. Instead of submitting and toiling and laboring at the work of God they go off and stand, as I have mentioned, with those who have labored much and lean upon them. If his neighbor says to one of them, "Depart, brother, to your usual place and stand there to sing with the brethren, for you are able to do so," he will reply, "If I listen
230 to those who are here and stand closer to them, I will sing better than where I usually stand." If the brother tells him again, "You may not stand here, brother, without being ordered to by our superior," he will go off as soon as he hears this and ask the superior, pretending weakness and infirmity of body, until he attains his end. He says, "Father, it is in order that I may hear the first canonarch[2] that I stand in the first or second row, next to so and so." Thus he makes himself equal to him who has endured many labors. When he has attained his end he can no
240 longer endure standing up in the choir. Gradually he who in every other way is anxious to number himself among the first counterfeits an outward piety and pretends a modesty in behavior. He rushes to welcome those who come to the monastery, whether they are friends of the other [monks] or prominent people, and frequently goes off to see the brethren whom they visit in order to become well known to them, pretending that he is helped by their conversations and their interpretations of the divine Scriptures.

[§ 7. "CHARITABLE" MONKS WHO LIVE DAINTILY.]

He then begins to run through the monastery and go from cell to cell, as he says to each one, "Believe me, brother, I have
250 such love for you that if I do not see you I do not consider that I

---

2. The monk who intones the text or other variable parts of the Office, which is then sung by the others—a device useful when there were but few books available, and which also enabled all to understand the sense of what was being sung.

have even lived that day." If among those whom he visits and tells this one is found who fears God, he will say in reply, "May God remember your love, brother, for what good do you see in me?" But that man will then say, "But what virtue is not yours? Who is as gentle, devout, wise, intelligent, and sincere as you? What is greatest of all, you have a father's affection and love all your brethren." When he says this his aim is to have a meal with him. The spiritual brother converses with him "according to the grace that is given to him" *(2 Pet. 3:15)* about the things that pertain to the salvation of the soul and, to his best ability, refuses   260
his praises and corrects his brother. If, however, he is otherwise and, on the contrary, carnal and unstable, he is at once filled with conceit by that man's praises and replies to him, saying, "And what is greater than love, O father and brother? Nothing whatever, and blessed is he who has gained possession of it," and other things that he knows the flatterer will accept and will encourage him in his praise. When he has been beguiled, so to speak, by those insincere praises, such a man becomes conceited in the emptiness of his mind. If he belongs to those who have means he will then not allow him to leave but bids him eat with him. So as he entertains him with food he receives empty com-   270
pliments in return, which, though they dissolve into the air, yet inflict great harm on his soul. If this is not the case, after long and useless conversations he tells him, "Please do not blame me, brother. Love knows that I have no food fit for you to join me over it. But since you have such kindliness and love toward our lowliness, we shall from now on enjoy together as friends whatever the Lord will supply us for food and rejoice with you." From then on an unceasing concern enters the minds of them   280
both, and they do not cease to seek occasions on which they may cultivate and strengthen their apparent friendship by gorging themselves on food.

When he has thus bound himself to everybody by pretended love, or rather by deceit, he sometimes himself invites someone, at other times he is invited by them, and so never lacks a table with abundant delicacies to satisfy him. He thus becomes a pig and is addicted to pleasures and constantly pampers his stomach—I hesitate to say his paunch. As he then eagerly fills   290
his belly by means of the alms he collects he goes off every eve-

ning after compline into his cell[3] and says to the one who serves him, "Look, poor fellow, I am desperately thirsty. Make me something warm and give me a drink of it and relieve my thirst." The other, as usual, is immediately attentive and a very prompt servant, and joins him in his feasting and drinks the strongest possible wine and guzzles it down, with the darkness ensuring that it is in secret. After he has had a drink his appetite

300 is aroused. Imperceptibly he is as it were led astray by the tasty food; without realizing it he eats it greedily and fattens his stomach and makes it intractible so that it does not respond to the impulse of the soul. Then a thought tells him, "Dismiss your attendant and stand for your usual prayer." But another thought replies and tells him, "And how will you be able to stand up when you are all full and stuffed? Take a little nap and help nature to digest the food and then get up before the Office. Then, when your body is mobile, you will pray the better." He obeys this thought and lies down and falls asleep, and if he

310 awakes he does not rise, but says, "It is early, I will sleep a little longer." So, as he procrastinates, the time for the Office of Orthros [lauds] arrives. He then rises and turns up for the Office, with his conscience accusing him of his carelessness and slackness.

So, as we have said, as he is accustomed he frequently goes off to the cells of his friends and his favorite fathers and stays late, joining them in eating and drinking and conversation. When he then returns to his own cell he has profited neither from vespers nor yet the morning Office, since he is incapable

320 of thinking or practicing anything that is spiritual. Even in his own cell, if anyone happens to come to see him, he spends the whole night in the same way, sometimes even criticizing and condemning the lives of others. So he continues and wastes his whole lifetime in "dissipation and drunkenness and cares" (*Lk. 21:34*) that do not profit.

[§ 8. FAILURE IN SPIRITUAL EXERCISES MEANS LACK OF VIRTUE.]

But why have I expounded all these things? In order that I

---

3. The monastic rules strictly forbid eating, drinking, conversation, and leaving one's cell after the last Office of the day, which is compline.

may show you, brethren, that he who lives such a life will never be able to shed a [penitential] tear from his eyes. How can he, when he is always pampering his stomach and, like the heathen, is constantly preoccupied with what he shall eat and drink *(Mt. 6:31ff.)* and enslaved, as to a mistress, to the pleasure of the gullet? But suppose that he avoids the things we have mentioned and does not go off to the cell of another nor entertain anybody in his own cell, nor give himself to gluttony, drinking, or idle talk, but shuts his door and stays alone inside his cell. What use is it, if his activity is not spiritual and with knowledge, but he sits to read something in order to learn it by heart so that he may recite it at the time of the Office, or even do so in the presence of his friends and thus appear to be clever? Let us suppose that this is not the reason why he attends the [reading of the] divine Scriptures, but rather that he may profit from them and hear God's word. Then he rises to stand for prayer. His prayer may consist of two or three psalms, or ten, or a hundred; he may make as many reverences as you wish. But if he has done all these things, and nothing more, and then lies down to sleep, what has he profited by being thus occupied, and thus only, if his prayer and his reading do not bear fruit and blossom in his soul through the tears of penitence? This fruit consists in the absence of passion, humility attained together with gentleness, knowledge together with the wisdom of the Spirit. Everyone who labors with knowledge at the spiritual work of God's commandments will, without any doubt whatever, acquire the virtues mentioned above in proportion to his arduous labor and as its fruit. But he who labors in appearance only, without these virtues blossoming out of his labors, does not work in accordance with God but only to please men *(Gal. 1:10)* and will of course fail to attain the better [gifts].

[§ 9. SPIRITUAL GIFTS BESTOWED ON A HUMBLE AND CONTRITE HEART.]

If, then, each of those whom we have mentioned spends his life in this way, will he ever attain to tears and compunction like him who from the beginning of his renunciation has wholly given himself to endure afflictions and suffer according to God? Will he be able to cast away the malice, wickedness, and hardness of heart that accompany him from the world, and achieve

370

380

390

400

humility? In no way! He who holds that opinon and so legislates, whoever he may be, deceives himself. It is impossible for iron that has not been heated in the fire to shine as brightly as iron that has been so heated, or to become malleable in some other way and be forged and wrought into a useful tool. So he who is careless and slack and lives such a harmful life as I have described cannot reach the level of him who from the beginning has accepted good examples for his life, who has obeyed his spiritual fathers and lived a virtuous life, nor can he enjoy the same gifts and endowments of the Holy Spirit. And with good reason! He who advances rapidly is the one who is humble in heart, who thinks the most humble thoughts and is contrite in mind *(cf. Ps. 51:19)*, and chooses more zealously to follow the divine Scriptures. He endures every tribulation and bears every trial and in addition numbers himself among the lowliest of all; he thinks over his actions and his faults and daily blames himself and sees himself as a sinner. It is the divine grace that instructs him in that which brings salvation when he "has no man" *(Jn. 5:7)* to help him. Bit by bit it drives out from his soul the faults and wickedness he has from the world and brings in virtues in their place. But he who is full both of uncleanness and presumption and is unwilling to be humbled before the mighty hand of God *(1 Pet. 5:6)* and to reveal the secrets of his heart to his spiritual father and cleave to him with understanding—he who refuses to do and to endure all things that lead to virtue and to God and bring to perfection the man who is in accordance with God—he becomes worse than he was in the world. The material spirit returns and takes up his dwelling in him *(Mt. 12:43ff.; Lk. 11:24ff.)*, together with the seven spirits of wickedness. So his brother, who has entered the monastic life with him, so far surpasses and excels him as the runner who runs without handicaps outstrips him who is restrained and weighed down by fetters of iron. So he loses out and continues in his previous faults or falls into even worse ones, because, when he entered and took upon himself to contend for virtue he refused from the beginning to choose and to do that which is good.

[§ 10. TEARS AND CONTRITION "CLEAN THE HOUSE
OF THE SOUL."]

Therefore, as I said earlier, compunction is the fruit of

practice and the means whereby the fruits are obtained. Or, rather, it produces virtues, it creates them, as all inspired Scripture bears witness. Therefore he who wishes to rid himself of passions or attain virtues must diligently seek compunction before all [other] good things and together with all the virtues. Apart from it he will never see his own soul purified. Without purity of soul he will never attain to purity of body. Without water it is impossible to wash a dirty garment clean, and without tears it is even more impossible to wash and cleanse the soul from pollution and stains. Let us not make vain excuses *(Ps. 141:4 LXX)*, which harm the soul or, rather, which are totally false and bring about perdition, but let us seek this queen of the virtues with all our soul.

He who seeks her with all his soul will find her *(cf. Mt. 7:8)* or, rather, it is she who will come and find him who takes pains to seek her. Even if his heart is harder than bronze, iron, or diamond, yet when she comes she will make it softer than any wax. For she is a divine fire that melts mountains and rocks *(cf. 1 Kings 19:11f.)* and levels all things *(Is. 40:4)*, and transforms them into gardens and so changes the souls that receive her. In their midst he becomes a flowing fountain, water of life that constantly leaps and bounds *(Jn. 4:14; Rev. 22:1)*, that waters them abundantly and flows down as from a reservoir to those that are near and those that are far off, and fills to overflowing the souls that receive the word with faith. It first cleanses from their filth those who partake of it, then it washes away the passions with it and scours them off, rubbing them off like the scars on wounds. (By these passions I mean wickedness, envy, vainglory, and all such things as are their concomitants.) Further, it is like a flame that runs about and gradually causes them to vanish as it constantly burns them away like thorns *(Ps. 118:12)* and consumes them. She it is that first inspires the longing for becoming completely free and cleansed from them, and then the desire for the good things laid up and ready with God for those who love Him *(cf. 1 Cor. 2:9)*.

All these things the divine fire of compunction effects with tears, or rather by means of them. Apart from tears, as we have said, not one of these things has ever come to pass, nor will it come to pass either in our own case or that of others. No one will ever prove from the divine Scriptures that any person ever

410

420

430

440

was cleansed without tears and constant compunction. No one ever became holy or received the Holy Spirit, or had the vision of God or experienced His dwelling within himself, or ever had Him dwelling in his heart, without previous repentance and compunction and constant tears ever flowing as from a foun-

450 tain. Such tears flood and wash out the house of the soul; they moisten and refresh the soul that has been possessed and enflamed by the unapproachable fire *(cf. 1 Tim. 6:16).*

[§ 11. HOW SPIRITUAL AFFLICTION ASSURES US OF VIRTUE.]

Those, then, who claim that it is impossible to mourn and weep every night and day are witnesses to their own lack of all virtue. For our holy fathers declare, "He who desires to cut off passions cuts them off by weeping, and he who desires to obtain virtues obtains them by weeping." It is thus clear that he who does not daily weep neither cuts off his passions nor achieves virtues even if he seems to be pursuing them all, as he imagines.

460 Tell me, of what use are the tools of a craftsman's trade in the absence of one who knows how to handle the material and work it into a suitable object? What does a gardener gain if he tills the whole garden and sows it and plants it with every kind of vegetable, unless the rain falls on them from above or if there is no water to irrigate them? Nothing whatever! Likewise, he who pursues all the other virtues and toils at them will gain nothing apart from this holy and blessed mistress, the author of all the virtues.

470 A king without the armies under his command is weak and is easily overcome by all; he does not even appear to be a king but is like any other man. Likewise great armies and forces without their king or general in command of them are readily scattered and destroyed by their enemies. So think of mourning in relation to all the other virtues. Look on all the virtues of beginners in terms of an army encamped and mobilized, and on blessed sorrow and weeping as if were it their king and commander, by whom the whole army is drawn up and marshaled

480 for battle. The general encourages them, prepares them for combat, reinforces them, instructs how and when to use their arms, the appropriate kinds to use against different adversaries and under what circumstances to use them, what scouts to send out

and what guards to post. He determines also what parleys should be held with enemy envoys and with what envoys to hold them, for it is sometimes possible by a mere conversation to rout all enemies, and sometimes to do so by refusing to entertain any overtures from them at all. He instructs them how and when to set ambushes and to lie in wait and post concealed units and what soldiers to detach for this purpose and in what places. In this manner [penitential] sorrow disposes the virtues; without it, however, the whole multitude of virtues is easily overcome.   490

[§ 12. CONTINUAL NEED OF PENITENCE, SORROW, AND TEARS.]

For this reason, brethren, let penitence be the task of us all that not only accompanies all others but takes precedence over them. With it is joined weeping and the tears that follow on it. There is no weeping without repentance, there are no tears apart from weeping, but these three things are interconnected so that it is not possible for the one to appear without the other. Let no one say that it is impossible to weep daily! He who says that it is impossible to repent every day subverts all the divine Scriptures, not to mention the very command of the Lord that says, "Repent, for the kingdom of heaven is at hand" *(Mt. 4:17)*, and again, "Ask, and it will be given you; seek and you will find; knock and it will be opened to you" *(Mt. 7:7; Lk. 11:9)*. For if you say that it is impossible daily to repent and to weep and shed tears, then how can you say that it is possible for men who are subject to corruption ever to attain to a humble mind, to rejoice at all times and pray without ceasing *(1 Thess. 5:17)*, let alone attain a heart that is pure from all kinds of passions and evil thoughts so that one may see God *(Mt. 5:8)*? You would not, for you would in that case be demoted to the ranks of unbelievers *(cf. Lk. 12:46)* instead of being with believers. If God has spoken of these things as being possible for us, if He says that they are and daily proclaims it, and you flatly contradict Him by claiming that for us they are not feasible but impossible, you are not at all different from unbelievers.   500   510

Do you wish, then, never to communicate without tears? Practice what you daily sing and read, and then you will be able continually to achieve this. What do I mean? Are you wholly ig-   520 norant thereof? Listen to him who says, "It is not the hearers of the law who are righteous before God, but the doers of the law who will be justified" *(Rom. 2:13)*. But let us not prolong the discourse. I will remind you of David's words: "I will not climb up into my bed; I will not suffer mine eyes to sleep, nor mine eyelids to slumber, neither the temples of my head to take any rest; until I find out a place for the Lord, an habitation for the God of Jacob" *(Ps. 132:3–5)*. And again, "There is no rest in my bones by reason of my sin, for my wickednesses have gone over my 530 head, and are a sore burden too heavy for me to bear; for my wounds stink and are corrupt through my foolishness, I am brought into so great trouble and misery, that I go mourning all the day long; I am feeble and humbled exceedingly, I have roared for the very disquietness of my heart" *(Ps. 38:4–8 LXX)*. [Similarly,] "I have become even as it were a sparrow, that sitteth alone upon the house-top" *(Ps. 102:8)*; "I am become like a pelican in the wilderness" *(Ps. 102:7)*, "for I have eaten ashes as it were bread, and mingled my drink with weeping" *(Ps. 102:9)*; and, "I am weary of my groaning, every night wash I my bed, 540 and water my couch with my tears *(Ps. 6:6)*. Saint John of "The Ladder" says, "Thirst and vigil have oppressed the heart, and from the oppressed heart waters have sprung forth" *(Scala Paradisi 6)*. He who wishes to find out in how many other passages he tells us of this will learn it from the book itself.

If you too then carry out in practice what you day by day sing and read or hear others read, without omission, with your whole heart, with humility and faith, in truth "I tell you good tidings of great joy" *(Lk. 2:10)*. If you persevere in doing this, 550 thirsting, watching, by being subject till death and obedient to your superior implicitly and without dissimulation, and endure every trial and slight and reproach and slander, not to mention blows and injuries from the most worthless brethren—if you do this with all thankfulness and without rancor toward them and pray for them, rejoice and exult *(Mt. 5:11)* with unspeakable joy *(1 Pet. 1:8)*! Because the divine and ineffable gift will come on you not only "in the evening and the morning and at noon-day" *(Ps. 55:18)*, but even when you eat and drink, and often in your conversation and when you sing and read and pray and lie down 560 on your bed. It will pursue you "all the days of your life" *(Ps. 23:6)* and accompany you on your journey. It will rest with you as you rest and serve with you when you serve; it will comfort and encourage you when your work causes you pain. Then you will know that the holy Symeon spoke very fitly and well that no one should communicate without tears, and that this is possible and truly suitable for all. It was not he who spoke and wrote these things, but the Holy Spirit through him. Since no one is without sin, even if he lived but a single day, and no one is able to keep his heart pure, it is evident that a man must not spend one single day of all his life without penitence and tears, as far as he is able. Even if he has not tears, at least he ought to seek them with all his power and soul. In no other way can he become sinless, nor may his heart become pure.

[§ 13. NO CONTRITION WITHOUT THE PRACTICE OF IT.]

If one refuses to lie on the ground and watch, and think on the multitude of his sins and the weight of his faults, if he continues to neglect his "wounds which stink and are corrupt" *(Ps. 38:5)* by reason of his carelessness and negligence, wounds of his passionate desire and inclinations, which lead him into insensibility—for this is the real foolishness—how will he attain to feel the judgment and condemnation that awaits sinners, and so weep in the pain of his heart?

How will one weep who refuses to be afflicted and undergo misery and be bent to the ground and walk all day in heaviness *(Ps. 42:6)*? If he refuses to suffer ill and be humbled exceedingly and "roar for the very disquietness of his heart" *(Ps. 38:9)*, and become like "a sparrow that sits alone upon the house-top" and as "a pelican in the wilderness" *(Ps. 102: 7–8)*? Unless in the disposition of his soul he becomes an alien to all, both in the monastery and in the world, without boldness toward either great or small, and "eats his bread like ashes" *(Ps. 102:10)*, and "is weary of his groaning" *(Ps. 6:7)* and "mingles his drink with weeping" *(Ps. 102:10)*, how, brethren, will he ever be able to "wash his bed" or "water his couch with tears" *(Ps. 6:7)*? Indeed not at all, never! Not only will he not envision this a reality in his own case, he will not even find a place for it in his prayer. He will not be able to "prepare a place for the Lord, nor a habitation worthy of the God of Jacob" *(Ps. 132:5)*, who is Christ the Lord, our Savior and our God. But if he does not prepare these things

570

580

590

600

beforehand, he does not communicate worthily and as he ought and receive his Lord and King into himself, even if he does so but once a year.

"The holy things for the holy!"—there are those who say this day after day and proclaim it to others as they shout it aloud. Would that they did it to themselves! You hear them say it. What then? Is one unworthy who is not a saint? No. But he who does not daily bring forth the secrets of his heart, he who does not display worthy penitence for them and for the sins he has unwittingly committed, he who does not always mourn and "walk in heaviness" *(Ps. 42:10)* and does not zealously practice what has been mentioned above, he is not worthy. But he who practices all these things and spends his whole life with groanings and tears is most worthy, not only on the feast day, but every day.[4] If I dare say so, he is worthy from the very beginning of his repentance and conversion to partake [daily] of these divine Mysteries. Such a person deserves leniency, because he is ready to persevere in these and similar practices to the very end, as he walks in humility and a contrite heart. By doing this and being so disposed he is daily enlightened in soul. Aided by partaking of the Holy Gifts he is the more quickly lifted up to perfect purification and holiness.

[14. THE UNWORTHINESS OF HIM WHO FAILS TO REPENT.]

Otherwise, there is no other means of washing or cleansing our soiled vessel and our defiled house. I on my part have learned nothing of the kind either from the Holy Scriptures or on my own. Every day we hear the apostle saying, "Let a man examine himself, and so eat of the bread and drink of the cup. For anyone who eats and drinks without discerning the body eats and drinks judgment upon himself" *(1 Cor. 11:28f.)*. Again, "Whoever eats the body and the blood of the Lord unworthily is guilty of profaning the body and the blood of the Lord, not discerning the Lord's body" *(1 Cor. 11:29)*. But if all inspired Scripture shows that he who does not "bring forth fruits of repentance" *(Lk. 3:8)* is unworthy, tell me then, how can anyone

---

4. Daily communion, except on certain nonliturgical days, was apparently not uncommon in the monasteries at that time.

be cleansed and, as far as he is able, worthily partake of the Mysteries? For the first fruit of repentance consists in these things. Just as the loathsome flow from the body and, if it may be so called, the pleasurable mingling of the heart with any passion so to speak constitutes a sacrifice offered by us to the devil, so the tears shed from the heart are a well-pleasing sacrifice offered to the Master, and purge away the shame of that passionate pleasure. This David showed when he said, "The sacrifice of God is a troubled spirit, a broken and contrite heart God will not despise" *(Ps. 51:19)*. Rightly so, for when our soul has attained to that state it thus daily humbles itself and never passes a day without tears, even as David says, "Every night wash I my bed, and water my couch with tears" *(Ps. 6:7)*.

[§ 15. INSUFFICIENCY OF A MOMENTARY REPENTANCE.]

Therefore I entreat you, my fathers and brethren, that each one of you eagerly exercise his soul with such practices. When your soul is pricked by compunction and gradually changed, it becomes a fountain flowing with rivers of tears and compunction. But if we make no effort thus to become clean, but prefer to continue in carelessness, idleness, and slackness, I on my part will say nothing troublesome out of regard for your charity. Except this—if any one of you ever happens to communicate with tears, whether you weep before the Liturgy or in the course of the divine Liturgy, or at the very time that you receive the divine Gifts, and does not desire to do this for the rest of his days and nights, it will avail him nothing to have wept merely once. It is not this alone that at once purifies us and makes us worthy; it is mourning daily and without ceasing till death. The Master Himself enjoined us so to do when He said, "Repent," and "ask, seek, and find" *(Mt. 4:17, 7:7; Lk. 11:9)*. How long? "Till you receive," says He, "till you find, till it is opened to you" *(Mt. 7:7f.; Lk. 11:9f.)*. What is it? Obviously, the kingdom of heaven!

[§ 16. THE GLORY AND DIGNITY OF THE PURIFIED SOUL.]

When, as we have said, this penitence, this unceasing penitence, is pursued with pain and tribulation until death, it gradually causes us to shed bitter tears and by these wipes away and cleanses the filth and defilement of the soul. Afterwards it produces in us pure penitence and turns the bitter tears into sweet ones. It engenders increasing joy in our hearts and enables us to see the radiance that never sets. Unless we strive with all zeal to attain it, spiritual fathers and brethren, we shall not be perfectly healed of all passions. We shall not acquire all virtues, nor shall 680 we ever be able daily to receive the divine Mysteries worthily or with tears that please God, or to contemplate the divine Light that accompanies them. Nor yet will we ever have a "pure heart" *(Mt. 5:8)*, nor be conscious of the Holy Spirit dwelling in us, nor will we be found worthy, as the saints, to see God either in this life or in the next, since, in my opinion, we shall depart hence when we are still blind. As Gregory the Theologian says,[5] we shall fail to see God "to the extent that each one comes from hence with dim sight," to the extent that we have willingly deprived ourselves of His light in this present life.

690 May we all be found worthy of seeing Him, whether as we are on the way to purification or when we have attained it! As for those who depart this life in neither state, the end of their sentence is uncertain. What is uncertain is also insecure, without hope and without assurance; for he who is not "strengthened by grace" *(Heb. 13:9)* will not, I think, ever from any other source obtain the hope that is without shame or doubt. He who lacks it, in what other way will he be "caught up together with the Saints into the air to meet the Lord" *(1 Thess. 4:17)*? Once our lamp has been extinguished here below, by what means will 700 it then be rekindled? Where and from what source shall we find the oil? Tell me, with what fire shall we kindle it? Where shall we turn, how shall we act in order then to be ready and bright with shining lamps to meet the Bridegroom *(Mt. 25:1–9)*? When we shall have risen up, as from sleep, we shall immediately, as you have heard, run to meet him. If then, when we sit and dwell in the tombs, and the trumpet blows *(Mt. 24:31; 1 Cor. 15:52)*, we have not taken our souls with us as lamps already lighted, but they are found to be either dim and on the point of going out or else, as the Gospel says, not burning at all, where shall we then 710 find the means either to light those that have already burned out or add a bit of oil to those that are going out? Indeed, we shall in

---

5. S. Gregory of Nazianzus, Or. 40, 45 (PG 36, 424 C).

no way be able. Let us therefore from henceforth be eager even now to kindle them by penitence accompanied with tears, so that they may shine brightly. So may we ourselves shine brightly and meet the Bridegroom at the resurrection of His brightness and enter with Him into the kingdom of heaven *(Mt. 25:10)* and enjoy eternal benefits. To these may we all attain in Christ our God Himself, to whom is due all glory, honor, and adoration, forever and ever. Amen.   720

V

ON PENITENCE

That it is not enough for us, in order to purify the soul, merely to distribute our possessions and to strip ourselves of our goods without afflicting ourselves. Of Adam's exile, and how, if he had repented after his sin, he would not have been driven out of paradise. How great a benefit his repentance effected after his fall. Of the Lord's second Coming and the condemnation of sinners. Finally, a reproof of those who live in malice and hypocrisy.

[§ 1. THE NEED OF REPENTANCE.]

10   Brethren and fathers,

It is a good thing to repent, and so is the benefit that comes from it. The Lord Jesus Christ, our God, knowing this and foreseeing all things, said: "Repent, for the Kingdom of heaven is at hand" *(Mt. 4:17)*. Do you want to learn why it is impossible for us to be saved without repentance, a heartfelt repentance such as the word [of Scripture] requires from us? Listen to the apostle himself as he proclaims: "Every other sin which a man commits is outside the body; but the fornicator sins against his own
20   body" *(1 Cor. 6:18)*. Again he says, "We must appear before the judgment seat of Christ, so that each one may receive good or evil, according to what he has done in the body" *(2 Cor. 5:10)*. One has thus frequent occasion to say: "I give thanks to God that I have not defiled a member of my body by any wicked action." This I cannot say for myself, for I am a worker of all lawlessness! So one has comfort from the fact that he is without any bodily sin. But to such a person the Master replies by telling the parable of the Ten Virgins *(Mt. 25:1–13)*, showing and making
30   clear to us all that there is no profit in bodily purity unless the

other virtues are present as well. Moreover Paul himself, in agreement with his Master, proclaims, "Strive for peace with all men, and for the holiness without which no one will see the Lord" *(Heb. 12:14)*. Why did he say, "Strive"? Because it is not possible for us to become holy and to be saints in an hour! We must therefore progress from modest beginnings toward holiness and purity. Even were we to spend a thousand years in this life we should never perfectly attain to it. Rather we must always struggle for it every day, as if mere beginners. This again he himself has shown us by saying: "Not that I have already obtained this or am already perfect" *(Phil. 3:12)*.

    Therefore I entreat you, my brethren, pay attention and listen to the words of a sinner, the least of your brethren. "Come, let us worship and fall down" *(Ps. 95:6)* before our holy God who loves mankind. "Let us come before his face with thanksgiving" *(Ps. 95:2)* "and weep before the Lord our Maker, for He is the Lord our God, and we are His people and the sheep of His pasture" *(Ps. 95:6–7)*, that "He may not turn away His face from us" *(Ps. 102:2)*. Let us repent with all our heart and cast away not only our evil deeds, but also the wicked and unclean thoughts of our hearts and obliterate them in accordance with that which is written: "Rend your hearts and not your garments" *(Joel 2:13)*. Tell me: What use is it if we distribute all our goods to the poor, but fail to make a break with evil and to hate sin? What [use is it] if, while we do not actively commit bodily sin, we mentally engage in shameful and unclean thoughts and invisibly commit sin and are governed and controlled by restrained passions of soul? I beseech you, let us cast away, together with our wealth, the habit of servitude to the evils we have mentioned. Nor let us stop at this, but let us eagerly wash away their defilement with tears of penitence.

[§ 2. THE USELESSNESS OF MONASTIC PROFESSION WITHOUT REPENTANCE.]

    Imagine the emperor himself, wearing his diadem and his royal purple, with boundless treasures of gold and silver, seated on high on a lofty throne, taking of his own accord some mud and soot and with his own hands smearing it all over his face so that all his senses are blocked and he is unable either to see or hear or to feel anything. Should he then change his mind and want to get rid of this evil, unless he went off quickly to his chamber to wash off all that mud and soot with plenty of water, it would be of no use to him if he were instead merely to sit on his royal throne and scatter all his treasures among the poor, and give away to them all his movable and immovable posses-

80 sions. Unless he had washed away the soot and the mud with water he would be an object of ridicule to those who saw him walking about like a scarecrow in the midst of the senate! Like-wise no one gains anything by distributing all his goods to the poor and taking on himself utter poverty and destitution unless he has made a break with evil and cleansed his soul by penitence and tears.

Every man who has committed sin, like myself who stands condemned, has stopped up the senses of his soul with the mud

90 of pleasure. Even were he to distribute all his goods to the poor and renounce all the glories of high office and the luxury of houses and horses, of flocks and herds and servants, and leave all his family, friends, and relatives behind, and in poverty and des-titution take the monastic habit, yet tears of penitence would be vital for his life, that he might wash away the mud of his of-fenses. Much more would he need it were he like myself and carried the soot and mud of his many evil deeds not only on his

100 face and hands, but on his whole body. It is not enough, breth-ren, that we merely distribute our goods; to cleanse our souls we must also weep and mourn from our hearts. I think that unless I show all eagerness to cleanse myself by means of tears for the defilement of my sins, but instead depart from this life still de-filed, I shall be fit to suffer derision on the part of God and His angels *(cf. Lk. 9:26, 12:9)* and be cast into eternal fire with the de-mons. Indeed, brethren, this is so! "For we have brought noth-ing into this world" *(1 Tim. 6:7)* that we might give to God as a

110 ransom for our sins *(Ps. 49:8f.)*. As the apostle says, "What shall a man give to God that he might repay Him?" *(cf. Rom. 11:35)*. This is the right judgment; this is the just and true humiliation. For the Lord says: "Think not that I have come to abolish the Law and the prophets; I have come not to abolish them but to fulfill them" *(Mt. 5:17)*. The fulfillment of the Law consists in this, that no one should defend himself in any matter, nor avenge himself *(Rom. 12:19)*, but that one should be exposed in every way to all men, like a corpse. Thus whatever men might

do to him he would not be moved thereby in any way, not be perturbed so that he would contradict them. Rather, he would simply abide in God's commandments and occupy himself with keeping His precepts, like some lion or a new gigantic Samson or someone more courageous than he, if one has ever existed or now exists.

[§ 3. SOME EXAMPLES OF PENITENCE AMONG LAYMEN.]

So it is possible for all men, brethren, not only for monks but for laymen as well, to be penitent at all times and constantly, and to weep and entreat God, and by such practices to acquire all other virtues as well. That this is true John of the golden words [i.e., Chrysostom], the great pillar and doctor of the Church, bears witness with me. In his discourses on David, as he expounds the fiftieth psalm,[1] he asserts that this is possible for one who has wife and children, men and women servants, a large household, and great possessions, and who is prominent in worldly affairs. Not only is he able daily to weep and pray and repent; he can also attain to perfection of virtue if he so wishes. He can receive the Holy Spirit and become a friend of God and enjoy the vision of Him. Such men before Christ's coming were Abraham, Isaac, Jacob, and Lot at Sodom, and (to pass over the rest who are too many [to enumerate]) Moses and David. Under the new grace and dispensation of our God and Savior, Peter the unlettered fisherman, who had a mother-in-law and other [relatives], preached the God who had been revealed. Who could count those others, more numerous than the rain drops *(Sirach. 1:2)* and the stars of heaven *(Gen. 15:5)*, kings, rulers, prominent men, not to mention poor people and those in modest circumstances? They have cities and houses and the sanctuaries of churches, which they have built with liberality; their homes for the aged and hospices for strangers remain and exist to this day. All the things they acquired during their lifetime they used with piety, not as though they owned them, but rather like ser-

---

1. I.e., Psalm 51 in most English versions, following the Hebrew reckoning. The reference in question does not appear to belong to any of the known works of this Father. It may be from some homily ascribed to him (PG 96, 144D–145C) of which the extant extracts show some correspondence to Symeon's passage.

150 vants of the Master who administers what He has entrusted to them according to His pleasure and who will, as Paul says, "deal with the world as though they had no dealings with it" *(1 Cor. 7:31).* For this reason they have become glorious and illustrious even in this present life, and now and to endless ages they will become even more glorious and illustrious in the kingdom of God. If instead of being timid, slothful, and despisers of God's commandments, we were zealous, watchful, and sober, we should have no need of renunciation or tonsure or the flight from the world. So listen to me, that you may be persuaded of what I have to say!

[§ 4. ADAM IN THE GARDEN.]

160 In the beginning God made man king of all the things that are on the earth *(Gen. 1:26, 28)*; indeed of all things that are under the vault of the sky. In fact sun, moon, and stars were brought into being for man. What then? When he was king of all these visible objects, did they harm him with regard to virtue? In no way whatever. On the contrary, had he continued to give thanks to God who had made him and given him all things, he would have fared well. Had he not transgressed the commandment of his Master he would not have lost this kingship, he would not have deprived himself of the glory of God. Since, however, he did this it was with good reason that he was cast out and exiled, and so spent his life and died. I will tell you something that no one, I think, has clearly explained, though it has been said in a somewhat obscure way.[2] What is it then? Listen to the divine Scripture as it speaks: "And God said to Adam" (that is, after his Fall) " 'Adam, where are you?' " Why does the Maker of all things speak in this way? Surely it is because He wishes to make him conscious [of his guilt] and so call him to repent that He says, "Adam, where are you?" "Understand yourself, realize your nakedness. See of what a garment, of how great glory, you have deprived yourself. Adam, where are you?" It is as though He spoke to encourage him, "Yes, come to

---

2. I.e., by S. Dorotheus of Gaza, a sixth-century abbot and monastic writer, whose writings had special importance for Byzantine monastic life. Symeon draws largely on him for the ideas and even expressions of this passage, but greatly expands on them.

your senses, poor fellow, come out of your hiding place. Do you think that you are hidden from Me *(cf. Gen. 3:7)*? Just say, 'I have sinned.' " But he does not say this! (Or rather, it is I, miserable one, who do not say this, for I am in this position!) But what does he say? "I heard the sound of Thee as Thou wast walking in the garden, and I realized that I was naked and I hid myself" *(Gen. 3:10)*. What then does God say? "Who told you that you were naked? Unless you ate of the tree of which I commanded you not to eat" *(Gen. 3:11)*.

[§ 5. ADAM IS DRIVEN OUT BECAUSE HE DOES NOT CONFESS HIS SIN.]

Do you see, dear friend, how patient God is? For when He said, "Adam, where are you?" *(Gen. 3:9)*, and when Adam did not at once confess his sin but said: "I heard the sound of Thee, O Lord, and realized that I am naked and hid myself" *(Gen. 3:10)*, God was not angered, nor did He immediately turn away. Rather, He gave him the opportunity of a second reply and said, "Who told you that you are naked? Unless you ate of the tree of which I commanded you not to eat" *(Gen. 3:11)*. Consider how profound are the words of God's wisdom *(cf. Rom. 11:33)*. He says: "Why do you say that you are naked, but hide your sin? Do you really think that I see only your body, but do not see your heart and your thoughts?" Since Adam was deceived he hoped that God would not know his sin. He said something like this to himself, "If I say that I am naked, God in His ignorance will say, 'Why are you naked?' Then I shall have to deny and say, 'I do not know,' and so I shall not be caught by Him and He will give me back the garment that I had at first *(cf. Lk. 15:22)*. If not, as long as He does not cast me out, as long as He does not exile me!" While he was thinking these thoughts—as indeed many do even now (and I myself am the first) when they hide their own evil deeds—God, unwilling to multiply his guilt, says, "How did you realize that you are naked? Unless you ate of the tree of which I commanded you not to eat" *(Gen. 3:11)*. It is as though He said, "Do you really think that you can hide from Me? Do I not know what you have done? Will you not say, 'I have sinned'? Say, O wretch, 'Yes, it is true, Master, I have transgressed Thy command, I have fallen by listening to the woman's counsel, I am greatly at fault for doing what she said and disobeying Thy

190

200

210

word, have mercy upon me!' " But he does not say this. He does
not humble himself, he does not bend. The neck of his heart is
like a sinew of iron *(Is. 48:4),* as is mine, wretch as I am! For had
220   he said this he might have stayed in paradise. By this one word
he might have spared himself that whole cycle of evils without
number that he endured by his expulsion and in spending so
many centuries in hell.

    This, then, is what I have promised to tell. Now listen to
the sequel and realize that the discourse is true and no lie whatever is in it. God said to Adam, "At the hour when you eat from
the tree of which alone I commanded you that you must not eat,
you will surely die" *(Gen. 2:17, 3:11).* Obviously this is the death
of the soul, and this is what took place the same hour. By this
Adam was stripped of the robe of immortality. God predicted
230   no more than this, and no more happened. For God had fore-
knowledge that Adam would sin, and wished to pardon him
when he repented. So, as we have said, He made no further pronouncement against him. But he denied his sin and did not repent even when God reproved him, for he said, "The woman
whom Thou gavest me, she deceived me" *(Gen. 3:12).* "Whom
Thou gavest me"—how thoughtless a soul, as though it said to
God, "Thou hast made a mistake; the woman whom Thou gavest me, she has deceived me." I, wretched and miserable man,
do the same, and I am unwilling ever to be humbled and to say
240   with my heart that I am to blame for my undoing. Rather I say,
"Such and such a person has urged me on to do and to say such
and such things; this or that person has advised me to do this or
that." O wretched soul that utters words full of sin! So as Adam
speaks thus, God says to him, "In toil and sweat you shall eat
your bread, and the earth shall bring forth to you thorns and
thistles" *(Gen. 3:18f.),* and, finally, "You are earth, and to earth
you must return" *(ibid.).* In other words, "I have told you to repent and return to your former state. But since you are so hard-
250   ened, from henceforth depart from Me. Your apostasy will be a
sufficient chastisement for you, because you are earth and to
earth you will return."

[§ 6. HOW EVE FAILED TO CONFESS.]

    Now you have known that Adam was condemned after his
transgression because he did not repent and say "I have sinned."

He was exiled and commanded to spend his days in toil and sweat and to return to the earth from which he had been taken. The sequel will make this clear. When He had left him God came to Eve. He wanted to show her that she too would justly be cast out, if she was unwilling to repent. So He said, "What is this that you have done?" *(Gen. 3:13)*, so that she at least might be able to say, "I have sinned." Why else did God need to speak 260 these words to her, unless indeed to enable her to say, "In my folly, O Master, I, a lowly wretch, have done this, and have disobeyed Thee, my Master. Have mercy upon me!" But she did not say this. What did she say? "The serpent beguiled me" *(Gen. 3:13)*. How senseless! So you have spoken with the serpent, who speaks against your Master? Him you have preferred to God who made you; you have valued his advice more highly and held it to be truer than the commandment of your Master! So, when Eve too was unable to say, "I have sinned," both were cast out from the place of enjoyment. They were banished from paradise 270 and from God. But consider how deep are the mysteries of God's love for men. Learn and be instructed that had they repented, they would not have been expelled. They would not have been condemned, they would not have been sentenced to return to the earth from which they had been taken *(Gen. 3:19)*. How? Listen further.

[§ 7. THE REPENTANCE OF ADAM AND EVE IN EXILE.]

After they had been cast out they were at once subject to sweat and bodily toil. They began to hunger and thirst, to be cold and shiver and to suffer the same things that we daily suffer. As they perceived more vividly their misfortune and fall, they realized their own perversity and God's unspeakable mercy. While they were walking about and sitting down outside 280 paradise they repented. They wept, they groaned, they beat their faces, they tore their hair and plucked it out and bewailed their own hardness of heart. Believe me! They did not do this for a day or two, or even ten, but all their lives. How could they lack occasion always and constantly to weep? They would think of that gentle Master, that unutterable delight, the unspeakable beauties of those flowers, that life free from cares and toil, and how the angels ascended and descended to them. As long as ser- 290 vants of a great lord of this present world, whom he has chosen to serve in his presence, observe, respect and honor him with genuine submission as their master and love him and their fellow-servants, they enjoy familiarity with him, his benevolence and love, and live in great ease and luxury. If, however, they fall into presumption and act proudly against their own master and haughtily toward their fellow-servants (*cf. Mt. 24:49*), they can

300 no longer be on familiar terms with him or enjoy his love and favor. He banishes them into a distant land, and by his orders they undergo thousands of trials; as they suffer weariness and are worn out they appreciate more and more how they have lost their former ease and have been deprived of the good things they once enjoyed. In the same way those who were first formed suffered after they had fallen from the blessings and enjoyment of paradise and been sent into exile. When they realized their

310 downfall they wept constantly and called on their Master's loving-kindness.

[§ 8. HOW GOD PITIES THOSE WHO REPENT.]

But how did God act, who is "rich in mercy" *(Eph. 2:4)* and slow to punish? When He saw them humbled He did not as yet cancel their sentence. He had pronounced it on them for their correction, and to prevent any one from setting himself up against the Maker of all things. But being God He foreknew man's fall and his repentance. So, before creating all things He foreordained the occasion and the time that He would recall man from his exile, judgments unutterable and unsearchable

320 *(Rom. 11:33)* for all that breathes. Were these judgments to be revealed to such as would record them time, paper, and ink would not suffice, nor would the whole world be able to contain the very volumes *(cf. Jn. 21:25)*. As He foreordained and predicted in His loving-kindness so He acted. Once those whom He had cast out of paradise for their shamelessness and impenitence heard and had shown proper penitence, worthily humbling themselves by weeping and mourning, He Himself came down to them. He who is the Only One begotten of the Only One, the only-begotten Son and Word, came from His Father who has no beginning, as you all know. Not only did He become like them, becoming Man, He undertook to die like them and chose for

330 Himself a violent and most shameful death. He descended into

hell and raised them thence. Would not He, then, who as you hear every day suffered such great things for them in order to recall them from that long exile, have had compassion on them if they had repented in paradise? How would He have failed to do so? By nature He loves man and has created him for the end of enjoying His blessings in paradise and of glorifying his Benefactor. Indeed, I believe this would have happened! But listen to what follows in order that you may learn the rest and be yet more persuaded by my word.

[§ 9. ALL MEN MAY RECOVER GOD'S LOVE.]

Had they repented while they were still within paradise, 340 they would have received that paradise and nothing else. But they were cast out because of their impenitence, and afterwards repented with great weeping and tribulation. As I have said, they would not have undergone this if they had repented inside paradise. So God their Master wished to honor and glorify them on account of these toils, sweat, and labors. And more than that, he also wished to make them forget all these evils. What does He do? Consider the greatness of His love for man! When He went 350 down into hell He raised them up from there and restored them, not to paradise whence they had fallen, but to the very heaven of heavens (cf. Ps. 68:34). When the Master had sat down on the right hand of God His Father, who is without beginning, what do you think He did to him who by nature is His slave, but has become His ancestor by grace? Have you seen how lofty is the height to which the Master has raised him because of his repentance, humiliation, mourning, and tears?

How great the power of penitence and tears! How great, brethren, the ocean of ineffable and unsearchable loving-kindness! For it is not only Adam whom God has honored and glori- 360 fied. All his seed, that is, we who are his sons, if we imitate his confession, his repentance, his mourning, his tears, and the rest that we have mentioned above share in this glory; so also those who have done so until now and will do so in the future, whether they are seculars or monks. "Verily," says the God of truth, "I will never forsake them" (Heb. 13:5), but will show that they are my brothers and friends, fathers and mothers (cf. Mt. 12:49f.; Mk. 3:34f.; Lk. 8:21), my kinsmen and fellow-heirs (cf. Rom. 8:17),

370 and I have glorified and will glorify them (cf. Jn. 12:28) both in heaven above and on the earth below (cf. Deut. 4:39), and there will never be an end of their life, their joy and glory.

Tell me, what profit would it have been to our first-formed [parents] if they had remained in the life in paradise, which had no pain and care, once they had become careless and by their unbelief despised God and transgressed His commandment? If they had believed Him Eve would not have trusted the serpent more than God, nor would Adam have trusted Eve more. They would have kept themselves from eating from the tree. But since they ate and failed to repent they were cast out. Nor did their 380 exile harm them, but they reaped the greatest benefits from it, and this turned out for the salvation of us all. When our Master descended from on high He by His own death destroyed the death that awaited us. The condemnation that was the consequence of our forefather's transgression he completely annihilated. By Holy Baptism He regenerates and refashions us, completely sets us free from the condemnation, and places us in this world wholly free instead of being oppressed by the tyranny of the enemy. By honoring us with our original free will He gives us strength against our enemy, so that those who are willing may overcome him more readily than could all the saints 390 who lived before Christ's coming. Unlike them, when they die they will not be brought down to hell, but enter into heaven with its delight and pleasure. At this present time they enjoy these in part. But after the resurrection from the dead they will be granted the fullness of eternal joy.

[§ 10. HOW JESUS CHRIST SETS US FREE.]

As for those who make excuses for themselves (cf. Ps. 141:4 LXX), let them not say that we are totally under the influence of Adam's transgression and so dragged down into sin. Those who think and speak to this effect claim that the coming of our 400 Master and our God was to no purpose and in vain. These are words fit for heretics, not believers! Why did He come down, and for what purpose did He taste death (Heb. 2:9)? Was it not that He might altogether cancel the condemnation of sin and set our race free from the slavery and oppression of our adversary and enemy? True independence consists in being in no way under the dominion of another. Because of him who had committed sin we were sinners, because of the transgressor we too were transgressors, because of the slave of sin we ourselves became slaves of sin *(cf. Rom. 6:17, 20)*. Because he was accursed and died we became accursed and dead. Because he was influenced by the counsel of the evil one and was enslaved and lost his independence, so we, as his children, were influenced, dominated, oppressed, and tyrannized. But God came down and was incarnate and became man like us, "but without sin" *(Heb. 4:15)*, and destroyed sin. He hallowed conception and birth and, as He grew up, bit by bit blessed every age. When He had reached mature manhood He began His preaching and taught us that we, especially those who are mere youths and not mature men, should not leap ahead in any way or surpass those who are aged in understanding and virtue *(cf. Wis. 4.8f.)*. He assumed that which was enjoined on us and kept all the commandments of His own God and Father *(Jn. 15:10, 5:18)*. Thus He canceled the transgression and set the transgressors free from their sentence *(cf. Rom. 8:2)*. He became a slave and "took on himself the form of a slave" *(Phil. 2:7)* and restored us slaves to the dignity of masters in that he made us masters of him who had been our tyrant. To this the saints bear witness, for even after their death they drive him and all his servants away like weaklings. He became a curse by being crucified; as it is said, "Accursed is everyone who hangs on a tree" *(Gal. 3:13; Deut. 21:23)*. He destroyed altogether the curse of Adam. He died, and by His own death He destroyed death. He rose, and did away with the power and activity of the enemy *(cf. Lk. 10:19)*, who had held sway over us through death and sin *(cf. Heb. 2:14)*. As He applied the ineffable and life-giving power of His Godhead and His flesh to the deadly venom and poison of sin, He completely delivered all our race from the action of the enemy *(cf. 2 Thess. 2:9)*. Through Holy Baptism and the Communion of His undefiled Mysteries, His Body and His precious Blood, He cleanses us and gives us life and restores us to holiness and sinlessness *(cf. 1 John 5:18)*. More than that, He sends us forth to enjoy the honor of liberty, so that we may not appear to serve our Master by compulsion, but out of free choice. In the beginning Adam was free and without sin and violence; yet of his own free will he obeyed the enemy and was deceived [by him] and transgressed God's commandment. So we have been born again in Holy Baptism and have been released from slavery and become free, so that the enemy cannot take any action against us unless we of our own will obey him. Before the Law and before Christ's coming many people, count-

450 less people, were able to please God without these aids and were found without reproach *(Gen. 17:1)*. Among these God translated and thus honored righteous Enoch *(Gen. 5:24)*. He took up Elijah into heaven in a fiery chariot *(2 Kings 2:11)*. If this is so, what excuse have we, who live after [the coming of] grace, who have enjoyed such great and wonderful benefits, who live after death and sin have been destroyed? After the regeneration of Baptism, the protection of the holy angels, and the overshadowing and descent of the Holy Spirit, shall we not be found equal

460 to those who lived before grace? Are we to be slothful, despisers of God's commandments who transgress them? But that we, if we persist in evil, are liable to greater punishment than those who sinned under the Law, Saint Paul made clear when he said, "If the message declared by angels was valid, and every transgression or disobedience received a just retribution, how shall we escape if we neglect so great a salvation?" *(Heb. 2:2f.)*.

[§ 11. THE CONSEQUENCES OF IMPENITENCE
HEREAFTER.]

Whenever, then, we fall into any kind of sin, let no one of us accuse and blame Adam, but rather himself. Like him let each

470 one of us exhibit worthy penitence, if he really wants to obtain eternal life in the Lord. But if you do not wish to do so, if you do not in every way take pains either to keep yourselves faultless by observing the commandments, or, when you have transgressed them in any way, to be penitent until death and vehemently bewail your own sin, but on the contrary persist in hardness of heart and your impenitence, listen to what the Lord says. "The earth will tremble on account of those who, after so great and marvelous wonders, after My appearing in the world, after all that teaching which I have spread abroad in the world,

480 still hesitate in unbelief and disobey My words. It will be rent in many pieces since it cannot carry on its back the senseless ones who in hardness of heart disobey Me. Before their feet they will see their approaching fall and will tremble. When the earth quakes and the heaven is shaken *(cf. Is. 13:13)* and rolled up like a scroll with a great noise *(cf. 2 Pet. 3:10)*, their inflexible and im-

102

placable hearts will be frightened by those horrible terrors as that of a rabbit about to be killed. The light will become dark *(Amos 8:9)*, the stars will fall *(cf. Is. 34:4)*, the sun and the moon will be extinguished *(cf. Mt. 24:29)* over them; from the crevasses of the earth a fire will come up and overflow like the depths of the sea. Just as at the time of the Deluge the windows of the heavens were opened *(Gen. 7:11)* and the water came down and gradually overwhelmed the nations, so the earth will be opened to its very foundations *(cf. Is. 24:18; Ps. 18:16)* and will gush forth fire. Not just bit by bit, but all at once, covering all the earth, and all will become a river of fire" *(Dan. 7:10)*.[3]

490

[§ 12. HOW AT THE FINAL JUDGMENT THE VERY GOSPELS WILL ACCUSE THE IMPENITENT.]

What will they do then who say: "If only they had let me alone; I did not want the kingdom of heaven"? What will happen to those who now mock *(cf. Lk. 6:25)* and say, "Why do you order us to weep every day?" Those who stir up controversy or complaints or even worse than these, how will they defend themselves? Will they say, "We have not heard"? Or "Nobody warned us"? Or "We did not know Thy Name, O Master, nor Thy might, Thy strength, Thy power"? He might then justly say to us, "How often I have told you beforehand and exhorted you, O miserable ones, through prophets, through apostles, through all My servants, even through Myself *(cf. Mt. 23:34)*. Have you not heard My Gospels say, 'Repent ye' *(Mk.. 1:15; Mt. 4:17)?* Have you not heard them say, 'Blessed are those who weep now, for they shall laugh' *(Lk. 6:21)?* Have you not heard Me cry aloud, 'Blessed are those who mourn' *(Mt. 5:4)?* But you have laughed unrestrainedly as you discussed among yourselves and prolonged your idle conversations *(Mt. 12:36)*, inviting each other to dinner and ministering to your stomachs. Have you not heard Me say, 'How narrow is the gate and how hard is the way that leads to life' *(Mt. 7:24)* and 'The kingdom of God suffers violence, and men of violence take it by force' *(Mt. 11:12)?* Yet you lie on soft beds and seek comfort by every means! While I

500

510

---

3. The source of the quotation is unknown—apparently some lost apocalyptic writing.

520 say, 'If any one would be first, let him be last of all, and the slave of all, and the servant of all' *(Mk. 9:35)*, you have chosen 'the best seats and the places of honor' *(Mk. 12:39)*. Have you not preferred positions of power and leadership and offices and high honors, and been unwilling to be subordinate and to serve in humility of spirit, in obscurity, poverty, and abandonment? When I said, 'Whatever you wish that men would do to you, do so to them' *(Mt. 7:12)*, have you not been concerned solely with your own comfort and desires and lusts? Have you not been covetous, rapacious, and unjust *(cf. 1 Cor. 6:9f.)* and served no one but yourselves? When I said, 'When one smites you on the right

530 cheek, turn to him the other also' *(Mt. 5:39)*, have not some of you laughed and others refused even to listen to this? Have you not said that I have commanded you something bad and unjust? When I said, 'If any one forces you to go one mile, go with him two miles' *(Mt. 5:41)*, not only have none of you done so yourselves, but have not most of you even compelled your own brethren? When I said, 'Blessed are you when men revile you and persecute you and utter all kinds of evil against you falsely for My sake' *(Mt. 5:11)*, you could not bear to hear a harsh word

540 spoken not merely by your equals but even by your superiors. When I said, 'Rejoice and be glad on account of your persecutions and tribulations' *(Mt. 5:11f.)*, did you not rather welcome praises and honor and glory to the extent that the other would make you weary of life itself? When I spoke of the poor as being blessed *(Mt. 5:3)*, did you ever heartily wish to become poor? When I said that the meek were to inherit the earth *(Mt. 5:5)*, did you not act like wild beasts toward those who did not do at once what you wanted? Again, when you saw men transgress

550 my commandments, were you not indulgent and easy-going toward them saying, 'Let be, the Lord has said, "Be not angry at anyone." ' When I said, 'Pray for those who ill treat you, love your enemies, and do good to those who hate you' *(Mt. 5:44)*, have you not said 'This is fine for the apostles, this belongs to the great saints, who else is able to do this?' You wretches, why did not you become holy? Have you not heard Me say, 'You shall be holy, for I am holy' *(1 Pet. 1:16; Lev. 11:44f.)*? But you have remained in the uncleanness of your defilements and your iniquities!"

THE DISCOURSES

[§ 13. THE EXAMPLES OF PENITENT WOMEN.]

As for the women, He says to them, "Have you not heard
people read in the churches 'The Life of Saint Pelagia the for- 560
mer Harlot,' 'The Life of Saint Mary of Egypt, the Former Prof-
ligate,' 'Theodora the Adulteress, who became a Worker of
Miracles,' as well as 'Euphrosyna the Virgin, called Smaragdus,'
and 'Xena, the True and Wonderful Stranger'? Have you not
heard how they have left parents, wealth, and even suitors and
served Me in obscurity and humility and have become saints?
Why have you not imitated those and similar women—you who
once were prostitutes, you who once were profligates, you who 570
are wives the married women who once were sinners, the
virgins those who were virgins like yourselves?"

[§ 14. FOR PERSONS OF PROMINENCE—THE EXAMPLE OF DAVID.]

To men who are kings and rulers He will likewise say:
"Have you not heard how David, when he had sinned, did not
contradict Nathan the prophet when he came to him and reproved him for his sin? He did not burst into anger, he did not
hide his offense, but rose up from his throne and fell down on
the ground before all the people and said, 'I have sinned against
my Lord' *(1 Sam. 12:13)*. He ceased not day and night from 580
weeping and lamenting. Have you not heard him say, 'For I
have eaten ashes as it were bread, and mingled my drink with
weeping'; and 'For the voice of my groaning my bones cleave to
my flesh; I am become a pelican in the wilderness' *(Ps. 102:10, 6,
7)*, and again 'I am weary of my groaning; every night wash I
my bed, and water my couch with my tears' *(Ps. 6:7)*? Have you
not heard him say, 'O Lord my God, if I have done any such
thing, if there be any wickedness in my hands, if I have reward-
ed evil unto them that did evil unto me, then let me fall empty
before mine enemy; then let mine enemy persecute my soul and 590
take me; yet, let him tread my life down upon the earth, and lay
mine honor in the dust' *(Ps. 7:4ff.)*? Why then have you not imitated him and those like him? Do you think that you are more
glorious or more wealthy than he, and therefore unwilling to be
humbled before Me? O miserable and wretched ones! You are

105

mortal and corruptible and yet you have wanted to be sole rulers and in control of the world! If somehow somebody in another country was unwilling to submit to you, you set

600 yourselves in array against him as if he were an insignificant slave of yours and you could not bear to tolerate his insubordination, even though he was your fellow-servant and you were no greater than he. But why have you refused to be subject to Me, your Maker and Master, and to serve Me with fear and trembling *(Ps. 2:11, 2 Cor. 7:15)*? When you exacted retribution of those who sinned against you, why did you not consider the sins you have committed against Me? As though there were no one who requires a reckoning of the blood of the oppressed *(cf. Gen. 9:5)*? As though there were no one who sees what you commit secretly? Or is it because you have forgotten Me and imagine that you have none who is above you and do not expect that you will ever have to stand before Me *(Rom. 14:10)* all naked and

610 exposed *(Heb. 4:13)*? Have you not heard Me say constantly: 'He who would be first of all, let him be last of all, and a slave of all, and a servant of all' *(Mk 9:35)*? How is it that you have not trembled and mourned in contrition within yourselves and feared lest you become haughty by reason of this false and vain opinion and so become transgressors of this my commandment and be given over to this fire? Have you not heard how that David, when he was being insulted by his general Shimei and called 'a man of blood,' with all his heart accounted himself lower than

620 him and instead of being angry prevented those who wanted to kill him *(2 Sam. 16:5ff.)*? Look at Moses, and Joshua the son of Nun, and David, and many others before My appearing, and now even more after My coming. You see that they are glorified with Me. Like you they were kings, rulers, and generals, and because of My fear they lived in humility and righteousness. They did not 'render to any evil for evil' *(Rom. 12:17)*, but often suffered contempt from their equals and their inferiors, and left to Me the vengeance for this *(Rom. 12:19)*. For the sins they committed against Me in all their lifetime they repented and wept

630 with fear and regret. They heard of this day of My coming and return and judgment and believed; but you have despised My commandments as though they came from some feeble outcast. Well, then, go off with those with whom you have chosen to as-

sociate, and whose words and deeds you imitate in action, and enjoy with them what has been prepared for them!"

[§ 15. HOW ALL CONDITIONS OF MEN WILL BE JUDGED.]

To the patriarchs He will likewise oppose the sainted patriarchs: John of the golden words [i.e., Chrysostom], John the Almsgiver, Ignatius, Tarasius, Methodius, and the rest, who not only by word but by deed were the reflection of the true God. Against the metropolitans He will set the saintly metropolitans: Basil, Gregory his brother and his namesake the Wonderworker, Ambrose, and Nicholas. In short, each patriarch, each metropolitan, each bishop, God will judge by the apostles and the holy Fathers who were illustrious before them in each metropolitan see and diocese. He will set them all opposite each other when you hear Him say, "The sheep on the right hand, the goats to the left" *(Mt. 25:33)*. He will say, "The place where these have worshiped and served Me, is it not the same as where you have spent your lives? Did you not sit on their thrones? Why did you not imitate their life and conduct as well? Why have you not been afraid to handle and eat Me, the spotless and undefiled, with unclean hands and yet more unclean souls? Have you not at all shuddered, have you not trembled? Why have you wasted what belonged to the poor on your own pleasures, your friends and your relatives? Why have you sold me, like Judas, for gold and silver? Why, when you had bought me as if I were a worthless slave, did you exploit Me to serve the passions of the flesh? Even as you have failed to honor Me, so I will not spare you. Depart from Me, you workers of iniquity, depart!" *(Lk. 13:27)*.

Thus fathers will be judged by fathers, friend and relatives by friends and relatives, brothers by brothers, slaves and free men by slaves and free men respectively, the rich by those who were rich and the poor by those who were poor, the married by those who have excelled in the married state, the unmarried by those who have lived unmarried. In short, on the awesome day of judgment every sinful man will see one who is like him opposite to him in eternal life, in that unutterable light, and will be judged by him. What do I mean? As every sinner looks on him

who is like him, the king upon the king, the ruler upon the ruler, the impenitent whoremonger on the whoremonger who repented, the poor man on the poor man, and the slave on the slave, he will remember that the other one was also a man, with the same soul, the same hands, the same eyes, in short with all other things in common, the same kind of life and the same
680   rank, the same occupation, the same resources. Yet, since he was unwilling to imitate him, his mouth will at once be stopped *(Ps. 107:42)* and he will remain without excuse *(Rom. 1:20)*, without a word to speak! When seculars see seculars and sinful kings see holy kings on the right hand, when those who bear the burden of life see rich men and those who bore that burden among the saints, and all those who will be in torments see men like themselves in the kingdom of heaven, then they will be put to shame and find themselves without excuse, just as that rich man saw Lazarus in the bosom of Abraham while he himself was roasting in the fire *(Lk. 16:23)*.

[§ 16. MONKS ARE JUDGED BY THEIR RENUNCIATION OF THE WORLD.]

690   What, then, shall we monks do—monks like myself, slothful and sinful? What disgrace and torment will seize us when we see those in secular life who had wives and maidservants and men servants singing praises with one accord with their wives and children in the kingdom of heaven? When we see those who have pleased God in their high office and wealth, in short, those of all conditions who have achieved all virtue and have lived in penitence and tears because of the fear of the Lord, standing in the joy and brightness of the righteous? When we consider that
700   we have forsaken fathers and mothers and brothers and sisters *(Mt. 19:22; Mk. 10:29)* and the whole world in order to save our souls, while they had wives and children, and some even wealth and honors as well as other pleasant things life provides? By our withdrawal [from the world] we became poor and were tonsured to become monks for the sake of the kingdom of heaven. Yet because of a little slothfulness and wickedness and by reason of our wicked desires we have ranked ourselves with the worldly, with whoremongers and adulterers and those who live in debauchery *(Lk. 15:13)* in worldly fashion! On that day what fear
710   and trembling and shame will seize us! Believe me, brethren,

when I tell you that our confusion will be a greater torment than the eternal punishment of the worldly! For when they see me, who made my renunciation with all my soul, standing with worldly men who now have children and are involved in public affairs or even serving in the army and about to receive the same punishment as they, they will turn and look at me and say to me, "And are you, O monk, who has forsaken the world, standing here with us worldly men? You too? Why?" How shall I then defend myself? What shall I say to them? Brethren, who will be able adequately to describe in words the greatness of the tribulation that I will then undergo? No one at all! What shall we say? How shall we be able in any way to make an answer? Shall we say that we have left the world and the things in the world? But we did not hate them wholeheartedly! True withdrawal from the world and the things that are in the world consists in this, that when we have fled the world we hate and abhor what pertains to it.

720

[§ 17. "THE WORLD" CONSISTS IN LUSTS AND PASSIONS.]

But what is "the world"? What are "the things that are in the world"? Listen! It is not gold, silver, or horses, or mules. All these things that serve our physical needs we ourselves possess. It is not meat, nor bread, nor wine, for we ourselves partake of these things and eat them in moderation. It is not houses, nor baths, nor fields, nor vineyards, nor suburban properties, for great and small monasteries consist of these. So what is the world? It is sin, brethren, and attachment to things and passions. Let John the Theologian, the disciple beloved by Christ *(Jn. 13:23)*, speak of "the things that are in the world." He says: "Do not love the world or the things in the world ... for all that is in the world, the lust of the flesh and the lust of the eyes and the pride of life, is not of the Father but is of the world" *(1 John 2:15f.)*. If we, then, who have left all the world behind and fled from it and have become naked do not beware of these things, what would it profit us merely to have withdrawn [from the world]? From whatever place we have come out and wherever we arrive, we shall find the same things. Whatever the place, men cannot live alone. Everywhere we make use of things that we need for sustaining our bodies. Everywhere there are wom-

730

740

750 en and children, and wine and every kind of fruit; physical sustenance consists in these and similar things. But if we have "the lust of the flesh and the lust of the eyes" and the pride of our thoughts, how shall we be able in their midst to escape from any kind of sin, without in any way being harmed by its sting? I know well that many of the saints of old guarded themselves from this, and those of the present still do so. They spend their lives in the midst of the things of this life, its concerns and its cares, and yet complete their lives in perfect holiness. Of them

760 and their like Paul bears witness, when he says "The form of this world is passing away, so that those who have wives should be as though they had none, and those who buy as though they had no goods, and those who deal with the world as though they had no dealings with it" *(1 Cor. 7:29ff.)*. From these examples we may learn how to deal with others. Thus he who is given to anger must not give way to it. He who pleads in his defense should not add any [mental reservation] in his heart to what he speaks; he who seeks justice for himself must be dead to the world in the disposition of his heart. He who has once attained to that state must eagerly seek and desire not even to spare his own body. Those who contend in the spiritual contest have attained this state, and in every generation still do so.

[§ 18. LOVE OF THE WORLD—ATTACHMENT TO IT.]

770 If we do not endeavor to attain to that state and to end our lives in it, what shall we say [for ourselves]? Shall we claim that we have despised glory and riches? Then He will surely tell us, "You have not forsaken envy and rivalry *(cf. Phil. 1:15)* and jealousy." The divine James, the apostle of Christ, tells us that these things alienate and separate us from God *(Wis. 1:3)*, saying, "If you have a bitter jealousy"—for it is possible to be jealous for a good purpose!—"and selfish ambition in your hearts, do not boast and be false to the truth; this wisdom is not such as comes

780 from above, but is earthly, unspiritual, devilish. For where jealousy and selfish ambition exist, there will be disorder and every vile practice" *(Jas. 3:14ff.)*. And a little later he says, "You ask and do not receive, because you ask wrongly to spend it on your passions," and he adds, "You adulterers and adulteresses! Do you not know that friendship with the world is enmity with God? Therefore whoever wishes to be a friend of the world

makes himself an enemy of God" *(Jas. 4:3f.)*. Note that he did not say merely, "The world is an enemy of God." He said it of friendship with the world, for by it we become adulterers and adulteresses. For a proof that this is true, listen to the Lord Himself as He says, "Every one who looks lustfully has already committed adultery in his heart" *(Mt. 5:28)*, and again, "You shall not covet anything that is your neighbor's" *(Ex. 20:17, Deut. 5:21)*. By these words He shows us that it is not only he who commits sin who is separated from God and becomes His enemy, but also he who loves it and covets something, or has an attachment in his heart to anything that is on earth. This constitutes friendship with the world. Thus it is clearly proven that, even if one is deprived of everything and commits no sin whatever in action, but merely likes it and favors it and, so to speak, is attached to it, he is an enemy of God. Thus John says, "If any one loves the world, love for the Father is not in him" *(1 John 2:15)*. So the Lord Himself says, "You must love the Lord your God with all your mind and with all your strength and with all your soul" *(Mk. 12:30)*. Therefore he who craves or has an attachment to anything else transgresses this commandment. But we, miserable and wretched men, have left behind the great and glorious and exalted things of the world and have entered the monastery. Yet some of us love shiny cloaks, others garments with gold embroidery, some girdles and scapulars, others sandals and shoes. Yet others love tasty dishes and drinks, some knives, pins, and daggers or yet more worthless objects. These things, brethren, have caused us to fall away from love of Christ who is King over all, and made us His enemies, and we do not care about it! For this reason we must anticipate our doom by repentance, and each one of us cast out from our souls every evil desire and wickedness, strife, jealousy, and vainglory. Otherwise we will be condemned to eternal fire together with publicans and sinners and rich men who have lived in dissipation *(cf. Lk. 15:13)*.

[§ 19. THE RIGHT HAND AND THE LEFT AT THE JUDGMENT.]

Let us therefore, brethren, take pains to show forth every virtue and heartily abhor all evil and every passion. Let us hate everything, great or small, that endangers our souls. Let us use

790

800

810

820

111

only those things in which our mind finds no delight and in which the heart takes no pleasure, so that we may not range ourselves on the left hand with the worldly, as we have said, because of things that appear insignificant, and see our brethren and fathers standing on God's right hand and condemning us. The abbots of each monastery would see those who had lived pleasing to God in the same monastery, while those who hold office would see those who had held the same offices and had shone as bright lights *(Dan. 12:3)*; the subordinates and manual workers those who had distinguished themselves in the same works and the same insignificant or more honorable services, crowned with the holy martyrs! Those who have defiled their youth will see those who have restrained it as with a bridle, those who in mature years have fallen by slothfulness those who have persevered from youth into old age in the warfare against the flesh and have preserved their chastity. Those who have acted like senseless boys even in old age to the very end will see those who received the tonsure as old men and who through the fear of God have cut off every evil habit acquired since their youth in a short time. Those "who laugh" will confront "those who weep now" *(Lk. 6:21, 25)*, those who live delicately and eat before the appointed time those who do not eat their fill even at dinnertime, those who are frivolous those who spend their time in constant sadness and pale fear because they remember that dreadful hour and their own sins. Those who have come from wealth and glory to enter the monastic life and yet refuse to be humbled even for a short time will face those who have come from utter poverty to spend their lives with us, and who because of their humility will stand above many others who are with them at His right hand, such as kings and patriarchs, because they are more glorious than they and truly adorned by their humility.

[§ 20. THE OBEDIENT AND HUMBLE MONK AT THE RIGHT HAND.]

Well, then, my dear brethren, have you understood what I have said? Do you realize what disgrace will then befall us? Have you taken it to heart? Have you come to the understanding of that hour, or must I repeat the same things for my own profit and that of those who are careless like me? Indeed it will so happen to us on that dreadful day! Many of our brethren will be found standing at God's right hand in glory, while many will be on the left and be condemned by them. How could it fail to be so? Suppose two young men renounce the world at the same time, whose occupations are the same, stonecutters perhaps, or carpenters, both of them young, pure of every bodily sin, born of poor parents. Will it not be so if the one chooses to become a practitioner of every virtue, while the other practices every evil and wickedness? Do we not see this happening in our midst every day? We see one of these two as a humble, docile, obedient [monk] who lives among us as a servant of God rather than of men, who serves all the brethren with faith and has a humble and contrite mind. As we have learned from his daily confessions and from those who often question him, he thinks and speaks by himself somewhat like this. When he answers people [who ask him] he says, "Reverend father, when I was in the world in my poverty I was barely able, with great weariness, to earn my own living. Now that I have come here, why should I neglect my work and eat the bread of the monastery for nothing, and be held accountable for it in the day of judgment? But since I have come to serve God I shall strive even to surpass, as far as I am able, the work that earns my food, and will without complaining be subject to my superior and to all my brethren until death, as to Christ Himself, so that I do not at all disobey them."

[§ 21. A PICTURE OF THE PROUD AND DISSOLUTE MONK.]

In contrast we see the vainglorious, insubordinate, and disobedient [monk] thinking and saying to himself: "Look: God has sent me a house, bread, wine, and abundant food. I have been numbered among the first and take precedence over those who have come after me. I am the brother of these men, whether or not they want it. From now on I shall eat and drink and sleep to my heart's content. What need have I to work from now on, that I should weary myself and that others should benefit from my weariness? If others impose some service on me I shall first of all plead weakness, but if they compel me I shall tell them: 'If I am unable to do this, can you strangle me, can you persecute me, when I have not the strength?' So I shall pretend to weep; I will

860

870

880

890

cry out; I shall use the pretext that my knees are weak *(cf. Is. 35:3; Heb. 12:12)*, I shall use the excuse that I am dizzy, I shall say that my head is troubled with bile, and for this reason I shall

900   have good excuse for eating from early morning. I shall begin to curse and blaspheme, I shall answer back to everything that I am ordered and complain. Surely when they have become discouraged [by this] they will leave me alone, however unwillingly. But if they ever give me unimportant tasks or an unimportant office, I shall treat it with contempt. For example, if I am assigned to tend the mules, I shall make the excuse that I know nothing about their care. I shall leave them ungroomed and uncared for with all their harness, so that they will be forced either to leave me alone or else to give me someone else to help me, so that I may take my ease as he performs all the jobs

910   and I do but a little. If they order me to become a baker, I shall hypocritically protest beforehand so that I shall not be condemned for disobedience and say 'Fathers, I have never seen how bread is made.' So shall I go off and make bread that is like mud. And so when they cannot bear to eat it they will not compel me to perform such a service.' " But if they set him to work in the kitchen, he will not know how to humble himself before his superior and make a prostration, but will say to him with arrogance: "Lord have mercy! Father, have you chosen me alone

920   from all these men to perform lowly services? Are there no other brethren in the monastery?" He says these things in order to refuse the service enjoined on him. But if he sees the abbot determined on it, he then goes off, not for the sake of God, but because he fears to be punished and whipped. As he goes off he says within himself, "Will the others have well-cooked and wholesome food to eat from that which I cook? If I do not make them rise from the table either fasting, or else vomiting what they have eaten, I am not myself!" In short, the wretched fellow does everything with much madness. Not only does he cause the

930   kitchen of the brethren and their vegetables to reek with smoke, even burning them; he also throws all things into the pots without washing them or cleaning them. He puts too much salt into them and makes them brine. What is hot he serves lukewarm. With disgust and indigestion they vomit the food. If a brother asks him to cook something or sends it to him to cook and prepare, he says without shame, "What nerve! So the master gives

orders to his slave! You can just wait to eat till I come around
and fix it!" So he does in all things. He is found eagerly running   940
only to those offices and services where he finds a way to steal
or purloin something. If he is not preferred above all others he
is sad in public, and out of sheer vexation he secretly complains
to those like himself. However, if he receives an order to this effect, one might say that it is as though he were raised from the
dead and from hell; he is at once cheerful in face and his eyes are
filled with joy. Even though in his great wickedness he is willing to dissemble so that he will not be caught, he still cannot
hide [his feelings] from those who notice him. If for no other
reason he can be recognized because he does not complain or de-   950
lay for a while—as he usually does in all other services—because
he is afraid to say anything for fear that someone else will be
designated instead of him and so he be left without something to
do.

With the two of them so disposed—the one submits in the
obedience of a good soul and in humility of heart and does not
grumble or complain, without acting deceitfully or stealing,
without giving offense, while, as we have written, the other acts
in the opposite manner—death comes and snatches them both
away. On that dreadful day the one—I mean the wicked one—is
placed on the left hand, all naked and put to shame. As he looks   960
about him he sees him who received the tonsure with him standing on the right hand, the one who ate and drank with him, his
contemporary, his colleague, who is completely [surrounded] by
great glory like Christ Himself. What, then, will he be able to
say or speak? Nothing at all, my brethren! He will groan and
tremble and gnash his teeth *(Mt. 24:51)* and go off into eternal
fire. Thus each of us sinners will be condemned by each of the
saints, and likewise unbelievers by those who believe, and sinners who have failed to repent by those who perhaps have   970
sinned more but have fervently repented.

[§ 22. THE IMPORTANCE OF SMALL THINGS.]

Therefore I urge and entreat you all, that if you realize that
you have done something wicked and have committed a sin and
have wounded and destroyed your souls, that you at least from
now on amend your lives. Let each of you exhibit a penitence
that befits your offenses and in every way strive to stand at the

980

990

right hand of our Savior and our God. As for those who recognize that they have failed in some venial matters, with all haste cast them away from you as well, lest, as all Scripture bears witness, you too be set at His left hand because of these minor matters. Do not consider them worthless and trifling, but think of them as important. He who willingly fails in small things, even though he keeps himself from great offenses, will be more severely condemned because, while he kept the greater matters under control, he was overcome by the lesser. Even one single passion will be enough to destroy us, as I said earlier, adducing the testimony of the holy apostles John and James themselves. But I will ask you [this] question in order to show you by an example that you should believe what I say.

1000

1010

Suppose, brethren, that a man fights against ten or twelve. As he joins battle with them he at the first onset repulses all the first line of champions, the bravest of them, all at once and wounds them and strikes them down. If he afterwards sees one or two of them, rather miserable and weak, who had been left behind approaching him from a distance with fear and cringing, will he not hasten to overpower them and tie their hands behind their backs to take them prisoner, or perhaps even kill them? If he fails to do so, will they not savagely kill him? Were he out of sheer bravado and arrogance to put his weapons down and take his ease, lie down and sleep out of contempt for them, has he not freely surrendered himself to those wretches to be enslaved by them? Will not both, or even one of them, come upon him and put him in chains and, when he has him at his mercy, lead him away into slavery or even kill him, and so make him an object of mockery? Would not all men say that the careless braggart, or rather, senseless fool, deserved to be killed? Whatever praise he might deserve for fighting those who were stronger than himself and overpowering them could not be compared to the blame, the reproach, the rejection, even the enslavement or death, that he would deserve because he was defeated by that one man.

[§ 23. HOW WE MUST FIGHT AGAINST MINOR PASSIONS
AS WELL.]

Thus, my dear brethren, it will be of no use to us whatever if we, after prevailing over the great passions, become subjugated by the minor ones. What do I mean? I will say the same thing over again and will not cease repeating it. We may guard ourselves from the defilement of the flesh, and abstain from envy and excessive anger and from theft. We may conquer homosexuality, pederasty, unnatural vice, and all licentiousness. But if we are slaves to gluttony or excess of wine *(Tit. 2:3)* or sleep, to sluggishness or slothfulness, to contradiction, disobedience, and complaining, and serve them like slaves subject to the whip, what will our abstinence from the other evil deeds avail for our benefit? If we surreptitiously take and eat slices of bread or anything else and snatch them from any place whatever and without the blessing of our superior, who will say that we are free from sin? If we purposely absent ourselves from the Offices unless we are very ill or because of some pressing need; if we are in charge of the fruits and do not keep ourselves from them (for what else was it that caused Adam to be expelled from paradise and gave him over to death?), what shall we gain by fleeing from the things we have mentioned? Suppose a man who had been wounded in his whole body were to be healed by means of many medicines, except for a tiny wound. He could not be called wholly sound as long as he bears a wound like a hole of a needle; were it possible to be rid even of the scar of that wound only then could he be called [perfectly] healthy by all. Let us not, therefore, think that these things are trifles. Rather, when we hear of others who have suffered punishment and been severely condemned on their account, let us with all our power flee from the harm that they do. Let no one, beloved, persist in any of these passions or in any other, but let him from henceforth abstain from them and so lay the foundation of repentance. Let him not desist and admit his defeat, [but fight on] until the enemy who assails him is put to shame and ceases from attacking him. Let not envy lord it over you, neither anger nor wrath nor clamor *(cf. Col. 3:8; Eph. 4:31)* from which foul talk and insults usually spring. Let not vainglory, pride, and conceit take hold of us and drag us to the abyss of hell, but let us drive these things far from us and lay hold of the virtues in their stead.

[§ 24. HOW TO ATTAIN TO FREEDOM FROM PASSIONS.]

Someone will possibly say, "Since the passions are so many and almost without number, who can search them all out and

1020

1030

1040

1050

117

abstain from them all, so that he is not dominated by any of them?" By the grace of Christ I will instruct you. He who always keeps his own sins in mind and constantly looks forward to the coming Judgment, and fervently repents and weeps, will overcome them all at the same time. As he is lifted up by repentance he "is more than a conqueror" *(Rom. 8:37)*. Not a single passion of those that I have mentioned will be able to reach his soul and touch it in its flight. But unless our mind is borne aloft

1060   by penitence and tears and by the humility of spirit that results from them to the height of mastery of the passions, we shall not have the strength to become free from all those we have mentioned. At one time we shall be stung by one passion, at another time by another one, and thus we shall not cease from being devoured by them as if by wild beasts. After death, since we shall have lost the kingdom of heaven because of them, we shall in turn be eternally punished by such [passions] as these.

[§ 25. FINAL ADMONITION.]

For this reason, my spiritual fathers and children, I urge

1070   you all, and I shall never cease to urge your charity, that no one of you neglect his own salvation *(Heb. 2:3)*, but that you in every way endeavor to be lifted up even but a little from the earth. Should this wonderful thing happen, which would astound you, that you should float up from the earth into the air *(1 Thess. 4:17)*, you would not at all want to descend to the earth and stay there! But by "earth" I mean the fleshly mind, by "air" the spiritual. Once the mind is set free from evil thoughts and through it we contemplate the freedom that Christ our God has bestowed on us *(cf. Gal. 5:1)*, we shall never again be willing to descend to

1080   our former slavery to sin and the fleshly mind. In accordance with the voice of Christ we shall not cease to watch and pray *(Mt. 26:41; Mk. 14:38)* until we depart for the bliss that lies beyond and obtain the promised blessings, by the grace and loving-kindness of our Lord Jesus Christ, to whom all glory is due forever and ever. Amen.

VI

[THE EXAMPLE AND SPIRIT OF SYMEON THE PIOUS]

On spiritual activity. The activity of the saints of old. How we may achieve it, in order that we like them may become partakers of the Holy Spirit.

[§ 1. LOOKING AT THE FATHERS OF OLD.]

Fathers and brethren,

There are some who think highly of themselves and, as they ought not, look on themselves as the equals of the saints who were of old, our fathers who carried God, in practice, knowledge, and perfection, and to [be inspired] by the same Spirit in whom they lived and moved (cf. Acts 17:28). But they commend themselves with words only (2 Cor. 3:1), not by actions, and are led astray by a spirit of presumption. So I have seen fit to address a few words to them in simple and plain fashion, as if I were speaking to a single person, because God said, "When you have turned again, strengthen your brethren" (Lk. 22:32), and because of the love for our neighbor that is enjoined on us all in common. So I shall begin now to speak in all simplicity and exhort your charity.

Do you wish, then, to hear what our holy fathers did when they stayed in their cells? Read their lives and first learn of their outward activities, and then I will tell you of the spiritual activity in which they were engaged. Those who compiled the lives of the saints described their outward activities, their lack of possessions, their fasting, their vigils, their self-control, their patience, as well as all the other things I will not recount to avoid prolonging my discourse. But they hardly described their spiritual activity except as mirrored in such actions, that those who

30 exhibit their labors and their faith by their deeds *(Jas. 2:18)* may by the very deeds know and participate in their spiritual gifts, while the others are not found worthy even to hear of such things. But since we have been brought down into so deep an abyss of folly that we think that the grace we have is equal to that of the fathers, although we do not practice what they achieved, let us bring the matter into the open and speak of them. Once we have information of the certain facts let us from thenceforth eagerly walk in their footsteps, even if we cannot attain to their level. So let us begin our discourse with them and gradually descend to our own level.

[§ 2. SAINT ANTONY OF EGYPT.]

40 What then did the great Antony do while he sat in the tomb, and was as yet without any knowledge of spiritual activity? Had he not shut himself up in the tomb as though he were a corpse, bringing with him nothing of the world, without any anxiety whatever in himself? Was he not completely dead to the world? As he lay in the tomb was he not seeking God, who was able to give him life and raise him up? Was he not satisfied with dry bread and water? Did he not suffer much harm from the demons and lie half-dead from their unbearable beating? He was taken into the church as though he were dead, but once he regained consciousness did he not of his own accord go back to
50 face his adversaries? Had he not returned to them and persevered to the end, but stayed in the world though he had delivered himself to death in intention and will, he would not have been found worthy of the vision of the Master, which he so greatly desired, nor would he have heard His sweet voice. But he sought with all his heart, he knocked without growing weary *(Mt. 7:7; Lk. 11:5ff.).* He persevered to the end *(Mt. 10:22; Mk. 13:13)* and received the reward of which he was worthy. Since, as we have said, he died in will for Christ, he lay as though he were dead until He came who gives life to the dead. He raised him up from hell—by which I mean the darkness of the soul—
60 and brought him out into the wondrous light of His countenance *(1 Pet. 2:9).* When he saw this and had been set free from those sufferings he was filled with joy and said, "Lord, where wast Thou until now?" It was one who did not know where He

was who said the words, "Where wast Thou?" But to say, "until now" showed that he had attained to the vision and awareness and knowledge of the Master's presence. If we, then, refuse so to renounce the world and like him to persevere and endure, how shall we be found worthy to see God in the Holy Spirit as he did, and to be filled with joy? Not at all!

[§ 3. THE EXAMPLE OF SAINT ARSENIUS.]

But, if you are willing, let us direct our discourse to another example. How did the great Arsenius act from the very beginning of his renunciation? He had forsaken the palaces and the kings, his silk-clad attendants and all his wealth, and had arrived all alone at the monastery as a poor beggar. Was he not anxious to hide who he had been, to flee from glory and human praise, so that he might receive the glory that comes from God (*Jn. 5:44*)? Was he then content merely to go that far? By no means! What did he do? It was not enough for him to rank himself as one poor man among other poor men—he looked on himself as a dog! When the abbot threw a piece of bread to him and it fell to the ground, he got down on all fours and took it, not with his hand but with his mouth, like a dog that picks up a piece of bread, and so ate it. When he sat in his cell he not only worked, but spent far less on his needs than what he had earned with his labor and drank water that was like stinking mud. For this reason, both when he prayed and when he worked, he constantly wept and was drenched in his tears. Further, as he prayed he remained standing from evening till early morning, and persevered to the end in poverty and lowliness. Why did he? That he might himself experience and see the very thing that the great Antony was granted to see and experience. How then is it not recorded that he too saw the Lord? Was it that he was not found worthy to see the Lord on the basis of all these toils? Not at all! He likewise was granted to see God, even though the narrator did not make this clear. If you want to be sure of this go over the chapters he (I mean Saint Arsenius) composed[1] and you will know from them that he too truly saw God.

70

80

90

---

1. The work in question seems to have been lost, since no extant writing by this father seems to mention this.

[§ 4. HOW LIVING IN THE HOLY SPIRIT INVOLVES
"VIOLENCE."]

100

110

120

130

He, then, who imitates [these fathers] by deeds and efforts
will certainly be found worthy of the same grace. But if one refuses to imitate their humility and their endurance, why should
he claim that it is an impossible thing? As for the superhuman
deeds of Euthymius and Sabas and the saints who followed
them, who will recount them? Whether it was before they had
received the grace of the Spirit or afterwards, it was never without many toils and labors, sweat and violence, difficulty and
tribulation, that anyone was able to break through the darkness
of the soul or see the light of the all-holy Spirit. "The kingdom
of heaven suffers violence and the violent take it by force" *(Mt.
11:12)*, since it is "through many tribulations that we must enter
the kingdom" *(Acts 14:22)* of heaven. The "kingdom of heaven"
consists in partaking of the Holy Spirit, for this is what the saying "The kingdom of heaven is within you" *(Lk. 17:21)* means.
So we must endeavor to receive the Holy Spirit within ourselves
and to keep Him. Thus those who are strangers to constant violence and difficulty, lowliness and tribulation, claim that they
have the Holy Spirit within them. Without the works and sweat
and the toils of virtue nobody obtains this reward. Therefore I
think that the common saying is true, "Show your works [first],
and [then] seek the reward."

As for me, I know one who, before he wearied himself and
did violence to himself, with upright thoughts and in simplicity
of heart diligently studied the divine Scriptures. After he had
spent but a few days and nights doing so without wearying himself, if I may say so, he was so greatly enlightened by the grace
from on high that it seemed to him that he had gone outside his
body and his dwelling and the whole world. Though it was
night it became like broad daylight. But since he had obtained
them without toil he very quickly made light of these riches. So,
by being careless, he lost all those riches at one time and went so
far as not even to remember that he had ever contemplated such
glory.

How those who have never been found worthy to receive
this glory or in any way to see it make the claim that they have it
wholly within themselves, I cannot understand. What hardness

of heart, what darkness, what ignorance and vain presumption! Where have they learned this, and from what Scriptures? Certainly "they have become vain in their thoughts and their foolish heart has been darkened" *(Rom. 1:21)*. They have remained in Egypt, that is, in the darkness of their passions and their pleasures.

Those who have longed to see "the land of promise" *(Heb.*   140
11:9), which the eyes of the meek, the humble, and the poor have been granted to see, accept every difficulty and tribulation. They completely abstain from all bodily pleasures, honors, and comforts of every kind. Furthermore they separate themselves from every person, great or small, and flee them without hatred in order that they may be found fit to walk on this earth before their course is cut off from the path of this present life. With a fervent desire to learn what to do in order to be reconciled to their Master Christ they humble themselves and, in accordance with the truth, feel that they are wicked and have committed many offenses. Nay, more, they live in sadness and sorrow as   150
those who have become God's enemies and transgressors of His commandments. For this reason the Lord not only grants them to know what they must do, but also the strength that comes from Him. He gives them endurance in order that they may do all that is necessary, so that they may see and possess Him who is God "who is above all and in all" *(Eph. 4:6)*. From henceforth they live as in heaven and have their citizenship there *(Phil. 3:20)*, even though they spend their lives in caves or on mountains *(Heb. 11:38)* and in [monastic] cells, or live in the midst of   160
cities. Thus they will always serve Him in joy and gladness and ineffable exultation.

[§ 5. THE WORDS OF SYMEON THE PIOUS.]

Such, then, is the activity of the saints and the practice of those who are led by the Spirit of God *(Rom. 8:14)*. Such in our own generation was also that most blessed saint, the pious Symeon, who "shone like the sun" *(Mt. 13:43)* in the midst of the famous monastery of Studion. Once he had been in the midst of the world and of worldly affairs, of friends and of relatives; yet he so completely renounced not only these, but life's cares, anxieties and pleasures as well, that he did not even remember them at all, but had banished that memory far away from himself.   170

Though he lived in the midst of a multitude of monks he once made this blessed statement, "The monk must be in the monastery as one who is, yet is not, does not appear, and is not even known." This he interpreted as follows, "As one who is in the body, but in spirit he is not; as one who does not appear except, through the Holy Spirit, to those who are pure in heart; as unknown, since he has no relations with anyone." How blessed are these words! By them is proclaimed his angelic life, which was
180   above [that of] men. By them he bore witness through the Holy Spirit that he had acquired "citizenship in heaven" *(Phil. 3:20)*. By them, as he spoke of having no relations with anyone, he made known how we live with God. No one can achieve this or speak of its reality if he is not completely and wholly united with God; were he even to speak of it he would be deceiving himself. He who says that he does not sin *(cf. 1 John 1:10)* "is blind and shortsighted" *(2 Pet. 1:9)*, but he who has God cannot sin because His seed abides in him *(1 John 3:9)* as said John, the great theologian and the thunder of the apostles *(cf. Mk. 3:17)*. But while he was still alive he said that he had God wholly with-
190   in himself, and after his death he shouted aloud that which he wrote with his own hand—"Gain God as your friend and you will not need the help of man," and again, "Gain God for yourself and you will not need a book." This he showed by his deeds, as he wrote a book by his own efforts, or rather by the Spirit that dwelled within him *(Rom. 8:11)*, though he had no literary education.

[§ 6. THE REFRESHING WATER OF HIS SPIRIT.]

This is what we too confess as we join our witness to that of our holy father. We do not hide his merit for fear that some men may think that we are boastful. Just as a cistern is filled by running water, so our holy father partook of the fullness of our
200   Master Jesus Christ and was filled by the grace of His Spirit, which is "living water" *(Jn. 4:10)*. A man may take water from a cistern that overflows and runs down on the outside till his thirst is quenched. Similarly we have seen and have received from our holy father that which overflowed and constantly poured over; we drank of it and washed our faces with it, even our hands and feet, and bathed our entire bodies *(Jn. 13:9f.)* and

our very souls with that immortal water. What a strange and wonderful mystery, brethren!

Do not refuse to believe this, for the word is not mine alone, nor did it happen only to me! Listen to John the Evangelist. What does he say about this water, or rather, about the Word, the Son of the Living God Himself, by whom John too became rich in the word? He says, "He who drinks of this water," that is, the physical water, "will thirst again, but he who drinks of the water which I will give him will never thirst again, but it will become in him a fountain of water springing up into eternal life" *(Jn. 4:13f.)*. This the Evangelist interprets by saying, "But this He spoke of the Spirit, which those who believed in Him were to receive" *(Jn. 7:39)*. With such water wickedness is washed away from the soul like dirt; without it, even with great effort, one gains nothing.

[§ 7. PRAISE TO GOD FOR THE BLESSINGS OF GOD THROUGH SYMEON THE PIOUS.]

Therefore, since we are not at all able to hide our Master's talent *(Mt. 25:25)* and keep silence about the gift that God has bestowed, we openly confess God's mercy. We who are unworthy have been more than abundantly refreshed by the water we received from God through our father. We have been filled without satiety to the glory of His holy Name. As far as in us lies, we, who are the last of all and "unprofitable servants" *(Lk. 17:10)*, have glorified and continue to glorify God who has glorified our holy father. Through our father God has glorified us, lowly and unworthy though we are. Let no one think that I am lying and speak against my soul and against my father, nor let him think that I am speaking vainly and boastfully, for I know that God will destroy "all those who speak falsehood" *(Ps. 5:7)*. The divine Paul so instructs me, when he says, "Blessed be the God and Father of our Lord Jesus Christ *(2 Cor. 1:3)*, who is blessed for evermore" *(2 Cor. 11:31)*, "I speak the truth and lie not" *(Rom. 9:1)*. "I know a man fourteen years ago, etc." *(2 Cor. 11:31)*, and again, "We have not received the spirit of the world, but the Spirit which is from God, that we might understand the gifts bestowed on us by God, which also we speak" *(1 Cor. 2:12f.)*. What advantage would I gain in any way for myself or

210

220

230

240

for my holy father by these praises? None whatever, any more than when I spoke about the other saints. I did not benefit them by my words, but I stirred up my listeners to zeal and urged them on to imitate them. So I shall not cease to speak of holy Symeon as I have spoken; I speak under the pressure of necessity,
250 and about ourselves as well, unworthy as we are. There are many who harm those who hear them by saying that nobody can be like that now, or in his deeds attain to what our great fathers achieved, or be found worthy of the spiritual gifts that were granted them. Their unbelief compels me, unwilling as I am, to say the things I never wanted to say, and so to proclaim publicly the reality of God's love for man in order to reprove the slothfulness and carelessness of those who make those claims.

Our blessed and holy father Symeon so greatly wearied
260 himself as to surpass many of the holy fathers of old. He endured such great trials and temptations as to be the equal of many of the more famous martyrs. Accordingly, God glorified him so that he became free from passions and a saint, and received within himself the wholeness, so to speak, of the Paraclete. Then, just as a father freely gives his son a share [of his estate], so he bestowed on me his unworthy servant, freely, without effort on my part, the Holy Spirit. Who among you, tell me—I hesitate to say so—has accomplished all that he did and (as far as he was able) spoke of, or even fully understand it?

[§ 8. DEATH TO THE WORLD, ACCORDING
TO PIOUS SYMEON.]

270 First of all he has written this in the manner of teaching a lesson, "Consider, brother, that what is called perfect retirement from the world is the complete mortification of self-will." What a blessed utterance! Or, rather, what a blessed soul that was granted to become thus and to be separated from the whole world! It is to these and to those who are like them that Christ, the Master, says, "You are not of the world, but I have chosen you out of the world" *(Jn. 15:19)*. "Come to me, and I will give you rest" *(Mt. 11:28)*. Those who walk in a different way and,
280 however slightly, follow their own wills or some other apparent good will never see that life which those see who are cut off from the world and have died to their own wills.

Do you then, brother, refuse to be humbled and submissive, afflicted and dishonored, despised and reproached? Or to become one of those who are obscure, foolish, insignificant, and have gone astray? Or to be the object of contempt on the part of everybody and counted as one of the epileptics who beg "in the streets and lanes of the city" *(Lk. 14:21)*? If so, how, tell me, can you become alien to self-will? If God has commanded us all patiently to endure the things that come on us to test and try—or, rather, not to test and try us, but to cleanse our souls—and we refuse to endure them, and the will not to suffer them (which is the earthy "mind of the flesh" [*Rom. 8:6f.*] is still alive in us, how shall we become dead [to the world]? In no way! Unless we become dead to the world and the things in the world *(1 John 2:15)*, how shall we live the "life that is hid in Christ" *(Col. 3:3)* when we have not died for the sake of God? How, as holy Symeon said, shall we contemplate God dwelling in us as light? In no way, brethren, let no one deceive you *(1 John 3:7)*.

290

[§ 9. THE IMITATION OF CHRIST.]

But perhaps you consider the blessed Symeon a fool, and are ashamed of imitating what he did? Then imitate Christ our God! Suffer for your own salvation even as He suffered for you. You have heard how they called Him possessed by demons, a deceiver *(Mt. 27:63)*, a glutton and a winebibber. People said, "You have a demon" *(Jn. 7:20)*, and, again, "Behold, a glutton and a drunkard, a friend of tax collectors and sinners" *(Mt. 11:19)*. Our blessed father, I mean holy Symeon, heard the same accusations for us, or rather because of us. In addition to these accusations you hear how the Lord was dragged away in bonds as if he were a murderer and a criminal *(Jn. 18:12)* and set before Pilate like a worthless man. He received a slap on the face from a slave *(Jn. 18:22)*; He was cast into prison and taken out from thence; He was led away by soldiers and lictors and handed over to the people by Pilate as he said, "Take him yourselves and crucify him" *(Jn. 19:6)*. Consider how He was abandoned in their midst, He who is above all the heavens *(Eph. 4:10)* and governs all things by His hand, how He was pushed from one side to the other, punched by men's fists, slapped *(Mt. 26:67)*, derided, scourged *(Mk. 15:15; Mt. 27:26)*, and led into the praetorium *(Jn. 18:29)*. He whom no creature is able to behold, not even the very

300

310

320 Seraphim, was stripped, bound to the pillar, and received the full number of forty stripes, which proclaimed that He was sentenced to death. What next? When He had received the scarlet robe in mockery He was slapped on His head and asked, "Who was it who struck you?" *(Mt. 26:69).* He was crowned with thorns, received mock homage, and was spat upon, and heard Himself mentioned in irony, "Behold, the King of the Jews" *(Mk. 15:26; Lk. 23:38).* When He was once more dressed in His own clothes His neck was bound with a rope and He was led away to death *(Mt. 27ff.; Mk. 15:16ff.).* He was then loaded with his own cross *(Jn. 19:17);* and when He had come to the place

330 He saw it fixed in the ground. So, being abandoned by His friends and disciples He was again stripped naked, hoisted up, and His hands and feet were nailed to it by the soldiers. As He was left hanging there, He was given a drink of bile *(Mt. 27:34),* He was pierced by lance *(Jn. 19:34),* blasphemed by a robber, and mocked as He heard men say, "You who could destroy the Temple and build it in three days, save yourself and come down from the cross!" *(Mt. 27:40)* and again, "If he is the Son of God, let him now come down from the cross and we will believe in him" *(Mt. 27:40ff.).* And so, after He had suffered all these

340 things He gave thanks and prayed for His murderers and commended His soul into His Father's hands *(Lk. 23:34, 46).*

[§ 10. TO BE GLORIFIED WITH CHRIST.]

Are not all these things, brothers, sufficient for you to imitate? But are you ashamed to suffer them? Through what other works or in what other way will you be glorified with Him? For He says, "Whoever is ashamed of Me and of My words, of him will I also be ashamed before My Father, who is in heaven" *(Mk. 8:38; Lk. 9:26).* Therefore Paul also says, "If we suffer with Him we shall also be glorified with Him" *(Rom. 8:17).* But if we are ashamed to imitate His sufferings, which He endured for us,

350 and to suffer as He suffered, it is obvious that we shall not become partakers with Him in His glory. If that is true of us we shall be believers in word only, not in deed. When deeds are absent, our faith is dead *(Js. 2:17, 26).*

For this reason, therefore, I say and will not cease to say that those who have failed to imitate Christ's sufferings through penitence and obedience and have not become partakers of His death, as we have explained above in detail, will neither become partakers of His spiritual resurrection nor receive the Holy Spirit. It is through the Holy Spirit that there will be a universal resurrection. I do not mean the resurrection of the bodies at the end *(Heb. 9:26)*, for then the angel will blow the trumpet and the dead bodies will rise *(1 Cor. 15:52)*, but I mean the spiritual regeneration and resurrection of the dead souls that takes place in a spiritual manner every day. This [resurrection] He gives who has died once [for all] and risen *(Rom. 6:9f.)*, and through all and for all those who live in a worthy manner He causes the souls to rise who have died with Him in will and faith and raises them up. This He grants through His all-holy Spirit as He even now bestows on them from henceforth the kingdom of heaven. To this may we all attain through the grace of our Lord Jesus Christ, to whom all glory is due forever and ever. Amen.

360

370

VII

ON ATTACHMENT TO ONE'S KIN

What is its illusion, and what are the pit and the bonds
that it brings on those who are caught in it. Of despair
and its different forms. The meaning of the text "He
who believes and is baptized shall be saved, but he who
does not believe shall be condemned."

Brethren and fathers,

Had I been able, as I ought, to keep silence at all times, I
should have been able to bewail my own faults and never undertake the work of a teacher. I should not have to instruct your
10   charity, or point out the ways of salvation to others in any way
whatever *(cf. Acts 16:17)*. Not that doing so is contrary to the
commandments of God—nay, rather, it is well pleasing to Him.
I, however, am unworthy of such a spiritual undertaking. So in
my lowliness I am afraid lest that word of David should be most
fitly spoken of me: "But unto the ungodly said God, 'Why dost
thou preach My laws, and takest My covenant in thy mouth?
Whereas thou hatest to be reformed, and hast cast My words behind thee" *(Ps. 50:16f.)*.

[§ 1. THOSE WHO REJECT GOD'S WORDS.]

20   So let us see, if you are willing, who is he "who hates to be
reformed" and who it is who "casts His words behind him." He
who does not obey God's laws hates the instruction that comes
from the words of the Lord. He "stops his ears" *(Ps. 58:5)* so that
he may not hear the word about the final retribution for sinners
or about that eternal fire and the punishments of hell and that
everlasting condemnation, from which retribution he who has

fallen into it cannot escape. He who fails to keep God's commandments before his eyes and observe them with all the strength and ability of his soul, but instead despises them and prefers what is contrary to them and does it, he it is who "casts His words behind him" *(Ps. 50:17)*. Let me make clear to you, in a word, the subject of this discourse. On the one hand God commands and explicitly proclaims: "Repent, for the kingdom of heaven is at hand" *(Mt. 4:17)*, and again, "Strive to enter by the narrow door" *(Lk. 13:24)*. On the other hand, when he who hears these things not only refuses to repent and compel himself to enter through the narrow door, but spends all the days of his life in distraction and dissipation of soul and every hour adds [new] evils to those he has already, and beyond necessity seeks bodily relaxation and care, this is a sure sign of the "broad and spacious road" rather than "the narrow and straitened one which leads to eternal life" *(Mt. 7:13f.)*. It is such a man who "casts God's words behind him" and does the things he himself wills, or rather, what the devil wills.

[§ 2. ATTACHMENT TO KINDRED.]

Wretch as I am, I have been the first to realize this. As I lie in a pit of mud *(Jer. 45:6)* I realize my own faults. I cry out from below and call to all who pass by outside, "Get yourselves far away, brethren, from this most horrible pit, and go by the straight way, which is Christ *(Jn. 14:6)*! Let no one turn aside to the right or to the left and fall in here where I am in my wretchedness and misfortune, and so be deprived not only of earthly benefits, but of heavenly ones as well! The most wicked one, the enemy of our souls, the devil by means of his manifold machinations time and time again casts most men, or nearly all, together as in heaps into such a pit. He often uses this one means, attachment to one's kinsfolk, like a lasso to drag them off. The enemy brings it around the neck of every one who has accepted this attachment and pulls and drags them off together to such frightful precipices and dangerous pits of sin from which there is no escape, and even plunges them into the abyss of despair. Once he has brought them down into the depth of hell and bound them *(Prov. 14:12)*, he leaves them there. I implore you, brethren, let us flee from this destruction

[§ 3. HOW TO CURE THOSE WHO HAVE BECOME ROOTED IN EVIL.]

With such treachery, such sophistry, he inspires such souls with despair and causes it to take root in them. It goes so far that they neither think that they have reached despair nor obey the divine Scriptures; indeed, those who tell them of such things they consider unfit to be trusted. They put their own opinion before everything else—or, rather, their own folly and senselessness; they feel no pain from the lasso around their necks, which is even worse than despair. It is one thing if a man despairs of his own salvation after falling into a multitude of evils, and another if he practices evil as though it were good and is convinced that he is doing right. In the former case, if he is taught about repentance and God's loving-kindness and learns that there is no abundance of sins that repentance cannot wipe away, and that "where sin abounded, grace abounded even more" *(Rom. 5:20)*, and that "there will be more joy in heaven over one sinner who repents *(Lk. 15:7)*, he may perhaps some day come to himself. He may be touched with compunction and want to be rid of those many faults and have his conscience freed from that intolerable burden. He will rise up and count all other things (that is, of this life) as nothing, and fervently enter on penitence. The other is harder to recall, and one must give up resorting to such remedies. How will he be willing to be cured when he does not at all believe that he is sick or wounded? In no way!

We, however, must to the best of our ability instruct and show them by means of spiritual sayings collected both from the divine Gospel and from the rest of Holy Scripture how they have been led astray and turned aside after beginning on the straight path; how the enemy, when he found them alone, deceitfully caught their necks in a noose and has led them off to precipices and pits of sins. After that we will show them how he has cast them down into the deepest pit, where and how he has brought them down into hell and tied their necks in a noose and so has departed and abandoned them there, unable to free themselves and to return to the earth. When they have been persuaded by the words of divine Scripture and have come to the realization of their own faults and have confessed them and agreed that such is their condition, we can then apply the remedies appropriate to their wounds by these very words.

[§ 4. INVOCATION BEFORE BEGINNING HIS EXPOSITION.]

But as I am about to engage in the exposition of the subject and undertake the verbal struggle, though I lack eloquence and learning, I ask you all to pray with me. Pray that the grace of the all-holy Spirit may shine more brightly and enlighten all my thought and mind, and so grant me to say something worthy, not because I deserve it, but that you may benefit. As the grace shines with its own light may it cause the words to resound and make plain whatever we said before. May it speak to us, as it were, and say, "This is the way, see how one loses it, see the enemy, see his rope [to catch us with]. See how the brother joyfully accepts his bonds, and where the devil drags him along and takes him away." Pray that when this grace has shown us everything in order, without omission, it may teach us how to escape from this snare, and so take us as free men to heaven.

This we will not be able to do unless we resume our discussion from the very beginning of [our] life, our entry into the monastic life, and start from that point. So our discussion will follow its road, as it were, and through the grace of the Holy Spirit achieve what it promised and clearly expound its subject to those who pay attention. Do not then grow weary, for to the extent that God inspires it our discourse will be profitable, for, as the wise man has said, "we and our words" and even our very breath "are in the hand of God" (*Wis. 7:16; Dan. 5:23*).

[§ 5. THE PRECEPTS OF THE LORD.]

Our Lord and God Jesus Christ, who is the genuine Son of God the Father, is of the same substance, nature, and glory. He shares with Him one and the same throne; He abides in the Father and the Father in Him (*Jn. 14:10f., 15:5*). Yet He has looked down on our misery and misfortune, or rather that servitude by which we were enslaved to the enemy who had deceived us through sin. He has shown us mercy by His ineffable love to men, and has willed to deliver us from slavery and most hateful error. He came down from on high without at all leaving the bosom of the Father, in the way that He [alone] knows. When He came down to earth He walked among us *(cf. 2 Cor. 6:16)* and had converse with us men, sinners though we were, and gave precepts of salvation to his holy disciples and apostles. He ascended back to His own Father with glory, after He had given them the precept and told them, "Go, and preach the gospel to the whole creation *(Mk. 16:15)*, teaching" all men "to observe," not this or that commandment, but "all that I have commanded you" *(Mt. 28:20)*. When He said "all things" He omitted nothing from what He commanded them to observe. What follows? "He who believes and is baptized will be saved; but he who does not believe will be condemned" *(Mk. 16:16)*.

So then, dear brethren, have you realized what is the meaning of these words "He who believes and is baptized," and again, "He who does not believe"? Or must I speak to your charity of this as well? The saying seems to be easily understood and simple, but it has thoughts hidden in the depth!

[§ 6. HOW THE SPIRIT OF FAITH EXTENDS TO THE LEAST PRECEPT.]

What he here calls "faith" is not merely the belief that Christ is God. It is that most comprehensive faith which includes all that concerns the holy commandments spoken by Him. It somehow contains all His divine commandments and believes that in them nothing is unimportant, not even a dot, but that everything down to the last iota *(Mt. 5:18)* is life and leads to eternal life *(Jn. 6:63, 68)*. Thus he who believes this is true of them and through Holy Baptism has pledged himself to observe all these things and to perform them without omitting anything will be saved. But he who in any way disbelieves His words, even to the extent of a single dot or one iota, as it is said, will be condemned as though he denied him altogether. Rightly so, for one may believe in Him in great matters, such as that He was God and without change became man; that He was crucified, died, and rose again; and that when He had risen He entered when the doors were shut and appeared to His disciples *(Jn. 20:19)*; that He was taken up and is seated on God the Father's right hand *(Mk. 16:19; Col. 3:1)*. One may believe that He is to come to judge the living and the dead *(1 Pet. 4:5)* and requite every man according to his works *(Rom. 2:6)*, that is, after

150

160

170

134

that He has first raised up all of us from Adam to those who will be born till the last day. Yet if he disbelieves when Christ says, "Truly I say to you, that on the day of judgment men will render account even for every careless word they utter *(Mt. 12:36)*, how can he be a believer and be counted with those who believe?

One may then believe in Christ with regard to those awesome mysteries that surpass understanding *(cf. Phil. 4:7)* and every human thought. His soul may be obedient and submissive to all that our Lord Jesus Christ Himself has done or will do. Yet he may disbelieve when he hears Him say, "He who would come after Me, let him take up his cross and follow Me" *(Mt. 16:24; Mk. 8:34)*. If he disbelieves when he hears Him say, "He who loves father or mother more than Me is not worthy of Me" *(Mt. 10:37)*, and, "If any one comes to Me and does not hate his own father and mother and brothers and sisters and wife and children, yes, and even his own life, he cannot be My disciple" *(Lk. 14:26)*, and "He who breaks one of these least commandments shall be called least in the kingdom of heaven" *(Mt. 5:19)*—how can such a person be called a believer? Shall he not rather be condemned as an unbeliever or even worse than an unbeliever? He confesses that he believes in Christ in the greater matters, but in the lesser he despises Him, the God and Master of the universe, as if He were a liar. In other matters he professes to believe Him as God, but distrusts Him as if He were any man when He says that men will give account even for an idle word in the day of judgment *(Mt. 12:36)*. He laughs, uses foul language, talks foolishly, and thinks that he will be saved, though Christ calls those who laugh miserable *(Lk. 6:25)* and those who mourn blessed *(Mt. 5:4)*. Though he does not deny himself or bear his cross *(Mk. 8:34; Mt. 16:24)*, he thinks that he is following Christ who was crucified for him. While he loves his parents more, he thinks from his soul that he is worthy of Christ *(Mt. 10:37)*. Thus, even those who supposedly come to Him by renouncing the world, yet do not hate all their own kinsmen and deny their own souls but, on the contrary, love themselves the more, they vainly think that they are disciples of Christ—those who break, not one and the least of the commandments, but many and great ones every hour, yet do not at all think that they are doing anything that contravenes them, but

180

190

200

210

rather suppose that as they so act they are great in the kingdom of God *(Mt. 5:19)*. What is the worst of all evils, they deny that these are at all transgressions of the commandment! In their folly they even try to persuade us, who hold fast to the word of truth *(cf. Eph. 1:13)*! But let us return to the subject at hand.

[§ 7. THE WILL FOR DETACHMENT.]

All things, then, that Christ our God enjoined upon the apostles, He likewise also commanded us to observe. We have the ability to observe them in the world, yet we do not will to do so because we are weak in faith and love toward Christ *(cf. 1 Tim. 1:14)*. That this is true, we have the witness borne by all who have pleased the Lord before the Law, under the Law, and after the coming of the Savior. Though they had children and wives and were occupied with the cares and concerns of all the affairs of this life they were pleasing to Him. They were separated from all these things by their will of detachment, and shone more brightly in faith and life than those who "are in mountains and caves" *(Heb. 11:38)*. Accordingly, with the help of the commandment of the Lord (since it was uttered for our sake and because of our weakness), we renounce all things and approach the narrow and straightened path and are, as it were, physically cut off from the world and the things in the world. We thus leave one country, place, and city and come to another dwelling in abode, to the arena of the exercise of the virtues as each one by his conduct and asceticism walks, hastens, or runs, as he himself wills. Why? In order that we may acquire detachment from the things that we have mentioned. It is for this reason that we leave the world and forthwith follow the Lord's commandments and obey His precepts, and start on the way that leads to heaven.

[§ 8. THE COUNTLESS TEMPTATIONS ON THE WAY.]

Now join me in examining carefully the force of these words. With me depict in your mind a road well worn by the feet of those who have made a good start on it. On either side imagine mountains, forests, precipices, peaks, and ravines, as well as plains, gardens, and places that are pleasant and shaded and very beautiful, with all kinds of fruit, with great numbers of wild beasts, of bandits and gangs of murderers scattered in various places. Under these conditions none of these things will be able to entice us or disturb our sense or cause us harm so long as we follow the saints who have gone before us and go by the same road that they walked. For when we go on the path of the commandments of our Lord and God *(Ps. 119:1ff., 32)* let us go on it without turning aside in the midst of all the perils I have mentioned. Then none of those bandits, none of those wild beasts will openly and shamelessly assault us or venture to come near us, especially if we follow a guide and travel in company with good companions on the way. From time to time, however, it happens that either from a distance or else from nearby some of them will look at us with murderous eye and use threats, while others will address us in friendly fashion with enticements and flatteries. They will also point out to us how attractive is each place in its location, how beautiful are its fruits, and will exhort us to rest briefly to seek relief from the hardships of the journey. They will suggest that we eat some of the fruits that are particularly sweet and pleasant to look at *(Gen. 3:6)* and devise many other snares and varied approaches, not only by day but even by night, not only when we are awake but also when we sleep. At times they will assail us with itchings and secretions, at other times by the taste of forbidden foods. At times they will meet us "with torches and lanterns" *(Jn. 18:3)* like robbers with sword in hand, and like robbers they still threaten us with death, intending to throw us into confusion and turn us aside from the straight path. Some of them will suggest to us that it is impossible to bear up under the difficulties of the way until the end, others that all this is useless and that it can be of no avail for those who weary themselves with it. Yet others will tell us that there is no end of this road nor ever will be. They will point out to us some who have not succeeded, in particular any who have spent a lot of time in asceticism and have not profited thereby, since they have seemed to run the way of the commandments but have done so without knowledge and godly intention, but rather by following their own devices and with presumption. In their case it is natural that they should waste even their steps that are pleasing to God, since they give way to fear and turn back *(cf. Mk. 13:16; Lk. 17:31)*, and by their carelessness give themselves up to the wicked one so that he can do toward them as he pleases.

260

270

280

290

But why do I want to expound all this time to you, my
spiritual brethren? It is because the ambushes and terrible machinations of our adversary the devil (*1 Pet. 5:8*) and his evil spirits
cannot be numbered! Most of these things I shall leave to be examined by the zealous and with these few remarks provide them
with a starting point, and will attempt to explain to your charity
300   that which I have promised. What do I mean? The bond of our
attachment to our kinsmen. The devil uses this to put us into his
chains, in particular those who have valiantly fought the other
passions and obtained the crown. By this means the wicked one
sends us off in misery to darkness and destruction.

Once again, examine with me carefully the sense of what I
say. Think of yourself on the road in question, having either just
started on it, or walked on it for years and suffered much harm,
in the way we have mentioned, from those wild beasts and bandits. Yet through the grace of Christ you have neither been deceived by flatteries nor been beguiled by the beauty of outward
310   appearances to pursue pleasure, nor yet influenced by fear or by
threats to turn aside from the straight way or stop your advance
or turn back, but instead you run more strenuously. While you
are so running do you think that Satan has left off from fighting
you, or that he will ever do so? By no means whatever! But he
knows that God has given us a commandment to forsake father
and mother and, in short, all our earthly family and even our
own selves as well *(Lk. 14:26)*, and also that we have made this
promise to God when we entered on the monastic life that we
should observe this commandment together with all the others.
320   Since he has not been able to prevail against you in all the matters we have mentioned, what does he do? First, he rouses and
renews in us the memory of our own kin. Then he borrows even
from the divine Scriptures words that have been said concerning other things and that were addressed to other people, and
with them muddies the waters and makes us to transgress the
commandment. So he says, "Divine Scripture says, 'Honor your
father and your mother' *(Ex. 20:12)*, and 'Do not ignore those
who are of your own seed' *(Is. 58:7 LXX)*, for according to the divine apostle, 'He who does not provide for his relatives has dis-

owned the faith' *(1 Tim. 5:8)*." He who is full of guiles naturally does not know that these words were not spoken with the intent that we should love our parents or our kinsfolk more than God and put them before our love of Him. They are to teach us obedience and that we might learn that if submission and honor are due from us to our parents, how much more are they due to God, who has created them and ourselves? Those who "are related to us by seed," O deceiver—how good it is to turn the argument back on him!—are not our relatives, but those who "are of the household of the faith" *(Gal. 6:10)*, whom you do not know, naturally, as you by guile sow in our minds *(cf. Mt. 13:25)* [the idea of] fleshly kinship, since you are anxious to drag us down to [the level of] affection for them and attachment to them.

[§ 10. THE DEVIL'S RUSES TO ATTACH US
TO OUR KIN.]

Now then, when we perceive this deception and become aware of it, whether on our own or by the help of others who are our guides or companions on the way of the Lord, what does [the devil] whisper to us as he imperceptibly moves the heart? He says, "You have at this point arrived at a standard different from that of the brethren who are with you and made an advance that none of them understands. You have attained to detachment and complete freedom from passion. So, if you wish, you may ignore and despise your kinsmen, and you will be in no danger from them." While he secretly suggests this, he may present to you that kinsman either mentally or even physically present and suggest words such as these and say to him, "How do you allow that which God has formed to perish, so that it becomes like the brute beasts *(Ps. 49:13, 21)* and through ignorance falls down into the number of those who have no reason? Will you not stretch forth your hand to him, will you not 'open his mind' *(Lk. 24:45)*, will you not make known to him God who has made him? What excuse will you have, or what will you say, on that dreadful day?" He then ceases and makes him to imagine him in his prayer and, as it were, shed tears of compassion and

offer him, so to speak, as an "acceptable gift" before God *(cf.*
360 *Rom. 15:16)* while he says within himself, "He who brings forth
one who is worthy out of the unworthy will be as my mouth"
(cf. Jer. 15:19), and again, "As you did it to one of the least of
these, you did it to Me" *(Mt. 25:40)*, and "He became a father of
the fatherless" *(Ps. 68:6; Job 29:16)* and the rest. But these things
are all a certain illusion and deceit of the wicked one.

But when someone is not moved by all these things but still
hesitates and answers the wicked one by saying, "Indeed, whatever I owe to my kinsman I do to the stranger, who according to
God is closer to me than a kinsman according to the flesh," the
370 guileful enemy then replies and says to him, "Certainly it is thus
that God cares for all men, and in this way all are led to know
Him and believe in Him, in your case both through your kinsmen and through strangers, and he again through you and others through him. But in these days who is like you? How can
you let him go away so that he does not at once become prey for
the wolf and lose his soul? You will pay the penalty if you completely abandon him!" Finally that brother is led astray and,
without resisting, for plausible reasons submits to the bonds of
attachment. Once bound by Satan he no longer objects but
380 obeys his words.

[§ 11. THE LOSS OF DETACHMENT.]

Consider with me the villany of this terrible bandit and de-
stroyer of souls! Once he through natural attachment has taken
a man prisoner he no longer walks with him on the road. For
the present he does not bother him with this matter, so that his
treachery will not be recognized. What then? He, as it were,
takes the end of the rope and goes off at a distance and hides
from him in the darknesss, since he is truly the prince of darkness, and leaves him with the care and worry about his kinsman.
He knows that he, instead of himself, constantly bothers and
390 pricks him! Once this has happened, whenever he gives in to
any worry about his kinsman he turns aside from the straight
royal road on which he began. The more he turns aside the
more the enemy, as it were, moves into the depth of his treachery and remains hidden as he penetrates more deeply, while he

holds the "rope" of that attachment in his hands and, as he holds it securely, endeavors not to be recognized at all.

[§ 12. THE DISASTROUS CONSEQUENCES OF ATTACHMENT TO KIN.]

Once the brother has departed from the road, note how he begins to say within himself, "He who saves a soul is like one who gains his own." He thus convinces himself that he has undertaken to perform a task that is an imitation of Christ. If he is well known to some people who are in the world he goes to see them and at times flatters them beyond their worth and praises them, while at other times he takes it on himself severely to reprove them. Sometimes he shows that he is a glutton and indifferent and talks with the aim of moving everyone to laughter. In a word, he adapts himself to please everyone in order to receive some gift in return. If, however, he sees someone give him nothing, without shame he does not hesitate to ask as he mentions his kinsman everywhere. Since those who hear are themselves worldly and beset with the same faults, they commend that miserable man the more and tell him, "You will have a great reward." These things cause attachment to grow and take root, or, rather, spiritually speaking, cause its passion, like a rope, to embed itself in the flesh of the neck and hold him securely and be impossible to untie. Further, it will gradually draw him away from pure prayer, and without his knowledge it will transform godly tears into their opposite. It will then lead him into hatred and envy of those who have more than he and are not generous in their gifts; furthermore it will make him sluggish and disobedient in all [matters of] obedience. He then lies and regards the matter as almsgiving, as though he gave to God what he spends on his kinsman. Further, he begins to steal from small things and is convinced that it is not stealing, but his mind is so beguiled by passion that his conscience does not condemn him for anything that he does in the interest of his family and kin. Thus, when our enemy the devil has pulled the poor monk down to these depths, he winds the end of that rope about that hardened and deeply rooted sin of the passion of attachment as about a pillar fixed deep in the bowels of hell and leaves

400

410

420

430   him there, certain that he will never tear himself loose from thence.

[§ 13. HOW WE MUST AVOID BEING BOUND
BY ANY PASSION.]

So we have spoken these few words, out of many, about those who are in the struggle. As for those who approach this road, this way of life, with indifference and contempt, why should we mention how great is their attachment to their relatives, when one sees how they fall into every snare of the devil *(1 Tim. 3:7)* like senseless birds? They expose themselves to every passion, they constantly become the prey of the wicked one
440   who "goes about roaring like a lion seeking whom he may devour" *(1 Pet. 5:8)*, and prefer to die rather than be drawn away from his teeth and his most terrible jaws *(cf. Ps. 22:22)*. But let us "who hear the word" *(Mt. 13:23)* with faith pray with all our will and mind that we may never be deceived or beguiled, nor by a single transgression, great or small, depart from the way that leads to heaven. May we not be taken captive by any passion, but walk in the way without turning aside and hasten to come to Jesus *(Phil. 3:12)*, who walks before us. Once we have taken hold of Him let us fall before Him and weep before His
450   goodness and fervently ask that He may never at all be separated from us nor allow us to depart from the way. He is that way, for He Himself has said, "I am the way and the resurrection and the life" *(Jn. 11:25, 14:6)*. Let us then seek Him out, let us endeavor to attain to Him, that we may lay hold on Him *(cf. Phil. 3:12)*. If we attain to this, if we live with Him and associate with Him, we shall ascend with Him and be assumed with Him into heaven, and that not merely when we depart this life, but even now. Rather, He will take us up and glorify us with Himself *(cf. Rom.*
460   *8:17)* and bestow on us the enjoyment of eternal benefits. These may we all obtain by the grace and loving-kindness of our Lord Jesus Christ, to whom be glory and might, now and ever, and unto ages of ages. Amen.

VIII

ON PERFECT LOVE, AND WHAT
IT IS IN ACTION

How we cannot be believers and Christians, nor become sons and children of God, unless we even in this
life through zeal become partakers of the Holy Spirit.

[§ 1. EXPOSURE OF THOSE WHO PRETEND VIRTUE.]

Brethren and fathers,

He who feigns virtue, and thus deceives and destroys many,
is truly miserable, and subject to condemnation and abhorrence
on the part of God and men. So it is obvious that he who is with-   10
out passion, and yet for the sake of the salvation and profit of
many pretends to be subject to some passion, is praiseworthy
and blessed as the ancient fathers teach. The devil played the
part of a serpent and of a counselor, and while he seemed to be
good and useful in reality he brought death and deprived man of
God and of all the fruits in paradise, and so showed himself to
be an enemy of God and a murderer *(Jn. 8:44)*. So he who pretends to be evil and seems to utter wicked words, [and does so]
to find out what the devil achieves through those who pretend
virtue and piety and to turn those who do evil to repentance and
salvation and confession of sins, he is really an imitator of Christ   20
(1 Cor. 11:1) and clearly a "fellow-worker with God" *(1 Cor.
3:39)* and a savior of men. But this work is only for those whose
sense is not redolent of this air[1] or of the sensuality of the world
and things that belong to it, whose minds are not affected by visible things but have departed from the lowliness of the body. I
speak of those who are equal to angels, perfectly united to God,

---

1. "Air" as the special sphere of demonic powers; see Eph. 2:2.

who have wholly possessed Christ in themselves by action and experience, by perception, knowledge, and contemplation.[2]

[§ 2. CHARITABLE CORRECTION OF ONE'S BRETHREN.]

30   It is most certainly an evil thing to overhear or spy on one's neighbor's conversations or actions, if done with the intention of criticizing or denigrating him, slandering him, or spreading abroad, when occasion serves, what one has seen or heard. However, it is not wicked if it is done in order to set one's neighbor on the right way with compassion, wisdom, and prudence, and to pray for him with tears from one's very soul. In fact, I have seen a man who with great effort and many pains took care that nothing done or spoken by his companions should escape him.

40   He did this, not to harm them—far from it!—but in order that he might dissuade them from evil deeds and thoughts, as he moved one by word, another by gifts, yet another in some other way. Indeed I have seen this man sometimes weeping over someone, or groaning over another. Sometimes he would strike his own face or his breast for somebody, as he took on himself the part of him who had sinned and looked on himself as though it were he who had done evil and so made confession to God and fell before Him in grievous sorrow. Yet another I have seen who

50   so greatly rejoiced over those who struggled and succeeded, and applauded their progress as though he himself were to receive the reward of their virtues and efforts instead of them. As for those who fell in word or deed, or who persisted in evil, he grievously mourned and lamented as if he himself were truly responsible for all these things and had to account for them and suffer punishment. I have seen yet another who was so zealous and filled with desire for the salvation of his brethren that he often implored God, who loves man, with all his soul and with warm tears that either they might be saved or else that he be

60   condemned with them. His attitude was like that of Moses (cf.

---

2. S. Symeon here enumerates the signs of our union with Christ and possession of Him, possibly even of successive stages of that union—action, experience, perception, knowledge, contemplation—contemplation in any case being the highest state. To be complete, this union must be both experimental and cognitive.

Ex. 32:32; Num. 14:10ff.) and indeed of God Himself in that he did not in any way wish to be saved alone. Because he was spiritually bound to them by holy love in the Holy Spirit he did not want to enter into the kingdom of heaven itself if it meant that he would be separated from them. O sacred bond! O unutterable power! O soul of heavenly thoughts, or, rather, soul borne by God and greatly perfected in love of God and of neighbor!

[§ 3. TRUE CHARITY.]

He, then, who has not yet attained to this love, neither seen a trace of it in his own soul nor in any way felt its presence, is still earthbound and among the things of the earth. Nay, rather, his nature is to hide himself beneath the earth like the so-called blind rat, since he is blind like it and capable of hearing only those who speak on the earth. What a terrible misfortune that we who have been born of God and become immortal and partakers of a heavenly calling *(Heb. 3:1)*, who are "heirs of God and fellow-heirs with Christ" *(Rom. 8:17)* and have become citizens of heaven *(Phil. 3:20)*, have not yet come to the realization of so great blessings! We are, so to speak, without feeling, like iron that is thrown into fire, or like a lifeless hide that cannot feel it when it is dipped in scarlet dye. This is still our attitude though we find ourselves in the midst of such great blessings of God and admit that we have no feeling of it in ourselves! Though we boast as if we were already saved and numbered among the saints, and make pretense and adorn ourselves with affected holiness like those who spend their lives in misery as performers in the music hall or the theater, we are like clowns and harlots who have no natural beauty and foolishly think to beautify themselves with cosmetics and unnatural colors. How different are the features of the saints who have "been born from above" *(Jn. 3:3)*!

[§ 4. ONE CANNOT BE A CHRISTIAN WITHOUT LOVE.]

When a baby comes forth from its mother's womb it unconsciously feels the air and is spontaneously moved to weep and wail. So we must know that, when he who is "born from above" *(Jn. 3:3)* comes out from this world as from a dark womb, he enters into the intellectual and heavenly light, and as he, so to

70

80

90

speak, peers slightly inside it he is at once filled with unspeakable joy. As he naturally thinks of [the darkness] from which he
has been delivered, he painlessly sheds tears. This is how one begins to be counted among Christians. But those who have not
entered into the knowledge and contemplation of such beauty,
100 who have not sought it with great patience, groanings, and tears
in order to be purified by these practices and so attain it, be
completely united with it, and have communion with it—how,
tell me, can they in any way be called Christians?[3] They are not
truly so! If "that which is born of the flesh is flesh and that
which is born of the Spirit is spirit" (*Jn. 3:6*), how can one who
has become a man by physical birth, but has never thought or
believed that one must be born spiritually or striven for this,
ever become spiritual and count himself among spiritual men?
110 He might enter by stealth, like one who wears filthy clothes,
and as he joins the bright-robed saints at the royal feast he will
be cast out, "bound hand and foot" (*Mt. 22:11ff.*). Because he is
not the son of light (*Lk. 16:8*) but of flesh and blood (*Jn. 1:13*) he
will be sent off to the eternal fire "which is prepared for the
devil and his angels" (*Mt. 25:41*). He who has received "the power to become a son of God" (*Jn. 1:12*) and an heir of the kingdom
of heaven and of eternal blessings, who has learned in many
ways what are the works and the commandments by which he is
to be raised to such honor and glory (*Ps. 8:6*), and then has de-
120 spised all this and preferred earthly and perishable things,
choosing a piggish life and thinking transitory glory better than
that which is eternal, how will he not justly be separated from
all the faithful and be condemned with the unbelievers (*Lk.
12:46*) and with the devil himself?

[§ 5. THE GREATNESS OF THE SONS OF GOD.]

Therefore I entreat you all, brethren and fathers, to strive
while it is yet time and we are still among the living. Struggle to
become sons of God (*Jn. 1:12*) and be accounted children of light
(*Eph. 5:8*), for it is that which gives us the birth from on high

---

3. S. Symeon maintains that union with God by knowledge and contemplation, or at least the striving for such a union, is a necessary qualification for being a Christian. His teaching is addressed to all Christians, not only monks.

(Jn. 3:3). Hate "the world and the things that are in the world"   130
(1 John 2:15), hate the flesh and the passions that spring from it.
Hate every evil desire and covetousness *(Col. 3:5)* even to its
least manifestation and object. This we shall be able to do if we
keep in mind how great is the glory, the joy, and the pleasure we
shall receive in time to come. Tell me, what can be as great "in
heaven or on earth" *(cf. Ps. 73:25)* than that one may become a
son of God, His heir, and fellow heir with Christ *(Rom. 8:17)*?
Nothing whatever! But because we prefer earthly things and
things that are at hand, and do not seek the blessings that are
"laid up in heaven" *(Col. 1:5)* nor cleave to them with longing,
we provide a sure proof to those who look at us that we are vic-   140
tims of the disease of unbelief, as it is written, "How can you believe, who receive glory from men and do not seek the glory that
comes from the only God?" *(Jn. 5:44)*. Then, when we have become slaves of passion we are nailed fast to the earth and what is
on it and altogether refuse to look up to heaven and to God. Being deceived by folly of soul we disobey His commandments
and fall away from His adoption of us as His sons.

[§ 6. THE KEEPING OF THE COMMANDMENTS
AS LEADING TO THE VISION OF GOD.]

Tell me, what is more foolish than he who disobeys God
and does not strive to attain to His adoption of sons? He who be-   150
lieves that God exists has great thoughts of Him. He knows that
God is the only Master, Creator, and Lord of all things, that He
is immortal, eternal, infinite, ineffable, incorruptible, and that
there will be no end of His kingdom *(Lk. 1:33)*. How should He
not be eager to lay down his life unto death *(cf. Jn. 15:13; 1 John
3:16)* for the love of Him, in order that he might be worthy, if
not to become His son and His heir, at least to become one of
His genuine servants who stand near Him? Every one who
strives to keep all God's commandments without fail becomes   160
both a child of God and a son of God born from above *(cf. Jn.
3:3)* and is known to all as a true believer and a Christian. But if
we despise the commandments of God and reject His laws,
which He will vindicate when He comes again, and this time
with awesome glory and power *(Mt. 24:30; Mk. 13:26; Lk. 21:27)*,
we show ourselves by our deeds to be unbelievers in terms of

the faith, and in terms of unbelief believers merely in words. Be not deceived: Without deeds mere faith will not profit us at all, for it is dead *(Jas. 2:17f.)*. The dead will not become partakers of life unless they first seek it by practicing the commandments.

170 As we practice them there grow up within us, like succulent fruits, love, mercy, compassion for our neighbor, gentleness, humility *(cf. Col. 3:12; Mt. 5:7, 5)*, endurance of trials *(Mt. 5:10)*, chastity, and purity of heart through which we shall be found worthy to see God, and in which the presence and enlightenment of the Holy Spirit are granted. It is this [presence] that gives new birth from above, and turns us into sons of God. It clothes us with Christ *(Rom. 13:14; Gal. 3:27)* and kindles our lamp *(Mt. 25:8)*. It shows us to be sons of light and sets our souls

180 free from darkness, and even here and now causes us to be conscious partakers of eternal life.

[§ 7. FINAL ADMONITION.]

Let us not therefore lean solely on one or other practice or virtue, such as fasting or keeping vigil or lying on the ground and various other mortifications, while we despise the keeping of the Lord's commandments, as though we were able to be saved through the one without the other. It is impossible, impossible! Let the five foolish virgins *(Mt. 25:1ff.)* persuade you [of this], as well as those who have performed many signs and wonders in Christ's name *(Mt. 7:22)* and yet, because they had not within themselves love and the grace of the Holy Spirit, they

190 heard the Lord tell them, "Depart from Me, you workers of iniquity" for "I know not whence you are" *(Lk. 13:25ff.)*. And not those alone, for there are many others with them, men who were baptized by the Holy Apostles and the saints who came after them, but were not found worthy of the grace of the Holy Spirit because of their abundant wickedness. They did not exhibit a life worthy of "the vocation wherewith we are called" *(Eph. 4:1)*, nor did they become children of God but instead remained flesh and blood *(1 Cor. 15:50)*, without ever having believed that the Spirit exists *(cf. Acts 19:2)* or seeking Him or expecting to receive Him. Wherefore such persons will never be

200 able to become masters of the desires of the flesh or the passions of the soul, nor will they display any nobility in virtue, for, as the Lord says, "Without Me you can do nothing" *(Jn. 15:5)*.

THE DISCOURSES

So I implore you, fathers and brethren, let us with all our
power endeavor to become even here and now partakers of the
gift of the Holy Spirit, so that we may obtain both present and
future blessings, by the grace and the loving-kindness of our
Lord Jesus Christ, to whom be glory forever. Amen.

IX

ON WORKS OF MERCY

Who it is that ministers to God by feeding the hungry
and giving drink to the thirsty, and such like. How one
may achieve this. How one will not benefit merely by
doing this to the poor while forgetting that he himself
is starved and denuded of God's righteousness, but
must do all this in one's own case and so feed Christ
and give Him drink.

[§ 1. SYMEON SPEAKS UNDER THE CONSTRAINT OF THE SPIRIT.]

Brethren and fathers,

I ought never to have ventured at all to address you, nor oc-
10 cupy the place of a teacher in the presence of your charity. As
you well know, an organ built by a craftsman does not play of
its own accord. Only when its pipes are filled with air and the
fingers of the player touch [its keys] in due order will it make its
sound and fill the ears of all with sweet music. So too in my own
case you must remember to ignore how poor an instrument I
am, and not be unkindly disposed toward what I am about to
say. Rather, look to the grace of the Spirit, which from on high
20 inspires and fills the souls of the faithful, to the very "finger of
God" *(Lk. 11:20)* that plucks at the strings of the mind and incites us to speak. Listen with fear and trembling *(Eph. 6:5)* to the
sound, as it were, of the Master's trumpet, or more correctly, to
the King of all things as He speaks to us as through an instrument. Listen with understanding and in great quietness!

[§ 2. THE SUPREME NEED OF SPIRITUAL FOOD.]

All of us men must be watchful and take heed to ourselves,
whether we are believers or unbelievers, small or great. If we

150

are unbelieving we must do so in order that we may arrive at knowledge and faith toward the God who has made us; if we believe, it is in order that we may live rightly and be found well pleasing to Him in every good work *(cf. Heb. 13:21)*. As for the junior monks, they should be subject to the seniors for the Lord's sake; as for the seniors, they should behave toward the juniors as toward their true children because of the Lord's commandment, "As you did it to any one of the least, you have done it to Me" *(Mt. 25:40)*. The Lord did not, as some imagine, say this merely of those who are stricken with poverty and destitute of bodily food. He said this no less of all our other brethren who are wasting away, not through any famine of bread and water, but from the famine of the neglect of God's commandments and failure to obey them *(cf. Amos 8:11)*. To the extent that the soul is more valuable than the body *(Mt. 6:25; Lk. 12:23)*, so much more is spiritual food necessary than bodily food. It is of this that I think the Lord spoke when He said, "I was hungry and you gave me no food, I was thirsty and you gave me no drink" *(Mt. 25:42)*, rather than of bodily food, which is subject to corruption; for He truly suffers thirst and hunger for the salvation of each one of us. Our salvation consists in abstaining from all sin; but apart from the practice of the virtues and the fulfilling of all the commandments it is impossible to achieve abstinence from all sin. It is by fulfilling His commandments that we usually "feed" our Master and God, the Lord of all; for our holy fathers tells us that just as the demons are fed by our evil deeds and so prevail against us, so, when we abstain from evil, they become weak through starvation and lose their vigor. So I think that He who became poor for the sake of our salvation *(cf. 2 Cor. 8:9)* is thus nourished by us, and suffers hunger when we neglect Him. Of this the lives of the saints can instruct and inform us. Since they are "more numerous than the sands" *(cf. Ps. 139:18)*, I will pass over many others and instruct your charity by taking the example of one holy woman.

[§ 3. SAINT MARY OF EGYPT.]

I know that you hear the life of Mary the Egyptian when it is read, not as though some one else were relating it, but as from herself. That woman, equal to the angels, revealed her poverty in the manner of a confession when she stated, "Even when men

offered me the price of sin, as often happened, I did not take it. I did this," she says, "not because I was well supplied with the necessities of life, for I made my living by spinning hemp, but rather that I might have many lovers ready for my passion."
70   When she was about to take ship and go to Alexandria she was so poor that she did not have the price of her ticket nor money for her expenses. But after she had made her vow to the all-pure Mother of God and fled into the desert, she bought loaves with a couple of coins that someone had given her, and then crossed the Jordan and stayed in the desert until her death. She saw the face of no person except Zosimas, and so did not feed any hungry pauper or give drink to any thirsty person or clothe the naked or visit those who were in prison or give hospitality to strangers *(cf. Mt. 25:35ff.)*. On the contrary, she had driven many into the pit of perdition, and had received them as guests
80   in the abode of sin! How then, tell me, will this woman be saved, and enter into the kingdom of heaven with the merciful? She had never forsaken wealth, nor given her possessions to the poor *(Mt. 19:21; Lk. 12:33)*, nor ever performed any work of mercy, but instead had become the cause of perdition for thousands of others. See how, if we claim that it is only by giving money and physical food that works of mercy are performed and the Lord is fed by these alone, and that only they are saved who so feed Him and give Him drink and minister to Him, and that those
90   who fail to do so perish, we reach an absurd conclusion, and thus cast many of the saints out of the kingdom! But it is impossible, it is impossible![1]

[§ 4. MATERIAL POSSESSIONS AND BONDAGE
TO COVETOUSNESS.]

The things and possessions that are in the world are common to all, like the light and this air that we breathe, as well as the pasture for the dumb animals on the plains and on the mountains. All these things were made for all in common solely for use and enjoyment; in terms of ownership they belong to no one. But covetousness, like a tyrant, has intruded into life, so that its slaves and underlings have in various ways divided up

---

1. It would seem that even then there were those who would apply the criterion of social utility to the pursuit of holiness.

that which the Master gave to be common to all. She has en-   100
closed them by fences and made them secure by means of watch-
towers, bolts, and gates. She has deprived all other men of the
enjoyment of the Master's good gifts, shamelessly pretending to
own them, contending that she has wronged no one. But this tyrant's underlings and slaves in turn become, each one of them,
evil slaves and keepers of the properties and monies entrusted to
them. Even if they are moved by the threat of punishments in
store for them, or by the hope of receiving them back a hundredfold *(Mk. 10:30)* or by sympathy for the misfortunes of men, and
take a few or even all of these things to give to those who are in   110
poverty and distress whom they have hitherto ignored, how can
they be accounted merciful? Have they fed Christ? Have they
done a deed that is worthy of a reward? By no means! I tell you
that they owe a debt of penitence to their dying day for all that
they so long have kept back and deprived their brothers from using![2]

[§ 5. SPIRITUAL DEEDS OF MERCY TOWARD CHRIST.]

We, on our part, have apparently become poor, even as
Christ our God, who though He was rich became poor for our
sakes *(2 Cor. 8:9)*. How shall we be accounted as showing mercy   120
toward Him, who for our sakes became like us, while we show
mercy toward ourselves? Think carefully of what I am saying!
For your sake God became a poor man. You who believe in Him
owe Him the debt of becoming poor like Him. He is poor according to human nature, you are poor according to the divine.
Consider, therefore, how you may feed Him! Pay careful attention! "He became poor that you might become rich," that He
might impart to you the riches of His grace *(Eph. 1:7, 2:7)*. For
this reason He assumed flesh, that you might become partaker
of His Divinity *(2 Pet. 1:4)*. When, therefore, you make ready to
entertain Him, it is said of Him that He is about to be your
guest. When you are hungry and thirsty for His sake it is reck-   130
oned as food and drink for Him. How? Because by these and
such like actions you cleanse your soul and rid yourself of the
famine and squalor of passions. God, who receives you and thus

---

2. An extremely interesting commentary on social and political conditions,
with precedent in S. John Chrysostom.

makes His own all that concerns you, desires to make you a god, just as He became man. Whatever you do to yourself He counts as though He undergoes it Himself and says, "As you did this to the least one, your soul, you did it to Me" *(cf. Mt. 25:40).*

By what other works have those pleased God who have "dwelt in caves and on mountains" *(Heb. 11:38),* save by love, re-
140   pentance, and faith? They have left all the world and have followed Him alone *(Mk. 10:28).* They have received and entertained Him as their guest through penitence and tears; they have fed Him and given Him drink when thirsty. Likewise indeed have all those who by reason of Holy Baptism are entitled sons of God, yet according to the world are insignificant and poor. Those, then, who realize in their souls that they are sons of God can no longer bear to adorn themselves for a transitory world, for they have clothed themselves with Christ *(Gal. 3:27).* Who among men clothed with royal purple will ever allow himself to put on a filthy and torn garment on top of it?
150   Those who do not know this and are naked, without the royal array, yet endeavor to put on Christ by means of penitence and the other good works that we have mentioned, clothe themselves with Christ Himself. They themselves are christs, just as they are sons of God by virtue of divine Baptism. But even if they were to clothe all the naked people that are in the world, but fail to do this and so leave themselves naked, what have they gained?

Again, we who have been baptized "in the Name of the Father, and of the Son, and of the Holy Ghost" *(Mt. 28:19)* bear
160   the name of Christ's brethren *(Heb. 2:11f.).* We are more than this, for we are also His members *(1 Cor. 6:15, 12:27).* As His brother and His member you may honor all others, give them hospitality, and care for them. Yet if you ignore yourself and, instead of striving by every means to attain to the summit of that life and honor which are pleasing to God, leave your soul in the famine of laziness or the thirst of indifference or imprisoned in the dungeon of this filthy body through gluttony or love of pleasure, lying in filth, squalor, and deepest gloom as though it were dead, have you not treated Christ's brother with contempt? Have you not abandoned Him to hunger and thirst? Have you not failed to visit Him when He was in prison *(Mt. 25:42f.)?*
170   Surely for this you will hear Him say, "You have not had mercy on yourself, you will be shown no mercy."

154

THE DISCOURSES

[§ 6. THE MEANING OF CORPORAL WORKS OF MERCY.]

But if anyone says, "Since this is so and we have no reward for the money and possessions we give, what need is there to give to the poor?" let him hear from Him who will judge him and requite to every man according to his works *(Rom. 2:6)*, as though he were speaking to him: "You fool, what have you brought into the world *(cf. 1 Tim. 6:7)*? Have you yourself made anything that is visible? Did you not come forth naked from your mother's womb? Will you not depart from life naked *(Job 1:21)* and will you not stand exposed before My judgment seat *(cf. Heb. 4:13)*? What money is there of yours for which you ask compensation? By what possessions of yours do you claim that you give alms to your brethren, and through them to Me? I have given you all these things, not to you alone, but to all men in common. Or do you think that I covet something and that I can be bribed like the covetous among human judges? For it is impossible that you have so thought in your folly. It is not that I covet any wealth, but that I have pity on you; it is not that I wish to take what is yours *(cf. 2 Cor. 12:14)* but that I wish to set you free from the condemnation that attaches to them that I so legislate, and for no other reason."

Do not think at all, brother, that God is at a loss and is unable to feed the poor, and for this reason commands you to show mercy to them and highly values this commandment. Far from it! But Christ has taken that which the devil through covetousness has wrought against us for our perdition, and through almsgiving has turned to our good to make it redound for our salvation. What do I mean? The devil has suggested to us that we appropriate the things that were provided for our common use and hoard them for ourselves, so that through this covetousness he might make us liable to a double indictment and thus subject to eternal punishment and condemnation—the one, of being unmerciful, the other, of putting our hope in hoarded up wealth instead of in God. For he who has wealth hoarded up cannot hope in God, as is clear from what Christ our God has said, "Where your treasure is, there will your heart be also" *(Lk. 12:34)*. He, then, who distributes to all from the wealth that he has stored up has no reward owing to him for doing this; rather,

180

190

200

he is to blame for hitherto unjustly depriving others of it. Further, he is responsible for those who from time to time have lost
210   their lives through hunger and thirst, for those whom he did not feed at that time though he was able, for the poor whose share he buried and whom he allowed to die a cruel death from cold and hunger *(cf. Jas. 2:15f.)*. He is exposed as one who has murdered as many victims as he was then able to feed.

[§ 7. HOW DISTRIBUTING ONE'S POSSESSIONS IS TO SET
ONE'S HEART FREE.]

Once the good and gracious Master has set us free from the indictment of all these charges He no longer accounts us as those who hold on to the goods of others. He counts them as our own, and promises to give us not merely tenfold, but a hundredfold *(cf. Mk. 10:30)*, if we distribute them to our brethren with cheerfulness *(Rom. 12:8, 2 Cor. 9:7)*. Cheerfulness consists in not
220   regarding these things as our own, but as entrusted to us by God for the benefit of our fellow-servants. It consists in scattering them abroad generously with joy and magnanimity, not reluctantly or under compulsion *(cf. 2 Cor. 9:7ff.)* Further, we ought cheerfully to empty ourselves of that which we stored up in the hope of the true promise God has made to us of giving us a hundredfold reward for this. For since God knows that we are all wholly possessed by the lust for possessions and mad desire for wealth and how difficult it is for us to tear ourselves loose from them, and how those who in various ways have been deprived of them despair of life itself, He has made use of the corresponding
230   remedy. He has promised to give us, as we have said, a hundredfold reward for that which we spend on the poor. This He has done, first, that we may be set free in this matter from the condemnation of covetousness, and second that we may cease to put our trust and hope in possessions and find our hearts set free from such bonds. Once we have been set free we can proceed without hindrance to the practice of His commandments and "serve Him with fear and trembling" *(Ps. 2:11)*, not as though we were doing Him some favor, but as receiving a benefit by be-
240   ing admitted into His service. Otherwise it would be impossible for us to be saved! The rich have been commanded to lay aside their wealth as being some kind of burden and hindrance to a

life pleasing to God, and thus to take up the Cross on their shoulders and follow the Master in His footsteps *(Mk. 8:34; Mt. 16:24)*, for it is wholly impossible for us to bear both burdens at once. As for those who are not in their case and live in moderate circumstances, or even go short of the necessities of life, they have nothing that impedes them if they wish to walk on the narrow and difficult way *(cf. Mt. 7:14)*. The former need no more than the intention to do so; the latter are already walking on that way, and must live with patience and thanksgiving. God, because He is just, will prepare a place of rest for those who are thus on the way to eternal life and enjoyment.

[§ 8. HOW ONE MUST CARRY HIS CROSS AFTER DISTRIBUTING HIS GOODS.]

But to give away all one's possessions and wealth without fighting valiantly against the assaults of temptations and all kinds of tribulations seems to me to pertain to a soul that is careless and does not know the end for which this serves. Just as gold tarnished in depth *(cf. Jas. 5:3)* cannot be properly purified and restored to its proper brightness unless it is cast into fire and thoroughly hammered with mallets, so when the soul has been tarnished with the rust of sin and become thoroughly useless it cannot be cleansed and recover its original beauty unless it meets with many trials and enter into the furnace of tribulations *(cf. Wis. 3:6)*. The word of the Lord hints at this when He says, "Sell what you possess and give to the poor, and take up your cross and come, follow Me" *(Mt. 19:21, 16:24)*. By "the cross" He alludes to temptations and tribulations. Those who renounce wealth and possessions and take refuge in the monastic life will gain nothing by merely casting them away, unless they persevere to the end in trials and tribulations and the grief that is pleasing to God *(2 Cor. 7:10)*. Christ did not say, "By the renunciation of your possessions you will gain your souls," but "by your endurance" *(Lk. 21:19)*. It is evident that the distribution of one's wealth to the poor and fleeing from the world are excellent and useful, but by themselves alone they cannot make a man perfect and pleasing to God without endurance of trials. That this is so, and that it has so pleased God, listen to Him as He tells the rich man: "If you would be perfect, sell what you

250

260

270

280

possess and give to the poor, and take up your cross and come, follow Me" *(Mt. 19:21, 16:24)*. As we have said, by "the cross" He alludes to the trials and tribulations.

Since, then, "the kingdom of heaven suffers violence and the violent take it by force" *(Mt. 11:12)*, and it is impossible for the faithful to enter it by any other way, unless they come through the narrow gate of trials and tribulations, the divine oracle rightly commands us, saying: "Strive to enter by the narrow door" *(Lk. 13:24)*. Again He says, "By your endurance you will gain your souls" *(Lk. 21:19)*, and, "Through many tribulations we must enter the kingdom *(Acts 14:22)* of heaven." He, then, who "scatters abroad" *(Ps. 112:9)* his possessions to those who are in need and retires from the world and its affairs in the hope of a reward burdens his conscience with the great pleasure that he takes therein and may at times even be deprived of reward because of vainglory. But he who has given all things to the poor and has endured troubles with thankfulness of soul and persevered in difficulties, and feels all the bitterness and pain of sufferings, keeps his mind inviolate in the present time. In the life to come he has great reward, in that he has imitated the sufferings of Christ and patiently waited for Him in the days when temptations and trials assailed him.

[§ 9. THE NARROW DOOR OF PENITENCE AND PURIFICATION.]

Therefore I entreat you, brethren in Christ, let us endeavor to act in accordance with the word of our Lord and God and Savior Jesus Christ. Since we have renounced the world and the things that are in the world *(1 John 2:15)*, we have done so in order that we may enter through the narrow door *(Mt. 7:13)*, which consists in cutting off our carnal mind and will and fleeing from them. For if we are not mortified in the flesh and its lusts and desires *(Eph. 2:3)* it is not possible for us to obtain relief and deliverance from our ills, nor the freedom that comes to us from the comfort of the Holy Spirit. Apart from this—I mean the coming of the Spirit—no one will see the Lord *(Heb. 12:14)* either in this world or in the world to come *(Mt. 12:32)*. Because you have done well in that you have scattered all your wealth abroad to the needy (as long as you have not left anything for yourself after the example of that Ananias [*Acts 5:1ff.*]), and in addition have renounced the world and the things that are in the world *(1 John 2:15)*, and have fled from [worldly] life and its cares and have run into the haven of life and have wrapped yourself in the outward form of religion *(2 Tim. 3:5)*, I am in agreement with you and praise you for your effort. But now you must strip yourself of "the mind of the flesh" *(Rom. 8:6f.)* even as you have discarded your [secular] attire. As you have put on your robe for Christ's sake, so you must acquire the habits of the soul and the spiritual mind itself *(Rom. 8:27)*. You must be clothed as well through penitence with that radiant garment which is the Holy Spirit Himself. This can happen only through the persistent practice of the virtues and by the endurance of afflictions. The afflicted soul is moved to tears through trials; as the tears cleanse the heart they make it into a temple and a resting place for the Holy Spirit. The mere clothing with the habit and the outward adorning of the human form do not suffice for our salvation and perfection. No less than the outward man, so must we needs adorn our inner man *(2 Cor. 4:16)* with the moderation of the Spirit, and completely offer up ourselves to God in soul and body. By bodily exercise *(cf. 1 Tim. 4:8)* we must exercise the body for the labors of virtue so that it may be vigorous and accustomed to the painful things that are pleasing to God and nobly bear the bitterness of fasting, the violence of abstinence, the necessity of vigil, all suffering of hardship. By piety *(cf. 1 Tim. 4:8)* we must train the soul to think as it ought to think *(Rom. 12:3)* and constantly meditate on the things that belong to eternal life, to be humble, meek *(cf. Mt. 11:29)*, and contrite, filled with compunction, to mourn daily and by prayer invoke on itself the light of the Spirit. These gifts usually come to it through most fervent penitence as the soul purifies itself by many tears. Apart from these not even its garment may ever be cleansed, let alone the soul itself rise to the height of contemplation. Just as a garment soaked in mud and dung is so thoroughly soiled that it cannot possibly become clean unless it is washed with much water and much stamping of the feet, so when the garment of the soul has been defiled with the mud and dung of sinful passions it cannot be washed clean except through many tears and endurance of trials and tribulations. Of the two fluids that the body by nature produced in us—that is, the tears that flow sown from above and that

320

330

340

350

360

which flows from the genitals—the latter defiles the soul when it is evacuated contrary to nature and to law, while the former, when they flow out of penitence, cleanse it. Those who have become defiled in soul by the guilty practice of sin and by the passionate movement of the heart that imprints in them the forms of irrational desires must become clean through many tears and attain perfect purity of the garment of the soul. Otherwise it is impossible to see God, who Himself is the light that enlightens the heart of every man *(cf. Jn. 1:9)* who comes to Him through penitence, since it is the pure in heart who will see God *(Mt. 5:8)*.

[§ 10. TEARS AND THE COMFORT OF THE SPIRIT.]

370

380

390

I therefore entreat you, my fathers and brethren and children, let us endeavor to attain to purity of heart, which comes from paying heed to our ways and from constant confession of the secret thoughts of the soul. For if we, moved by a penitent heart, constantly and daily confess these, it produces in us repentance for what we have done or even thought. Repentance gives rise to the tear from the depths of the soul; the tear cleanses the heart and wipes away great sins. When these have been blotted out through tears the soul finds itself in the comfort of the Spirit of God and is watered by streams of sweetest compunction. By these it is spiritually fructified day by day so that it produces the fruits of the Spirit *(Gal. 5:22f.)* and in due time yields them like an abundant harvest of grain as an unfailing supply of food for the incorruptible and eternal life of the soul. When the soul by a good zeal has reached this state it is identified with God and becomes the house and abode of the Divine Trinity. It sees its own Maker and God clearly, and as it converses with Him day by day it departs from the body and the world and from this air and ascends into the heaven of heavens. Borne aloft by the virtues and by the wings of God's love it rests from its labors together with all the righteous and is found in the infinite and divine Light, where the hosts of Christ's apostles, of the martyrs, of the blessed ones and of all the powers on high sing in chorus together.

Brethren in Christ, may we too attain such a state! Let us not fall short of our holy fathers, but rather by our zeal for goodness and by the practice of Christ's commandments "attain to mature manhood, to the measure of the stature of the fullness of Christ" *(Eph. 4:13)*. There is nothing that prevents us, if only we desire it! Thus shall we glorify God in ourselves and God will find joy in us. As we depart from this present life we shall find God as the great "bosom of Abraham" *(cf. Lk. 16:22)*, receiving us and cherishing us in the kingdom of heaven. To this may we all attain by the grace of our Lord Jesus Christ, to whom be glory forever. Amen.

400

X

[PERFECT HOLINESS]

On partaking of the Holy Spirit, on holiness and the complete absence of passion. That he who loves the glory that comes from men will derive no benefit from the other virtues, even if he excels in them all.

[§ 1. EARTHLY AND HEAVENLY GLORY.]

Brethren and fathers,

Do you not see how those who attend on an earthly king regard it as a great glory, that they are proud of it, and are considered objects of envy by those in the world? If, then, this is so in vain and transitory matters, how much more should we, who have been enrolled in the army of the heavenly King and have taken His service upon ourselves, rejoice and be glad that we have been found worthy to be taken into His service and called on to render worship to His Name? And if we shall ever be counted worthy to behold Him face to face and to be numbered among those who stand in His presence, how greatly that would surpass any praise for blessedness! But if one were to be numbered among His special servants and friends, and be counted worthy to hear the utterance and voice of the Master, what human mind, what human tongue would be able to describe the greatness of this glory and dignity? But if that "which no eye has seen, nor ear heard, nor the heart of man conceived, which God has prepared for those who love Him" *(1 Cor. 2:9)* is above human comprehension and above all visible blessings, how much more is God Himself who has prepared them! Not only is He above them, but also those who have been counted worthy to see Him and to stand before Him and have converse with Him, and who have become partakers and sharers of His divinity and His glory. They have become altogether superior to the good

162

things that God has prepared for them, since they have received   30
as their inheritance the very Lord who has prepared these good
things. That men have become such and continue to do so until
the present time, and that not merely after death, but, I say,
even while they are living this present life, this the whole inspired Scripture teaches. All the saints confirm this witness
through their own lives, among others our blessed father Symeon the Studite himself, whose memory we celebrate today, as
well as those who by their words praise the saints.

This our most holy father Symeon, of whose life and conduct, pleasing to God, we have read, lived such a life of asceti-   40
cism and exhibited such conduct in the midst of the city and in
the very midst of a most illustrious monastery that he surpassed
not only those who shone in his own generation, but even many
of the fathers of old, in the sublimity of his virtues and by
achievements beyond [human] power. Therefore, since he has
shown himself to us to be worthy of many praises and eulogies,
we praise him, call him blessed, and eulogize him according to
our ability.

[§ 2. CRITERIA OF HOLINESS AND OF BLESSEDNESS.]

The whole praise and blessedness of the saints consists of
these two elements—their orthodox faith and praiseworthy life,   50
and the gift of the Holy Spirit and His spiritual gifts. A third
point follows on them. When a man lives rightly, as a friend of
God, with orthodox faith, and when God bestows His gifts on
him and glorifies him through the gift of the Spirit, there follows the praise of the whole Church of the faithful and on the
part of all its teachers and their pronouncement of his blessedness. But if the basis of faith and works is not laid without fail
(cf. Heb. 6:1) it is impossible for any man ever to enjoy the
presence of the adorable and divine Spirit and to receive His
gift. Unless He is present in a man and is known to dwell in   60
him, it is in every way incongruous to call him spiritual. If he
has not become spiritual, how will he be holy? If he has not become holy, for what other work or activity will he be accounted
blessed, when God is blessedness? He who has no part in God,
or, rather, who does not possess Him wholly in himself, how
can I consider him to be blessed? It is impossible! Were the sun
without light, how could it be called a sun? If a man does not

partake of the all-Holy Spirit, how can he be called holy? For the Lord has said, "You shall be holy, for I am holy" *(1 Pet. 1:16)*. In order to encourage us, so to speak, to imitate Him by our deeds, the Compassionate One, as He visits us while we are in our sins, says: "Leave off from evil deeds and practice all good deeds; pursue every virtue and become holy as far as it is attainable, if you really want to have fellowship with Me. For I am holy, that is, pure and undefiled. This pertains to Me by nature; but if you abstain from the defilement of sins by practicing the commandments and partake of Me by the grace of the Holy Spirit, then you also will be holy." This is what is implied in "become."

[§ 3. ZEAL FOR GOOD WORKS.]

By abstaining from evil *(cf. Job 2:3)* and by the practice of good deeds *(cf. Ps. 34:15)* a person becomes holy. It is not as though he were sanctified simply by works, for no soul will be justified by the works of the law *(Rom. 3:20; Gal. 2:16)*, but rather that by practicing such actions he is brought into fellowship with the Holy God. I am sure that the Lord spoke this especially to those who had already received the grace of the Spirit in order to urge them not to presume on the gift and turn back to evil through apathy. It is as though He said, "Do not give yourself to idleness, O spiritual man who has received the grace of the Holy Spirit and thereby received Me. For idleness gives birth to wickedness, and wickedness engenders all kinds of evil. Therefore become holy by the daily practice of the commandments, if you wish that I shall be in you and with you, and that you should be in Me and with Me." But since the mind is something that is in constant motion and incapable of total inactivity, it is necessary that it should be concerned and eager to practice the commandments of God. So the whole life of men is filled with care and concern and cannot be wholly at leisure, even if many have striven to achieve it, though it is beyond their ability and power. But in the beginning man was created with such a nature, for in paradise Adam was enjoined to till [the ground] and care for it *(Gen. 2:15)*, and there is in us a natural bent for work, the movement toward the good. Those who yield themselves to idleness and apathy, even though they may be spiritual and holy, hurl themselves into unnatural subjection to passions.

[§ 4. HOW LOVE OF GLORY RUINS THE PRACTICE OF VIRTUES.]

A fountain that constantly flows with water vanishes, even if it stops but briefly, and turns into a pool instead of a fountain. So he who constantly cleanses himself by practicing the commandments and is cleansed and sanctified by God would likewise cease from holiness if he were even briefly to cease practicing them. He who knowingly is led astray even by a single sin falls completely from purity, just as a bucket of water is wholly polluted by a little dung. What I call sin is not merely what is committed by the body, but also the passions within us that we invisibly fulfill. Brethren, do not greet what I say with disbelief! Rather, be sure of this, that even if we practice every virtue and perform miracles and omit nothing either great or small from the commandment, yet desire nothing but the glory that comes from men and seek it, however slightly, by our endeavors and hasten to receive it, we shall be deprived of the reward for all the rest. For if we receive the glory that is from men and do not prefer that which comes from God *(Jn. 5:44)*, we shall be judged as idolaters, because we worship the creature rather than the Creator *(Rom. 1:25)*. But he who when earthly glory is given accepts it with pleasure and joy, and prides himself on it and rejoices over it in his heart, is judged like a fornicator. Such a person is like a man who chooses to live in virginity and avoid the company of women, yet, though he does not resort to them nor desire to live with them, when one woman comes to him he at once receives her with pleasure and takes his fill of the enjoyment of sexual union.

[§ 5. HOW PASSION AND HOLINESS ARE INCOMPATIBLE.]

This is also the case with every other desire and every passion. If anyone willingly abandons himself to envy, avarice, jealousy, strife, or any other wickedness *(cf. Rom. 1:29, 13:13)*, he will not obtain the crown of righteousness. Because God is righteous He cannot bear to have fellowship with the unrighteous; since He is pure He is not defiled with the impure. Since He is without passions He does not dwell with those who are passionate; since He is holy He does not enter into a soul that is defiled and wicked. He is wicked who receives the seed of the wicked sower into his heart and brings forth thorns and thistles *(cf. Mt. 13:24ff.)* as fruit for the devil. These are fuel for the eternal fire, consisting of envy, hatred, rancor, jealousy, rivalry, presumption, vainglory *(cf. Jas. 3:14)*, pride, guile, idle curiosity, slander, and any other abominable passion the flesh delights to fulfill, and which defiles *(cf. Mt. 15:11)* our inward man *(cf. Rom. 7:22; Eph. 3:16)*, according to the word of the Lord.

150

    Far be it from us, brethren, that we should ever bear the fruit of such tares, and that because of carelessness we should receive the seed of the evil one in our hearts. Rather, may we bear fruit for Christ thirtyfold, sixtyfold, and a hundredfold *(cf. Mt. 13:23; Mk. 4:8, 20)* of the things the Spirit has cultivated within us, that is, "love, joy, peace, kindness, goodness, long-suffering, faith, meekness, self-control" *(Gal. 5:22ff.)*. So may we be fed with the bread of knowledge *(cf. Sir. 15:3)* and grow in virtues and attain to the perfect man, "to the measure of the stature of the fullness of Christ" *(Eph. 4:13)*, to whom all glory is due forever. Amen.

160

XI

ON FASTING

That one should not embrace and zealously observe the benefit of the fast only in the first week of Lent, but that the zealous must continue the same zeal in all the weeks of Lent.

[§ 1. THE FIRST WEEK OF LENT.]

Brethren and fathers,

What we are about to say we ought to have addressed to your charity last Sunday. I was aware, however, that every one of us believers, [together with] the whole Christian people, both monks and laity, with fervent zeal accepts the blessing of fasting in the holy first week of Lent, and that each one of us willingly puts its yoke upon his neck *(Sir. 51:26)*. Even among those who greatly despair of their own salvation and live their lives without fear and reverence for God there is no one who rejects the law of fasting in that week. Rather, as far as he is able, he joins with all in observing abstinence. So I come today to speak a few short words to you about the present season.

As we have said, all faithful people spend the first week of Lent, which is now past, in a strenuous manner. But now that it is past and Saturday has arrived, it falls to the lot of the Church of God to celebrate, in accordance with tradition, the feast of the great martyr Saint Theodore,[1] or rather, the extraordinary act of salvation that God wrought through him for His most faithful people. Likewise on Sunday we all make commemoration of the Orthodox Faith[2] and sing hymns of thanksgiving to God,

---

1. S. Theodore Tiron, soldier saint martyred under the emperor Maximian, whose memorial is celebrated on the first Saturday of Lent.
2. The Sunday of Orthodoxy.

167

30   who is all-good. But the evil one, who is always envious of goodness, secretly steals up on each of the faithful and invisibly puts
on him the chains of slackness and carelessness. He persuades
him to despise and reject the salutary yoke of fasting *(cf. Ps. 2:3)*
and to return to his former habits. Therefore I remind you today and make my appeal to your charity, your paternity, that
you do not in any way obey him who wills you ill. Do not be led
astray by the bad habit of insatiable gluttony, nor turn back to
40   the old [habit of] satisfaction of evil desires. Rather, let us keep
this second week of Lent like the first, and likewise the remain-
der [of the season].

[§ 2. FASTING AS THE HEALER OF THE SOUL.]

Indeed, my fathers and brethren, let us act for our own
good by so doing, and let us not allow ourselves to lose what we
have gathered together in the past, but rather let us strive to add
to it and increase it. Let us not miserably allow what we have
built up in times past to be destroyed *(cf. Gal. 2:18)*. Let each one
of us keep in mind the benefit of fasting and what gifts from
God he has enjoyed in these few days and so become more eager
50   for the days to come. For this healer of our souls is effective, in
the case of one to quieten the fevers and impulses of the flesh, in
another to assuage bad temper, in yet another to drive away
sleep, in another to stir up zeal, and in yet another to restore purity of mind and to set him free from evil thoughts. In one it
will control his unbridled tongue and, as it were by a bit *(Jas.
3:3, 8)*, restrain it by the fear of God and prevent it from uttering idle or corrupt words *(Eph. 4:29; Mt. 12:36)*. In another it
will invisibly guard his eyes and fix them on high instead of al-
60   lowing them to roam hither and thither, and thus cause him to
look on himself and teach him to be mindful of his own faults
and shortcomings. Fasting gradually disperses and drives away
spiritual darkness and the veil of sin that lies on the soul, just as
the sun dispels the mist. Fasting enables us spiritually to see that
spiritual air in which Christ, the Sun who knows no setting,
does not rise, but shines without ceasing. Fasting, aided by vigil,
penetrates and softens hardness of heart. Where once were the
vapors of drunkenness it causes fountains of compunction to
spring forth. I beseech you, brethren, let each of us strive that

this may happen in us! Once this happens we shall readily, with   70
God's help, cleave through the whole sea of passions and pass
through the waves of the temptations inflicted by the cruel tyrant, and so come to anchor in the port of impassibility.

[§ 3. FASTING AS THE FOUNDATION OF ALL SPIRITUAL ACTIVITY.]

My brethren, it is not possible for these things to come
about in one day or one week! They will take much time, labor,
and pain, in accordance with each man's attitude and willing-
ness, according to the measure of faith *(Rom. 12:3, 6)* and one's
contempt for the objects of sight and thought. In addition, it is
also in accordance with the fervor of his ceaseless penitence and   80
its constant working in the secret chamber of his heart *(Mt. 6:6)*
that this is accomplished more quickly or more slowly by the
gift and grace of God. But without fasting no one was ever able
to achieve any of these virtues or any others, for fasting is the
beginning and foundation of every spiritual activity. Whatever
you will build on this foundation cannot collapse or be destroyed, because they are built on solid rock. But if you remove
this foundation and substitute for it a full stomach and improper
desires, they will be undermined like sand by evil thoughts, and   90
the whole structure of virtues will be destroyed *(cf. Mt. 7:26f.;*
Lk. 6:49). To prevent this from happening in our case, my brethren, let us gladly stand on the solid foundation of fasting. Let us
stand firmly, let us stand willingly! He who is compelled to
climb the rock of fasting against his will cannot fail to be
dragged down by his desire and thrown headlong into eating in
secret. And so, as he nibbles, he becomes, I think, food for the
evil one, for fasting is a divine law and those who presume to
transgress it are seized by the devil, who flogs them like an exe-   100
cutioner. If this does not happen immediately or quickly it is because God is patient with us and accepts our penitence. Yet we
shall not altogether "escape his hand" *(Tb. 13:2)* either in this
life or in the world to come, if we persist in sin without repent-
ing thereof. If we act in this way we shall share in the devil's
condemnation, and at his hand and together with him we shall
receive eternal punishments by the just judgment of God. We
may be hidden from our superiors, yet we cannot be hidden
from the Master and God of our superiors.

[§ 4. FASTING AND DEVOTION.]

110 Let us then beware, brethren, not only of eating in secret, but also of eating our fill from the dishes set before us on the table. Indeed I entreat you without ceasing to call to mind this sacred week that has passed. Take into account, as I have said, not only the benefit you have derived from fasting and vigil, from prayer and psalmody, but also your sorrow, your devotion, and your silence. At the time the monastery seemed to me to be uninhabited by man and inhabited only by angels, since I heard no
120 worldly word but only the glorification we offered to God, which is also the work of angels. I believe that just as you fulfilled the function of the angels, so also the angels took their part with you and sang with you. Do not then allow yourselves to be separated from their company by much and idle talking, nor by disorderly voices or loud shouts, so that you cause the demons to come near you as in times past. Rather, let each man take heed to himself and carefully work at his handiwork and his appointed service, as rendering service to the Lord and not
130 to men *(Eph. 6:8)*. For it is written, "Cursed is he who does the work of the Lord with slackness" *(Jer. 48:10)*.

[§ 5. MUTUAL INVITATION TO THE SPIRITUAL FEAST.]

Brethren, fail not to encourage one another during the offices to listen carefully to the sacred readings. At a physical banquet we encourage and invite our neighbors to eat of it, and those whom we like best we constrain to eat. So at this banquet, which nourishes the soul, we have the obligation to encourage our neighbors to pay attention, lest we be condemned for failing in mutual love and lose our right to be Christ's disciples. For he
140 says, "By this all men will know that you are My disciples, if you have love for one another" *(Jn. 13:35)*. At the physical banquet he who does not compel his friend to feast of it often does him the greatest service. At the spiritual feast, by which I mean the hearing of the oracles of God, he who acts in this way causes untold harm to those who are his neighbors. To fill oneself with physical food often causes harm and damage to both body and soul. On the contrary, the words spoken by the saints both enlighten the mind and sanctify the soul, and thereby impart sanc-
150 tification even to the body itself and make it healthier and more vigorous.

170

THE DISCOURSES

[§ 6. HOW TO FEED ON THE WORDS OF LIFE.]

Let everyone then pay attention to the reading *(cf. 1 Tim. 4:13)*! The words of the saints are words of God and not of men. Let him put them in his heart and keep them securely *(cf. Lk. 2:19)*, since God's words are words of life *(cf. Jn. 6:68)* and he who has them within himself and keeps them has eternal life *(Jn. 5:24)*. Were you often guests at a sumptuous banquet I doubt that any one of you would be so indifferent that he would fall asleep and only take from it for his own need, and not be anxious before departing to take with him something for the morrow that he would eagerly share with some of his friends or even with the poor. But here the words of life are offered to you, which make those who feed on them immortal! Tell me, is it right for anyone to be inattentive or to fall asleep and snore as if he were a living corpse? How great the loss! How great the insensitivity and sluggishness! He who sits at table and has no desire for the food set before him is clearly lacking in physical health. So he who hears the divine reading without unspeakable pleasure and spiritual desire, and fails to take immaterial and spiritual delight in the immaterial oracles of God and intellectually fill all his senses with their sweetness, is weak in the faith *(cf. Rom. 4:19)*. He has never tasted the spiritual gifts; for in the midst of many good gifts he wastes away with hunger and thirst. Just as a corpse, when it is being washed with water, cannot feel it, so this man feels nothing when God's life-giving streams of His word flow over him.

You have the word of life in yourselves *(cf. Phil. 2:16)*. You have come to be fed with this bread of the word *(cf. Jn. 6:27)*; you are not dead, but have become living instead of dead. You have tasted of the true life and have obtained compassion for your neighbors *(cf. Phil. 2:1; Col. 3:12)* from God who is compassionate. Therefore do not fail to stir up, to encourage, to instruct your neighbors and all others, as best you are able, as your own members, or rather, as those who are members of Christ and sons of God. Be anxious to educate them, reprove them, rebuke them *(cf. 2 Tim. 4:2)*, not in order to cause them pain, but rather to deliver them from the Father's wrath and indignation. Your purpose is not to harm them, but rather to confer on them the greatest benefits by preparing them to accomplish the things that their God and Father wills. If you act in this way and each

160

170

180

171

190   of you stirs up his brother to increased effort of love and good works *(Heb. 10:24)*, we shall quickly be lifted up to the summit of virtues and show ourselves to be fulfillers of the commandments of God. So shall we all together attain to the kingdom of heaven in Christ Himself, our God, to whom is due all glory forever and ever. Amen.

XII

OF ABSTINENCE AND ENDURANCE

For the practice of the virtues in the season of Lent. Of silence. How those who contend in truth ought to act throughout Lent.

[§ 1. SYMEON PROTESTS HIS UNWORTHINESS.]
Brethren and fathers,
Since I am constantly weak in soul and body through my failure and slackness of will and disposition, I would rather keep silence and merely look to my my affairs till I could overcome my own defects and they could be brought under the control of good thoughts. Oh, that I could wholly enjoy peace of spirit and be delivered from disturbance of the mind of dust and earth and enter into the harbor of our blessed rest! But you chose me to be the head of your sacred company, and so it is necessary for me to exhort your charity, since the salvation of your fraternity affords me consolation. Though I am weak in soul, yet you will be saved through the prayers of Him who is my Father and yours. Therefore, though I am unable to open my mouth and am scarcely able to write my discourse and address a timely reminder to your brotherhood, yet I earnestly implore your charity that, as true servants of Christ and lovers of your brethren, you pray for me in my wretched condition, in order that I too may obtain salvation with you, and that as I walk on the way of God's commandments I may be reunited with you, my beloved brethren.

So I exhort and entreat you in Christ Jesus to take heed to yourselves. Let each of you think with sober judgment and "not think beyond what he ought to think" *(Rom. 12:3)*. Do not look

173

30   on my careless and distracted life, but follow the footsteps of our
Lord and Savior Jesus Christ, before whom we must needs give
an account of ourselves as to a just and unerring Judge. Grant
me this cause for boasting *(2 Cor. 12:1)*, that though I by my
carelessness were all alone to.be brought down to hell's abyss,
yet I rescued you from the snare by crying aloud, and that
though I must needs greatly bewail my slackness, yet I may find
satisfaction merely in seeing you fly on high above the snares of
the devil. Therefore, beloved, keep without fail all the commandments of God, that you may be saved like a gazelle from a
trap and like a sparrow from a snare *(Ps. 124:7; Prov. 6:5)*.

[§ 2. THE ZEAL OF MONKS FOR FASTING.]

40   The first commandment is to love God with all one's heart
and [the second is] to love each other *(Mt. 22:37ff.; Mk. 12:29ff.)*
even as God Himself loved the world *(Jn. 3:16)*. Genuine love is
known by these marks: It is not puffed up, it does not exalt itself, it is not jealous *(1 Cor. 13:4)* of one's brother, but is zealous
for the good. It is not boastful *(1 Cor. 13:14)*, it does not complain, it does not trifle *(1 Cor. 10:10, 7)*, nor does it enter into arguments over anything, whether great or small. Love avoids
taking its fill, not merely of various kinds of food, but, if possi-
50   ble, even of water, particularly during these days of Lent. For
he who now repents with zeal and diligence receives from on
high forgiveness of his offenses of the whole past year, according to divine Scripture. You know that fervent penitence accompanied by tears that spring from the depth of the heart will melt
and burn up the filth of sin like a fire and make pure the soul
that has been defiled. In addition, penitence through the visitation of the Spirit generously imparts an abundant flow of light
to the soul, whereby it is filled with mercy and good fruits *(Jas.
60   3:17)*. I pray, therefore, fathers and brethren, let us use fasting
both during this third week of Lent and in those that follow, as
we daily add fervor to fervor and zeal to zeal, until we arrive at
the Sunday of Easter with souls and bodies alike resplendent.
        As you see, we have with God's help run the course of this
second week of Lent with good courage and ardent wills! I bear
witness that you have in no wise fallen short of the blessings of
the fast. Rather, you have spent whole nights in psalmody with
full attention and maintained strenuous abstinence and contin-

ue so to do, being content with the greens and pulse set before you. I even know that some of you, out of a contrite and humble spirit *(cf. Ps. 34:19, 51:19)* of mind, sat in your midst before these simple meals on our table and judged yourselves unworthy to partake of them. Further, as you took heed to yourselves and your handiwork, your remained in modest silence, with souls wholly filled with tears of compunction, prayer, supplication, and spiritual effort from your constant genuflections. You have been changed with a wondrous change and have acquired a most ascetic and beautiful look.

[3. BEYOND LENT—LIFELONG SOBRIETY.]

Now then, since we are about to strip ourselves for the final effort of Lent, I entreat you, let us strive in this sacred week of the most noble fast to maintain the same norm for our own effort as in the weeks already past. We shall need great sobriety and great zeal, so that we do not spend our days like those who are in the world. You know how, once the first week is past, they consider that they have passed through all of Holy Lent. Not only do they so imagine, but they explicitly say so to one another and to everyone else. But we must beware, most greatly beware, that we do not imagine and speak to one another as they do, and so appear to deny our profession! To us who flee the world and are crucified to it, who have been totally consecrated to God, it is not the present season only that has been given to us for a law of abstinence, but the whole length of our present life. In it we have the obligation to observe abstinence without any excuse.

Do we not have an obligation to do this at all times? Have we not taken the vow to be hungry, thirsty, and ill clad *(cf. 1 Cor. 4:11)* and to endure all things and bear them with joy? Ought we not particularly to do so in the season of the Lenten struggle? But if we are unwilling to do this all the days of our life, instead preferring laughter, idle talk, trifling, and arguing, how do we differ from unbelievers and pagans? In reality, not at all! For if seeking and worrying about bread and wine and clothing causes us to be like pagans *(cf. Mt. 6:31f.; Lk. 12:29f.)*, to whom will the conduct that I have mentioned make us equal, when it is worse and more sinful than these things? Will not the prophet's word be fulfilled in our case: "He became comparable

110 to the senseless beasts and was made like unto them" *(Ps. 49:13, 21 LXX)*?

Brethren, let us obey God, who daily through His apostles proclaims to us and says, "We are no worse off if we do not eat, and no better off if we do" *(1 Cor. 8:8)*. Again he says, "Do not be anxious about your life, what you shall eat or what you shall drink, or what you shall put on, but seek first the kingdom of God and His righteousness, and all these things will be yours as well" *(Mt. 6:25, 33)*. But to prevent anyone from saying, "If He delays giving and I have nothing to eat, what shall I do?" He says, "Look at the birds of the air, how they neither sow nor 120 reap, nor gather into barns, and yet your heavenly Father feeds them" *(Mt. 6:26)*. In addition He says, "O you of little faith, are you not of more value than many sparrows?" *(Mt. 10:31)*. So that we should not grumble with faintheartedness about food and drink, He explicitly cries aloud to us, saying, "Blessed are those who hunger and thirst for righteousness, for they shall be satisfied" *(Mt. 5:6)*.

[§ 4. TO AVOID GRUMBLING OR IMPATIENCE
UNDER PRIVATIONS.]

Therefore, if you believe Christ and confess that He is without deceit, but then, when you are hungry or thirsty and have nothing to eat or drink and ask the cellarer for bread or wine or something to eat and he gives you nothing (perhaps because he 130 is too busy!), think and call to mind the Lord's words and say to yourself: "I am hungry and thirsty, but I wait patiently for the Lord *(Ps. 40:1)*, and He will act according to my weakness and will not forsake me." Be thus patient, brother, and you will have great reward from God. Do the same in all the other trials that you encounter. In this way you will become an object of admiration in this present life, and in the life to come you will be numbered with the holy martyrs. How many of the brethren in Christ often long for some cold water as they lie in a corner, yet 140 perhaps give thanks to God instead of being moved to anger and uttering blasphemy? As for ourselves, by God's grace we have an unfailing supply for every physical need and, through His generous gifts, more besides! So if any one of us has nothing at all and yet complains, he is condemned for lacking patience. But if he has much and yet, because he lacks some little thing, stirs up envy and strife and goes so far as to utter blasphemous words, what pardon will he deserve? But as I say these things I know that I condemn myself and my words will quickly convict and condemn me. Yet, I pray, let them serve you as a reminder! 150

[§ 5. EDIFICATION FROM SOBRIETY AND WORK.]

Therefore, call to mind the benefit of the days of fasting now past, how you have spent them, how great your zeal and fervor. I beseech you, strive to spend the whole of this Holy Lent likewise. Each of you ought to reflect on your good conduct (cf. Jas. 3:13; 1 Pet. 2:12), how great was your devotion and humility, as well as your silence, your zealous observance of the rule of the divine Office and for your handicraft. Indeed I urge you, do not forget the fasting that slays the passions, the abstinence that cleanses, and do not neglect to act in the same way! 160 Even if it often happens that the food changes and you derive consolation from it, keep your resolve unshaken and your rule unchanged! In particular, if you eat more of the usual food, labor with greater zeal in the work of God to prevent the comfort from becoming for you an occasion of slackness and extraordinary harm rather than of thanksgiving and benefit. Indeed, my brethren, be sober! As I told you, follow what you did last week and observe the week that is beginning without eating fish, and let your conduct be in the fear of God (1 Pet. 1:17). Do not forsake your special tasks and your handicraft to walk about aimlessly and in dissipation and so expose yourselves to the demon of accidie.[1] But if any of you find another brother standing up or sitting down when you pass by, zealously make a prostration and go on your way. Possibly the idle brother will come to his senses and he too will be ashamed of himself and return to his work. So, as each of you does this, you will escape condemnation for idleness and idle talk.

[§ 6. RESTRAINING IDLE TALK.]

Have you not heard what that blessed man Zosimas says— he who wrote an account of the life of blessed Mary [of Egypt]— 180 what he tells about the holy men who were in the monastery

---

1. This could well be described as "spiritual boredom"—a malady well known to all spiritual writers of East and West.

into which he too, by God's providence, was received at that time? How they left the monastery and spent the whole of Lent in the desert? No one of them ever joined another, but if one of them should by chance meet another he would avoid him and run away from him. They could not bear to be with each other. Likewise, he relates that when they returned to the monastery no one ever asked another what he had seen or what he had done in the desert, but they all lived and behaved themselves as though they were "strangers and exiles" *(Heb. 11:13)* and men of different speech. In my opinion they did this for no other reason than that they strictly observed the rule of uttering no idle word with their mouths *(cf. Mt. 12:36; Eph. 4:29).* If then these men could spend so many days and so many years without conversing with each other at all, what about us, who cannot even avoid conversation and idle talk for these few days? But why should I speak of days? We cannot contain ourselves for the space of a single hour! What should we do, my good brethren, if God the Judge of all men should suddenly come—He who will demand an account from us even for one idle word in the day of judgment *(cf. Mt. 12:36)*—and find us in this state? And how shall we control the other passions if we have an uncontrolled tongue? Which of all the other passions, tell me, is easier [to control] than this? The flesh with its physical lust and ardor rises in rebellion against the spirit *(cf. Gal. 5:17)* and wages violent war against the soul. The belly wants to be fed with [various] foods, for it was made for this purpose. If then we do not control the habit of the tongue, which is a light and easy task, how will we ever be able to gain control over those great and violent passions, which have so much power over our very nature and even, so to speak, over desire and pleasure?

[§ 7. A WAY OF GUARDING ONE'S TONGUE.]

Let us then, brethren, begin from this day forward to run with all our strength, and cast behind us all the passions that tyrannize us, so that we may soar as golden-winged eagles light of wing and attain to the Lord's Passover,[2] where Christ our God has entered as our Forerunner *(cf. Heb. 6:20).* If you are

---

2. I.e., Easter. The Greek word for both is "Pascha."

agreeable, we will by common consent make it a law among us that, except on Saturdays and Sundays, if two are found abandoning themselves to idleness and carrying on useless conversations, they will have nothing else to eat on that day except dry bread and salt and cold water at mealtime, and that they will partake of it standing, at the lower end of the table. If we strictly keep this law you will preserve yourselves blameless in the matter of idle talk and argument. Likewise you will be serving God for whose sake you "set a door before your lips and keep a watch over your mouths" *(Ps. 141:3)*. By doing this you will greatly comfort me, your unworthy father, and fill my poor soul with delight. You will derive no little profit for your own souls as you instruct yourselves with a good rule and an admirable custom for the sake of God's love. In consequence you will be worthy of esteem and admiration on the part of all men. Through you God will receive glory, because in this generation you will be found imitators of the lives of the saints. Such, in my opinion, are not readily to be found or seen at this present time, either [in the country] where we live, or among the [foreign] monks and monasteries of which we hear.

[§ 8. FINAL EXHORTATION.]

Therefore I entreat your charity, my holy fathers and servants of God, do not ignore the words of your unworthy father, nor let my sayings appear to you as mere nonsense. Even though I am weak and filled with tens of thousands of faults, yet look and realize that I have given you no advice beyond that which is in the commandments of God and the divine Scriptures. Make, then, a good beginning. Give me a little encouragement, so that I may recover my strength by your holy prayers, and lift up my head, wipe my face, wash my eyes, and rise up from the great sleep of slackness. In return for the great benefits that you have conferred on me, your unworthy servant, may I be able to requite your love, if not as I ought, yet as I am able, with such good words as God's grace grants me to speak when I open my unclean mouth *(cf. Eph. 6:19)*. Indeed, my brethren, I pray that you do not ignore my request, but even as you granted me to speak before your reverences, although half-dead and altogether dumb, so grant me also your wills. It is as you cut them off that you will live the life of the martyrs and athletes of

Christ. I, on my part, will from this day forward again and again repeatedly give all my soul *(cf. Jn. 15:13)*—and my body as well—as a voluntary death on your behalf. This I pray will be as
260 food for me on my way to the life to come, in Christ Jesus our Lord, to whom be glory and power with the Father and the Holy Spirit, now and always, forever and ever. Amen.

XIII

OF CHRIST'S RESURRECTION

In what it consists—how Christ's resurrection takes place in us, and in it the resurrection of the soul. The mystery of this resurrection. Delivered on the Monday of the second week of Easter.

[§ 1. THE DAY OF RESURRECTION.]

Brethren and fathers,

Already Easter, that joyful day, that day of all gladness and delight, the day of Christ's resurrection, has arrived in the circle of the year. But rather, it happens daily and eternally in those who know its mystery, and so has filled our hearts with unspeakable joy and gladness. Likewise it has broken off the labor of the all-holy fast, or, rather, it has perfected our souls and encouraged them as well. So, as you see, it has come and invited all the faithful together to rest and to thanksgiving. Let us therefore give thanks to the Lord, who has brought us over the sea *(Wis. 10:18)* of Lent and led us with joy into the harbor of His resurrection. Let us give thanks to Him, both those who have nobly and zealously completed the course of Lent with fervent resolve and struggles of virtue, and those of us as well who have been weak in this matter through neglect and weakness of soul. He it is who in great generosity gives crowns to the zealous and duly rewards their labors, and also in mercy and loving-kindness grants forgiveness to the weaker. He sees the dispositions and intentions of our souls rather than the labors of our bodies, by which we exercise ourselves in virtue, whether we increase our asceticism out of eagerness of soul or practice less than the zealous ones because of the weakness of our bodies. According to our intentions He measures out the prizes and the gifts of the Spirit to each one, whether He grants fame and glory to one

181

who is zealous or leaves him still in lowliness and in need of more strenuous purification.

[§ 2. CHRIST'S RESURRECTION MYSTICALLY
REPRODUCED IN US.]

But, if you will, let us look and carefully examine what is the mystery of that resurrection of Christ our God which takes place mystically in us at all times, if we are willing, and how Christ is buried in us as in a tomb and how He unites Himself to
40   our souls and rises again, and raises us with Himself. Such is the aim of our discourse.

Christ our God was hanged on the cross and nailed on it *(cf. Col. 2:14)* the sin of the world. He tasted death *(Heb. 2:9)* and went down to the uttermost depths of hell *(cf. Eph. 4:9)*. Again, He returned from hell into His own spotless body, from which He had in no way been separated as He descended thither, and forthwith He arose from the dead. After that He ascended into heaven with great glory and power *(Mt. 24:30)*. So, likewise, as
50   we have now come out of the world and entered into the tomb of repentance and humiliation by being assimilated to the sufferings of the Lord *(Rom. 6:5; 2 Cor. 1:5; Phil. 3:10)*, He Himself comes down from heaven and enters into our body as into a tomb. He unites Himself to our souls and raises them up, though they were undoubtedly dead, and then grants to him who has thus been raised with Christ that he may see the glory of His mystical resurrection.

[§ 3. UNION WITH THE MYSTICAL REALITY.]

Christ's resurrection is thus our resurrection, ours who lie here below. He who has never fallen into sin *(Heb. 4:15, 7:26)*, as it is written, nor lost anything whatever of His own glory, how
60   will He ever be raised up or be glorified, since He is always glorified above all and remains the same, "far above all rule and authority *(Eph. 1:21)*? As has been said, Christ's resurrection and His glory are our glory. Through His resurrection in us it comes into being in us, is shown to us, and is seen by us. Once He has appropriated what is ours, that which He works in us He attributes to Himself. The resurrection of the soul is union with life. The body is dead and cannot live or be called alive unless it receives the living soul in itself and is joined to it, though

not mingled with it. Likewise the soul cannot live unless it is ineffably and without confusion united to God, who is truly the 70
life eternal *(cf. 1 John 5:20).* Before this union in knowledge, vision, and perception it is dead, even though it is endowed with intellect and is by nature immortal. There is no knowledge without vision, nor vision without knowledge. This is what I want to say—there is vision, and in the vision there is knowledge and perception; but I say this about spiritual things, for in the physical realm there is perception even apart from vision. What do I mean? A blind man who hits his foot against a stone feels it, but a dead man does not. But in spiritual things, unless the mind comes to the contemplation of the things that are above thought, it does not perceive the mystical activity. He 80
who has not arrived at contemplation in spiritual matters and claims that he perceives the things that are above intellect, word, and thought is like him whose eyes are blinded and who has a sensation of good or bad things that he experiences, but does not know what is in his hands or at his feet, even if they are for him a matter of life or death. Since he is deprived of the faculty and perception of vision he in no way perceives the bad or the good things that come upon him. Thus he will often lift up his staff to ward off his enemy and possibly strike his friend instead, while his enemy stands before his eyes and laughs at him.

[§ 4. WHO IS ABLE TO EXPERIENCE THE RESURRECTION.]

Most men believe in the resurrection of Christ, but very 90
few have a clear vision of it. Those who have no vision thereof cannot even adore Christ Jesus as the Holy One and as Lord. As it is written, "No one can say, 'Jesus is Lord,' except by the Holy Spirit" *(1 Cor. 12:3),* and, elsewhere, "God is spirit, and those who worship Him must worship in spirit and truth" *(Jn. 4:24).* That most sacred formula which is daily on our lips does not say, "Having *believed* in Christ's resurrection," but, "Having *beheld* Christ's resurrection, let us worship the Holy One, the 100
Lord Jesus, who alone is without sin." How then does the Holy Spirit urge us to say, "Having *beheld* Christ's resurrection," which we have not seen, as though we had seen it, when Christ has risen once for all a thousand years ago, and even then without anybody's seeing it? Surely Holy Scripture does not wish us

183

to lie? Far from it! Rather, it urges us to speak the truth, that the resurrection of Christ takes place in each of us who believes, and that not once, but every hour, so to speak, when Christ the Master arises in us, resplendent in array *(cf. Ps. 93:1)* and flashing with the lightnings of incorruption and Deity. For the light-bringing coming of the Spirit shows forth to us, as in early morning, the Master's resurrection, or, rather, it grants us to see the Risen One Himself. Therefore we say, "The Lord is God, and He has given us light" *(Ps. 118:27)*, and we allude to His second Coming and add these words, "Blessed is He that cometh in the Name of the Lord" *(Ps. 118:26)*. Those to whom Christ has given light as He has risen, to them He has appeared spiritually, He has been shown to their spiritual eyes. When this happens to us through the Spirit He raises us up from the dead and gives us life. He grants us to see Him, who is immortal and indestructible. More than that, He grants clearly to know Him who raises us up *(cf. Eph. 2:6)* and glorifies us *(Rom. 8:17)* with Himself, as all the divine Scripture testifies.

[§ 5. A FAITH THAT LIVES IN DEEDS.]

These, then, are the divine mysteries of Christians. This is the hidden power of our faith, which unbelievers, or those who believe with difficulty, or rather believe in part, do not see nor are able at all to see *(cf. 1 Tim. 6:16)*. Unbelievers, those who believe with difficulty, or believe in part, are those who do not show their faith through works. Apart from works the demons also believe *(Jas. 2:19)* and confess Christ to be God and Master. "We know who you are" *(Mk. 1:24)*, they say, "you are the Son of God" *(Mt. 8:29)*, and elsewhere, "These men are the servants of the Most High God" *(Acts 16:17)*. Yet such faith will not benefit the demons, nor even humans. This faith is of no use, for it is dead, as says the divine apostle, "Faith apart from works is dead" *(Jas. 2:26)*, just like works without faith. How is it dead? Because it has not in itself God who gives life *(1 Tim. 6:13)*. It has not laid hold of Him who said, "He who loves Me will keep My commandments, and I and the Father will come and make Our home with him" *(Jn. 14:21, 23)*, so that by His coming He may raise from the dead him who has attained faith and give him life, and grant him to see Him who has risen in him and who has raised him up. For this reason such faith is dead, or, rather, they are dead who have faith apart from works. Faith in God is always alive, and since it is living it gives life to those who come with a good intention and receive it. Even before they have practiced the commandments it has brought many out of death into life and has shown them Christ our God. Had they persevered in His commandments and kept them until death they too would have been preserved by them—that is, in the state to which faith alone had brought them. But since they "turned aside like a bent bow" *(Ps. 78:57)* and speared themselves on their former actions, they inevitably at once made shipwreck of their faith *(1 Tim. 1:19)* and miserably deprived themselves of the true riches, who is Christ our God.

      150

So I urge you, let us keep God's commandments with all our might, so that we may not share in their fate, but enjoy both present and future blessings, that is, the very vision of Christ. To this may we all attain through the grace of our Lord Jesus Christ, to whom be glory forever. Amen.

      160

XIV

ON PENITENCE AND THE BEGINNING OF THE MONASTIC LIFE

How a person by practicing the commandments advances in due order on the way to virtue, and so arrives at perfection.

[§ 1. THE DIRECTION OF AN EXPERIENCED GUIDE.]

Brethren and fathers,

He who has despised all things visible and even his own soul *(cf. Lk. 14:26)* in order to exhibit genuine penitence in accordance with the Lord's commandment *(Mt. 4:17)* and begin this enterprise does not imagine that he can learn this on his own. He goes to a man who is an experienced craftsman and
10   submits himself to him with great fear and trembling and with earnest attention. He learns from him as he teaches him the spiritual work of virtuous actions and what one who is penitent must do. By "fear and trembling" I mean the fear that he may not attain to such an ideal, and that he may be condemned to eternal fire as being incompetent in the practice of the commandments. He accounts the words of his teacher as though they came from the mouth of God, as causing life or death depending on whether they are observed or neglected, and so he observes with exactness. So—to avoid prolonging my discourse
20   with many words—once he has begun he hangs on God's promises with unwavering faith. Day by day he makes progress as God pleases, and so advances on the way and grows in spiritual maturity and becomes a perfect man in Christ our God *(cf. Eph. 4:13; Col. 1:28)*.

THE DISCOURSES

What then are the promises of our Lord Jesus Christ, God's Son Himself, on which he hangs? Listen intelligently to that which He promises us. "Indeed I tell you, there will be joy in heaven over one sinner who repents" *(Lk. 15:7)*, and again, "Him who comes to Me"—that is, by this way—"I will by no means cast out" *(Jn. 6:37)*. Again He says, "Let him who is thirsty come to Me and drink" *(Jn. 7:37)*, and, "He who believes in Me shall never die" *(Jn. 11:26)*. Elsewhere He says, "Draw near to Me and I will draw near to you" *(cf. Jas. 4:8)*, and, "Come to Me, all who labor and are heavy laden, and I will give you rest" *(Mt. 11:28)*. In yet another place, "He who has My commandments and keeps them, he it is who loves Me; and he who loves Me will be loved by My Father, and through the Spirit I and the Father will come to him and make our abode with him" *(Jn. 14:21, 23)*. And He says, "If you who are evil men know how to give good gifts to your children, will not your heavenly Father give the Holy Spirit to those who ask Him?" *(Lk. 11:13)*.

Hope therefore in these promises of God with unwavering faith, as we have said, and with much zeal and unremitting effort resolutely fulfill all His commandments. This is the first commandment, "Repent, for the kingdom of heaven is at hand" *(Mt. 4:17)*, and further, "Ask, and it shall be given you, seek, and you will find, knock, and it will be opened to you; for everyone who asks receives, and he who seeks finds, and to him who knocks it will be opened" *(Mt. 7:7f.; Lk. 11:9f.)*. Since God wanted to teach us about those things, how one ought to ask, and with what words and actions, He said, "He who would be first among you let him be last of all and servant of all" *(Mk. 9:35)*. For "he who exalts himself will be humbled, and he who humbles himself will be exalted" *(Lk. 14:11)*.

He who ceaselessly keeps all these things in mind, and others like them, and occupies himself with them day and night *(cf. Ps. 1:1)*, and thinks of them with mind and sense and puts them zealously into practice, will gradually be separated from memory of the world, of secular affairs, of possessions, and of his own family and friends, and correspondingly draw nearer to spiritual things. As he daily advances he will notice how the thoughts

of the passions to which he is prone are gradually withdrawing, then how these passions themselves diminish, and how the heart is softened and comes to humility; then in turn how the heart gives rise to thoughts that bring about humbleness of mind. But yet as he perceives this he will scarcely thereby arrive at compunction and tears. Nevertheless he arrives at this through many tribulations *(Acts 14:22)*, and the more he is humbled the more he feels compunction. Humiliation brings about affliction, but affliction feeds the humility that is its source and
70   makes it grow. This activity, which is exercised by the fulfilling of the commandments, washes away—what a marvel!—every stain from the soul. It expels every passion and every evil lust, by which I mean not only those of the body but also of the world. Thus a man will be set free in soul from every earthly desire, and that not only from physical bonds—it is as when one puts off a garment and is completely stripped. Rightly so, for the soul is first stripped of its insensitivity, which God's apostle calls a "veil," that "lies on the hearts" of the unbelieving Jews *(2 Cor. 3:15)*, but not on theirs alone. Even now everyone who does
80   not practice the commandments of the new [covenant of] grace with all his might and with a fervent heart has such a veil lying on the understanding of his heart and he cannot be lifted up to the height of "the knowledge of the Son of God" *(Eph. 4:13)*. Then, just as he who has been physically stripped naked sees the wounds of his body, so he who has been stripped spiritually may clearly see the passions that cling to his soul, such as ambition, avarice, rancor, hatred of his brethren, envy, jealousy, contentiousness *(cf. Phil. 1:15)*, and all the rest. So he applies the commandments to them as medicines, and trials as cautery, and is
90   humbled and sorrowful, and fervently seeks God's help. He clearly sees the grace of the Holy Spirit coming to him and tearing all these [passions] away from him one after the other and eliminating them until it has entirely freed his soul from them all. The coming of the Paraclete grants freedom to the soul, not merely in part, but completely and totally. Not only does it expel the passions mentioned above, but also all boredom, carelessness, slackness, and ignorance, all forgetfulness, gluttony, and
100   love of pleasure. Thus it renews and restores a man both spiritually and physically, so that such a person seems to be clothed,

not with a corruptible and gross body *(cf. Wis. 9:15)*, but with one that is spiritual *(cf. 1 Cor. 15:44)* and immaterial and even now ready for the rapture *(cf. 1 Thess. 4:17)*. These are not the only effects the Spirit's grace works in him; it does not even permit such a man to see the objects of sense, but instead makes him, while he sees, to be as though he did not see with the [physical] sense. For whenever the mind is united to the objects of intellect it finds itself entirely beyond the realm of sense, even though it appears to be looking at sensible objects.

[§ 3. THE MYSTERIES MAN EXPERIENCES IN HIS SPIRITUAL FULLNESS.]

He who thus occupies himself with these things lives in accordance with the words of the saint—"Our citizenship is in heaven *(Phil. 3:20)*, because we look not to the things that are seen but to the things that are unseen" *(2 Cor. 4:18)*. He receives light and enlightenment; day by day he grows in spiritual maturity and eliminates that which belongs to the childish mind on his advance to the perfection of manhood *(cf. Eph. 4:13f.; 1 Cor. 13:11)*. Therefore he is changed in the faculties and activities of his soul in accordance with the measure of his stature, and becomes bolder and more vigorous in the practice of God's commandments. As he fulfills them day by day he is purified anew to the extent that he practices them. He becomes radiant, he is illuminated, there is granted to him to see revelations of great mysteries the depth of which no one has ever seen nor is at all able to see *(cf. 1 Tim. 6:16)* who has not striven to attain the height of such purity. By mysteries I mean things that are seen by all without being understood by them. From the Spirit who renews him he obtains new eyes as well as new ears. From henceforth unlike an [ordinary] man, he does not see the objects of sense with physical vision; he sees them spiritually as one who has become superhuman, and sees them as images of things invisible, and their forms are to him formless and shapeless. One might say that he no longer hears any human voice or voices, but only the voice of the Living Word whenever it speaks through a human voice. By its hearing the soul admits Him and no other, and permits Him to enter because he is well known

110

120

130

and loved; it gladly welcomes Him when He has entered, even as the Lord said, "My sheep hear My voice *(Jn. 10:27),* but they do not hear the voice of strangers" *(Jn. 10:5).* As for other men, though he hears all their words he does not accept them within. He does not at all permit them to enter but turns away from them and sends them away. Sometimes he does not even notice

140   their presence or their knocking for admission, but even though he hears them he is as one who is deaf and hears not. This is his attitude toward them!

[§ 4. HOW GOD'S MYSTERIES OVERPOWER US.]

Accordingly, as soon as he has attained this state, God dwells in him and becomes for him all that he desires, or, rather, more than he desires. For God who is all goodness fills the soul in which He dwells with all goodness *(cf. Ps. 107:9)* as far as our nature is capable of receiving it, because God is infinite and cannot be contained by any created nature. I speak of those blessings that "eye has not seen and ear has not heard, neither have entered into the heart of man" *(1 Cor. 2:9)*—certainly not the

150   heart of him who has not attained that state. So God who dwells in him teaches such a man about things to come and things present, not by word, but by action and experience and reality. As God removes the veil from the eyes of his mind he shows him what is His will and what is useful for him. As for other matters, He persuades him not to be inquisitive about them or seek them or be curious about them, for he cannot boldly look into even the things that God reveals to him and shows him. When he stoops low to inquire into the depth of the riches and wisdom and knowledge of God *(Rom. 11:33)* he immediately becomes dizzy and is struck with amazement as he thinks of himself and

160   who he is to be counted worthy to behold such things. As he looks on the greatness of God's loving-kindness he is struck with amazement. He considers himself with all his soul to be unworthy of the vision of such goodness and does not wish to look closely at them or fully understand them. He is constrained by trembling, fear, and reverence to cry, "Who am I, Lord, and what is my father's house *(1 Sam. 18:18),* that Thou shouldst reveal such mysteries to me, unworthy as I am, and hast won-

drously made me not only to have a vision of such good things, but even to participate and share in them!"

[§ 5. THE VISION OF GOD IN HIMSELF.]

Such a man who has been lifted up over all creation is unwilling to go back and be curious about created things. Since he possesses the very Master of the angels he cannot endure inquisitiveness about the essence and nature of the angels who serve Him, because he is aware that it is not pleasing to God that a man should be curious about that which is beyond man. Since we have been commanded not to be curious about the divine Scriptures, even less ought we push our curiosity "beyond that which is written" *(1 Cor. 4:6)*. Such a man sees God as far as it is possible for a human being to see Him, and to the extent that it pleases God that he should. He is anxious constantly to behold Him and prays that he may see Him forever after death. He is content to enjoy nothing else but the vision of God and asks for nothing else. So he does not want to forsake his Master and his God, who fills him with light and from whom he has the enjoyment of the unending life, and instead turn his attention to his fellow-servants. Such a man on whom God looks, or whom He illuminates from above, himself contemplates God's exceeding glory. It is impossible for others to see what he is, or what is the glory in which he finds himself, nor can he understand it. Every holy soul is set free from all vainglory, since it is clothed with the royal garment, the most radiant vesture of the Spirit, and is filled with God's superabundant glory *(cf. 2 Cor. 3:10)*. Not only does it disregard the glory of men, but even if it is honored by them it pays no attention to it. Since God sees the soul and it in turn sees Him, it will in no way ever desire to look on another man or be looked on by him.

Therefore I beseech you, brethren in Christ, let us not desire to learn by mere words that which is beyond utterance; it is equally impossible both for those who teach about such matters and for those who listen to them. Those who teach about intellectual and divine realities are not able to supply clear proofs, strictly speaking, from examples, or to express their truth concretely. Nor are their pupils able to learn by mere

170

180

190

200

words the meaning of that about which they speak. It is by practice and effort and labors that we must be anxious to grasp these things and attain to comptemplation of them. May we thus be initiated into [the meaning of] the words that deal with such [realities], and may God be glorified in us when we are in that state! By the knowledge of such things may we glorify Him and He glorify us, in Christ Himself who is our God, to whom is due all glory forever. Amen.

210

XV

THE LIGHT OF GOD

Of the passionate, unbelieving, and wicked disposition.
What is the union of God with the children of light,
and the manner in which it is realized in them. Finally,
an attack on those who presume unworthily on the
high-priestly office.

[§ 1. THE DARKNESS OF UNBELIEF.]

Brethren and fathers,
There is a constant opposition between light and darkness,
faith and unbelief *(2 Cor. 6:14)*, knowledge and ignorance, love
and hatred. When God said in the beginning, "Let there be
light" *(Gen. 1:3)*, and it came into being, at once the darkness
vanished; but when the day departed the night took its place.   10
While Adam was preserved by his faith in God he was in immortal glory and in paradise. But when the enemy had turned
him aside into unbelief he was condemned to die and he was cast
out of paradise *(Gen. 3:23)*. Instead of the divine and spiritual
knowledge he received fleshly knowledge. Since he had been
blinded in the eyes of his soul and had fallen from the life imperishable, he began to look with his physical eyes. He turned the
vision of his eyes on visible objects with a feeling of passion and
"knew Eve his wife, and she conceived and bore Cain" *(Gen.*   20
4:1). Such knowledge is in reality ignorance of all goodness, for
had he not first fallen from the knowledge and contemplation of
God he would not have been brought down to this knowledge.
Thus his son Cain would not have killed Abel his brother, had
he not first been inflamed with hatred and envy against him *(cf.*
Gen. 4:3ff.).
Those, then, who from their birth are under the dominion
of darkness and are unwilling to contemplate the spiritual light

193

30

from which their forefather fell look on those who have come to
that light and speak of the things of the light as adversaries and
enemies, since their words wound them. When a sunbeam in
some way penetrates into a dark house it pierces and cuts
through the darkness like an arrow. So the divinely inspired
word of a spiritual and holy man is like a two-edged sword *(Heb.
4:12)* in the heart of a carnal man. It causes him pain and pro-
vokes him to contradict and to hate because of his ignorance and
unbelief.

[§ 2. HOW IGNORANCE OBSCURES THE SENSE OF CHRIST.]

But he who imagines that he knows, even though he knows
nothing, were he even to see an angel from heaven *(Gal. 1:8)*
coming down to him, yet he would send him away as though he
were an evil demon. Even if it were an apostle or a prophet of
40   God, he would turn him away like another Simon Magus. What
utter obtuseness that a blind man should consider the seeing
man to be blind, and that he who talks nonsense should think
that the words of the sensible man are nonsense! The blind man
disbelieves those who tell him at night that the sun is not shining, and in his disbelief thinks that it is night at high noon. He
thinks both are deceiving him whether by day they tell him that
there is light, or at night that it is dark, and in his doubt sends
his informants packing. So those who sit in the darkness of passions and whose minds are blinded by ignorance, or, rather,
those who have not acquired "the mind of Christ" *(1 Cor. 2:16)*,
50   think that he who has the mind of Christ is foolish, and that he
who has it not is sensible. Of these the prophet David rightly
states, "The ignorant and foolish perish together" *(Ps. 49:11)*.
Therefore such men twist the whole of Scripture according to
their own desires *(cf. 2 Pet. 3:3, 16)* and corrupt themselves in
their own passions. But it is not divine Scripture that suffers
from this, but those who disfigure it!

You, then, who have a right judgment of things, tell me
how will the blind on their own rightly discern the thoughts of
the light if they by their presumption refuse to be taught? He
who is blind in his eyes, how will he read the letters that are in
60   the light when he does not see the light? He who is blind in his
mind and has not the mind of Christ *(1 Cor. 2:16)* in himself,

how can he consider the thoughts that are stored up in the light of Christ? Even though he reads their visible record thousands of times with his physical eyes, the record that has been committed to writing, yet I do not think that such a person will ever be able to contemplate things that are spiritual, immaterial, and full of light in a place that is material and in darkness.

[§ 3. GOD AS THE LIGHT OF THE SOUL.]

Let no one deceive you! God is light *(1 John 1:5)*, and to those who have entered into union with Him He imparts of His own brightness to the extent that they have been purified. When the lamp of the soul, that is, the mind, has been kindled, 70 then it knows that a divine fire has taken hold of it and inflamed it. How great a marvel! Man is united to God spiritually and physically, since the soul is not separated from the mind, neither the body from the soul. By being united in essence man also has three hypostases by grace. He is a single god by adoption with body and soul and the divine Spirit, of whom he has become a partaker. Then is fulfilled what was spoken by the prophet David, "I have said, ye are gods, and ye are all the sons of the Most High" *(Ps. 82:6)*, that is, sons of the Most High according to the 80 image of the Most High and according to His likeness *(Gen. 1:26)*. We become the divine offspring of the Divine Spirit *(Jn. 3:8)*, to whom the Lord rightly said and continues to say, "Abide in Me, that you may bring forth much fruit" *(Jn. 15:4, 8)*. He speaks of the multitudes that are being saved by them as "fruit." He adds, "Unless the branch abides in the vine it withers, and is cast into the fire" *(Jn. 15:4, 6)*, therefore "abide in Me, and I in you" *(Jn. 15:4)*. How He abides in us and how we in turn abide in Him, the Lord Himself taught us when He said, "Thou, Father, art in Me, and I in Thee *(Jn. 17:21)*, and they are in Me, and I in them" *(Jn. 17:23, 21)*. Desiring to confirm this He re- 90 sumes his discourse and says, "That they may be in Me, and I in them, even as Thou, Father, art in Me, and I in Thee" *(Jn. 17: 21, 23)*. To assure His hearers He adds these words besides, "As Thou hast loved Me, so have I loved them" *(Jn. 17:23)*, and they have known that Thou hast sent Me" *(Jn. 17:25)*. It is evident that just as the Father abides in His own Son *(Jn. 14:10)* and the Son in His Father's bosom *(Jn. 1:18)* by nature, so those who have been born anew through the divine Spirit *(Jn. 3:3, 5)* and by His gift have become the brothers of Christ our God and sons of God and gods by adoption, by grace abide in God and God in them *(1 John 4:12ff.)*.

[§ 4. THE SPIRITUALLY BLIND.]

100 But as for those who have not become such, and who have not been changed at all in action, knowledge, and contemplation, how are they not ashamed to call themselves Christians? How dare they open their mouths and shamelessly speak of God's hidden mysteries *(Eph. 3:9; Col. 1:26)* with indifference as though they were lying on a bed? How do they not blush to count themselves among Christians and number themselves among those who are spiritual? How do they fail to tremble to sit with the priests and to perform the priestly and liturgical ministries of the Body and Blood of the Master? I am wholly baffled by this! As I have said, it is the blindness of mind and the
110 insensitivity and ignorance that accompany it and the presumption it produces that cause them to trample on the true gold, the most precious stone, the Lord Jesus Himself, the Christ, as though He were mud! What shocking audacity! It causes each of them as it were to climb up a high ladder and stand on it, so that he may appear to rise above the multitude and be admired by it. What sort of Christian would give such men the name of Christians?

But this we have addressed to those who profess to know everything and speak of it, who think that they are something, though they are nothing *(Gal. 6:3)*. By our discourse we have
120 shown, as on a pillar, who are Christians and what is their nature, that those men may compare themselves to the model and find out how far they fall short of those who are truly Christians.

[§ 5. SEEKING THE LIGHT WITH TEARS
OF PENITENCE.]

But to you, who are Christ's servants, who are anxious to learn and have prepared your ears to hear, the Master of all things shouts through His holy Gospels, saying, "While you have the light, run to the light, lest the darkness overtake you" *(cf. Jn. 12:35–36)*. By repentance run in the way of His commandments *(cf. Ps. 119:32)*. Run, run, while it is still the time when He shines on you, before the night of death overtakes you *(cf. Jn. 9:4)* and you be sent away into eternal darkness. Run, seek, knock, that the door of the kingdom of heaven may be opened to you *(cf. Mt. 7:7; Lk. 11:9)* and you may enter within it and have it within you *(cf. Lk. 17:21)*. As for those who depart from this present life without attaining to it, how will they ever find it once they have gone there? Accordingly, it is here that we have been commanded to ask, to seek, and to knock by means of penitence and tears, and the Master has promised to give it to us if we do so. If then we refuse to do this and to obey Christ our Master, so that we may endeavor to receive the kingdom within us while we are still in this life, will we not deserve to hear Him speak to us when we have departed thither and say, "Why are you now seeking the kingdom which you refused when I was giving it to you? Were you not unwilling when I earnestly entreated you to exert yourselves to receive it from Me? Have you not despised it and preferred to enjoy corruptible and earthly things? By what deeds or words will you be able to find it from now on?"

Therefore, fathers and brethren, I exhort you, let us keep God's commandments with all eagerness, in order that we may obtain the eternal life and kingdom. May we never hear in this life [these words addressed to us], "He who does not obey the Son shall not see life, but the wrath of God rests upon him" *(Jn. 3:36)*, nor in the world to come, "Depart from Me *(Mt. 7:23)*, I do not know where you come from" *(Lk. 13:25)*. Rather may we listen to that blessed voice as it says, "Come, O blessed of My Father, inherit the kingdom prepared for you, because you fed Me when I was hungry for your salvation by practicing My commandments, you gave Me drink, you clothed Me, you welcomed Me, you visited Me *(cf. Mt. 25:34ff.)* by cleansing your hearts from every spot and defilement of sin. Now enjoy My blessings whose enjoyment is ineffable, and is eternal and immortal life." May we all obtain this, through the grace of our Lord Jesus Christ, to whom be glory forever. Amen.

XVI

[ECSTASY IN THE LIGHT]

On the activities of the Holy Spirit. The contemplation of His mysteries. How they are revealed to the pure in heart. A useful preliminary account of a young monk who received the Holy Spirit at the prayers of his spiritual father.

[§ 1. THE STORY OF A NOVICE—THE PURSUIT OF THE LIGHT.]

Brethren and fathers and children,
A young man has told me this story:[1]
"I was the apprentice of a venerable father, of one who was equal to the great and exalted saints. From him I often heard of divine illuminations sent from heaven to those engaged in the spiritual struggle, consisting in a flood of light, and conversations between God and man thereby, and I marveled. So great", said he, "was my desire and longing for such a blessing that as I thought thereof I forgot all things earthly and heavenly, to the extent even of eating and drinking and bodily relief.

"This man, however, was a great saint (he is now among the saints!), a man endowed with the gift of prophecy. When he saw

10

---

1. Nicetas Stethatos, the biographer of Symeon, followed by other ancient editors, identified the "young man" in question with Symeon himself, and does not hesitate to incorporate the data in his life of Symeon. His spiritual father would thus be Symeon the Pious. There are some problems about the details. It would appear that the vision described in Catechesis 22 was experienced by Symeon while he was still a layman aged twenty, while this vision took place when Symeon had entered the monastery of Studion some eight years later, in 977. Stethatos's own explanation, chapters 5 and 19, that these were two separate experiences, would seem to be most satisfactory, though it does not eliminate all difficulties.

me carrying out the things that he enjoined on me to the exclusion even of eating and drinking, wholly absorbed in myself and   20
as though I was wasting away through some poison, out of endless compassion he gave me a strict command and so, unwillingly, I ate, for," as he said. "I was afraid of being charged with disobedience. The more I partook of food, the more the fire consumed me and I could not bear the constraint. I poured out tears like rivers and so I often left the table. In my senselessness I thought that he was setting obstacles in the way of my desire out of ignorance of the great pain that I suffered within. In this state I, miserable wretch, did not know that he was aware even of the   30
hidden thoughts of my heart, as will appear from what follows.

"It happened one day that we were going into the city[2] in which he had his dwelling, in order that we might visit his spiritual children. We spent the whole day among them, for there were many whom he helped even by his mere presence. At evening we came back to our cell, hungry and thirsty from much labor and the heat, for, however hot the day, he would never take the slightest nap, in spite of his age, though he was about sixty years old. When we sat down to partake of some bread I did not   40
eat, for I was worn out by fatigue. I thought that if I were to take food and drink I should not at all be able to stand for prayer and seek what I desired. These," said he, "were my thoughts, as I was sitting, as though I were beside myself."

[§ 2. THE COUNSELS OF SYMEON THE PIOUS.]

"When the saint saw me and considered the labor that I had endured with him he realized why I had undergone these things, since, as I have mentioned, he was endowed with prophetic insight. Moved with great compassion he spoke to me and strictly commanded me, 'Eat, my child, and drink, and from   50
henceforth be not sad. Had not God willed to have mercy upon you, it would not have pleased Him that you should come to us.' So we ate," said he, "and drank, and more than we needed, for he too ate to put himself on the level of my weakness. Then when the meal was finished he said to me, 'Know this, my boy, that it is neither fasting, nor vigil, nor bodily effort, nor any oth-

---

2. I.e., toward the center of Constantinople, since the monastery of Studios was on its western outskirts.

60 er laudable action that pleases God so that He appears to us, but only a soul and heart that is humble, simple, and good.' When I heard this I marveled at the words and the admonition of the holy man. More than ever I was burning with ardor. With keenness of mind I called to mind in a single instant all my sins and was flooded with tears. I fell at his holy feet and laid hold of them and said, 'Pray for me, O saint of God, that I may find mercy through you, for none of the good things that you have mentioned belong to me, but only many sins, as you well know.' The holy man showed me even more compassion and shed tears. Then he bade me rise from the ground and said, 'I am confident that God, who has bestowed abundant grace on me, will bestow a double portion thereof on you simply because of the faith you

70 show toward Him and toward my humble self.' So I received this word as though it came from God Himself and thought of that which Elijah did to Elisha *(2 Kings 2:9–10)*. I believed that however unworthy I was, yet God is gracious to men, and quick to fulfill the desire of those who fear Him *(Ps. 145:19)*. So again I made a bow of reverence and asked for his prayer and departed for my cell, having been told by him merely to recite the Trisagion[3] and go to sleep."

[§ 3. THE LIGHT AND THE ECSTASY.]

"So I entered the place where I usually prayed and, mindful

80 of the words of the holy man I began to say, 'Holy God.' At once I was so greatly moved to tears and loving desire for God that I would be unable to describe in words the joy and delight I then felt. I fell prostrate on the ground, and at once I saw, and behold, a great light was immaterially shining on me and seized hold of my whole mind and soul, so that I was struck with amazement at the unexpected marvel and I was, as it were, in ecstasy. Moreover I forgot the place where I stood, who I was, and where, and could only cry out, 'Lord, have mercy,' so that when

90 I came to myself I discovered that I was reciting this. But Father," said he, "who it was that was speaking, and who moved my tongue, I do not know—only God knows. 'Whether I was in

---

3. The hymn "Holy God, Holy Mighty, Holy Immortal: have mercy upon us," one of the most frequently used forms of prayer in the Orthodox Church, occurring in the Divine Liturgy and the offices as well as in private devotion.

the body, or outside the body' *(2 Cor. 12:2, 3)*, I conversed with
this Light. The Light itself knows it; it scattered whatever mist
there was in my soul and cast out every earthly care. It expelled
from me all material denseness and bodily heaviness that made
my members to be sluggish and numb. What an awesome marvel! It so invigorated and strengthened my limbs and muscles,
which had been faint through great weariness, that it seemed to
me as though I was stripping myself of the garment of corruption. Besides, there was poured into my soul in unutterable fash-   100
ion a great spiritual joy and perception and a sweetness
surpassing every taste of visible objects, together with a freedom
and forgetfulness of all thoughts pertaining to this life. In a marvelous way there was granted to me and revealed to me the manner of the departure from this present life. Thus all the
perceptions of my mind and my soul were wholly concentrated
on the ineffable joy of that Light."

[§ 4. THE PAIN CAUSED BY THE WITHDRAWAL
OF THE LIGHT.]

"But when that infinite Light which had appeared to me—
for I can call it by no other fitting or appropriate name," so he   110
continued, "in some way had gently and gradually faded and, as
it were, had withdrawn itself, I regained possession of myself
and realized what its power had suddenly done to me. I reflected on its departure and considered how it had left me again to
be alone in this life. So severe was the grief and pain that over-
came me that I am at a loss properly to describe how great it
was: A varied and most vehement pain was kindled like a fire in
my heart. Imagine, father, if you can," said he, "the pain of being separated from it, the infinity of love, the greatness of my   120
passion, the sublimity of this greatest of blessings! I on my part
cannot express in words or comprehend with my mind the infinity of this vision."

[§ 5. THE ENJOYMENT OF SUCH A LIGHT.]

"But tell me, most venerable father and brother," said I,
"more clearly and exactly what were the effects of what you
have seen." But that dear man, full of the divine Spirit, who had

been found worthy of such contemplation, at once replied with a voice most gentle and flowing like honey, "Father, when it appears it fills one with joy, when it vanishes it wounds. It happens close to me and carries me up to heaven. It is a pearl [of 130 great price] *(Mt. 13:46).* The light envelops me and appears to me like a star, and is incomprehensible to all. It is radiant like the sun, and I perceive all creation encompassed by it. It shows me all that it contains, and enjoins me to respect my own limits. I am hemmed in by roof and walls, yet it opens the heavens to me. I lift up my eyes sensibly to contemplate the things that are on high, and I see all things as they were before. I marvel at what has happened, and I hear a voice speaking to me secretly from on high, 'These things are but symbols and preliminaries, for you will not see that which is perfect as long as you are 140 clothed in flesh. But return to yourself and see that you do nothing that deprives you of the things that are above. Should you fall, however, it is to recall you to humility! Do not cease to cultivate penitence, for when it is united to My love for mankind it blots out past and present failures.'"

When I had heard these things from him, fathers and brethren, I was almost ecstatic and trembled all over. I noted at once the great height of contemplation and knowledge to which he had readily ascended, solely because he loved and trusted his 150 spiritual father. From mere beginnings he had been granted to see and enjoy such great blessings, as if he had already cast human weakness aside and become an angel instead of a man.

[§ 6. THE PURSUIT OF PURITY OF HEART.]

I therefore entreat you, brethren in Christ, let us cast far from us every attachment and every care of this present life. Let us hate the pleasures of the flesh, bodily comfort, slackness, and idleness, by which that which is worse prevails over that which is better. Come, let us arm ourselves with genuine faith *(cf. Eph.* 160 *6:16)* toward God and toward our fathers and teachers who live according to God. Let us acquire a contrite heart, a soul humbled in mind, and a heart that by means of tears and repentance is pure from every stain and defilement of sin. So shall we too be found worthy in due time quickly to rise to such heights that even here and now we may see and enjoy the ineffable blessings of the divine light, if not perfectly, at least in part, and to the extent to which we are able. So shall we both unite ourselves to God and God will be united to us. To those who come near us we shall become "light" and "salt" *(cf. Mt. 5:13–14)* to their great benefit in Christ Jesus our Lord, to whom be glory forever. Amen.

170

XVII

OF CONTEMPLATION, REVELATION, AND THE PRAYER OF ILLUMINATION

How he who is possessed by the love of God and has attained to the depth of humility is activated by the Holy Spirit.

[§ 1. SYMEON'S OWN ASCENT TO THE LIGHT.]

Brethren and fathers,

How great is the condescension and the love of God toward men! Before the unutterable goodness of God I am struck with
10 amazement, I am filled with wonder. So I cry out, "O wondrous miracle, power of God's commandments, how they change those who practice and observe them!"

Once I had started out on the way and had in slight measure returned to my senses from the abyss of evil and darkness I was obsessed with fear as I was tormented by the evils within me. Yet it was really love and striving for goodness that contributed most to turn me toward it. But all that it accomplished was a flight from evil that impelled me toward the good. In the midst of these things there was this alone that held me back—my ingrained propensities and evil habits of sensuality. By the
20 persistent practice of prayer, the meditation on God's oracles, and the acquiring of good habits this fades away. As the sun gradually rises the darkness recedes and disappears. So as virtue shines, evil, like darkness, is driven away and is proved to be without substance, and from then on we shall always continue in goodness just as we have previously been evil. Through a little patience and a very slight effort of will, or, rather, by the

help of the living God, we are re-created and renewed. We are cleansed in soul, body, and mind, and we become that which we [really] are, though we know it not because we are shrouded by passions, and in addition we receive [gifts] of which we are not worthy.

Even I, who am of all men most insignificant and useless, have received some of these gifts—how good it is thankfully to proclaim the blessings of God, who loves men!—by the grace of my Savior Jesus Christ. By grace I have received grace *(cf. Jn. 1:16)*, by doing well I have received [His] kindness, by fire I have been requited with fire, by flame with flame. As I ascended I was given other ascents, at the end of the ascent I was given light, and by the light an even clearer light. In the midst thereof a sun shone brightly and from it a ray shone forth that filled all things. The object of my thought remained beyond understanding, and in this state I remained while I wept most sweetly and marveled at the ineffable. The divine mind conversed with my own mind and taught me, saying, "Do you realize what My power has done to you out of love for men because of but a little faith and patience that strengthens your love? Behold, though you are subject to death, you have become immortal, and though you are ruled by corruption you find yourself above it. You live in the world and yet you are with Me; you are clothed with a body and yet you are not weighed down by any of the pleasures of the body. You are puny in appearance, yet you see intellectually. It is in very deed I who have brought you into being out of nothing."

[§2. THE TERRIFYING AND ATTRACTIVE BEAUTY OF GOD.]

To these words I replied with trembling and joy, saying, "Who am I, O lord, but a sinner and unclean, that Thou hast at all looked on me and vouchsafed to have converse with me? O Thou who art undefiled, invisible, and inaccessible to all men, how is it that Thou showest Thyself to me as being accessible and gentle, radiant with beauty through Thy refulgent glory and grace?"

These words I heard mystically and in a wondrous way I answered. But the supernatural struck me with amazement; it was terrifying and forced me to shrink back. The ineffable beau-

205

ty of that which appeared to me wounded my heart and attracted me to infinite love. That love prevented me from turning to
60 things below, as though I were already completely freed from
the bonds of the flesh, and I rejoiced—and then I was again
wholly human. I received the certain knowledge of the forgiveness of my sins, yet I saw myself as a greater sinner than all other men. It was impossible for me to disbelieve Him who spoke
to me, yet I was afraid to believe because of the descent from
that exaltation.

[§ 3. TAKING REFUGE IN SELF-ABASEMENT.]

There are times when I, without willing it, mount to the
height of contemplation; with my will I am drawn down from it
because of the limitations of human nature and [find] safety in
abasement. I know many things that are unknown to most men,
yet I am more ignorant than all others. I rejoice because Christ,
70 "whom I have believed" *(2 Tim. 1:12)*, has bestowed on me an
eternal and unshakable kingdom, yet I constantly weep as one
who is unworthy of that which is above, and I cease not. I dare
not open my mouth and ask forgiveness for my actions; yet for
the sake of others I speak boldly out of love and, to speak foolishly *(cf. 2 Cor. 11:23)*, people listen to me! I stand before Him as a
son, yet my attitude is that of a stranger who dares not speak. I
hear Him say, "Well done, faithful servant" *(Mt. 25:21)* and the
rest, yet in reality I find that I have not kept even one talent of
all those that were given me *(cf. Mt. 25:24f.)*. It seems to me that
80 I reach the very summit of blessings, yet I am lying as a prisoner
down in the abyss of my sins, engulfed in despair. It is when I
am abased below all others that I am lifted up above the heavens
(cf. Eph. 4:10) and am once more united in love to Christ our
God. Before Him I hope to stand, once I am rid of the burden of
this earthly flesh, and even closer to Him, and in addition be yet
more clearly initiated into the eternal joy and exultation of the
love that is on high.

[§ 4. WORDS OF ENCOURAGEMENT TO HIS HEARERS.]

I have decided to write[1] these things, my brethren, not as
one who wishes to pursue glory, for such a man is a fool and a

---

1. This would appear to be message in writing from Symeon to his pupils,

stranger to the glory that is on high! Rather, I have done so in order that you may be aware of God's infinite love for us men, of the nature of that very light burden *(Mt. 11:30)* of the commandments of Christ our Savior and God, and of the great price of the gift He bestows. As you learn of it, may you be filled with longing to obtain His love, or else may you fear and tremble at failure to obtain it as if it were eternal death! In addition you will be taught the sublimity of self-abasement and the sure proof of perfect love, as well as experience the richness of God's condescension and know the gift of His great and inexhaustible self-emptying for us *(Phil. 2:7)*. Learn in how awesome a manner our earthly [being] is re-created, and how those men live who have consented to believe in Christ crucified, that is, those who imitate His obedience and self-abasement and desire to turn from evil to good. Learn also how those men are changed who forsake all things out of love for Him who has loved us, and yet are not thereby deprived of things present or to come; how those who are dark become light in wondrous fashion as they draw near to the Great Light; how those who come from below, even as Moses of old, become gods as they are united to things above *(Col. 3:1)*. While they live and move among all men they are by no means defiled by their converse with others. When they do well to those who come to them they suffer no loss of what is good, but as they impart to others they receive more mercy than they give. Rather, as they love others they become like Him who is the Lover of mankind. The higher they ascend the more they abase themselves; the more they humble themselves the higher they are lifted up *(Mt. 23:12; Lk. 14:11)*. By humbling themselves they go without what they need, yet they lack nothing *(2 Cor. 4:8)* because they are fed by the eternal life *(1 John 5:20)* of holy love.

Behold, I have revealed to you, my friends and brethren, the mysteries that are hidden within me *(Col. 1:26)*. Already I see my end drawing near, how near, I do not yet see[2]. [I have told you this] in order that you may know the ways of penitence, the ascents and the progress of the beginning and the

90

100

110

120

---

rather than one delivered orally.

2. This would appear to indicate that this discourse belongs to Symeon's old age.

middle and the measures of perfection. So may you endeavor to imitate, if not someone else, at least the one who has begotten you all and loved you with [all] his soul, who has fed you with the milk of God's word *(cf. 1 Pet. 2:2)* and refreshed you with the life-giving bread *(Jn. 6:33)* and has shown you how to walk in the way of the saving commandments of God, to whom all glory is due, now and always, forever and ever. Amen.

XVIII

[ON WORTHY AND UNWORTHY SUPERIORS]

Of the designs of the evil one, which he insinuates to the vain and ambitious when their shepherd departs this life. How necessary it is with all diligence to prevent those who seek the office but are unworthy, and, on the contrary, to thrust spiritual and holy men into it and to cooperate with them. A final admonition to the shepherd.

[§ 1. WRONG MOTIVES FOR SEEKING OFFICE.]

Brother, if you have become superior of a people and a flock, look well to yourself and examine yourself *(1 Cor. 4:8)*, with what intention and in what way you have attained such a position. Perhaps you will find that you have sought it, though merely in thought, with the intention of obtaining honor from men, or for the sake of presiding over them or for the glory of the office. Perhaps you cannot endure being governed by another brother because you think that no one else is more devout or learned than yourself. It may be that you want to be able to satisfy your physical wants more fully than all others by being waited on or taking rest, or else to be able to help some of your family or relatives, and gain friends among those who walk according to the flesh *(cf. 2 Cor. 10:2)*. You may wish to gain repute by being abbot and to become well known by the kings and rulers of the world. Your motive may have been jealousy—not so much that you wanted the office, but rather that such and such a brother should not have it, and so you were eager for it. Perhaps it was because you were ashamed before men, lest all should hear, or some when they came should see that someone else was preferred to you and that they would then condemn

10

20

209

you as one who was not virtuous. If such is the case, know well that your promotion was not pleasing to God! So in order that I may better inform you of the suggestions that the evil one inspires in those who dwell in a monastery, hear how Satan plots and schemes.

[§ 2. THE DEVIL'S SUGGESTIONS TO THE DEVOUT.]

30   When the shepherd departs to the Lord *(cf. 2 Cor. 5:8)* and the community must elect another, the enemy begins to make his suggestions and to speak to each man in accordance with his particular passion, his desire, his own condition. If, then, there are in that flock some who are more devout, he makes these suggestions to each one and says, "If you became shepherd and abbot here, you would be able in every way to help and save them and share your virtues with them, since this brother or that one in fact will not do so." If he is well known among those who are

40   in the world he suggests to him, "You might be able to attract many to the monastic life and take them out of the world, and you might become a mouthpiece of Christ, for He says that he who brings the worthy forth from the unworthy will be as my mouth" *(Jer. 15:19 LXX)*. Such people would be able to renounce great fortunes and give their wealth to the monastery, and the abbey would be able to grow and become like those of saints Euthymius the Great and Sabas and Pachomius. In addition you would be able to attain greater humility, so that your brethren would see it and imitate it; you would live in the abbey as the least of all *(cf. Mk. 9:35)* and bear the burdens of everyone, the

50   weaknesses of all *(cf. Rom. 15:1; Gal. 6:2)*. Thus you would not only profit many, but you yourself would be profited in soul, and have great refreshment in body" *(cf. Mt. 11:29)*.

[§ 3. THE SCHEMING OF THE DEVOUT BROTHER.]

These, then, are the things that he suggests to the earnest members of the monastery. Each of them begins to reveal his own intention to some brother in whom he has confidence. So he speaks to him in a witty and modest fashion, so as to avoid the accusation of being ambitious, "Now then, Dom[1] so-and-so, if the brethren were sensible, would not they make me abbot?"

---

1. Using the Western Benedictine title to render its Eastern equivalent.

He, perhaps, answers and says, "Believe me, father, I know that you are a modest man, since I have thought this for a long time, but I was wary of saying so, for fear that you might blame me for speaking against your views." Then again he says, "You have spoken well, brother. Believe me, I do not need the office. But I would rather not see an unsuitable man get it and upset the monastery and cause grief to the brethren. Should the brethren want me to be abbot, I should certainly appoint you administrator, this man cellarer, that man bursar, while I should be entirely free to engage in spiritual things undistracted by temporal affairs." This the brother hears, that he will make him administrator, and so goes off to confide this to the brethren whom he said he would appoint to office.

[§ 4. WHAT THE DEVIL SUGGESTS TO THE WORLDLY MINDED.]

Such things two or three of the more devout might do out of ignorance of the machinations of the evil one *(cf. Eph. 6:11)*. To those who are worldly and careless of their own salvation the enemy suggests and insinuates the following [motives]: pleasure, glory, and honor on the part of all men. "So that none of these hypocrites and pseudo-pious men should get it," he says, "make sure that you do! For if you do not, you will have to stand before the future abbot with your hands tied and be dishonored by him. While he will ride on thoroughbred mules you will have to walk and get tired; he will have special meals prepared for himself with bread and wine, while you will have to do with vegetables and herbs like everybody else. He will be the first and sit on a throne, while you will be in the midst of the others or even in the lowest place among them; for he has a special regard for this one and, if he becomes abbot, he will honor him more than you and give him precedence over you, and then how will you bear the disgrace before the brethren? Further, such and such a man is more devout than you, and perhaps he will be preferred by him. Moreover, perhaps he will give the tonsure to some who are illustrious and renowned, and they will honor him as the abbot, while he honors those whom he has tonsured as men of position and will give them precedence over you, while he sends you off to sit on a stool or even lets you stand and attend on them. What do you intend to do about this? You dare

not speak up, for there are those who love him and who will at once silence you. Perhaps they will even strike you when you
100 contradict, and your disgrace will be even worse. If you quit the monastery you will be condemned, everyone will mock you and blame you, and you will find no rest elsewhere, for wherever you go you will have to take last place because you are a strange monk. You cannot endure this and remain in your monastery. Therefore, strive with all your might that none of the more pious monks should overcome you."

[§ 5. THE SCHEMING OF THE WORLDLY MINDED BROTHER.]

Then he reflects and says within himself, "Everybody knows that this or that brother is more devout, so that they will seek [to promote] him and overlook me. I will go and get hold of that brother and that one, for they love to be at ease, to amuse
110 themselves, to enjoy themselves, and constantly leave the monastery and spend their time wherever they please. I will make them my allies, and whatever they tell me, they too will strive diligently to see me become their abbot."

He therefore goes off and acts in accordance with his vain reflection. Again he says to himself, "This brother is devout and has no need of this position, but he has relatives and friends and wishes to help them with the resources of the monastery. I will go and talk to him, and similarly make an ally out of him." So he constantly goes about the monastery and, one by one, canvasses
120 each [of his brethren] and promises to fulfill the wishes of them all, while he is in great agony and trembling for fear of failing to achieve his aim.

From these schemings and many others many divisions, dissensions, and disputes arise in the monastery. On the one hand the more devout seek both their own welfare and that of the others; on the other hand the more worldly seek nothing but their own glory, immediate advantage, and physical pleasure; the majority seek a guide according to their own desires and rally around such a person. But you, my spiritual brother, listen with
130 attention, I pray, to my words, for I do not speak of myself, but that which He who alone is wise and compassionate would speak to you.

212

THE DISCOURSES

[§ 6. SYMEON'S WISE COUNSELS.]

If you live in the midst of the brethren of a monastery, refuse to set yourself in opposition to the father who has tonsured
you, even if you should see him commit fornication or be drunk
and, in your opinion, badly conducting the affairs of the monastery, even if he strikes you and insults you and you suffer many
other troubles at his hand. Do not associate with those who revile him *(cf. Jer. 15:17)*, nor go along with those who plot against
him. Endure him to the end, without curiously inquiring into
his faults. Whatever good you see him do, put your mind on 140
that, and seek to remember that alone. Whatever you see him do
or speak that is unsuitable or evil, blame it on yourself and regard it as your own fault and repent in tears. Treat him as a holy
man and ask for his prayers.

[§ 7. SUPPORT THE MOST SPIRITUAL CANDIDATE.]

Should death befall him, and the brethren wish to elect another abbot, consider well whether you in conscience know a
brother in the monastery who is your equal or even your better
in word and deed and good works, one whom the brethren for
these reasons prefer to have as abbot. Refuse to become an anti- 150
christ, that is, one who opposes God's will and a good and gentle
brother, whether by saying things or entering into schemes that
in any way cast suspicion of scandal on him, with the aim of de-
terring some of the brethren from loving and trusting him. On
the contrary, you must with all joy and humility accept and sincerely cooperate with the desire of the brethren. But if you
know another who is more devout than him who is receiving the
votes, tell the brother who is about to be elected privately, "My
brother, by God's grace you are a devout and spiritual man. As 160
you know, we must do all for the glory and the salvation of our
souls. You know that our brother so-and-so is devout and virtuous. If you so order, we will make him abbot, and he will be a
good shepherd over all the community. Let us also strive together for him with all our might, in order that we, be sure of this,
may have our reward on account of him and together with him,
and keep our consciences pure. It will be God himself whom we
do service to and all will commend us because we have not put

213

ourselves forward, but him whom God willed" *(cf. 2 Cor. 10:18).*
170 If the brother in question has humility and a soul free of ambition and without any antipathy toward the other [candidate], he too will say the same things to him and God will reassure him against any other evil suspicion. Surely he will accept your words and at once obey you. Then, both of you, speak to the whole brotherhood, and the will of God will be done.

[§ 8. CONTINUED FIRM SUPPORT OF THE GOOD CANDIDATE.]

But if you speak without passion in favor of the more spiritual brother, and your brother does not listen to you, but is
180 moved to justify and commend himself, know that he is possessed by ambition. Endeavor in every way, as a servant of Christ, in the pure witness of your conscience *(cf. 2 Cor. 1:12; 1 Tim. 3:9),* that the more spiritual brother become abbot. If he, at the suggestion of the enemy, or even to test you, says to you, "But you should be chosen, since I will not have him whom you mention, but I would be happy to have you," do not be dragged down by his passion or be involved in his fall. Keep the virginity of your soul intact for Christ *(cf. 2 Cor. 11:2),* inviolate by any desire for lustful pleasure. Do not let fear turn you aside from
190 the good candidate to accept the choice of a wicked one *(cf. Ps. 34:15, 36:27),* by saying within yourself, "Let me not appear to be obstructing and contradicting in the matter of that man by saying that he is not worthy of being a superior, for he might be elected in spite of me and inflict many troubles on me." But if you are one of the leading members and you are asked for your opinion, boldly speak the truth and strengthen the unstable in goodness. If you are among the lowest and those who do not readily distinguish between the righteous and unrighteous man, follow those who are most devout and most spiritual.

[§ 9. THE AGITATION OF THE AMBITIOUS IS TO BE OPPOSED BY PRAYER.]

200 But if, perchance, the majority or even all concur in the choice of the bad candidate, and to this end have busied themselves to obtain helpers from without, then yield and do not either cooperate or obstruct. Let the bad break themselves on him whom they have chosen to lead them, since they will gain noth-

ing thereby but trouble for themselves and no benefit, for God often gives the disobedient people a ruler according to their heart *(cf. Ps. 20:5; Jer. 3:15)*. Let these things be firm and unchangeable for you.

But after the death of the superior you may see the whole brotherhood around you unstable, entirely moved by the spirits of wickedness *(cf. Eph. 6:12)*, pulled asunder and collapsing by 210 reason of the lusts and pleasures of the flesh, without any base or foundation on the rock *(cf. Lk. 6:48)*, but entirely confused. You may find that each brother stretches out his hands, one here, one there, to grasp, not at that which saves him, but for that which drags down his body and soul together into hell and darkness and the fire of lusts, while others swell with pride and are crazy for power and have an unrestrained desire for it. If that is the case, then be merciful, compassionate; be lenient, take pity, and mourn over such people and weep tears. Since you 220 have been vouchsafed to see clearly, represent in your mind the wounds of your brethren, how your [fellow-] members have been fractured, how the whole body has collapsed. Entreat God with all your heart, with toil and tears, to stop the flow of so great an evil and to turn back the hearts of the brethren toward goodness. Look to the inclination of your own heart, that it does not apply the petition to yourself, for your own preferment, lest it obtain for you, instead of blessing, God's curse and wrath *(cf. Gen. 27:12)*.

[§ 10. SADNESS AT WITNESSING THE USURPATION OF APOSTOLIC OFFICE.]

If then you take this course of action, and see some of the brethren agree on an evil course, and run about to deceive the simpler brethren, as well as with all eagerness and even with 230 gifts draw in outsiders to help them, then grieve and lament with pain of heart, that we monks have come to such audacity and darkness that we attempt to be shepherds of Christ's sheep without Christ, and do so for the sake of bodily pleasure and enjoyment, financial gain, and to be honored by men. Woe to me, wretched and miserable man! We strive by all means to receive the dignity of the apostles, and even buy their authority with gold *(cf. Acts. 8:18–20)*, without fearing God or being ashamed in 240 the presence of those who see it! No one dares ascend the throne of the emperor without his consent. An unlearned man dares not take on himself the part of a grammarian or teacher of rhetoric, or an illiterate man attempt to read before the people. But it is the dignity of the apostles to which you aspire or which you receive, before you have received the grace of the apostles or see the fruits thereof cultivated in you! How, brother, can you bear to think of the greatness of that audacity? Tell me, my dear, if all

250 this great and populous city were to invite you and say, "We will make you a praepositus and the emperor's grand master of the robes;[2] walk up alone into the palace and speak to the emperor on our behalf *(cf. Esther 4:8)*, and ask him to do this thing and that for us." Would you dare to do this or accept the dignity when you have never entered the palace and are personally unknown to the emperor and a stranger to all the palace officials? Surely you would admit that you would never have the audacity to perpetrate this! You would rather accuse those who tell you

260 such things of being mad and out of their minds. You would laugh at them, and reject the proffered office as bringing on you disgrace and punishment rather than honor.

If then we are powerless to do such things in human affairs, brother, do you not think that it is a frightful thing rashly to take to yourself the apostolic dignity? Do you consider it a small thing to draw near to the light unapproachable *(cf. 1 Tim. 6:16)* and become a mediator between God and man *(cf. 1 Tim. 2:5)*? Do you lightly despise laying your hands on this thing *(cf. 2 Sam. 6:6–7)*? Woe to me, my brother! I fear that we have fallen into total darkness, and therefore do not know the objects of our audacity! For if we knew it, we would never have reached such

270 a point of arrogance and audacity that we should mock at things divine and show greater honor and fear to the earthly king than toward Christ, the immortal King *(cf. 1 Tim. 1:17)*. Let us, therefore, never cease to judge ourselves *(cf. 1 Cor. 4:3)*. As for those who unworthily attempt to approach such an office, let us by all means turn them back and prevent them from such an enterprise. Let us strive, as far as we are able, to debar them from this

2. The Praepositi were the personal attendants of the emperor at great receptions, charged with transmitting his orders, while the grand master of the robes (protovestiarius) occupied the second highest office in the palace, and was in charge, not only of ceremonial robes, but of many valuable treasures and of vast sums of money.

unreasonable attempt. so that we may also deliver them from judgment and that we may live more securely.

[§ 11. QUALIFICATIONS OF THE CANDIDATE— VIRTUE.]

But, as we have said, you may see no brother in the monas- 280
tery whose life is commendable, none who is spiritual in word and deed, but anyone who happens to be available simply rushing at the pastoral office without being worthy, and so striving both to harm the brethren and to ruin his own soul. You must then examine yourself carefully to make sure that you are free from all ambition, without a trace of bodily pleasure and lust, entirely pure from love of money and remembrance of past wrongs, perfectly gentle and free from anger. You must have such love toward God that the mere mention of the name of Christ kindles you with desire for Him and moves you to tears. 290
In addition, you must mourn for your neighbor and account as your own the failures of other men, and regard yourself from your soul to be a greater sinner than all others. Finally, you must see in yourself the abundant grace of the Holy Spirit enlightening the interior of your heart and making it into a very sun, and clearly experience the miracle of the bush *(Ex. 3:2)* taking place within you, so that you are inflamed by union with the unapproachable fire, yet not consumed thereby because your soul is set free from all passion. Then you must so abase yourself that you regard yourself as insufficient and unworthy, knowing 300
well the fraility of human nature, but confident in the grace that comes from on high and in its sufficiency undertake the task with eagerness under the constraint of its fervor, and repel every human calculation and give your very soul for your brethren moved only by God's command and the love of your neighbor. Besides what I have said, if your mind is stripped of every worldly thought and clothed with the luminous role of humility, to the extent that you do not feel in your heart the least attachment to your partisans or antipathy to your opponents, but treat them all equally in simplicity and goodness and 310
the innocence of your heart, even then you must not dare to approach the office without the advice of your spiritual father. Humble yourself, and do it with his prayer and his command,

and accept the office solely for the sake of the salvation of the brethren.

[§ 12. THE COUNSEL OF THE SPIRITUAL FATHER.]

But [you must do this] in the knowledge that your spiritual father is a partaker of the same Spirit and has been found worthy to know and receive Him, so that he may not speak things that are contrary to the divine will, but according to His gift
320 and measure tell you what pleases God and profits your soul, so that you may not be found obedient to man instead of to God and thus be deprived of glory and the divine gift bestowed on you. If then you find a good and spiritual advisor to help you, know that your endeavor will be the more secure and your mind will increase in humility. All these conditions, and many others besides, if you look carefully *(Is. 6:9)*, you will truly find and recognize by yourself, or, rather, you will learn them from the sun of glory, if you at least have ever looked on that sun.
330 How difficult is this advance, how hard it is to know that it is good in God's sight! How much more difficult is the undertaking and administration of the task, endurance in the face of temptations, subtle discernment in the face of opposition! For this reason we have thought it necessary to make clear to your charity through this catechesis these few points from the experience and knowledge of which we have been found worthy. Concerning the rest we have restrained our mind and our hand, lest we should be found divulging what happens in the monasteries. Leaving all other matters behind we direct our word to the shepherd.

[§ 13. THE VIRTUES OF A SUPERIOR.]

340 Look carefully at your heart *(cf. Is. 6:9)*, O spiritual father! Or, rather, constantly wash out the eyes of your mind and endeavor that it may be pure and untroubled, since by it you will be able to see your own heart, and also well and fittingly to discern and administer the welfare of the sheep that have been entrusted to you—that is, the fathers and brethren. As you have heard, the church is a body *(cf. Eph. 1:23; Col. 1:24)* of which the superior is a head. Just as the other members of the body each have a single function *(cf. Rom. 12:4; 1 Cor. 12:12ff.)*, such as the foot for walking, the hand for holding and for working, so the

head is that which holds the whole body together *(cf. Col.* 350
1:17–18, 2:19), since it holds together in itself all the senses and
the mind and speech itself. So in the monastery all the brethren
do not have all abilities, but one has the natural aptitude for one
activity or office, another for another. Thus it is hardly to be
wondered at that you hardly ever find more than one or two of
the virtues at the same time in any of your subjects, for they are
separate members of the one body *(cf. 1 Cor. 12:27)*. But it is required of the superior that he have all the virtues in himself, not
only those of the soul but also those of the body—or, rather, one
should say, in addition to the virtues the great and mystical
gifts. For just as a man's head has its beauty and its value from 360
its external configuration and handsome appearance, but is useless and without value for any purpose unless it has intelligence
and all its senses intact and inviolate, so must it be with the superior. It is not merely the virtues of soul and body that must
adorn him and make him illustrious. In addition they must be
the more enhanced by the spiritual gifts, since virtue and spiritual gift are different things. The virtues are achieved by our
personal effort and acquired by our own labor, but spiritual
gifts are bestowed by God on those who struggle.

[§ 14. GOD INCREASES VIRTUE.]

What do I mean by this? Fasting and abstinence are a vir- 370
tue, for they quench the lusts and calm the fevers of the body.
But this is the work of our free will; but to practice it without
forcing oneself and without effort and to achieve purity and perfect freedom from passion is a gift of God and a most exalted
grace. Again, to be in control of one's temper and anger belongs
to a wondrous struggle and extreme effort, but to attain to their
complete quiescence and obtain serenity of heart and perfect
gentleness is the act of God alone and a transformation at His
hand *(cf. Ps. 77:11)*. Again, to scatter and distribute all one's 380
goods amongst the poor *(cf. Ps. 112:9)* and to become a pauper
who begs alms is a matter of our own will, but to desire nothing
but to endure the furnace of poverty with joy and gladness is a
mystical and divine working. Thus every excellent and good action that is done in accordance with the commandment of the
Lord becomes a virtue. Just as the farmer wearies himself by
merely ploughing, digging, and sowing the seed on the ground,

but it grows and produces fruit early and late *(cf. Jas. 5:7)* by
God's gift, so it is in reality, as you will discover, in spiritual
390   matters. It belongs to us to engage in every activity and with
much toil and weariness to sow the seeds of virtue, but by God's
gift and mercy alone the rain of His loving-kindness and grace
falls and causes the unfruitful soil of our hearts to bear fruit.
When the grain of the word *(Mk. 4:14; Lk. 8:11)* falls on our
souls it receives the moisture of God's goodness; it germinates,
grows, and becomes a great tree *(cf. Mt. 13:31–32; Lk. 13:19)*, that
is, it attains to mature manhood, to "the measure of the stature
of the fullness of Christ" *(Eph. 4:13)*.

[§ 15. THE SUPERIOR'S DUTIES.]

400   So it is necessary for you, the shepherd of Christ's sheep, to
acquire, as we have said, every virtue of body and spirit. You are
the head of the body of the Church of Israel *(cf. 1 Kings 8:14)*,
which is under your rule, so that the brethren may look to you
as a good pattern, and imprint on themselves those excellent and
royal traits of character. May your trumpet never cease to resound! Some it should warn of the sword that comes on the disobedient and stubborn, so that even if they ignore you you may
save your soul from the terrible wrath of God *(cf. Ezek. 33:3ff.)*.
410   Others you must warn, teach *(cf. 2 Tim. 4:2)*, exhort; sometimes
you must "be urgent in season and out of season, convincing,
and rebuking" *(2 Tim. 4:2)* those who need reproach and chastisement, and interrupt their efforts toward evil, as God's apostle commands you. Open your heart *(cf. 2 Cor. 6:11ff.)* to all your
brethren equally, and show an equal love to the whole brotherhood that depends on you. Honor each man according to his
worth and the greatness of his virtue, according to his due, and
do not prefer even him whom you regard as first in the service
of your flock over him who is spiritual and virtuous. Those who
420   serve in various offices bear the dignity of the seven deacons recorded in the Acts of the Apostles *(cf. Acts 6:5)*. They are "like
ministering spirits sent forth to serve" *(Heb. 1:14)*, and if like
them they serve without guile and faithfully, and without greed
for gain *(cf. 1 Tim. 3:8)*, they will deserve a great reward both
here below and on high. But those who persevere in prayer and
silence and the ministry of the word *(cf. Acts 6:4)*, in patient
practice of the best works, bear with you the dignity of the very

chief apostles themselves. You will have them as fellow-workers in the Gospel *(cf. 1 Thess. 3:2)* of your spiritual teaching, as they take up the burdens of the brethren *(cf. Gal. 6:2)* and ease your 430 labors, as though they were precious stones rolling about in the midst of the rest.

[§ 16. THE CARE OF SOULS.]

In this work you will have no rest for your body, no enjoyment. Your nights and days alike will be spent in concern for the souls entrusted to you, lest a single one of them become the prey of wild beasts, be devoured by the bear of concupiscence or swallowed up by the dragon of wrath, or torn in pieces by the vultures of the thoughts of pride, lest the one mind [of the community] become many, and the mind of one be a variance with itself. You will wish to preserve your flock safe and sound and 440 fruitful for Christ our God, the Chief Shepherd, that they all may bear fruit, may be full of virtues, enlightened with the knowledge of God, not mangy, nor with slit ears, or lame, or with any other fault. Thus you will save many and make them perfect in perfect works, in no wise lacking in anything *(cf. Jas. 1:4)*, entirely chaste, leading them to your Christ pure from unclean works. So you will make yourself worthy of abundant recompense from on high, in the same tabernacle as the apostles and pastors of Christ, and reigning with the Son of God Himself unto unending ages.

Let your life be a straight rule lying in the midst of your 450 brethren and fathers, so that the crookedness of others may be straightened thereby. You must have no love for material things, nor for glory, or pleasure, for food, for wine. You must not be boastful, frivolous, or avaricious, nor hot tempered, nor conceited, nor violent, nor hold grudges or repay evil for evil. Rather, you must have detachment, hate glory, hate every pleasure of life and all ease of the flesh. Be humble, simple, filled with compunction, kind, gentle, without ill temper or covetousness, recollected, silent, well ordered, patient, faithful, self-controlled, 460 conscientious, vigilant, energetic, zealous, taking heed of the souls entrusted to you as if they were your own members. If it were necessary you would lay down your own life for each one of them *(cf. Jn. 10:11)*, preferring no matter of the world to your love for them. Since you have been preferred over others to be

the shepherd of the rational flock of your Master and God, you must in accordance with His word be the last of all *(cf. Mk. 9:35)* in your attitude and pleasing to God by humility, in order that you may be strong to bear the infirmities of the weak *(cf. Rom.*
470 *15:1).* As a physician you must cure the passions and diseases of those who are sick in soul; as a shepherd you must bring back that which has strayed *(Jas. 5:20; 1 Pet. 2:25).* That which is healthy you must make fruitful in virtues, that which is mangy and incurable you must cut off from your rational flock, so that it will not infect the healthy sheep with its disease.

[§ 17. A MODERATE COURSE.]

Hasten then to increase the flock of your Master! Do not turn aside to relaxations or pleasures of the body, nor vilely squander the wool and the fat *(cf. Ezek. 34:3, 39:19)* of Christ's sheep by hoarding up the goods of the monastery for your own benefit rather than of the brethren, so that you may enjoy your-
480 self. Do nothing whatever, do not say anything for the sake of human glory, that does not pertain to the good of your monastery. Do not love to go on constant travels on thoroughbred mules with escorts preceding and following you. It should be sufficient for you to go out once a month to transact the more urgent business of your flock; the rest you can leave to the various bearers of office, who will keep you free from distraction so that you can persevere in the ministry of the word and the care of the brethren, that is, with prayer. Do not prepare expensive
490 meals for yourself, and leave the children neglected with poor and unseasoned ones, but have a common table for yourself and the children, except for cases of illness or the reception of friends who share your mind and way of life. Whether the meal is one of boiled herbs and vegetables, or of fish once a week on Sundays and feasts of our Lord, let it be prepared by the cellarer for all in common.

[§ 18. A ZEAL ADAPTED TO EACH ONE.]

Do not give in to ill temper, anger, and clamor *(cf. Eph. 4:31)* against your children and brethren unless there is some cause that portends danger to the soul. Rather, teach them with gentle words and voice how each one should live *(cf. 1 Thess. 4:1)*
500 and behave himself in the midst of the brotherhood *(cf. 1 Tim.*

3:15). You must teach the young and unstable to spare both themselves and the other brethren so that they cause no harm to those who see them by their behavior, their disorderly conduct, their brazenness, and their undisciplined youthful activities. As for those who have grown old in asceticism, teach them with wise words to be patient under the trials the enemy inflicts on them. Teach them humility, contrition of heart *(cf. Ps. 51:19)*, compunction, tears, care and persistence in prayer, the blessed sorrow, and how to be and become, both in word and deed, profitable to the rest. As for priests, teach them reverence, silence, meditation on God's Scriptures, the exact knowledge of the apostolic canons and traditions,[3] doctrinal orthodoxy, purity of heart *(cf. Mt. 5:8)*, perseverance in prayer and compunction. Teach them how to attend on God's sanctuary in the fear of God and with trembling, the sacred action of the mystery, the revelation of the mysteries of God. For to them it is given to "know the mysteries of the kingdom of heaven" *(Mt. 13:11)*, as the Lord says, that they may be God's salt and light to whole brotherhood and to those without, by having the word of life in themselves *(Phil. 2:16)*.

[§ 19. THE DUTY OF CORRECTION.]

But should you some time be moved with reasonable anger to chasten the disorderly with rod and staff *(cf. Ps. 23:4; 1 Cor. 4:21)*, in order that you may in some measure check evil and repress pestilential corruption among them, and prevent the spread of evil in practice and disposition, this has not been found unsuitable by the apostles in their ordinances, nor by our God-inspired fathers. Every movement and every act on our part that represses and repels evil and is helpful for righteousness and virtue is worthy of praise, pleasing to God, and acceptable to all the righteous. Jesus is witness, in that he beat the obstinate Jews with a whip *(cf. Jn. 2:15)*, because they had made the house of prayer into a house of merchandise and He upset the tables of the money-changers *(cf. Mk. 11:17)*. Do not, out of

---

3. A collection of some eighty-five rules, entitled "Apostolic Canons," included in the collection of John the Scholastic, Patriarch of Constantinople 566–577, and sanctioned by the Quinisext Council in 692. While attributed to the apostles, they were probably compiled in Syria toward the end of the fourth century. They form part of the Canon Law of the Orthodox Church to this day.

pretended gentleness, motivated solely by the praise of men, overlook some small action contrary to the commandment of God *(cf. Mt. 5:19)* subversive of the apostolic canons and ordinances, dishonoring the evangelical life and the monastic state. Imitate Jesus your God, who was moved with indignation *(cf.*
540 *Mk. 1:43)* and without passion disturbed Himself *(Jn. 11:33)*. Act to vindicate God's commandments and the canons ordained by his apostles. Guard your strictness toward all even in the examination of each man's thoughts, that you may know who may stand together with those who pray and communicate, and who should be separated to do penance with tears and stand with the penitents. Beware of being partial and thus knowingly or unknowingly making the Church of God, instead of a holy temple, into a cave of robbers *(cf. Mt. 21:13)* or a house of harlots. For this you will not escape the terrible punishment of God's wrath *(cf. Rom. 2:3)*!

[§ 20. THE CARE FOR HOLY THINGS AND PERSONS.]

550   Know this, that for each of these classes the eyewitness of the Word *(cf. Lk. 1:2)* and His disciples have assigned a fitting place. You must the more carefully attend to the reading of their ordinances and canons that you may know what are the mysteries hidden from those who believe in Christ, and that you do not fail by doing what is contrary to godliness. As it is written, "You must make your spiritual sons reverent" *(cf. Lev. 15:31 LXX)*, and teach them to reverence the sacred and divine places
560 and vessels of the consecrated temple of God and His liturgy, since it is written, "Blessed is the man who out of reverence trembles before all things" *(Prov. 28:14 LXX)*. Know this, that it is only to those who have been ordained and to those who by struggles and penitence with abundant tears have been purified and sanctified by partaking of the mysteries of Christ, the most devout monks, that the fathers and apostles have bestowed the honor of the liturgy of these things and the touching thereof. You will not permit to all who wish it to enter into the sanctuary of God, but, as I have said, only to those of your more devout brethren and fathers who have been ordained and
570 consecrated. As for the rest, [and especially] those of the brethren who walk disorderly *(2 Thess. 3:6)*—note what I say to you!—you will forbid them to enter! Well you know that many

have been cut off from this present life because they despised these things! If this happens through your carelessness, the blood of those who for this cause are cut off from this life will be required at your hands *(cf. Ezek. 33:6)*.

These things, O shepherd of Christ's sheep, and many others besides, you must know exactly and zealously perform them as you watch over your flock. If, therefore, you know that you have attained so great a sufficiency and have been favored with 580 such spiritual gifts that all who draw near you, whether of your own flock or strangers, are enlightened by the light of good deeds and inspired wisdom and knowledge *(cf. Col. 2:3)* that radiates from you, then confidently feed the sheep of Christ *(Jn. 21:15)*. Feed them with the prudent word of the grace that has been effectually given to you, in accordance with the rule and law that has been given to you above. Lead His lambs into the salutary pastures *(cf. Jn. 10:9)* of His commandments, until they grow and attain "to the measure of the stature of the fullness of Christ" *(Eph. 4:13)*, and you will have a great reward therefrom by sharing the throne and tabernacle of His apostles. But if not, 590 then if you are persuaded by me who has a concern for your salvation, withdraw to yourself! For our God is a consuming fire *(Heb. 12:29)*. To Him be glory forever. Amen.

XIX

[SYMEON'S SPIRITUAL CONCERN]

That one ought not to trust in the mere words and promises of men, but confirm the trustworthiness of the words from their deeds. The nature of the disposition of the true teachers, and their love toward their disciples. What are their affections and their care. How they intercede for them before God.

[§ 1. THE UNCERTAINTY OF MAN'S WORD.]

Brethren and fathers and children,

Each of you knows the beginning of your affection for me,
10 how it arose, and for what reason. Likewise it is you who know the measure of your love and faith toward God. I on my part do not know how to speak with accuracy of something that is invisible, and to gain knowledge about such matters through words alone is impossible. It often happens that a person suddenly achieves in action something that he has not promised in words, while he has agreed to something by an oath, but when the time comes he changes his mind and completely refuses to do it. This is what you find in most cases. Indeed those who are not tossed about by the great waves of this life are very rare, as are those who are not choked by its thorns (*cf. Mk. 4:7*) or be-
20 guiled by its pleasures or enslaved by its riches, which are the cause of all falsehood. Accordingly, to put one's trust in mere words and base oneself on them as if they were solid facts is fitting only in the case of God's words and the promises He has made us. He alone is unchangeable and never has He been found to utter falsehood. But in the case of unstable men, who turn and stray in all directions, he who leans on nothing but their words leans only on wind and enjoys vain dreams. Of all

things nothing shows how unstable and changeable man is more than his reasoning. Only when it has rejected all changing and created and visible things it penetrates the darkness that envelops it and is mingled with that which is invisible and permanent. Since this is how I think of the matter, and I know that you join in bearing witness of what I say, listen to the reason why I so speak to you, and the suffering I have undergone.

[§ 2. THE CASE OF FATHER THEOPHYLACT.]

You have come to us with fervent love and faith. You were compelled by no one, but came of your own volition, as I could make out from your words and your faces. Thus when I saw you and heard such words from you, filled with the love of Christ, I accepted your faith and your purpose. In a passionless way I became very partial toward all of you. Though I have been enjoined to love all equally, yet I admit I conceived a special love for you. It is Father Theophylact[1] who is the occasion of my opening remarks, and it is to him that I specially directed them. He has come back to my humble person and that with greater enthusiasm and a most fervent love, which cannot be hidden, and shines brightly to those who see clearly. I received him as a brother and loved him as though it were myself, if he will believe what I say! My soul was sensibly moved and kindled by affection when I heard him speak the words and make his vow to Christ. I had never expected to hear those words from his mouth, words that God Himself recorded and that wounded my heart like an arrow. More than that, they became like a fire in it (*cf. Jer. 20:9*) that constantly consumes and burns me up. I do not hide from you what I suffer on your part, though I have never wronged you! Day and night they have caused me equal pain; they have banished sweet sleep and forced me to refuse nourishment. I have no thirst for water, but only for seeing the outcome of what he has said. I have no desire at all to see the visible sun, so great is my desire to see my brother approach the spiritual Sun with fervor. So much is this so that hot tears flow and are offered to Christ for my desire, that he may be washed clean by them and spiritually lift up the eyes of his mind and

---

1. Otherwise unknown. It would appear that he had left the community and then returned to it afterwards.

recognize his Maker. I utter groans from the depth of my heart
that I may bring the soul I have loved out of the abyss of evils. I
lie prostrate and lament continually, that I may lift up him
70 whom I love well, who is prostrated on the ground. I cry aloud
as I invoke the Almighty Lord, that He may snatch from the
bonds of the ruler of this world (cf. Eph. 6:12) him who has allowed himself to be held by them. I do other things that I should
not commit to writing to tell you about them; God alone knows
them, they are addressed to Him. If I lie, and even accidentally
speak a single word I have not fulfilled in deed, may I not be
counted among them that believe in the Lord. May I not see the
glory of the saints, but fail of the object of my hope, for which I
have left the world behind!

[§ 3. SYMEON'S CONCERN FOR HIS MONKS.]

Such are the things I have suffered at your hand, the injuries I have undergone. Tell me, on your part, is there any one of
you whom I have caused such pain? Brethren, show me, who am
tyrannized by love, a love equal to my own! Confirm your
words with deeds, that I may find but a little refreshment. If
80 you truly love me, bare to me the designs of your hearts (1 Cor.
4:5). Let me know not only by words, but in deeds, that God is
with you and that I have not labored in vain (Phil. 2:16)! If that
is not your wish, why do you come and lay burdens on me, and
leave me even more heavily burdened? Yet it is a burden that,
paradoxically, causes me both unspeakable joy and infinite sorrow, joy because I pray for you and rejoice at the prospect of re-
90 gaining you, sorrow because I fear that you will be suffocated
by the world, and on being deceived by it (cf. Mt. 13:22; Mk.
4:19) lie to Christ. The very thought thereof causes me to tremble and be beside myself! It is this that consumes my soul and allows me neither rest nor joy. For this reason I mourn, and truly
go about in heaviness (cf. Ps. 42:9), and tearfully wish for death
(cf. Jon. 4:8), for I do not consider it a gain to be saved all by myself, nor do I want to glorify God apart from you. If then my defense is sufficient, make your defense if you wish, and tell me on
whose side you are. Establish your word with action, so that I
100 may either have joy or else sorrow in the same way. But this is
my hope as I invisibly look toward the Lord, and I pray that you
will not lie, nor dissemble with words, but rather show in deed

what you have promised in words. Do not hesitate before this! Let no thoughts of unbelief arise in your hearts *(cf. Lk. 24:38)*, but listen to my words, which are accompanied by pain, and see that I shall speak nothing vain or deceitful.

[§ 4. TAKE REFUGE IN GOD!]

Look up to heaven above and to the earth below *(Is. 8: 21–22)* and consider how many and how great are God's works, all done for us! See and examine carefully that not one of them is permanent, but that among all these visible things the soul of man alone is invisibly seen and believed to be immortal. It is united to the body and dwells in it; it sees all things and considers material and created things and the things that are composed of physical elements. But once it has been severed from them the soul finds itself immediately outside all knowledge and is reckoned solely among the realities that are immaterial and objects of thought. If then the light of the commandments of Christ shines on it, it finds itself in the infinite light of His gracious Godhead and enjoys unutterable and unending joy. But if it is shrouded in the darkness of sins, alas! then in the same manner it is in unending darkness mingled with fire *(cf. Wis. 17:5–6)*. Since this is the case, and you admit that it is, why then do we delay to flee from the bitter darkness? Why do we say, "Woe to those who love the world and love pleasure" and do not realize that we are among them? Why do we utter these words, "Blessed in truth are those who seek the Lord and put their trust in Him" *(Ps. 78:7)*, while you do not consider and flee from your own misery? Why do you think that you confess and believe in God when you are unwilling to know Him and serve Him? Where do you place your hope when you abandon the blessings you have at hand and attach yourselves to vain and transitory things?

[§ 5. NOT TO STOP BELOW IN A GAME OF SHADOWS.]

I wish to address my speech to each one of those who attach themselves to the vanity of things present. Tell me, how can you say, "I understand it all, I am mortal, and visible things are a shadow and death comes unexpectedly, the glory of the righteous is eternal and the disgrace of sinners has no end," and yet you do not renounce evil things? If you really see, how is it that

you stumble like a blind man and your whole body and soul are covered with black marks? If you know what is good, how is it
140 that you do evil, as though you did not know? If you know that all visible things are a shadow and all pass away, are you not ashamed of playing with shadows and hoarding transitory things? Like a child you draw water with a bucket full of holes; do you not realize it and take it into account, my dear friend? As though there were nothing more serious than appearance and illusion, as though reality has been taken from them?

[§ 6. LAYING HOLD ON GOD.]

O man, do you believe that Christ is God? If you believe, fear, and keep His commandments. If you do not believe, why not ask the demons *(cf. Mt. 8:29; Mk. 3:11)* whom you perhaps believe to be more trustworthy? Learn from those whose slave you are and whom you follow that there is no other God but He
150 *(Deut. 4:35)*. To Him no one is equal, nor can become equal *(Is. 40:18)*. He is the Ruler of all things, the Judge of all, the King of all, the Maker of light, and the Lord of life. He is the Light that is ineffable, inaccessible *(1 Tim. 6:16)*, and He is the Only One. By His appearing He causes all His enemies to vanish before His face *(cf. 2 Thess. 2:8; Ps. 68:2f.)*, as well as those who do not perform His commandments, just as the sun when it rises drives away the darkness of the night. Yet the Lord our God, who is unlimited among the unlimited and infinite among the infinite, will show Himself only to those who are worthy according to
160 the measure of their faith in Him. The sinners, however, will be as though they were enveloped with darkness in the midst of the light *(cf. Wis. 17:20f.)*, disgraced in the midst of joy, wasted away in the midst of gladness, terribly burned and punished in various ways by their own passions, even as the righteous will be crowned by divers virtues.

This, then, I have found with my physical eyes contained in the inspired Scriptures. I have been taught it spiritually by the Spirit for your instruction; out of great love I have not withheld
170 it, but have written it down. Behold, I have reported all to you, I have not hidden my talent *(cf. Mt. 25:25)*, I have not begrudged you your salvation. From henceforth let every one choose what he wishes. As for me, I am now free of any blame on your account, in Christ Jesus our Lord. Amen.

XX

[THE IDEAL SPIRITUAL GUIDE]

On the renunciation and elimination of self-will, addressed to those who had asked Symeon to write to them how one ought to spend the ascetic life. How to this end it is excellent and useful to have an experienced guide or spiritual father, in order that one may learn the things that pertain to virtue and the difficult practice of the ascetic art. Of faith in our spiritual fathers, and of the contemplation of the light that enlightens every soul that progresses in the love of God.

[§ 1. CHRIST, THE SOURCE AND END OF ALL THINGS.]

My dear and well-beloved brethren,

You have often wished to hear a profitable discourse from my   10
mediocrity. But because of your quick departure I would not
tell you by word of mouth[1] the things that I should say, as if
they were merely incidental. As you therefore asked me to write
to your charity, I was rightly anxious to do so. It is not in order
to admonish you, for I am unworthy to do that, but rather because I love you greatly, to counsel and remind you of the things
that I know to be profitable and helpful to the soul for fleeing
the world and ridding itself of passions and attaining to love of
God and perfect tranquillity.   20

Therefore, as I address one who thirsts for the salvation of
his soul, I thought it proper to choose no other starting point
than the very eternal Source Himself, Christ our Savior and our
God. For His sake we make our discourse and undertake every
task. He is the Goal of every endeavor with good hope, and of

---

1. This discourse would appear to have been written as a letter, rather than
delivered orally.

every desire. For those who begin He is the unbreakable foundation, for those in the middle He is the hope that cannot be con-
founded, for those at the end He is insatiable love and life
without end. It is His holy voice that I have heard speaking to
30 all without distinction: "He who does not leave father and
mother and brothers and all that he possesses and take up his
cross and follow Me is not worthy of Me" *(cf. Mt. 10:37–38,
19:29, 16:24; Lk. 14:26–27; Mk. 8:34, 10:29)*. I have learned from
Scripture and from experience itself that the cross comes at the
end for no other reason than that we must endure trials and
tribulations and, finally, voluntary death itself. In times past,
when heresies prevailed, many chose such a death through martyrdom and various tortures. Now, when we through the grace
of Christ live in a time of profound and perfect peace, we learn
40 for sure that cross and death consist in nothing else than the
complete mortification of self-will. He who pursues his own
will, however slightly, will never be able to observe the precept
of Christ the Savior.

[§ 2. THE GUIDANCE OF A SPIRITUAL FATHER.]

I will address my discourse as though it were to a single
person, and so I will say to you: Brother, constantly call on God,
that He may show you a man who is able to direct you well, one
whom you ought to obey as though he were God Himself,
whose instruction you must carry out without hesitation, even
if what he enjoins on you appears to you to be repugnant and
50 harmful. If your heart is moved by grace to even greater confidence in the spiritual father whom you already have, do what he
tells you and be saved. It is better for you to be called a disciple
of a disciple rather than to live by your own devices and gather
the worthless fruits of your own will. If the Holy Ghost sends
you to another, do not hesitate at all, for we hear that it was Paul
who planted, and Apollos who watered, and that Christ gives
the growth *(1 Cor. 3:6)*. So, brother, do as we have said, and go to
the man whom God shows you, either mystically in person, or
60 externally through His servant. You should look on him and
speak to him as to Christ Himself, and so revere him and be
taught by Him what is profitable. Supposing you hear him say,
"Depart from the land of your will and the family of your own

point of view" *(cf. Gen. 12:1)*, do not argue, do not be ashamed, do not be overcome by conceit. If he tells you, "Come to the land of obedience which I will show you" *(cf. ibid.)*, run to it, my brother, with all your strength. Do not give sleep to your eyes *(cf. Prov. 6:4)*, do not bend your knees *(cf. Judg. 7:5)* overcome by sluggishness or apathy. Perhaps it is there that God will appear to you and show you that you must be the father of many spiritual children *(cf. Gen. 17:4f.)*, and bestow on you that   70
land of promise *(Heb. 11:9)* which only the righteous will inherit *(cf. Mt. 5:5)*. If he brings you to the mountain, climb it with eagerness, for I know well that you will enjoy the vision of Christ transfigured and shining more brightly than the sun with the light of Godhead. Perhaps you will fall down because you cannot bear to see what you have never contemplated, and you will hear the Father's voice from on high and see the cloud overshadowing you, and the prophets testifying that He is the God and Lord of the living and the dead *(cf. Mt. 17:1ff.; Mk. 9:2ff.; Lk. 9:28ff.)*.

[§ 3. FOLLOWING CHRIST WITH HIM.]

If he urges you to follow him, go confidently through the cities with him *(cf. Mt. 9:35)*, for you will derive the greatest benefit if you look to him alone. If you see him eating with har-   80
lots and publicans and sinners *(cf. Mt. 9:11; Mk. 2:16; Lk. 15:2)*, do not think anything passionate and human, but rather think of all such things as are without passion and holy and remember the saying, "I have become all things to all men, that I might win all" *(1 Cor. 9:22)*. With these thoughts in mind, see him condescending to human passions. What you see with your eyes do not believe at all, for the eyes too make mistakes, as I have learned by experience. When you follow him and obey what he says, do not look aside at those who are with you *(cf. Jn. 21:19–20)*, nor say about anyone, "Lord what about this man?" *(Jn. 21:21)*. Rather, pay constant attention to yourself and keep   90
death before your eyes, and think over and reflect by what virtue you will glorify God *(cf. Jn. 21:19)*. Do not become proud when you are honored by those who are greater than yourself because of your teacher. Even if there are many who obey you on account of his name, rejoice only if your name is written in

the heaven *(cf. Lk. 10:20)* of humility. Even if you see the demons tremble at your very shadow *(ibid.)*, do not ascribe it to yourself but only to the intercession of your father. If you do that, they will fear you the more!

[§ 4. WITH HIM AT TABLE.]

If he bids you sit at table, if it is next to him, accept it with
100 gratitude. With silence show him reverence and honor, and do not touch anything that is set before you without his blessing, nor give anything to anyone else or dare to show him preference in any way without his approval and command. But if he calls you last of all, do not say, "I shall seat myself at his right hand or his left," for you know that this has been prepared for others *(cf. Mk. 10:37, 40)* and have heard the saying, "If any one would be first he must be last of all" *(Mk. 9:35)*. Accept the lower place as the means of obtaining the higher *(Lk. 14:10)*, and love your teacher as the one who by means of lowly things obtains for you
110 the greater. Do not, out of audacity, put your hand to the platter as the first with him *(cf. Mt. 26:23)*, for you know who was rash enough to do this *(cf. Mt. 26:25; Jn. 13:26)*. Should he wish to wash your feet, reverence him *(cf. Jn. 13:5f.)* as if he were the Lord and Teacher *(Jn. 13:13)* and refuse the act. But if you hear him say, "If I do not wash you, you have no part in me" *(Jn. 13:8)*, then eagerly offer him your whole body to be washed *(Jn. 13:9)* in order that you may learn from what happens to you the great sublimity of the humility that makes us divine and thus be the more greatly profited thereby, if you are conscious thereof, than if you were washing the feet of your father. If he should
120 say after sitting down at table, "One of you will betray me" *(Mt. 26:21; Mk. 14:18; Jn. 13:21)* or "is a cause of offense to me" *(cf. Mt. 16:23)*, do not hide your treachery, but if you are conscious thereof, confess it. If you are not, fall on your face at his feet and ask him with tears, "Is it I, master?" *(Mt. 26:25)*. For we all make many mistakes *(Jas. 3:2)*, and out of ignorance. But to fall on the breast of your father is not good for you. Even though John out of his great love for Christ took this liberty with Him as though with a man *(cf. Jn. 13:23)*, yet he too when he had done everything was ordered to call himself an unprofitable servant along with all the rest *(Lk. 17:10)*.

THE DISCOURSES

[§ 5. WITH HIM AS AT THE PASSION.]

If you see your guide performing miracles and receiving 130
glory, believe and rejoice and give thanks to God that you have
obtained such a teacher. Be not scandalized when you see him
dishonored by those who are envious, perhaps even struck and
dragged off *(cf. Mt. 26:67)*. Like the ardent Peter take the sword
and stretch forth your hand and cut off not only the ear *(cf. Mt.
26:51)*, but the hand and the tongue of him who attempts to
speak against your father or to touch him. If you, like him, receive a rebuke, you will be the more praised because of your
great love and faithfulness. Even if you, since you are human, 140
give way to fear and say, "I know not the man" *(Mt. 26:73)*, then
at least weep bitterly *(Mt. 26:75)* over it and do not be overwhelmed with despair. I am sure that he will be the first to take
you back to himself. Suppose you were to see him crucified like
a criminal *(cf. Lk. 23:32)* and suffering at the hands of criminals,
if possible, die with him. If it is not possible, do not join with
the evil men as an evil man and a traitor, nor have part with
them in innocent blood *(cf. Mt. 27:4, 24)*, but though for a moment you have forsaken your shepherd like a cowardly and
timorous man remain faithful to him. If he is released from im-
prisonment, return to him again and venerate him the more,
like a martyr. If he dies from ill treatment, then boldly seek his 150
body *(cf. Mk. 15:43)* and pay him more honor than when you at-
tended on him while he was alive, and so anoint it with per-
fumes and give it a costly burial *(cf. Mk. 16:1; Jn. 19:40)*. Though
he will not rise again on the third day, yet he will rise on the last
day with all men. Believe that he will stand before God with
confidence even though you have placed his body in the grave,
and invoke his intercession without hesitation. He will help you
here and will preserve you from all adversity; when you depart
from the body he will receive you and prepare an eternal dwell- 160
ing *(cf. Jn. 14:1–2)* for you.

[§ 6. WITH THE TEACHER IN GLORY.]

If after the aforesaid things he calls you apart and bids you
to live as a solitary and tells you, "Stay here without going forth
until you are clothed with power from on high" *(cf. Acts 1:8)*, lis-

ten to him with firm hope and insatiable joy. Such a teacher, my brother, is truthful and trustworthy. Even now the same power of the most Holy Spirit will come upon you *(Acts 2:2, 3)*. It will not appear visibly in the form of fire or with a great noise and violent wind *(ibid.)*, for those things happened then for the sake of those who did not believe. Your mind will see him in the

170 form of a spiritual light with deep calm and joy. This light is the prelude of the eternal and primordial light; it is the reflected brightness of everlasting blessedness *(cf. Heb. 1:3)*. When this appears every passionate thought will vanish and every passion of the soul be dispelled, and every bodily disease healed. Then the eyes of the heart are purified and see that which is written in the Beatitudes *(cf. Mt. 5:8)*. Then the soul sees, as in a mirror, even its slightest failures; it is brought down to the abyss of humility. As it perceives the greatness of the glory it is filled with all joy

180 and gladness; it is struck with amazement at this wonder beyond all hope and flows with tears as from fountains. Thus the man is entirely changed; he knows God and is first known by Him. It is this alone of all things earthly and heavenly, of both present things and things to come, of things troublesome and joyful, that makes a man despise them all. At the same time it makes him a friend of God and a son of the Most High, and, as far as this is attainable to men, a god *(cf. Ps. 82:6)*.

[§ 7. HUMILITY AND CHARITY.]

I have written these things to your charity, that you may

190 have in writing the things you asked to hear from my wretched person, and so be able to read them whenever you wish. But if you believe that the most Holy Spirit commands you these things out of His providence and for your benefit by means of myself, all these things will happen to you in order as I have told you. Whatever we have omitted, though they are many, Christ Himself will teach you through Himself.

If, however, they seem incredible and disagreeable to you, forgive me for counseling you what I have learned. Follow all the better things you understand, but take heed, brother, that you do not follow the worse things as well, though unwillingly! In truth those who have the skill properly to direct and heal rational souls are rare, and especially at the present time. Many,

200 perhaps, have made a pretense of fasting and vigil *(cf. 2 Cor. 6:5,*

11:27) and a form of godliness, or have even achieved it in fact. As for learning many things by heart and teaching them in words, this is easy for most men, but as for eliminating the passions and acquiring the capital virtues so that they cannot be lost, very few are found [who do this]. Now we call "capital virtues" humility, which eliminates the passions and obtains heavenly and angelic impassibility, and love, which never ceases or fails *(cf. 1 Cor. 13:8)* but continually presses on to that which lies ahead *(cf. Phil. 3:13)* as it adds desire to desire and love to love. It supplies perfect discernment, and by itself is a good guide to 210 those who follow after it and infallibly carries us across the spiritual sea *(cf. Wis. 10:18).* It is this that I pray may be granted you by God, and especially now, that you may discern your affairs in a manner pleasing to God and may so act and endeavor that you may find Christ, as He even now cooperates with you, and in time to come will bestow on you abundantly the enjoyment of the illumination that comes from Him. Do not follow the wolf instead of the shepherd *(cf. Mt. 7:15)*, nor enter into a flock that is diseased *(cf. Ezek. 34:4).* Do not be alone by yourself, lest you be seen carried off by the wolf who destroys souls, or succumb to one disease after the other and so die spiritually, or, 220 as you succumb, you attain to that woe *(cf. Eccles. 4:10).* He who gives himself in the hand of a good teacher will have no such worries, but will live without anxiety and be saved in Christ Jesus our Lord, to whom be glory forever. Amen.

XXI

ON THE REMEMBRANCE OF DEATH

How Symeon's thrice-happy brother Antony attained a good end. In conclusion, his funeral eulogy.

[§ 1. ANTONY'S PURITY.]

Brethren and fathers,

I pray to God, who has had mercy on me and granted me that all things should be ordered for the salvation of all and that your souls should be well directed toward the life that is above, where our brethren and parents who have gone before await us. There our thrice-happy and blessed brother Antony has passed,
10 after living a good and holy life in this place. His was a true penitence, as he courageously confessed things few monks consider to be faults. He was pure and had obtained a heart that was pure *(cf. Mt. 5:8)* from passionate thoughts. So that holy man looked on faults that I myself consider to be altogether insignificant as great sins and confessed them. Since he was protected by God's grace he lived his life in virginity and was pure both in body and heart. From the day that he entered the gate of the monastery and made his vow to Christ he did not defile the garment of
20 his flesh or of his soul either by thoughts harbored in the mind or by mental consent or by any action. As I once sat close to his bed and wept, he confided in me and said, "Why do you weep, brother? I have not denied my faith in God, but I have kept it *(2 Tim. 4:7)* even as I have kept Him in whom I hope. From the time that I came to this holy monastery—I say this without boasting, but trusting in God and in our holy father's prayer—I have committed no fleshly sin. Yet as I ate and drank I have spent my days in negligence. But I commend myself to God's

loving-kindness, for He knows all things, and knows what He 30
will do with my lowliness."

What more is to be found in the last words and utterances
of the great Fathers than in those of our own brother? He frankly revealed to us his purity and virginity while his soul reaped
the benefit of the steadfastness of his humility. At the same time
he observed the saying, or rather commandment, of the Master
that says, "When you have done all things, say, 'We are unprofitable servants, we have only done our duty' " *(Lk. 17:10)*.

After this he privately met with our holy father[1] and with 40
sorrow told him the same things. These moved our holy father
to astonishment no less than ourselves. As well, all those who
heard it after his death were amazed. Not one of us expected
that such a treasure of purity and chastity was concealed in him.

[§ 2. SYMEON'S JOY AND SADNESS AT HIS DEATH.]

In this way, after he had been clothed with the holy and angelic Great Habit,[2] [he died] with great ardor, shedding many
tears, with unshaken faith and perfect knowledge. This neo-
phyte, this newly enlisted soldier, was the last one to join our 50
ranks in this present life and the first one to leave behind the
vanity of the world. He departed to his own Master with
unspeakable joy *(1 Pet. 1:8)* and left us wretched ones with un-
consolable sorrow. Whenever I think of that which I used to do
and say to him—as you yourselves know, vain as I am, I was
zealous for his soul's salvation—yet I am beside myself; my
mind, my thought, and my heart burn within me *(Ps. 39:4)*!
How I deceived myself! In my vanity I thought to instruct a
man from whom I ought rather to have received instruction!
For as I thought of his virtues as defects I was in great pain and
was impatient for the salvation of the soul of our longed-for 60
brother! (For so it is fitting not to lie!) I boast in Christ; again, I
am under the pressure of ineffable joy *(1 Pet. 1:8)*, because I have
thus taken leave of my brother at his departure from this life
and was found worthy to see him depart to Christ *(cf. 2 Cor. 5:8)*

---

1. I.e., Symeon the Pious. This discourse would thus have been given before
his death in 986 or 987.

2. Eastern monks are divided into two categories, those of the "Lesser Habit" and those of the "Great Habit," two different grades of monastic profession,
but equally binding.

with such actions and practices. God, who examines our
thoughts and our reasonings, knows that from the beginning I
had great zeal and concern for him, and that I shed many tears
for his sake. God, who loves mankind, did not overlook the
70   prayer of such a wretch as myself (cf. Ps. 55:1), for it is with mutual love, with humility and faith toward us, that he has flown
up to heaven, leaving merely his body in our hands.

[§ 3. ANTONY'S LAST MOMENTS.]

When I lamented and said, "Brother, do not forget us, for
now you are dying and leaving us behind," he calmly replied,
"Oh no, I trust in God." When he had uttered this last word
with his most pure lips he departed to God after saying this, not
80   once, but twice. For when I first asked him, "Do not forget us,
dear brother," he promised afresh that he would not forget us.
When he had stretched out his feet and arranged his hands in
the form of a cross, with the attitude and gesture of an untroubled soul he fell asleep in profound peace in most gentle sleep.
He slept the sleep that befits the righteous, without showing
any attachment to the things that surrounded him. He did not
think of his kinsfolk nor mention any friend in this life; he made
no disposition of any corruptible thing. Since he had hated and
90   despised all things here as if they were dung or mud, and was
denuded of all desire and attachment to things visible, he passed
on to the spiritual palace as one who had truly become a worthy
inhabitant and inheritor of it. How fittingly! For if God has
commanded us in our nakedness to clothe our brethren (Mt.
25:36, 40), how much the more will He become the garment and
covering for my very dear brother, who for His sake had
stripped himself of all the world and the things of the world,
and has gone to Him in his nakedness?

But now that we have all once again looked over the life of
100   our brother, let us, I entreat, imitate his faith, his struggles, his
confession, his penitence, so that we too, when we arrive at our
departure from the body, may like him, without fear and pertur-
bation, depart from the body and go off to God. Let us thus
dwell in Him with good hope and find our rest in eternal taber-
nacles, the dwelling place of all those who rejoice (Ps. 87:7),
where the choir of our blessed and holy fathers abides.

[§ 4. A PLEA FOR ANTONY'S INTERCESSION.]

But now, O most dear brother beloved by God, triply longed for, be mindful of your promise and do not forget those your last words, which were most sweet to me. Intercede for us, your brethren, and for all your kind. You know in what evils we find ourselves, now that you have come to happiness and many blessings; for he who has been freed from darkness knows exactly how great is the misery of those who are still confined in it. We ask you then, implore God even now from your whole brotherhood in Christ, even as you have never ignored anyone who asked of you, or withheld even your necessary food from those in need. Pray for your brethren who depend on your longing, who are unable to cover up their sense of loss or continue to restrain their sorrow, that you may have us with you and receive us there. Propitiate God in His infinite goodness that He may cause us to dwell with you, and prepare a place for us (*Jn. 14:2*) in advance where we may rest by means of your good deeds here below, that by your help we may be with you there, as we were in this present life, and live together with you and rejoice with you, being found worthy to dwell there and behold the blessed life that is without pain. Just as we had prepared for you in advance a monastery and a dwelling when you fled from the world into the monastic life, so now, when you have gone before us into that unutterable and divine and immaterial existence, receive us gladly, or, rather, seek for us and travel and labor with us with a fraternal love for your brethren. Deliver us from those who try to put obstacles in our way and prevent us from coming to you, and remember that we of the brotherhood in this life came to your aid and shared in your toils. Now we stand in even greater need of your cooperation than you did of ours when you undertook to escape from the nets of the world.

[§ 5. SYMEON'S DEMANDING LOVE.]

Many are the burdens, O dearest brother, that weigh down our humble souls and bodies. The most terrible of these is our isolation and our great concern for the brethren who are with us. You know how my zeal for this is a veritable mania! You now know for certain my attitude toward you, how I chastised

110

120

130

140

you without hate or abhorrence and in every way preserved you by my monitions out of the great affection and fervent and inflexible love that I bore you. I know well that now you see clearly, having come out of the darkness and mists of this body. You see my soul in all its nakedness and its very thoughts, even as you are now stripped of the body. Having become like God you see all our affairs in a manner more like His. So do not break your promises toward us, nor forget a brother who loved you exceedingly and who, without speaking audaciously, laid down his very life for you (*Jn. 10:15*). But through your acceptable prayers give us a helping hand, that we may be granted to attain to you and dwell with you in our Lord and God and Savior Jesus Christ Himself. So may we make our dwelling in Him, as we live with the ineffable light in the imperishable life, in the joy unspeakable, in the unutterable glory and brightness that is seen in the Father and the Son and the Holy Ghost and adored forever. Amen.

XXII

ON FAITH

An instruction on those who claim that it is impossible to attain to perfect virtue in the midst of the concerns of this life. By way of a preamble, an edifying discourse.

[§ 1. HOW FAITH IS ATTAINED.]

Brethren and fathers,

It is good that we should proclaim God's mercy to all men and make known His compassion and unutterable goodness toward us to our neighbors. As holy David tells us, "I therefore, as you see, did not fast, I did not keep vigil, nor did I sleep on the ground, yet 'I humbled myself' *(Ps. 116:10)* and, in short, the Lord saved me." To say it yet more briefly, "I but believed, and the Lord took me up" *(Ps. 116:10, 27:10)*. While there are many things that prevent us from achieving humility, there is nothing that hinders us from finding faith. If we heartily desire it, faith at once becomes active. It is a gift of our Master and a quality of nature, even though it remains subject to our own freedom of choice, for even Scythians and barbarians have faith in each other's words. But listen to me, in order that I may show you with actual facts what inward faith effects, and I will tell you an experience that was related to me by a truthful person, which will confirm what I have stated.

[§ 2. "GEORGE" READS MARK THE HERMIT.]

A man by the name of George,[1] still young in years, about twenty years old, lived in Constantinople in our own time. He

---

1. As Nicetas Stethatos in his biography of Symeon recognized, "George" is the saint himself. The events would have taken place about 970.

was handsome in appearance, elegant in body, manners, and gait, so much so that some for that reason harbored evil suspicions about him—that is, such persons as merely looked at the outward covering and passed harsh judgment on the conduct of others. He made the acquaintance of a certain holy monk[2] who lived in one of the monasteries of the city. When he made known to him the state of his soul, he received from him a simple command to keep in mind. The young man also asked him for a book that contained accounts of the life of the monks and their ascetic practices, so the old man gave him the treatise of the monk Mark with instructions about the spiritual law.[3] The young man accepted it as though it had been sent by God Himself. In the hope that he would gain some great benefit from it he read it through with longing and with attention. While he derived profit from all its passages, there were three only that, if I may say so, he fixed in his heart. The first was the one that reads as follows: "When you seek healing, take heed to your conscience. Do what it says, and you will find profit." The second one goes: "He who seeks the workings of the Holy Spirit before he practices the commandments is like a slave bought with money, who when he has been bought seeks manumission as soon as the price has been paid." The third goes: "The blind man who cries out and says, 'Son of David, have mercy upon me' *(Mk. 10:47–48)*, is the man who prays with his body without as yet possessing spiritual knowledge. But the blind man of old, when he had received his sight and saw the Lord, no longer confessed that He was Son of David, but Son of God, and so worshipped Him" *(Jn. 9:35ff.)*.

[§ 3. HOW "GEORGE" PRAYED WHEN HE WAS STILL IN THE WORLD.]

On reading those things the young man marveled, and in his wonder he believed that he would be helped by careful attention to his conscience, and that he would experience the activity of the Holy Spirit by practicing the commandments, and that by

---

2. Evidently Symeon the Pious of the monastery of Studios.
3. Mark the Hermit (d. after 430, near Ancyra), "Of the Spiritual Law," together with another work of his, "Of Those Who Think to Be Justified by Works," from which the quotations that follow are derived.

His grace he would receive spiritual sight and see the Lord. He
was wounded by love and desire for Him, and sought the prime-
val beauty through hope, even though it might not appear to
him. As he assured me by an oath, he did no more than carry out
the simple command that old man had given him, every evening   60
before he laid himself to sleep on his bed. So when his conscience told him, "You must perform additional reverences and
say more psalms, and repeat 'Lord, have mercy,' for you can do
it," he obeyed with eagerness and without hesitation. He did all
these things as if God Himself had told him so. From that time
on he never went to bed with his conscience reproaching him
and asking him, "Why have you not done this?" So, as he constantly followed its demands and as it daily demanded more of
him, in a few days' time his evening prayers became much longer. During the day he managed a patrician's household[4] and dai-   70
ly went to the palace, engaged in worldly affairs, so that no one
was aware of his pursuits. Every evening tears welled from his
eyes; more and more frequently he prostrated himself with his
face to the ground, with his feet together, without moving from
the spot where he stood. With all diligence he recited prayers to
the Mother of God, accompanied with groans and tears. As   80
though the Lord were physically present he used to fall at His
spotless feet; like the blind man he asked for mercy and that he
might spiritually receive his sight. So as his prayer grew longer
every evening he continued till midnight. During the time of his
prayer he in no way grew weak or slack. Not a member of his
body moved, his eye did not turn or look up, but he stood mo-
tionless [in prayer] as though he were a statue or an incorporeal
spirit.

[§ 4. THE VISION OF THE LIGHT.]

One day, as he stood and recited, "God, have mercy upon
me, a sinner" (Lk. 18:13), uttering it with his mind rather than   90
his mouth, suddenly a flood of divine radiance appeared from
above and filled all the room. As this happened the young man

---

4. Probably that of his maternal uncle. In the Byzantine civil service, pro-
consuls and patricians were the highest ranks after the magistri, and were conferred on the holders of the highest offices of the empire and on certain
members of illustrious families.

lost all awareness [of his surroundings] and forgot that he was in a house or that he was under a roof. He saw nothing but light all around him and did not know if he was standing on the ground. He was not afraid of falling; he was not concerned with the word, nor did anything pertaining to men and corporeal beings enter into his mind. Instead, he was wholly in the presence of immaterial light and seemed to himself to have turned into light. Oblivious of all the world he was filled with tears and with ineffable joy and gladness. His mind then ascended to heaven and beheld yet another light, which was clearer than that which was close at hand. In a wonderful manner there appeared to him, standing close to that light, the saint of whom we have spoken, the old man equal to angels, who had given him the commandment and the book.

When I had heard this account I thought both how greatly the intercession of this holy man had availed for him, and also how God in His providence had shown the young man the sublime height of virtue to which this holy man had attained.

Once this vision was over and the young man, as he told me, had come to himself, he was moved with joy and amazement. He wept with all his heart, and sweetness accompanied his tears. Finally he fell on his bed. At that very moment the cock crowed and announced the middle of the night. Soon afterwards the church bells rang for matins and he himself rose to sing psalms as usual, without ever thinking of sleep that night.

[§ 5. THE LIGHT AS THE FRUIT OF FAITH.]

As God knows, who brings these things to pass by the judgments He alone understands, these things happened even though that young man had done no more than what you have heard. But he did them with right faith and unhesitating hope! Let no one say that he did this to test [God], for he had not spoken or thought of this even in his imagination, for he who tries and tests has not attained faith! But that young man, as he declared under oath, took so much to heart what his own conscience said that he regarded all material things of life with indifference and even approached food and drink without taking pleasure in them or doing so with frequency.

Have you heard, brethren, how great things faith in God can accomplish when it is confirmed by actions *(cf. Jas. 2:18)*?

Have you understood that youth is not to be rejected, and that old age is useless without understanding and the fear of God? Have you learned that [living in] the midst of the city does not hinder us from practicing the commandments of God as long as we are zealous and vigilant? That solitude and retirement from the world are useless if we are slack and careless? No doubt we have all heard of David. We admire him and say that David was unique and there was no other—and behold, "something greater than David is here!" *(cf. Mt. 12:42)*. He received the witness from God and was anointed to be a prophet and a king; he was inspired by the Holy Ghost and had many proofs of the things of God. When he had sinned he was deprived of the grace of the Spirit. He lost the [power of] prophecy and was cut off from his accustomed communion with God. No wonder, as he remembered the grace from which he had fallen, that he sought for these things to be restored to him *(cf. Ps. 51:12–13)*! This man, however, had never received such gifts in his mind. He had given himself entirely to the things of this world and looked only to transitory things, and his mind imagined nothing higher than the things of earth. Oh, how great are Thy judgments, O Lord! He merely heard about these things and at once believed. He believed so firmly that he showed his faith in deeds appropriate to it. By these deeds his faith received wings and reached heaven. It attracted the compassion of Christ's Mother, and by her intercession God was propitiated and sent down on him the grace of the Spirit. This grace gave him strength to reach up to heaven and granted him to contemplate that light to which all strive, yet very few attain.

[§ 6. THE EXCELLENCE OF THE ILLUMINATION OF THE SPIRIT.]

This young man had not observed long fasts, he had never slept on the ground. He had not worn a hair shirt, nor received the tonsure. He had not left the world in his body, but in spirit, after keeping but a few vigils; yet he appeared to be greater than Lot, who was so famous in Sodom *(cf. Gen. 19)*. Nay, rather, though he was in the body yet he was an angel, held down yet not held down by it, seen yet not restrained, human in appearance yet in thought without flesh, in appearance "all things to all men" *(1 Cor. 9:22)*, yet alone to God who alone knows all

140

150

160

things. Thus, when the visible sun sets, this sweet light of the spiritual star takes its place, as a pledge and confirmation in advance of the unceasing light that will follow on it. Rightly so,

170 for the love of that which he was seeking took him out of the world and nature and all affairs, and caused him to belong wholly to the Spirit and to become light. It did all this to him while he was living in the midst of the city and was in charge of a house and cared for slaves and free men, and was carrying out all the duties and activities that pertain to [ordinary] life.

But enough of this, whether to praise the young man in question, or to move us to love and imitate him. Would you rather that I told you even greater things, which you might not be able to accept? Yet what will you find that is greater and more perfect? Indeed, nothing else is greater, as Gregory the Theolo-

180 gian said: "It is written, 'The beginning of wisdom is the fear of the Lord' *(Prov. 1:7)*. For where there is fear, there is the keeping of the commandments. Where there is the keeping of the commandments, there is the purification of the flesh, and from the cloud that besets the soul and prevents it from clearly seeing God's ray of light. Where there is purification, there is illumination. Illumination is the fulfillment of those who desire either the greatest of all supremely great things, or even that which is above all greatness."[5] By this saying he showed that the illumination of the Spirit is the infinite goal of every virtue. He who attains to this illumination has arrived at the end and limit of all things that can be perceived and has found the beginning of the knowledge of spiritual things.

[§ 7. THE NEED OF ENTERING THE KINGDOM.]

These, my brethren, are the wonders of God. When God

190 brings His hidden saints to light it is in order that some may emulate them and others be without excuse. Those who wish to remain amid distractions as well as those who live a worthy life in communities, in mountains, and in caverns *(Heb. 11:38)* are saved, and God bestows on them great blessings solely because they have faith in Him. Thus those who fail to obtain them because of their carelessness have nothing to say [in excuse] on the

---

5. S. Gregory of Nazianzus, Or. 29:8, P.G. vol 36, 344A.

day of judgment. He who has promised to save by faith alone does not lie, my brethren! So show mercy to yourselves and to us, who love you and often lament and shed tears over you—for God, who is compassionate and merciful, commands us to be such! Believe in the Lord with all your soul! Leave behind you the earth and all things that pass away! Draw near to Him *(cf. Ps. 34:5)* and attach yourselves to Him, for yet a little while and "heaven and earth will pass away" *(Mt. 24:35)*. Without Him there is no place to stand, no limit, nothing to hold back sinners as they fall. God is infinite and incomprehensible; tell me, if you can, what place will there be for those who fall outside His kingdom?

    Lamentation comes upon me; my heart is consumed, and I pine away for your sake, when I remember that we have such a generous Master, so full of loving-kindness to us men that in return for simple faith in Him He grants us such gifts as surpass our understanding, our hearing, our thinking, such as "the heart of man has not conceived" *(1 Cor. 2:9)*. But we are like brute beasts and prefer nothing but the earth and the things that, through His great mercy, it produces to satisfy the needs of bodies! These are for our moderate sustenance, so that our souls may make the journey to the things that are above without hindrance, as they are likewise fed with the rational food of the Spirit according to the extent that they have been cleansed and ascend.

[§ 8. THE FEWNESS OF TRUE CHRISTIANS.]

    This is man's nature, and for this we were created. To this end we were brought into being, that having received some small benefits in this life we may, by giving thanks to God and loving Him, enjoy in that life blessings far greater that endure forever. But alas! We have no concern whatever for the blessings that are to come and are even ungrateful for the blessings that are at hand, and so, to tell the truth, we become the equals of demons or even worse! Therefore we deserve an even worse punishment in proportion to the greater benefits we have received, for we know that God for our sakes became like us (apart from sin) *(Heb. 4:15)*, in order that He might deliver us from error and set us free from sin. But why should I say this? We truly be-

200

210

220

230

lieve all these things, but in word only; we deny them by our deeds! Is not Christ's name spoken everywhere, in cities, in villages, in monasteries, on the mountains [where hermits dwell]? Search, if you will, and examine carefully whether men keep His commandments. Truly, among thousands and tens of thousands you will scarcely find one who is a Christian in word and deed. Did not our Lord and God say in the Holy Gospel, "He who believes in Me will also do the works that I do, and he will
240   do greater works than these" *(Jn. 14:12)*? Who of us dares to say, "I do the works of Christ and I rightly believe in Christ"? Do you not see, brethren, that we risk being found unbelievers in the day of judgment, and that we will then suffer a punishment worse than those who do not know of the Lord? We must necessarily be condemned as unbelievers, unless Christ is shown to be a liar—and that, my brethren, is impossible, impossible!

[§ 9. FLEEING THE WORLD.]

I have not written these things to prevent you from withdrawing from the world or to encourage you to decide to live in the midst of the world. Rather, I have done so to show all who
250   may read this account that God has granted the ability to do good to anyone who wishes to do it, wherever he may be. Indeed, this narration encourages withdrawal! The man in question, though he moved in the midst of the world and had no thought of monastic profession or of poverty or obedience, yet received such mercy from God because he sincerely believed and called on Him. How much greater blessings should they hope to gain who have forsaken all things and all persons belonging to the world, who, as God Himself commanded, for His sake have given up even their very souls to death *(cf. Lk. 14:26)*?
260   Indeed, he who with unhesitating faith and wholehearted resolve has begun to practice goodness, and has begun to experience the blessing thereof, will know at firsthand that the care of the world and life in it is a great hindrance to those who have resolved to live in accordance with God. What we have related about this young man is amazing and unexpected, and we have never heard that anything like it has happened to anyone else. Even though it may have happened in some cases or will happen in the future, yet men should know that they will be deprived of so great a blessing unless they promptly withdraw from the

world. This is the very thing that I learned from that young man.

[§ 10. HOW "GEORGE" WENT ASTRAY AFTER HIS VISION.]

I later met him after he had become a monk, in the third or fourth year of his monastic life, when he had reached his thirty-second birthday.[6] I know him very well, because he had been my friend and my childhood companion. So he told me again: "After that marvelous change and the supernatural help I received, not many days passed and I was assailed by constant temptations of ordinary life. I found that they hindered my private activities and deprived me little by little of goodness. I was anxious to get away from all the world and in solitude seek Him who had appeared to me, because I was convinced, brother, that the reason that He at all vouchsafed to appear to me was in order that He might draw me, unworthy as I was, to Himself and separate me from all the world. Since, however, I was unable to do this at once I gradually forgot all that I have told you. I fell into total darkness, so that I could not at all remember, even in thought, anything either great or small of what I have mentioned. Rather, I fell into more evils than had ever before befallen me, and I reached such a state as though I had never thought or heard of Christ's holy words. It went so far that I looked on that holy man, who had once shown me mercy and given me that trifling command and sent me that book, as though he were any other person, without the slightest thought of the things that I had seen because of him. I tell you all this," he said, "in order that you may learn into what a pit of destruction I was brought, wretch that I am, on account of negligence, and that you may marvel at God's ineffable goodness that He afterwards showed me, and be amazed at it."

[§ 11. HOW GOD'S MERCY RESTORED HIM TO FAVOR.]

"Yet, I cannot tell how, unknown to myself, there remained love and trust in my wretched heart toward that saintly old man. I think that it was on account of this that God, who loves men, through his prayers showed mercy on me after so many

270

280

290

300

---

6. I.e., in 981, when Symeon had been a priest and abbot for about a year.

310

320

years. Through him He snatched me out of the abyss of evil and delivered me from great error. Though I was unworthy I did not completely avoid him. I confessed to him what had happened, and when I happened to be in the city I frequently visited his cell, although I did not heed my conscience and failed to keep what he commanded. But, as you now see, the merciful Lord has overlooked the multitude of my offenses. By His providence He has caused me to become a monk at the hand of that saintly old man, and has granted me, who am truly unworthy, to stay with him always. With great toil, many tears, strict solitude, and perfect obedience, with complete elimination of my own will and with many other very difficult pursuits and practices, I have been going forward without stopping or delaying on my course. So I have been vouchsafed again in some dim fashion to see a small ray of that most sweet and divine light, but until now I have never been found worthy to see a vision such as I saw at that time."

330

These things, and many others besides, he told me with tears. As for me, wretched man, when I listened to his holy words, I noted that he was entirely filled with the grace of God and that he was truly wise, even though he did not speak as one who had secular wisdom. Further, since he through practical experience had gained exact knowledge of the very realities, I asked him to tell me how faith could become capable of working such marvels, and to instruct me by expounding it in writing. So he began to tell me and did not disdain to write down what he told me. We shall not go on to speak of them now; we have served them up as a festive table on other occasions for those who with faith approach what has been written down.

[§ 12. FINAL EXHORTATION.]

Therefore I entreat you, brethren in Christ, let us also run with diligence the race of Christ's commandments (cf. Ps. 119:32), and "our faces will not be ashamed" (Ps. 34:5). To every one who persistently knocks He opens the gates of His kingdom, and straightway gives the Most Holy Spirit to him who asks (cf. Lk. 11:13). It is impossible that he who seeks with all his soul should fail to find (cf. Mt. 7:7–8), that he should not be enriched with the riches of His gifts. Thus you too will enjoy His unutterable blessings, which He has prepared for those who love Him *(1 Cor. 2:9)*. In accordance with His superior wisdom, in this present time [you will enjoy them] in part *(cf. 1 Cor. 13:12)*, but in their fullness in the world to come, in the company of all the saints from the beginning, in Christ Jesus our Lord, to whom be glory forever and ever. Amen.

XXIII

ON PENITENCE AND THE FEAR OF GOD

The nature of that struggle of soul and pain of heart which he must endure who repents with a contrite spirit. The words and the prayers that he addresses to the Lord, who loves mankind.

[§ 1. THE INWARD PAIN CAUSED BY SIN.]

Hearken to my words, my youngest sons, my dear ones, whom I have acquired! Listen to me, if you truly love me and seek me as a father. What man whose heart has been smitten
10   with poison and whose inward parts are in violent pain and anguish will be concerned with minor abrasions of the skin of his body or worry about them? The hidden pain of his heart will cover up every pain or irritation on the surface of his body. The anguish of his heart will not allow him to see and discern what is on his body, but because of the distress and pain of his heart he forgets about the wounds that are on his body. He rips his clothes apart with his hands and scratches the sores of his body
20   with his fingernails. He forgets his parents and friends and looks at no man with his eyes, nor will he turn an angry face on anyone who curses him. He pays no attention to his estates or his possessions, he abandons his wealth to those who would rob him. He does not eat his bread with pleasure, for it is filled with bitterness (cf. Jer. 15:17). He takes no pleasure in drinking wine, for he is sated with suffering. With great anger he will reply to those who invite him to a drinking party, "Get away from me, for death is crushing my heart, and how can I tell whether it will shortly take it? I hate to stay alive, for this life is death, and
30   I did not realize it." He will not go up to take rest in bed, but

254

rolls on the ground and gasps for breath; he will cry aloud and moan and pay no attention to those who see him relieving himself or who scold him when he cries out. His eyes will be like streams, gushing with water as from a spring, instead of means of vision. That man will esteem every [other] person as happy as an angel, whether he belongs to the present or to the past or those who have not yet known the world. Even every beast and every reptile creeping on the ground, and everything that has *the breath of life (cf. Gen. 7:14–15)*, he will think to be happy, as he says, "How blessed are all the things that God has created, who spend their time without pain and in joy of life and soul, while I alone am burdened with the weight of my offenses and am judged with the fire of judgment and suffer pain in solitude upon the earth!" He has the same opinion of every soul and reveres it as though it were holy to the Lord and venerates it as though it were pure of all [offenses]. He makes no distinction between the righteous and the unrighteous, but looks on all as equal, pure and impure alike. He alone is separated from all creation that is below the heaven, and sits on the dunghill of unspeakable sins, encompassed by the darkness of ignorance and sorrow, a darkness without end. He will scratch the pus of his wounds, not with a potsherd like Job *(Job 2:8)*, but with his fingernails because of the extreme pain of his heart. Though Job was stricken in his flesh, yet he had a soul that was under God's protection *(cf. Job 2:6)*; but that man has seen his soul poisoned by sins no less than his body, and therefore his pain is ten times worse than the plague of Job. After that his kinsmen according to the flesh and all his acquaintances and friends in the world will leave him; for when they have been with him for a short time and wept over his inconsolable affliction and seen how his soul cannot be comforted, they will look on him as an object of horror and each of them will go home.

40

50

60

[§ 2. TURNING TO THE LORD.]

When he has been left alone he sees himself in the midst of solitude, misery, affliction, and pain. So he will weep in the pain of his soul, and in his despair cry out to the Lord Almighty:

"Behold, O Lord, Thou seest, and there is nothing Thou dost not see. I am the work of Thy hands, yet I have not performed the works of Thy commandments, but in my folly I have

70　followed after all wickedness. Thou art good, yet I did not know Thee; but now I have heard of Thee and I tremble and do not know what to do. I have perceived Thy judgment, and no word in my defense was found in my mouth. I have done nothing to compensate for a single 'idle word' *(Mt. 12:36)* of my mouth. Even if a man perform all righteousness, he would do it as a slave and a debtor; he would find nothing to repay for his sin, for 'mercy is with Thee' *(Ps. 130:7)*. For sin is death *(cf. Rom. 5:12, 6:23)*, and who is there who dies because of it and raises himself up? Indeed, no one! Thou alone art He who died and didst rise again, for Thou hast committed no sin, nor was guile

80　found in Thy mouth *(cf. 1 Pet. 2:22)*. But who is he who dies in his sins and does not repent? Yet it will avail him nothing!

　　"Thus, O Almighty Master, I too repent for having committed evil deeds, yet my repentance serves not to justify me, for repentance is but the recognition of sin *(Rom. 3:20)*. Now, O all-seeing Lord, Thou seest that I have nothing but my body, but it profits me nothing to be deprived of riches. I am wounded all over and nowhere is there left me an opportunity of salvation, for I have been left abandoned and hell has swallowed me up

90　alive. And Thou, O Lord, seest it; Thou alone canst bring me up and heal the pain of my heart, for Thy hand is able to do all things and reaches the uttermost abyss, working all things at Thy pleasure. I dare not say, 'Have mercy on me,' for I am unworthy; but Thou, O Lord, seest [me].''

[§ 3. THE LORD GRANTS HEALING.]

　　So God in His compassion will speedily hear him and will hasten to grant him relief from his pain and deliverance from the distress of his heart. For since He loves man He cannot bear to see the work of His hands in such need and in such intoler-

100　able pain. If that man has done without fail everything that we have mentioned He will deal with him and with all those who in faith listen to this true pattern and account of repentance in accordance with His great and unutterable mercy. (This actually happened and was then recorded in writing!) He will pour on him His goodness and change his sorrow into joy *(Ps. 30:12)*. He will change the bitterness of his heart into the sweetness of wine, and will cause him to spew forth the poison of the dragon *(cf. Ps. 14:3)* that was burning up his innards. No more will he remember his former pains or all the evils he suffered. As for the money and property and wealth he abandoned at the time that he was smitten with penitence, he will not even return to seek them *(cf. Mt. 24:17f.; Mk. 13:15f.)*, nor will he want anything else. The Most High God will grant him health, a gift greater than all the treasures of the earth, and health will inspire ineffable joy in his heart. The joy in his heart will be tenfold greater than his past affliction, and this joy will drive out every pain that comes to his body from without. That man will realize that thenceforth the wounds of his body will not reach his heart, that outward affliction will not affect the joy that is in his heart. The knowledge of this will the more add to the joy that he has in his heart.

As for his neighbors who in time past had seen his outward afflictions, but are ignorant of the hidden joy that has come upon him afterwards, they will groan at him, saying, "Look at the man who never knew joy in his life, and whose life was all affliction and pain; his days are no different from those of criminals who suffer punishment by the lash for their offenses."

[§ 4. THE JOY THAT FOLLOWS ON HEALING.]

That man, however, is aware that his time is filled with gladness and joy. The joy of his heart mocks death and "hell has no dominion over it" *(Rom. 6:9)*, for such joy has no end. For all these reasons he has ten thousand times more joy than all the kings who rule the earth, than all who enjoy health and soundness of body, than all who are possessed of wealth and purple robes and fine linen, than all who are proclaimed as happy by the mouths of those who speak falsely. He knows that poverty accompanied by such joy is greater than all the world and the things it contains, for heaven will cover, hell will devour, death will have dominion over all the things that belong to his body and to all his life. On the other hand, the joy that has come to his soul from his healing cannot be overcome by any of these things, since it does not come from this world. It has not come to him from his glory, nor from abundant wealth, nor from his bodily health, nor from the praise of men, nor from anything else that is under heaven. It is the result of the affliction and bitterness of his soul, together with his encounter with the Spirit of God who is above the heavens. As the Spirit presses and fil-

110

120

130

140

150

257

ters his heart [as in a winepress], so it produces a joy that is genuine and unmixed with affliction. For this reason death will have no dominion over it—no blemish will be found in it. But it will be like wine that has been strained and is held up against the sun[light] shining brilliantly and showing its color more clearly and flashing joyfully on the face of him who drinks it as he faces the sun.

[§ 5. THE MYSTICAL INTOXICATION.]

But in these matters there is one thing that I cannot understand. I do not know which pleases me the more, the sight of the sun's rays and the delight of their purity, or the drinking and the taste of the wine that is in my mouth. I would say it is the latter, yet the former attracts me and appears more pleasant to me. Yet as I look at it, I derive more pleasure from the sweetness of tasting, so that I am not sated with seeing nor filled from drinking. For when I think that I have drunk my fill, then the beauty of the rays that pass through it redoubles my thirst and I crave it again. The more I am eager to fill my stomach, my mouth burns ten times as much and I am inflamed by the thirst and desire for that most transparent drink.

He who is judged by this good judgment will fear no further punishment or torment, nor will he be afraid of the trials that come upon him. His thirst will never be quenched for all eternity, and the sweet and transparent drink will never fail him. The sweetness of the drink and the joy-bringing beam that comes from the sun will drive away every sorrow from his soul, and will make that man to "rejoice always" *(Phil. 4:4)*. No one will be able to prevail against him by harming him *(cf. Jer. 15:18 LXX)*, nor will anyone be able to prevent him from having his fill from this cup as from a fountain. As for him who rules the earth by wickedness, the ruler of darkness, who rules over all the water of the sea and plays with the world as one who holds a little sparrow in his hand, with all his army and all his power he will not approach the heel of his foot and will not dare boldly to look upon him. For the shining of the wine and the beam of the sun as they shine on the face of him who drinks penetrate to his inward parts, to his hands, his feet, his back, and transform him wholly into fire. They give him the power to burn and melt the enemies that approach him from every side. He becomes dear to the sunlight and a friend of the sun. To the transparent wine belonging to the rays that issue from it he becomes like a beloved son, for the drink is his nourishment purging the infection of his putrified flesh. That purging becomes his complete healing, and his health does not permit him to feed on some other food that causes disease, but gives him an infinite burning desire to drink of that wine and by it purify himself and achieve health. The beauty of that health and the delight of the appearance that results from that health have no limit.[1]   200

[§ 6. THE MYSTICAL WINEPRESS.]

So, my beloved children, my sons whom I have acquired, who listen to my words, it will happen that everyone who has sinned before God Almighty will feel fear in his heart of the judgment and of God's turning away from him. The fear of the Lord and the realization of His just retribution wastes away the flesh and breaks the bones, just as the stone moved by the mechanism presses the grapes that are in the winepress and crushes them completely. First men trample on the clusters,   210
then they crush them under the stone and press out all the juice from them. So when a man enters into the fear of God, that very fear causes him to be trodden under foot by all others. When that fear has completely pressed down and crushed the pride and vainglory of his "mind of the flesh" *(Rom. 8:6f.)*, then holy humility, that very light and gentle spiritual stone, comes down from above and presses out all the moisture of carnal pleasures and passions. This does not render useless the soul that has been pressed down; rather, it waters the soul with floods of tears. It   220
causes the living water *(Jn. 4:10)* to spring forth to heal the wounds inflicted by sin as it washes away the pus and the sores, and so makes that man altogether "whiter than snow" *(Ps. 51:9)*.

How blessed, then, is that man who hears these words and accepts them with faith and performs them *(Mt. 7:24)*! When he has found great blessings that surpass mind, word, and thought,

---

1. The symbolism of the mystical "intoxication" derives from passages such as Psalm 23:5: "My cup shall be full," and the accusation by the detractors of the apostles in Acts 2:13 that they were "drunk with new wine." While the theme is a traditional one, the development and imagery in Symeon's case is original, as an image of man's total transformation by the Holy Spirit. Thus the "sun" in the preceding would symbolize Christ, the "wine" the Holy Spirit.

230   he will call my miserable hand blessed for having written these things. He will give glory to the merciful Lord, who is rich in pity, because He, through a defiled and unclean tongue and a defiled mouth, has committed them to writing as a pattern for conversion and repentance and for an unfailing and most true road for those, who with all their soul desire to be saved. It is such who will inherit the kingdom that is in God our Savior Himself, to whom be glory forever. Amen.

XXIV

ON SPIRITUAL KNOWLEDGE

How the treasure of the Spirit hidden in the letter of Holy Writ is not plain to all, even if they are willing, but only to those who possess Him who "opens the mind to understand the Scripture" *(Lk. 24:45)*.

[§ 1. THE CLOSED CHEST OF HOLY WRIT.]

Brethren and fathers,

Spiritual knowledge is like a house built in the midst of secular and pagan knowledge, in which there is laid up, like a solid and well-secured chest, the knowledge of the inspired Scriptures   10
and the inestimable riches they contain. Those who enter into the house will never at all be able to see those treasures unless this chest is opened for them. But it does not belong to human wisdom *(cf. 1 Cor. 2:13)* ever to be able to open it, so that the riches of the Spirit deposited in it remain unknown to all who are worldly.

A man might pick up the entire chest and carry it on his shoulders without knowing what treasure is contained in it. So a person may read the Scriptures and commit them all to memory   20
and carry them with him as if they were but one psalm, and yet be ignorant of the gift of the Holy Spirit hidden within them. It is not by the chest that its contents are exposed, nor is it by the Scripture that the contents of Scripture become clear. How is this so? Listen!

[§ 2. THE TREASURE THAT LIES WITHIN.]

You see a small chest, firmly secured on every side. By means of its weight and its external beauty you conjecture, or perhaps believe from what you have heard, that it contains a

treasure. You pick it up quickly and go off with it. But tell me,
30   what will it profit you if you constantly carry it about closed
and locked without opening it? As long as you live you will never see the treasure it contains; you will not see the sparkling of
its precious stones, the luster of its pearls, the flashing gleam of
its gold. What will you profit, if you are not found worthy to
take even a small part of it to buy some food or clothing? But if,
as we have said, you carry the chest about with you entirely
sealed, even though it is filled with a great and costly treasure,
will you not be worn out with hunger, thirst, and nakedness?
You will not profit at all!

40   Pay heed to me, brother, and apply this to spiritual things.
Think of the chest as the Gospel of Christ and the other divine
Scriptures. In them there is enclosed and sealed up eternal life
together with the unutterable and eternal blessings which it
contains, though unseen by physical eyes. As the Lord's word
says, "Search the Scriptures, for in them is eternal life" *(Jn.
5:39)*. As for the man who carries the chest about, think of him
as one who learns all the Scriptures by heart and always quotes
them with his mouth. He carries them about in the memory of
50   his soul as in a chest containing God's commandments as precious stones *(cf. Ps. 19:11)* wherein is eternal life. For Christ's
words are light and life, as He Himself says, "He who does not
obey the Son shall not see life" *(Jn. 3:36)*. Together with the
commandments [it contains] the virtues, like pearls.

[§ 3. THE COMMANDMENTS, GATES OF KNOWLEDGE.]

From the commandments spring the virtues, and from
them the revelation of the mysteries that are hidden and veiled
in the letter. From the fulfillment of the commandments comes
the practice of the virtues; through the practice of the virtues
the commandments are fulfilled. Thus by means of these the
60   door of knowledge has been opened to us *(cf. Lk. 11:52)*; or, rather, it has been opened, not by them, but by Him who has said,
"He who loves Me will keep My commandments, and My Father will love him, and I will reveal Myself to him" *(Jn. 14:23,
21)*. When, therefore, God "lives in us and moves among us" *(2
Cor. 6:16)* and perceptibly reveals Himself to us, then we consciously contemplate the contents of the chest, the divine mys-

teries that are hidden in the divine Scripture. Let no one deceive himself—in no other way it is possible for the chest of knowledge to be opened to us, and for us to enjoy the good things that it contains and partake of them and contemplate them.

But what are these good things of which I speak? They consist in perfect love (that is, toward God and our neighbor), contempt of all things that are visible, mortification of the flesh and "its members that are on the earth" *(Col. 3:5)*, including evil desire. Just as a dead man has no thought whatever and perceives nothing, so we ourselves shall have no thoughts of evil desire or of passionate sentiment at any time. We shall not feel the tyrannical oppression of the evil one, but be mindful only of the commandments of our Savior Christ. [We shall think of] immortality, of the incorruption of eternal glory, of the kingdom of heaven, of [our] adoption as sons through the regeneration of the Holy Spirit. Thereby we become sons by adoption and grace, we are called "heirs of God and fellow-heirs of Christ" *(Rom. 8:17)*, and together with these things we acquire "the mind of Christ" *(1 Cor. 2:16)* and through Him see God and Christ Himself dwelling in us and moving among us in a way that we can know *(2 Cor. 6:16)*.

All these things are granted to those who hear God's commandments and do them; they enjoy them abundantly together with those unutterable and ineffable things that are above these things, through the opening of the chest of which we have spoken, that is, the uncovering of the eyes of our minds and the contemplation of the things that are hidden in Holy Writ. But others, who lack the knowledge and experience of any of the things of which we have spoken, have no taste of their sweetness, of the immortal life derived from them, since they lean on the mere study of the Scriptures. Nay, rather, this very study will judge and condemn them at their departure [from this life] even more than those who have not heard the Scriptures at all. Some of these men err through ignorance and pervert all the divine Scriptures *(cf. 2 Pet. 3:16)* as they interpret them in accordance with their passionate desires. They wish to commend themselves *(cf. 2 Cor. 10:12)* as though they were to be saved apart from the exact observance of Christ's commandments, and so they altogether deny the power of the Holy Scriptures.

70

80

90

100

[§ 4. THE TREASURY OF THE MYSTERIES OPENED BY THE HOLY SPIRIT.]

This is natural, for the things that are sealed up and closed, unseen and unknown by all men, are opened up by the Holy Spirit alone. When they have thus been unveiled they become visible and knowable to us. How then will those who claim that they have never known at all the Holy Spirit's presence, radiance, illumination, and His coming to dwell in them have the power to know or perceive or think of them in any way? How shall they apprehend such mysteries, who have never at all experienced in themselves the recasting, renewal, transformation, reshaping, regeneration, that He brings about? Those who have not yet been baptized in the Holy Spirit *(Mt. 3:11),* how can they know the change that comes over those who have been baptized in Him? Those who have not been "Born from above" *(Jn. 3:3),* how shall they see the glory of those who have been "born from above" (as the Lord said), those who have been born of God *(Jn. 1:13)* and have become the children of God *(Jn. 1:12)?* Those who have refused to experience this, but by their negligence have missed this glory—for they have received the power to become such *(cf. Jn. 1:12)*—tell me, what knowledge will enable them to understand or in any way imagine what the others have become?

God is Spirit *(Jn. 4:24),* invisible, immortal, inaccessible, imcomprehensible. Those who are born of Him He makes to be such as Himself, like the Father who has begotten them. They may be touched and seen in body only; in other respects they are known to God alone and know only Him; or, rather, they wish to be known to God alone *(cf. Gal. 4:9)* and constantly strive to look to Him and are anxious to be seen by Him. To express it differently, just as the illiterate cannot read books like those who are literate, neither can those who have refused to go through the commandments of Christ by practicing them be granted the revelation of the Holy Spirit like those who have brooded over them and fulfilled them and shed their blood for them. The man who takes a sealed and closed book cannot see what is written in it nor can he understand its subject as long as the book remains sealed *(Is. 29:11),* even though he may have learned all the wisdom of the world. Likewise even he who, as

we have said, has learned all the divine Scriptures by heart will
never be able to know and perceive the mystical and divine glo-   140
ry and power hidden in them without going through all God's
commandments and taking the Paraclete with him. [The Para-
clete] will open to him the words like a book and mystically
show him the glory they contain. Indeed, with the eternal life
that causes them to spring forth, He will as well reveal the blessings of God hidden in them, blessings that are veiled and utterly
invisible to the despisers and the negligent. This is to be expect-   150
ed, since they have nailed all their senses to the vanity of the
world and are passionately attached to the pleasures of life and
to physical beauty. But since the vision of their souls is dimmed,
they are unable to see and contemplate the intellectual beauties
of God's unutterable blessings.

[§ 5. HOW THE EYES OF FLESH CANNOT SEE SPIRITUAL BEAUTY.]

One whose bodily eyes are weak cannot at all look on a
brightly shining sunbeam; if he stares at it he at once loses such
sight as he still has. So he whose spiritual eyes are weak and
whose senses are subject to passions cannot contemplate the excellence or beauty of a body without passion or harm to himself.   160
Whatever peace of thought he possessed before, whatever calm
of evil desire, he loses them as he lingers to reflect on the passion. Consequently such a person is wholly unable to perceive
even his own infirmity. For if he has thought that he was sick it
was because he believed that there were others who were
healthy, and perhaps he blamed himself for being the cause of
his sickness and was concerned for getting rid of it. Now, however, such a person holds that all men are subject to passions and
looks on himself as their equal, and claims that it is impossible
for him to be better than all others. Why is this? So that this   170
wretched man may with them succumb to passion, since he is
unwilling to rid himself of such an evil. Had he been willing, he
would have had the strength, for he would have received the
ability from God. For as many of us as were baptized into His
Name have received from Him the power to divest ourselves of
our past inborn corruption like an old garment, and to become
sons of God and clothed with Christ (*cf. Col. 3:9f.; Gal. 3:27*).

[§ 6. FINAL ADMONITION.]

But far be it from us, brethren, to become like those who take this attitude and think such thoughts, men of earth, and utterly dried up. Rather, may we follow Christ, who has died for us and has risen *(2 Cor. 5:15)* and exalted us to heaven. Let us continually follow in His footsteps, being cleansed by penitence from the defilement of sin and clothed in the bright garment of incorruption *(cf. 1 Cor. 15:53f.)* that belongs to the Spirit, in the same Christ our God, to whom is due all glory, honor, and adoration, forever and ever. Amen.

XXV

[THE INTERACTION OF BODY AND SOUL]

On the changes of soul and body, some of which happen to us from the air, some from the elements, and some from the demons.

[§ 1. THE VARIED STATES OF SOUL.]

Brethren and fathers,

The monk must know not only the changes and transformations that take place in the soul but also their causes: the nature of these causes, and their origins. At times a sudden joy arises in the soul, at other times sorrow comes on it and a great burden. Sometimes compunction comes easily to it, sometimes the same soul becomes hardened and is as hard as a rock. Again, at times it becomes gentle and humble *(cf. Mt. 11:29)*, and a little later distracted, irascible, and angry at all the brethren. At times it becomes soft and slack, without eagerness for any good work *(cf. Tit. 1:16)*; at times it is roused and vigilant and eager for all obedience, so that it incites and spurs on its fellows to that which is good. Sometimes it is devout and recollected, at other times dissipated and shameless. Sometimes it is lovingly mindful of those who are absent and summons them to itself; at other times it is unwilling to look at them or even at those who are in its company. Sometimes it is internally oppressed as though it would renounce life itself *(cf. Jonah 4:8)*; at other times is it so elated and increases so greatly in joy that it cannot contain itself, even by doing violence to itself.

[§ 2. STATES OF MIND.]

Such are the usual manifestations of the natural movements of the soul and the body, whenever we are in an aggressive

30

mood with regard to the practice of virtue and the fulfillment of the commandments. But just as the state of the soul undergoes changes, in the same way the state of our minds undergoes changes and is somehow transformed. Sometimes it is keen in understanding, and even keener to reflect on the things it has grasped or seen and to discern them quickly; at other times it becomes sluggish and slow in both respects. Sometimes the same mind seems to be dull witted, and even speechless and dumb, so to speak; at other times sprightly of wit and speech, quick to hear and to understand. Sometimes it seems to be blind, at other times sharp-sighted, forcing itself to penetrate into the depth and height of contemplation beyond the measure of human nature. At times the mind is simple and free for all contemplation,

40

without any memory whatever of evils that have befallen it in the past and without ever thinking of them at all; at other times it is complex, such as thinking of things that do not happen, and it schemes and plans ill. It becomes like a flame in green wood smothered by smoke and not only plans ill against those who are at hand, but very often forms vain and false imaginations concerning some who are absent. When this happens, even though the heart is very sorrowful, it is no help at all that it does not consent to the mind, but is unable to turn it aside from those vain reasonings.

[§ 3. HOW THE MIND IS TO BLAME FOR THE LUSTS
OF THE BODY.]

50

So much, then, for the changes of our minds and our intellectual and divine souls. As for the irregularities that concern our bodies, even though they may seem easy to diagnose and recognize on our part, yet this is not the case. The body in particular is subject to much change that, for the most part, has a natural cause. The soul is by nature and essence immutable, and so is the mind, which the Creator has formed simultaneously with it. Both of them are moved by free choice, and by their own will they lay hold on virtue or vice, that is, for all eternity they become partakers and heirs of either light or darkness.

60

That is to say, the soul and the mind adhere to the one or the other of these by their own free will and choice, as I have said, either to goodness, so that they become good, or to wickedness, and so become wicked. The body, however, is by nature subject to change because it is composite; in essence it is changeable since it is created out of corruptible and changeable matter, being a mixture or a compound of mutually opposite elements. Its essence is composed of hot and cold, as those who are knowledgeable in those matters say (and it is true), of dry and moist. As such the body has neither liberty nor will, and, if I must say so, not even movement, unless one were to call its mutability 70 and its tendency to move toward corruption a natural movement of its substance, which would be an irrational one. But if it is irrational, it is clear that it is also nonsinful and without condemnation before God. Rightly so, for that which follows its nature does not fall under condemnation. But fiery lust and the desire for marriage, sexual union, voluptuousness, gluttony, greed in eating, excessive sleep, idleness, pretentiousness in dress, and all the other things that, as most people think, the body seeks for—it is not the body as such, since it does not seek them when it is dead, but the soul that through the body seeks pleasure by their means. Since it has once mingled itself with clay and found pleasure in wallowing in mud like a pig *(2 Pet.* 80 *2:22),* so to speak, it is eager for the flesh with which it is mingled. Let nobody therefore think that he is being driven to these things and compelled by his own body! It is not true. But how? Listen and consider.

[§ 4. ADAM AND EVE WITHOUT CONCUPISCENCE IN EDEN.]

"God formed man, taking dust from the ground" *(Gen. 2:7).* I have shown you the body, now show me, on your part, what sort of passions it has. But you have nothing at all to say! What then? "And the Lord breathed into his face, and man became a living soul" *(ibid.).* So he arose from the ground and walked. 90 Clearly it was the spirit that was in him that moved him, that is, his body, as its master with authority over it. But fiery lust and movement, or irrational madness and desire, as yet did not at all exist, but in him was life without internal discord and his existence knew no pain. Let us then see whether it was because he lacked a wife or was without food that stirred him up to desire. Was he moved either to lust for sexual union or to gluttony? What does [Scripture] say? "God made to grow every tree that is pleasant to the sight *(Gen. 2:9),* and "Adam and Eve were in the

100 garden naked and were not ashamed" *(Gen. 2:25)*. Do you see that neither the fact that Eve was female, nor that they were both naked, caused either of them to lose self-control? They were indeed naked, and did not know each other, nor were they ashamed, nor were they compelled by the nature of the body to have intercourse. It was after they had sinned and transgressed and had been expelled from paradise, despoiled of God and fallen from His divine glory, that, as it is written, "Adam knew his wife and she conceived and gave birth" *(Gen. 4:1)*.

110 Accordingly, my dear man, if you love God genuinely and you also persevere in His love *(cf. Jn. 15:9, 10)*, you will never be dominated by any passion, nor will you be reduced to subjection by any necessity of the body. For since the body cannot be moved to anything apart from the soul, so the soul that is united to God by love cannot be led astray to the pleasures and cravings of the body, nor indeed to any other desires of anything visible or invisible, whether desire or passion. For by the sweet love of God the impulse of its heart, or, rather, the whole inclination of its will, is bound. When once, as I have said, it has

120 been bound to its Maker, how can it be inflamed by the body or in any way fulfill its own desires? In no way!

[§ 4. THE PHYSICAL CHANGES OF THE BODY.]

As for the changes that naturally ensue and take place in the same body, they are obvious, for they happen in the case of all the saints. Sometimes the body is said to be healthy, when its components are not at variance with each other; at other times it is compelled to give way to sickness, whenever any of the four elements becomes excessive or deficient, that is, when one prevails over the others or is dominated or suppressed by them.

130 Thus arise fluxes, mutilations, perhaps even the corruption of the entire organism. Yet our soul suffers no damage from these causes, for, while most of them are produced by excess in food and drink, some are produced by the alternation of winds and air. When it is cold, the bodies that are cold by nature are harmed and weakened, because they become too cold, while those that are of a warm composition become better balanced and stronger. But when the air again becomes hot, the cold are

140 warmed and revived, just as when the sun's rays shine on the flies and other insects and make them stronger and more mo-

bile. Those, however, that have a warmer matter are heated to excess and are enfeebled and become weak and useless for all activity and motion. So each body in accordance with its own temperament is similarly subject to change from the alternation of the air and the winds. But even apart from these a change independently comes about from excessive eating and drinking or from extreme fasting, and not from these alone, but also from excessive sleeping or wakefulness and from exertion or inactivity of the body. Another change again is that of the matter that is 150 in the body and the natural heat that moves within us, which is like a fire that gives off steam like coals that are being put out with water, and which sometimes reach only the head, at other times penetrate the whole body.

[§ 5. THE HEAVINESS OF THE BODY—A SPIRITUAL TRIAL.]

In addition to all these things there is yet another trial, which in His providence our good God and Master permits the demons to inflict on us to train us in humility. In what does it consist? The very weight of our body, which apart from any 160 other cause, solely on account of vanity, or pride, or the mutual accusation of carelessness, or for many other reasons, delivers us to this demon for the destruction of our flesh *(1 Cor. 5:5)* and the affliction of the soul. But it is also for the testing and the greater training of the soul, in order that we may recognize God's compassion and mercy toward us, and turn our whole love toward Him with full purpose, and attain to an exclusive desire for Him.

[§ 6. THE INTERACTION OF SOUL, MIND, AND BODY.]

Not all know these things. As for the alterations of the soul and the changes of the body, each of those who are in a middle 170 state with regard to virtue recognize some of these things whenever such things happen to them. As for those who are in complete darkness, we have nothing to say. In the case of the changes and turns of the mind we have mentioned above, it is only those who are free from passion and perfect, who are pure and free in soul as well as in mind, who know these. Not even they know it, for it does not come from themselves, but from Him to whom they belong and by whom they have been taught.

180 Sometimes the vicissitudes that take place in the mind cause the soul to become oppressed and gloomy by depriving it of part of the joy that belongs to it; yet it takes courage and raises up the mind. Sometimes the mind shares in the sufferings of the soul, and so is compelled to be in the night; yet it does not accept it, but forces itself to remain in the light and perhaps even succeeds in giving light to the soul. Sometimes both are tyrannically oppressed by the vicissitudes of the body, at times burdened from without, yet while they are aware of their burden they keep intact their equilibrium and their peace. At other times they are agitated and perturbed from within and totally subject to passions, to the extent that the sufferer loses hope of ever returning

190 to his past equilibrium and calm. So then the soul and the mind are troubled by the body, the mind by the soul itself, and the soul in turn by the mind and the body. It is not always both the soul and the mind that are perturbed by the body. Sometimes it is the soul alone that suffers, while the mind says to it, "What is wrong with you?" and comforts it. At other times the mind is blinded and covered with a veil, while the soul remains free and by the power of the divine fire expels the darkness, removes the veil *(cf. 2 Cor. 3:14)*, and makes the soul to see clearly.

[§ 7. HOW TO GOVERN OUR SOULS WELL.]

200 This is why I told you, fathers and brethren, that it is necessary not only to know the turns and changes and alterations that come upon us, but also to know their origins and the manner in which they come—their causes, what winds of thoughts blow, and whence the floods of passions and trials come to assault us. By knowledge of the symptoms we may securely strengthen the house of the soul *(cf. Mt. 7:24–25)* and steer the rudder of the ship properly with skill and understanding. The knowledge of all this comes from a life lived continually in strict discipline

210 and with a rule. What is required of a monk is that he fix in himself a standard and a pattern and that he know how he ought to spend every day, so that he may run well in the practice of virtue, and not stumble, through lack of experience, as he runs the race. In this way he will level for himself the rough and difficult way *(cf. Lk. 3:5)*; he trains himself by disposition and habit to run it and benefit from it. As he advances toward God and "keeps the ways in his heart" *(Ps. 84:6)*, he will be well pleasing

to Him as he advances from the lesser things to the greater and more perfect. He will acquire knowledge of all the things we have mentioned and become a teacher of virtue for many others. By his word and life he will give light to those who encounter   220 him, since he is himself enlightened from above, and reveals deep things to those who with desire seek to learn the depths of the Spirit *(cf. 1 Cor. 2:10)*, in Christ Jesus our Lord, to whom be glory forever. Amen.

XXVI

[THE DAY OF THE MONK]

On the beginning of an exceedingly useful and salutary life—appropriate for those who have newly renounced the world and the things in the world and have gone into the monastic life. A very profitable instruction for beginners.

[§ 1. THE ELEMENTS OF THE MONASTIC LIFE.]

Brethren and fathers,

Every person who has newly renounced the world and the things in the world *(1 John 2:15)* and fled to this life in the arena of monks: If it is for God's sake that he has made this renunciation he must choose to learn this art of arts! If he does not want his withdrawal from the world to be in vain he must from the very beginning apply himself to that which pertains to virtue with all eagerness and most ardent will. So, in order that we may supply in writing an introduction to the elements of the science of sciences, that is, our ascetic practice, to those who have newly come from the world to enter, as it were, this school, we set forth these things as a preamble, as in a rule, for them and for those who will succeed them, just as we ourselves have received these principles by tradition from our fathers.

[§ 2. HOW THE MONKS MUST ASSIST AT THE OFFICES.]

Let it be noted that he who has already outwardly laid aside *(cf. Col. 3:9)* the earthly man *(cf. 1 Cor. 15:47–49)* with his attitude of mind, and by assuming the monastic habit clothed himself *(cf. Eph. 4:24; Col. 3:10)* with the heavenly man *(1 Cor. 15:48–49)*, must rise at midnight before the Night Office[1] and

10

20

---

1. I.e., Orthros, corresponding roughly to Latin matins and lauds. In its monastic form (now universal in the Orthodox Church) it is a very long service,

274

recite the prescribed prayer. After so doing he must rise with all to go to the service of praise, and with attention and vigilance go through the whole service. He must pay particular attention to the beginning of the hymnody, that is, the six psalms,[2] the psalm verses,[3] and the lections,[4] with great concentration, without relaxation of body or putting one foot in front of another or leaning on walls or pillars, but holding his hands securely together, the feet equally on the ground, and the head immobile without nodding here and there. The mind must not wander off, nor the thoughts be occupied with curiosity or interest in the more careless brethren as they talk or whisper to each other. On the contrary, the eye and the soul must be kept free from distraction and pay attention to nothing else but the psalmody and the reading and, as far as possible, to the meaning of the words of the divine Scripture that are being sung or read, so that not one of these words may pass in vain, but rather that his soul may derive nourishment from all of them and attain to compunction and humility and the divine illumination of the Holy Ghost.

So, my fathers and my brethren and children, I entreat you all as one man, and recommend it to you as a salutary law, that each of you endeavor to lay such a foundation for the work of virtue. For, to put it more accurately, it is God's work, through which we receive from Him of His generosity rewards proportionate to our efforts. If possible, let none of you spend the time of the Office and the reading without tears! For if you so accustom yourself, O brother, to carry out this work, you will make progress in a short time and attain "to mature manhood, to the

---

about two hours. It is this which is being described in this Catechesis. The monk is to recite the preliminary prayer in his cell before betaking himself to the church.

2. In two groups of three, 3, 38, 63 and 88, 103, and 143, recited at the beginning of the office.

3. The section of the psalter recited at Orthros. The whole psalter is divided into twenty kathismata, of which two or three are recited at Orthros and one at Vespers, so that the whole is recited once a week. The kathisma derives its name from being recited sitting.

4. From the Synaxarion (lives of saints, homilies for great feasts, etc.) or the works of Fathers such as S. Chrysostom, S. Ephrem, S. John Climacus. The catecheses or instructions for monks, begun by S. Theodore of Studios, and continued, e.g., by Symeon, were preached at Prime.

measure of the stature of the fullness of Christ" *(Eph. 4:13)*. If you force yourself so that you do not go through the appointed office of the Church without tears, you will acquire this excellent habit, and during the psalm verses and the troparia[5] you sing your soul will be fed. It will receive the divine thoughts into itself, and through that which is recited your mind will be carried up to things spiritual. And as you weep sweet tears your time spent in church will be as if you were in heaven itself with the Powers that are on high.

60 So make this a law for yourself, that you never leave before the last prayer of the Office, unless there is urgent necessity or physical need. As we have said, remain standing in your place, for, as it is written, "He who endures to the end will be saved" *(Mt. 10:22)*. Not only will he be saved, but he will receive help, at first without perceiving it; later he will perceive it, and soon he will receive it in the illumination that comes from Almighty God.

[§ 3. WORK AND SILENCE BETWEEN THE OFFICES.]

Once the morning Office of praise is finished do not, as soon as you have left the church, start talking to one man and the other and so be distracted in idle talk. Rather pray in the
70 solitude of your cell, and when you have recited the appointed prayer with tears and great recollection, take on some physical labor and at once go off to perform it. If it is some appointed task, go off to that task; if it is manual labor, go off to it; if it is study, go off to study. Refuse altogether to sit in your cell without some occupation, lest idleness teach you every kind of evil *(Sirach 30:37)* of which one may not even speak. Do not go about the monastery to inspect those who work or perform services, but observe that silence and detachment from all things in which true solitude consists. Take heed to yourself alone and to your manual work, whatever it is.

80 Do not enter into the cell of anyone without the permission of him who is your father according to God, unless you have been sent by the superior or by some office holder of the monas-

---

5. Short rhythmic hymns characteristic of the Byzantine divine office.

tery. When you go there, endeavor neither to speak nor to hear a word apart from the necessity for which you were sent. When you have performed your errand, return quickly. If on your way you see a brother by himself, or sitting down with others and chatting outside the time, make a reverence and pass in silence. Do not go to sit with them, but be mindful of the psalmist's saying, "Blessed is the man that hath not walked in the counsel of the ungodly, nor stood in way of sinners: and hath not sat in the seat of the scornful" *(Ps. 1:1).* For such people are a plague, as Paul says, "Bad company ruins good morals" *(1 Cor. 15:33).* If a plague is anything, so is also corruption. Do not then, beloved, sit with those who talk idly, and do not say, "I too want to hear what you are saying," but as I have said, make a reverence and pass by. Observe silence and solitude, silence by saying to yourself, "What good have I to say, who am altogether mud, and a fool? Besides, I am a stranger and unworthy to speak and listen and to be numbered among men." Observe solitude and detachment from all things by thinking these thoughts and saying to yourself, "Who am I, who am rejected and worthless, base and poor, that I should enter anyone's cell? When he sees me, will he not turn away from me as from an abomination? Will he not say, 'Why did that wretch come to me to defile my cell?' " Set your sins before your eyes, and say this not by moving your lips, but from the depth of your soul. Even though at the beginning you cannot say this from your soul, yet will you gradually come to this, as grace helps you. Just listen to me in my lowliness, brother, and start to do this; merely begin to do and practice and say these things, and God will not forsake you! He loves you greatly and desires you to come to the knowledge of the truth and to be saved *(1 Tim. 2:4).*

[§ 4. AT THE SERVICE.]

So, brother, when you have spent the hours before the Liturgy in this way, go back to the service with haste and great eagerness. Stand according to the rule we outlined in the case of the morning Office of praise, and by no means forget sorrow. Stand with trembling as though you were seeing the Son of God being offered in sacrifice for you. If you are worthy and have re-

120   ceived the necessary absolution, approach with fear and joy to communicate in the ineffable blessings.[6]

[§ 5. SERVICE IN THE REFECTORY.]

When you have gone out after the last prayer, go to the table with everybody, and do not separate yourself from your brethren. If you have been ordered to serve [at table], attend to it as were you waiting on Christ and not on man *(Eph. 6:7)*, with an attitude of genuine love toward all as toward saints, or rather (as we have said) as were you about to serve Christ Himself. Embrace every one of them, so to speak, in your soul. In your intention put yourself altogether at their disposition, being assured of the fruit of holiness by waiting on them.

[§ 6. RECOLLECTION DURING MEALS.]

130   If, however, you sit at table with them all, take note of what I command you in the Lord, as my beloved father and brother. Do not hasten to stretch forth your hands to the food set before you on the table before your senior brethren have begun to eat, or before the blessing has been given from on high by the priest. When you have begun to eat together with your fathers and brethren, take heed to yourself. Sit in total recollection and silence without talking to anyone at all, but pay attention to the reading *(cf. 1 Tim. 4:13)* and so be nourished in soul, no less than

140   in body, from the inspired utterances of the Spirit. Since you are a twofold being, that is, composed of soul and body, you must likewise have twofold nourishment and a twofold table; having a physical and earthly body you must be fed with physical food from the earth, and having an intellectual and divine soul, you must be fed with intellectual and divine food of words.

[§ 7. DISCRETION AND HUMILITY AT TABLE.]

Do not be curious about the portions that are set before you on the table, which happens to be larger or smaller, but accept with all thankfulness the amount that is given to you. But eat it

---

6. It would appear that the Liturgy was offered daily in the monastery of S. Mamas, except on the nonliturgical days of Great Lent. Communion would be frequent, even on the part of novices, but would depend on the permission (absolution) of one's spiritual father.

with restraint; in all respects avoid satiety, considering yourself
to be unworthy of the common table of the brethren. Let such   150
be your private thoughts, as you say to yourself, "Who am I, the
worthless and unworthy one, that I should have become one
who shares the seats and the table of these saints?" As you are
thus saying these words within yourself, with your soul consider yourself alone to be a sinner. Just as a poor man dressed in
rags, were he to be found in the midst of rulers and rich men
dressed in splendid and costly clothing, would be ashamed and
draw back and would not venture to approach any one of them
or be near him, so let your attitude be toward them all. Always   160
choose the lowest place for yourself and be ashamed to be found
seated in the presence of any of them *(cf. Lk. 14:9f.)*, as if they
were all rich in virtues, while you are poor and naked *(cf. Rev.
3:17)* and unworthy of even being with them and seeing them.
When you are about to touch food think these thoughts again
and remember your sins and say to yourself, "Will it not be to
my judgment and condemnation if I touch anything that is set before me? God has made these things and provided them for our
food; ever since I was a child I have disobeyed and have not kept
His holy commandments. How shall I partake of His benefits,
like these holy fathers, since I am unworthy and subject to con-   170
demnation? I am an evil servant *(Mt. 25:26)*, far from the sight of
my Master, ungrateful and unthankful. Under what pretense
can I eat and drink and rejoice with the saints, when I have not
yet repented and received full pardon from God, who loves
mankind, like those who have never sinned, or who, when they
have sinned, have received His pardon? By no means! I shall eat
and drink merely to stay alive; I shall make myself waste away
and grieve by condemning myself, that God may look on me   180
from on high and see my distress and my voluntary affliction,
and have mercy and pardon my many evils." Think of these
things; remember them constantly!

[§ 8. ABSTEMIOUSNESS IN FOOD.]

Furthermore, when you eat your bread determine to eat
only so much, that you avoid satiety and so, as far as you can endure it, eat much less than your appetite demands. Similarly
drink one or two cups only, and only at the appointed time of
the day. When you eat do not listen to the thought that suggests

190

200

to you to choose between the things that are set before you and to partake of them, but beware of eating that which looks good to you, and eat only that which is set before you. Even if it were to happen that there should be fruits or other articles of food in front of you and one of them should appear desirable and your thought says to you, "That one is fine, take it and eat it," be careful not to give in or touch it. For no other reason was Adam cast out of paradise, than that the fruit of the tree looked beautiful to him and good to eat, and so he ate of it *(cf. Gen. 3:6)*; so he was cast out and expelled and condemned to death and corruption. Accordingly, those who would return to that paradise, or, rather, to the kingdom of heaven, must observe self-control without any transgression, even to this point, to avoid falling bit by bit into greater and harmful desires.

[§ 9. AGAINST THE ASSAULTS OF THE DEMON
OF GLUTTONY.]

210

220

If the brethren who sit with you urge you to eat or drink anything to excess, do not answer anyone, save by joining your hands and rising briefly and bowing your head and saying in a gentle tone of voice, "Excuse me!" At all times make this reply to everyone, and give preference to no one about what you leave over, nor receive anything from anybody. If you are not drinking wine, do not at all try to obtain any, and especially do not give any to one of your brethren, unless he should happen to have come from a strange [monastery] to seek you out for some needful business. Never accept an invitation to have lunch with anyone, nor to eat or drink in the evening, nor to eat after dinner. All sorts of evils arise from these occasions; they are the ambushes of the devil *(cf. Eccles. 11:29)* and his snares *(cf. 1 Tim. 3:7; 2 Tim. 2:26)*. They look fine, but contain the poison of death within them. He who believes me will flee from them, and he who observes my words with the help of God's grace will continue without being wounded or harmed by them. Others, however, without knowing it, choose to live a worldly life under a monastic habit, and they do not perceive the abysses and chasms into which they fall.

As for you, beloved brother, have the will to observe these things, even if you have to die; otherwise you will not have the strength to escape the demon of gluttony. But know that if you observe these things, the devil will not bear the sight of you. He will stir up against you all who are negligent; they will reproach you and mock you, they will be jealous of you and make fun of you and bring thousands of trials on you, in order that they may make you give up your good intention and your salutary practices. But if you endure them, beloved, you will find great help   230 and comfort from our God and Savior. Therefore, even if others sit down at dinner and eat, while you are not eating, whether or not you are waiting at table, do not forget to say this to yourself, "Had I but been penitent and myself found forgiveness for my sins, I too might have rejoiced and eaten with my brethren. But since I, wretch that I am, have made myself unworthy through my shameful actions, I here receive in accordance with my deeds!" As you say this, control your stomach, as far as you are able. As for the first place *(cf. Mt. 23:6)*, never seek it or want it,   240 but rather detest it heartily as a cause of pride and an occasion thereof. It is humility that will exalt you, and by being last you will become first of all *(cf. Mt. 19:30; Mk. 9:35)*. For it is written: "Every one who exalts himself will be humbled, but he who humbles himself will be exalted" *(Lk. 18:14)*.

[§ 10. AFTER THE MEAL.]

After you have risen from the meal with all the community and have given thanks to God and have been dismissed by the priest, run off to your cell in silence, shut your door *(cf. Mt. 6:6)*, and pick up your book. When you have read it for a short time, if it is summer, lie down on your mat and take a short nap, for if   250 you have abstained from filling yourself and eaten modest fare, with bread, a moderate amount of water, and vegetables or pulse, you will sleep less and rise again the sooner. If it is winter, after reading a little take hold of your manual work and continue with it until the wood[7] gives the signal for the singing of the Office of lamp-lighting.[8]

---

7. The semantron, a large board suspended and struck with a hammer, like a gong, still used in some monasteries.

8. The evening office, or Vespers, the opening service of the daily office, celebrated as the lamps were lit at nightfall.

[§ 11. THE EVENING OFFICE.]

Then, when you have returned to the service, stand with fear and attention before God as you sing to Him and make con-
260 fession to Him, without speaking a word to anyone. When the service of lamp-lighting is over, if you have the strength to de-prive yourself completely of eating and drinking and have final-ly made up your mind to eat only once a day, you will derive no little benefit from your attendance at the evening Office, and your night prayers and vigil. If you have not, then content your-self with one dry biscuit and a cup of water, unless you suffer from sickness or infirmity of stomach. After you have offered your evening prayers to God together with your brethren,[9] make a reverence before the feet of your superior, as at the feet
270 of Christ Himself. Receive his blessing, kiss the holy icons of the saints, and go in silence to your cell without saying a word to anyone.

[§ 12. READINGS AND PRAYERS OF THE VIGIL.]

Once you have closed your door, pick up your book, and read about six pages with attention. Then stand for prayer, qui-etly sing psalms and pray to God as one who is heard by no one else. Stand with boldness and collect your thoughts and do not allow them to roam elsewhere; join your hands, place your feet evenly together, and stand in one place without moving. Close your eyes to prevent them from looking at anything else and
280 your mind from wandering. As for your mind itself and your whole heart, lift them up to heaven and to God, invoking His mercy from on high with tears and groans. Let your psalms be prescribed by your spiritual father, such as contain words of penitence and compunction, enough to suffice for your ability and your disposition. Your singing of psalms and number of genuflexions and the length of time that you stand must corre-spond to your ability and your fortitude, so that you will not suffer the reproaches of your conscience as it says, "You still
290 had the strength to stand and sing and to make confession to

---

9. I.e., compline, often recited in private by the monks in their cells, but at S. Mamas celebrated by the whole community together in the church. It con-cluded with a request for pardon and blessing from the superior, and the venera-tion of the holy icons.

God." In addition you must have prayers of confession as well appointed for the morning and the evening. When you have finished your prayer once again read a little, then take your manual labor and watch through the night until the first watch, that is, the third hour of the night. Then, when you have risen again in this way and recited the [psalm] "Undefiled" (Psalm 119),[10] sign your whole body with the cross, and lie down on your mat. After you have slept until midnight, do afterwards as has been outlined for you above.

[§ 13. CONFESSION TO ONE'S SPIRITUAL FATHER.]

Indeed you should also confess the thoughts of your heart to your spiritual father every hour, if possible. But if not, do not put it off till evening, but after the morning Office examine yourself *(cf. 1 Cor. 4:3)* and confess all that has befallen you. Have unhesitating faith in him, even if the whole world reproach him and abuse him. Even were you yourself to see him committing fornication, do not take offense or diminish your faith in him, for you obey Him who said, "Judge not, and you will not be judged" *(Lk. 6:37)*.

If you do this every day and struggle in this way, God will not delay visiting you from on high *(cf. 2 Pet. 3:9)*. Indeed He "will send thee help from his holy habitation" *(Ps. 20:3)*, and the grace of His most Holy Spirit will overshadow you *(cf. Lk. 1:35)*! As you progress bit by bit toward your work you will grow in spiritual stature, and attain "to mature manhood, to the measure of the stature of the fullness of Christ" *(Eph. 4:13)*. You will be illuminated by the light of knowledge, like the sun, and give its light to all who draw near to you and encounter you, and glorify God both by life and by word, who has given to you the gift of His Holy and life-giving Spirit, to whom glory is due forever. Amen.

10. A characteristic feature of the Byzantine midnight Office, here obviously recited by each monk in his cell.

XXVII

[THE LEAST OF THE COMMANDMENTS]

That we should not be careless in practicing God's commandments, nor despise a single one of them, but strive to observe them all at the same time, so that we may not be cast out from the wedding feast as those who despise it. That we should courageously endure trials.

[§ 1. HOW WE MUST REACH OUR DESIRED HAVEN.]

Brethren and fathers,

Do you not hear the Lord and His apostles shouting to us, "Whoever keeps the whole law but fails in one point has become
10   guilty of all of it" *(Jas. 2:10)*? And again, "He who strives exercises self-control in all things" *(1 Cor. 9:25)*. In order to make clearer what he means he says in addition, "Whatever overcomes a man, to that he is enslaved" *(2 Pet. 2:19)*. So, brethren, he who is enslaved to any single passion is also dominated by it and is unable to obey the commandments of the Lord. How could he do so, as long as he is subject to an alien master *(Mt. 6:24; Lk. 16:13)*? But why do we not of ourselves realize the true meaning of the words of our Lord and the apostles, by duly following the indications from the things that we see?
20   We see that those who sail on the ocean are not said to have made a safe journey if they have sailed a certain number of miles and then, when they have come near their harbor, find themselves in danger and succumb to it, but only those who reach the port and get out on dry land. Similarly, those who travel by road and hasten to arrive in some city are not said to have completed their journey in safety if, when they have crossed such

284

and such a river and gone over such and such a mountain and escaped the robbers that lurk there, they subsequently fall into the
hands of some murderer or wild beast and are killed, or fall into
some pit and are suffocated. It is those who by God's help have   30
escaped from every trial and every treacherous plot who are said
to have reached the city that was their destination. Even they
may be careless or negligent after they have escaped all adversities, so that nightfall takes them by surprise and the city gates
are shut while they are still outside it, without knowing what
the next day will bring on them.

Think with me of this city as the kingdom of heaven, of the
day as the death of each one of us, and of the following day as
the Coming of the Lord God, which is the day of judgment. He   40
who has not hastened to come inside the kingdom of heaven
while he is still in the day of this life below, but is found outside
it at the departure of his soul, has the night of death fall on him.
He does not know what will happen to him on the following
day, the day of judgment, and whether or not he will be allowed
to enter.

[§ 2. THE DEER THAT DOES NOT ALLOW ITSELF
TO BE CAUGHT.]

If an antelope or a deer or any such animal has escaped a
certain hunter and his dog or avoided a certain trap, it is not said
to have escaped in safety if someone else catches up with it and
it falls into his hands. Only when it has completely avoided be-   50
ing hunted down or caught by any trap has it truly escaped. So
think of the hunters as evil demons, of the dogs as deceitful men
who teach falsehood, perverse and wicked men who are unwilling to amend their lives but presume to teach others. We must
think of these as baying hounds and flee from them, for by their
words they bite and scatter the sheep of Christ and deliver them
into the hands of the hunters.

As for the robbers, think of them as being wicked and
shameful thoughts that suddenly fall on him who strives, and
cause him either to flee and detach himself from his caravan in   60
the hope of saving himself, or else they seize him by the consent
and agreement of his mind and so tie him securely and tightly
and strike at him by the irritations and impulses of the flesh. As

they forcibly drag him off by unnatural lust they cast him down the precipice of evil action into the pit of sin.

70   [§ 3. THE PRECIOUS VESSEL THAT CONTAINS
ALL VIRTUES.]

It is therefore necessary to abstain with all one's power from all evil actions. At the same time we must cleave to all good works and keep God's commandments with fervent desire and all eagerness, without despising any of them, whatever it may be, as being least *(Mt. 5:19).* For he who says, "Would that I had never done this evil thing, nor committed this offense, for that one or that one is nothing," clearly subverts all God's commandments at one time and is a rebel against them. Now, O man, imagine some precious vessel made out of all God's commandments, such as faith, the fear of God, humility, silence from idle speech *(Mt. 12:36),* obedience unto death *(Phil. 2:8),* the elimination of every inward will and movement of the heart, unremit-

80 ting penitence and compunction, constant prayer, custody of the eyes, detachment from one's neighbor, and equal charity toward all, of absence of avarice, chastity, hope in God and perfect love toward Him, and of all other virtues that are their consequences. Each of these is as it were a leaf by itself, whether of gold, silver, bronze, or precious stone, and the rest in their order of other materials, all united into one and joined and fitted to-

90 gether by the Spirit. As has been said, they form the man into a useful vessel, into which the grace of God is poured like new wine *(cf. Mt. 9:17; Mk. 2:22; Lk. 5:37f.).* Tell me then—if any of the aforesaid virtues should be missing, out of which and by which the vessel is composed and constituted, would God allow any of the gifts of His Spirit, even in small measure, to be poured into it, if there were in it even an apparently tiny hole left by the missing leaf, that is, the place of the missing virtue? By no means! That which had been poured in would gradually leak out of the hole and imperceptibly vanish.

[§ 4. HOW THE VIRTUES GIVE STRENGTH TO THE
VESSEL OF OUR BODY.]

How can we think of ourselves as perfect and complete ves-
100 sels without the many virtues of which we have not yet acquired the incorruptible and inexhaustible riches? How, by our very

few good deeds, isolated from each other by our sins, can we imagine that we carry the Holy Spirit as a treasure within ourselves? In truth, as it has been said, "We have become futile in our thinking and our senseless minds have been darkened, and claiming to be wise we have become fools" *(Rom. 1:21f.)*. Saint Paul indeed proclaims, "It is the God who said, 'Let light shine out of darkness,' who has shone in our hearts, and we have this treasure in earthen vessels" *(2 Cor. 4:6f.)*. By "vessels" he refers to our bodies, as he says elsewhere, "Do you not know that your body is a temple of the Holy Spirit within you? And you are not your own" *(1 Cor. 6:19)*. By "earthen" he hints at the infirmity of our nature. Such bodies cannot be broken or torn asunder because of the irresistible power of the treasure that is within them. Therefore he adds these words, "The transcendent power belongs to God and not to us" *(2 Cor. 4:7)*. And that I may make this even clearer to you, he says as follows, "Do not think that the treasure that is in you is contained and guarded by you, but rather that you yourself have been guarded by the treasure that is in you, and that you have been prepared by the grace that is in you to become a vessel useful to God" *(cf. 2 Tim. 2:21)*. What is [especially] wonderful is that even if the vessel be broken by others than ourselves, by enemies, yet the treasure remains intact. The action of the treasure makes the vessel stronger and more secure, for that treasure is no other but God Himself. Thus the same apostle says about this matter, "I can do all things in Christ who strengthens me" *(Phil. 4:13)*.

[§ 5. THE TREASURE—THE BLESSED TRINITY.]

But let us examine how through such words he speaks of the Trinity as indivisible and as abiding in us. He says, "It is the God who said, 'Let light shine out of darkness'"—that is, the Holy Spirit—"who has shone in our hearts" *(2 Cor. 4:6)*. Thus the Lord also said, "I will send you another Paraclete, even the Spirit of truth" *(Jn. 14:16f.)*. Again [the apostle] said, "We have this treasure in earthen vessels" *(2 Cor. 4:7)*, that is, in hearts of flesh *(cf. 2 Cor. 3:3)*. When he wishes to show you that the treasure is nothing else but the One who shines, and that His is the same dignity and the same Essence, he added, "The transcendent power belongs not to us, but to God" *(2 Cor. 4:7)*, that is, to Him who dwells in us by the illumination of the Spirit. For it is

110

120

130

140

the Holy Trinity that is the treasure we possess, as has been said, by the exact keeping of all the commandments, and who possesses us completely through His love of mankind, His power, and His grace. He guards and protects us on every side inviolate, stable, and unshaken. Even though we are weak and
150 unsteady and briefly fail or fall, yet He who is our treasure holds us and unites us to Himself and makes us to cleave to Himself. He fills up all that is lacking in us, and makes us firmer and more solid.

Accordingly I entreat you, brethren in Christ, present yourselves without spot of any sin to the Lord *(2 Cor. 11:2)* and bring with you the observance of all His saving commandments. Thus the Artificer, God the Word, will take them as raw material composed of gold and silver and precious stones, and will Himself fuse them all together, and through His commandments fashion us into useful vessels *(cf. 2 Tim. 2:21)*. But let us
160 not bring Him some of them and omit the others. Nor let us offer Him all of them and yet appear before the Master, Christ our God, as careless and contemptuous with regard to even one of them, lest in His wrath He reject the others as well and bid us to be cast out from the wedding feast *(Mt. 22:13)*. If this happens to us nothing will avail us thereafter even though we knock for a long time and say, "Lord, Lord, open to us" *(Mt. 25:11)*. He will then say, "Depart from Me! I do not know you *(Mt. 25:12)*, either as [belonging to] the faithful, or as those who have been obedient unto death and have fulfilled what I have commanded. So, depart from Me!"

[§ 6. HOW SOME FAULTS THAT ARE CONSIDERED TRIFLING IN REALITY ARE GRIEVOUS.]

170 Well do I know that I, miserable and altogether wretched as I am, will hear these words, for I have not fulfilled a single commandment of my God. Then there will be those who, like myself, have been insubordinate and disobedient toward God's commandments who vainly calculate and say, "But I have not committed fornication! Swearing is nothing. I have not committed adultery! But what sin is it to have stolen a penny or a piece of bread?" And again, "I should attain bliss, if I do not commit the foul and sacrilegious vice of homosexuality. But what sin is there in being insulting or jealous, in being flippant or frivo-

lous?" Then again there are those who in their folly think high- 180
ly of themselves for being pure from the practice of sins of the
flesh, and think that they are like angels of God, but take no account of the virtues and passions of the soul. They have nothing
but contempt for all the rest of the Lord's commandments and
do not force themselves to fulfill them. They refuse to do anything that is strenuous or to undergo any suffering for a commandment of God, and live carelessly.

What benefit, brethren, is there from abstaining from fornication and other impure acts of the body and yet seek after glory
and strive for money? The one corrupts the body, the other cor- 190
rupts the soul. Moreover, glory from men and love for it makes
us to be unbelievers, according to the word of the Lord when He
says, "How can you believe, who receive glory from one another
and do not seek the glory that comes from the only God?" (*Jn.
5:44*). What good is it to be innocent of homosexual acts, but to
waste away with envy, hatred, and jealousy toward your neighbor? Hatred toward one's brother makes him who feels it into a
murderer, for the apostle says, "Any one who hates his brother
is a murderer" (*1 John 3:15*). According to the sacred canons a 200
sodomite and a murderer are subject to the same penalty, and if
they fail to repent they will be subject to eternal condemnation.

[§ 7. HOW ONE MUST NEGLECT NOTHING.]

What about never getting drunk on wine, but insulting
one's brother? According to God's apostle both are rejected
from the kingdom of heaven, for he says, "Be not deceived; neither fornicators, nor homosexuals"—and he adds—"nor drunk-
ards, nor revilers, nor robbers will inherit the kingdom of God"
(*1 Cor. 6:9f.*). What, tell me, is the use of fasting if it is not joined
with gentleness? What is the use of gentleness if it results in the 210
destruction of the soul and the transgression of a single commandment of God? Just as he who resists him who strikes him
by striking back dishonors God Himself, who said, "To him
who strikes you on the cheek, offer the other also" (*Lk. 6:29*), so
he who patiently endures him who blasphemes God sins against
Him who is being blasphemed. By acquiescing he consents to
his blasphemy by his so-called patience. Why, brother, are you
confident in your obedience when you are enslaved by glut-

tony? "No one," He says, "can serve two masters" *(Mt. 6:24)*, for it is impossible for one who is a slave of his belly to become a slave of God. Why do you boast of reciting many psalms when your mind is wandering and you do not realize the sense of what you are saying? If you even on that pretext neglect the services that are enjoined on you and the offices of the monastery that have been prescribed by your superior, I will say nothing. But you know that you have heard God's Scripture say, "Cursed is he who does the work of the Lord with slackness" *(Jer. 48:10)*. Why do you boast how weary you become from physical labors when you neglect the activity that is within? Do you not hear Paul saying, "Bodily training is of some value, but godliness is of value in every way" *(1 Tim. 4:8)*? What if someone succeeds in both, but condemns the brethren who are with him or who are in the world? For He says, "With the judgment you pronounce you will be judged, and the measure you give will be the measure you get" *(Mt. 7:2)*. But as for him who succeeds in all that has been mentioned, and commits nothing of what has been forbidden, nor condemns his careless brethren, but who when the time of trial comes receives spitting, blows, and insults—if he does not endure them without being perturbed, or even is perturbed in heart but utters no unseemly word, yet in his outward demeanor shows that the impulse of his soul is obviously moved to anger and replies with an insulting word or retaliates in any way—how can he dare to call himself a servant and imitator of his Master, and not, on the contrary, his enemy?

[§ 8. OUR HEARTS AS TABLETS ON WHICH EVERYTHING, BOTH GOOD AND BAD, MAY BE INSCRIBED.]

Those, then, who are God's friends and who love Him, and who have Him within themselves like an inviolable treasure, go to receive such insults and humiliations with unspeakable joy and delight. With all sincerity they love those who so treat them and act toward them even more as though they were benefactors. But those who say, "At the very time of strife and contention we are as men affected by anger and wrath, and sometimes we defend ourselves by words and even acts against our brethren, yet afterwards we have no hostility against them in our minds but forgive them everything, especially when we reconcile ourselves to them," to me they seem like a plain tablet on which the enemy who wars against our souls, whenever he finds opportunity, inscribes by means of them his wicked and abominable sentences and then goes away. Then they in turn efface what they have written under the impulse of the evil one. Yet they do not decide to inscribe Christ's words in their place, so that the adversary on his return may find them written on the tablets of our hearts (cf. 2 Cor. 3:3) and be turned away in defeat and confusion. By carelessness and negligence each man leaves his tablets uninscribed, so that when the Lord sends to have His precepts written on one of them, they eagerly write those of the enemy. By accepting those that are bitter and lethal they banish far from themselves those that give life and "are sweeter than honey" (Ps. 119:103).

[§ 9. THE IMITATION OF CHRIST.]

Jesus our Lord and God, who has never fallen into sin, was smitten so that those sinners who imitate Him should not only receive the forgiveness of the sins they have committed, but also become partakers of His divinity (2 Pet. 1:4) because of their obedience. He who does not accept this in humility of heart because he is ashamed to imitate the Master's sufferings, of him will Christ also be ashamed in the presence of the angels (Mk. 8:38) and of His Father who is in heaven (Mt. 10:33). This is what I mean to say—He was God, but He became man for the sake of us men. He was slapped, spit upon, crucified, as though He who is impassible in His Godhead were teaching and telling each one of us for whom He suffered: "O man, if you wish to become a god and obtain eternal life and to be with Me, that which your ancestor failed to obtain because he wished for it in an evil way, then abase yourself even as I abased Myself for your sake. Cast aside the boastful pride of the devilish mind; accept being beaten, spat upon, buffeted, and endure those things until death and be not ashamed of it. But if you are ashamed to suffer for the sake of My commandments even as I, who am God, suffered for your sake, I on My part will consider it a disgrace for you to be with Me at My coming with glory (cf. Mk. 8:38), when I shall say to My angels, 'This man was ashamed at My humiliation and was unwilling to forsake the glory of the world and become like Me. But now when he has been stripped of corruptible glory and I am glorified in the immortal glory of My Father, I am ashamed even to see him! Let him therefore be cast out, let him be taken away like the ungodly, that he may not see the glory of the Lord!'" *(Is. 26:10)*. Those words they will hear who keep all the commandments in appearance only, but do not accept the insults and dishonors and reproaches of men because they feel disgrace and shame before them, and are unwilling to endure their buffets and blows.

[§ 10. THE HUMILITY OF CHRIST AND
OF HIS DISCIPLE.]

300   Tremble with awe, O men! The insults God suffered for the sake of our salvation you too must endure! God is slapped on the face by the basest of slaves *(Jn. 18:22)*. He gives you an example of victory, yet do you refuse to undergo this at the hands of a man of like passions as yourself? You are ashamed of becoming an imitator of God *(Eph. 5:1)*, how then will you reign with Him *(2 Tim. 2:12)* and share in His glory *(Rom. 8:17)* in the kingdom of heaven if you do not endure that man? For if God, as far as you were concerned, had been ashamed to become man for your sake and had left you until now where your transgression had
310   made you to fall, would you not, O wretch, have remained with the unbelievers and ungodly in the recesses of hell? Do you believe that Christ is God? "Yes," you say. You believe that the God who has made heaven and earth is the One who, without being emptied, emptied Himself from the Father's bosom *(cf. Phil. 2:7)* and came down on the earth from the infinite height of Godhead and His unutterable glory and became an insignificant and poor man for the sake of you, who are clay and ashes and dust. Are you not, then, willing to come down from your imaginary high throne and be humbled before your brother? In appearance he may stand lower than you, but perhaps he is your
320   superior in virtues. Will you not cast away the garment that you think is splendid and ask for that man's sackcloth and humility? Do you not see that all these things are in reality but a plaything, a cover-up for ugliness, rather than glory and splendor? Do you not wish to become in all things like your Maker and your God by humbling yourself with your brethren? If you disdain becoming like Him, do you not know that you are making yourself greater and more glorious than Him? You show your-

self to us as yet another Annas or Caiaphas or Pilate and as a tyrant, not with the purpose of causing the Maker of all things to
sit with you, but rather to make Him appear before you as a
prisoner in the dock.

330

[§ 11. BEARING THE CROSS WITH CHRIST.]

So much for the rich and the rulers and those who sit above
others and raise their eyebrows with haughty mien. But what
about those who have left all things and become poor for the
sake of the kingdom of heaven? What shall we say? Behold, you
have become poor, brother, and have imitated Christ, your Master and God. Look at Him now as He is with you and accompanying you in your life, He who is above all the heavens *(Eph.
4:10)*. Behold, you walk on your way together; someone meets
you on the way of life, he slaps your Master in the face, and so
he does to you. Your Master does not talk back, do you resist?
But you say, "Yes, but He said to him who slapped Him, 'If I
have spoken wrongly, bear witness to the wrong; but if I have
spoken rightly, why do you strike Me?'" *(Jn. 18:23)*. This He
said, not, as you suppose, in the spirit of contradiction, but because "He committed no sin; no guile was found in His mouth"
(1 Pet. 2:22). On the other hand, He said this to show His innocence, lest it be thought that he who said, "Is that how you answer the high priest?" *(Jn. 18:22)* was right in striking Him as
one who had committed an offense. But this is not at all true of
us, for we are guilty of many sins. For later on, when He had endured things that were far worse, He was not found speaking a
single word. On the contrary, we hear of Him praying for those
who had crucified Him *(Lk. 23:34)*. Though He was the object
of derision He was not angry, and are you annoyed? He submit-
ted to being spat upon, struck, and scourged, and yet you cannot
endure a harsh word! He accepted the cross and a shameful
death and the agonies of the nails; do you refuse to perform the
lowliest services? How will you be a partaker in His glory *(1 Pet.
5:1)* when you refuse to be a partaker of His shameful death? Indeed it is in vain that you have left the world behind, when you
are unwilling, as He commanded you, to take up your cross
with the help of the word of truth, "Sell what you have and give
to the poor" *(Mt. 19:21)*. He said this to the young man, and
with him He commanded us, "Take up your cross, and come,

340

350

360

370

follow Me!" *(Mt. 16:24)*. Granted, you have distributed your wealth, yet without taking up your cross, as has been said, which means that you cheerfully endure the assault of all trials. So you have been abandoned on the way of life and have been miserably separated from your most gentle Master and your God!

But I implore you, fathers and brethren, let us keep all the commandments of Christ. Let us endure the trials that come on us unto death because of our longing for the kingdom of heaven. So may we become partakers of the glory of Jesus *(cf. 1 Pet. 5:1)* and share in eternal life and become heirs of the enjoyment of ineffable blessings in Christ Jesus our Lord, to whom be glory forever. Amen.

XXVIII

[DISCERNMENT, LIGHT, AND PRIESTHOOD]

On the mortification to which the Spirit impels those who struggle, which gives life before death. How those whom grace raises above law consciously receive in themselves the grace of divine light: for those who have not received this light already in the present life are still under the shadow of the law and are judged by it. The qualities of the superior and of the priest, who have received from on high the power of binding and loosing. How all are manifest to him who truly exercises the priestly office and is illuminated by the divine light, both those who walk by the Spirit of God and those who have not yet put off the earthly man.   10

[§ 1. RUNNING ON THE WAY OF SALVATION.]

Brethren and fathers,

Take heed how you listen! Christ our God says, "Search the Scriptures" *(Jn. 5:39)*. Why does He say this? First, that we may be taught the way that leads to salvation. Second, that by practicing the commandments we may walk without turning aside, and attain to the salvation of our souls *(1 Pet. 1:9)*.

What, then, is our salvation? Jesus the Christ, like the angel   20
who stood before the shepherds, said, "Behold, I bring you good news of a great joy which will come to all the people; for to you is born this day in the city of David a Savior, who is Christ the Lord" *(Lk. 2:10f.)*. Then let each of us, beloved, eagerly run with all our strength! We must not encumber ourselves with anything that is heavy, or worldly, or hard to carry. Nothing should force us to slow our pace and thus prevent us from reaching and

entering the city of David. I entreat you, through the grace that
is at work in you, do not neglect your salvation *(cf. Heb. 2:3)*, but
30   rise as from the sleep of evil presumption and negligence! Let us
not stop or sit down until we have left the world and found our
Savior and our God and see Him above, and worship Him and
fall down before Him *(cf. Ps. 95:6)*. Even then let us not stand
still until we have reached the point where He Himself tells us,
"You are not of the world, but I chose you out of the world" *(Jn.
15:19)*.

[§ 2. BEING CRUCIFIED TO THE WORLD.]

How does one arrive at the state of not being of the world?
By crucifying oneself to the world, and the world to oneself, as
Paul also says, "The world has been crucified to me, and I to the
40   world" *(Gal. 6:14)*. What is the relation of these words to the former? The words differ, but they both mean the same thing. Just
as he who is outside the house does not see those who are shut
up inside it, so he who is crucified to the world or mortified no
longer has any awareness of the things that are in the world.
Again, just as the dead body has no awareness whatever of living
bodies or even of dead bodies that lie beside it, so he who has
come out of the world in the Divine Spirit and is with God can
have no awareness of the world or of the things that belong to
the world.
50   In this way, brethren, our souls therefore die before death
and rise again before the resurrection of the body in deed, in
power, in experience, and in truth. When the mortal attitude
has been eliminated by the immortal mind and mortality has
been driven out by life, then, as though it had risen from the
dead, the soul manifestly sees itself, just as those who rise from
sleep see themselves. It recognizes God who has raised it; as it
perceives Him it gives Him thanks and worships Him and glori-
60   fies His infinite goodness. On the other hand, the body is entirely without breath, motion, and memory in relation to its own
desires, but in these respects becomes altogether dead and lifeless.

[§ 3. FREEDOM THROUGH GRACE.]

Under these circumstances it often happens that a man, so
to speak, forgets even his natural faculties, because his soul lives

its life intellectually, on a plane above nature. No wonder, for, as [Scripture] says, "Walk by the Spirit, and do not gratify the desires of the flesh" *(Gal. 5:16)*. For once the flesh is dead by the coming of the Spirit, as we have said, from then on it leaves us undisturbed. You will live without hindrance, since "the law is not laid down for the just" *(1. Tim. 1:9)*, as God's apostle says, 70 because he lives a life that is higher than the law. As he says, "Where the Spirit of the Lord is, there is freedom" *(2 Cor. 3:17)*, a freedom from the slavery of the Law. For the Law was a guide and a custodian leading us by the hand, teaching us righteousness and telling us, "You must do such and such," and on the contrary, "You must not do such and such." But grace and truth *(Jn. 1:17)* are different. In what way? "You are to do and say all things in accordance with the grace given to you" *(Rom. 12:3)* "and speaking through you" *(Mt. 10:20; Mk. 13:11)*. As it is written, "They shall all be taught by God" *(Jn. 6:45)*, learning goodness not by writings and letters *(cf. 2 Cor. 3:3, 6)*, but by being 80 taught by the Holy Ghost. Not by word alone, but in the light of the word and in the word of the light are they mystically initiated into things divine. For He says, "Then you will become teachers both for yourselves and for your neighbors; more than that, you will be the light of the world and the salt of the earth" *(cf. Mt. 5:13f.)*.

[§ 4. FROM THE SHADOW OF THE LAW TO THE LIGHT OF GOD.]

Those who lived before grace, since they were under the Law *(Gal. 3:23)*, found themselves sitting under its shadow *(Heb. 10:1)*. Those who have come after grace and the day have arrived have been delivered from the shadow, the slavery of the Law *(cf. Gal. 3:23, 4:3)*. They have risen above the Law, having climbed, as it were, the ladder of the life of the Gospel. They have been 90 lifted up on high to share the life of the Lawgiver, and have themselves become lawgivers rather than keepers of the Law.

Is there then one who "has ears to hear" *(Mt. 11:15)*, so that he may be able to hear the sense of that which the Spirit says *(cf. Rev. 2:7, 11)*? Is there even now someone who has acquired "the mind of Christ" *(1 Cor. 2:16)* so that he may rightly discern what He has written, in a manner worthy of God? Can anyone be found even now who has Christ speaking in him *(cf. 2 Cor. 13:3)*, so that he may be able rightly to interpret the mysteries that are hidden in the words? As [the apostle] says, "We speak the wisdom, but not that of this age which is doomed to pass away, but the wisdom hidden in a mystery" *(1 Cor. 2:6f.)*. It is hidden from most, yet revealed and known to us who walk in the fear of God and who always look to Him. We do not speak of that which we do not know, but "we bear witness of that which we know" *(Jn. 3:11)*, for "the light" already "shines in the darkness" *(Jn. 1:5)*, both by day and by night, both within and without—within in our hearts *(2 Cor. 6:16)*, without in our minds. It shines on us without evening, without change, without alteration, without form. It speaks, works, lives, gives life, and changes into light those whom it illuminates. We bear witness that "God is light," and those to whom it has been granted to see Him have all beheld Him as light. Those who have received Him have received Him as light, because the light of His glory goes before Him, and it is impossible for Him to appear without light. Those who have not seen His light have not seen Him, for He is the Light, and those who have not received the Light have not yet received grace. Those who have received grace have received the Light of God and have received God, even as Christ Himself, who is the Light, has said, "I will live in them and move among them" *(2 Cor. 6:16)*.

[§ 5. PENITENCE—THE GATEWAY TO THE LIGHT.]

But those who have not yet experienced this or been found worthy thereof are all subject to the Law, which was prior to grace. They are slaves *(cf. Gal. 4:7)* and disciples of slaves, hearers of the Law *(cf. Rom. 2:13)*, children of the slave-woman *(Gal. 4:31)* and sons of darkness *(cf. 1 Thess. 5:5)*, even though they may be emperors and patriarchs, prelates or priests, whether rulers or subjects, lay persons or monks, ascetics or superiors, poor or rich, physically ill or in good health. All who sit in darkness *(cf. Lk. 1:79)* are sons of darkness and are unwilling to repent. For penitence is the gateway that leads out of darkness into light. He who does not enter into the light *(cf. Jn. 3:20)* has not properly gone through the gate of repentance; for had he done so, he would have been in the light. He who does not repent commits sin, because he is not penitent, for "whoever knows what is right to do and fails to do it, for him it is sin" *(Jas.*

4:17). He "who commits sin is the slave of sin" *(Jn. 8:34)* and "hates the light and does not come to the light, lest his deeds should be exposed" *(Jn. 3:20).* But now we have willingly and of our own accord entered into the light through penitence and are convicted and judged *(cf. Eph. 5:13),* but this happens mystically and in secret in the innermost chamber of our souls. We undergo this for our purification and for the forgiveness of our offenses by the mercy and love of God toward men, as God alone, as well as we ourselves, understands our condition. On the other hand, when the Lord comes to those who now hate the light and are unwilling to come to it *(Jn. 3:20),* the light that now is hidden will be revealed and all that they have hidden will become manifest. Whatever each of us men is now, as we wrap ourselves up and refuse to reveal our condition by penitence, the light will then make it clear and manifest to God and to all men. 140

[§ 6. AT THE JUDGMENT—THE SHAME OF BEING IN THE DARKNESS.]

Look at the great disgrace of this! It is as though one of us were in a house with its doors locked, seen by nobody who is outside it. Supposing he were to sin freely and commit adultery or pederasty or other foul acts, and he were then suddenly exposed to view while perpetrating wickedness, he would be greatly disgraced. Or, to take another example, suppose someone were to plot against the emperor and to commit his plans to writing, or even to speak and plan something treasonable while he was hidden inside a house. Suppose then the emperor with all his senate and his usual armed guard were to come on him and surround the house. At once he would have lost his hiding place and he would be discovered in the midst of his plotting. How great would be the punishment and condemnation that he would suffer! In the same way it will happen [on the day of judgment] to all who are in the world. "The night will become as light as the day" *(Ps. 139:12);* every house and cave, even heaven and earth themselves, will be removed. All who have not been clothed with Christ *(Gal. 3:27),* that is, those who have not received the light, as we said earlier, those who have not previously been in it and become light *(Eph. 5:8),* will appear naked and will be filled with much shame from every quarter. In addition, every act of each person, whether good or bad, every word, 150 160 170

every thought, every memory that has arisen in us from our
very birth till our last breath, will then be gathered together and
be revealed in every member of mankind. With what, brethren,
may we compare that disgrace, that unique disgrace? What punishment is greater than that fear and confusion of those who, as
we have said, are then found in darkness and without the light-
180   giving Spirit? How can that man live, how can he act, who sits
in the darkness? Can he avoid the sudden flash of light that ex-
poses every defilement of thought and deed? Let us hasten, then,
my brethren, from henceforth even now to enter the narrow
gate *(Mt. 7:13)* through penitence and to see the light that is
within it! Indeed I beseech you, let us not be fainthearted in
knocking and seeking and asking before the door is opened to us
and we receive *(cf. Mt. 7:7f.; Lk. 11:9f.)*. Further, let us continue
[to do so] till we enter within and receive the light and have it
burning in our hearts without ceasing.

[§ 7. AS A PASTOR, THE PRIEST HIMSELF MUST BE IN THE LIGHT.]

190   But let us not deceive ourselves *(1 Cor. 3:18)*! Let us not follow after the desires of our flesh and "play the harlot in our do-
ings" *(Ps. 106:39)*. Let us not set ourselves up as teachers, that
is, by becoming superiors and prelates and priests, while we despise God and our own salvation. For when Jesus said to Nicodemus, "Unless one is born again from on high, he cannot see
the kingdom of God," and Nicodemus replied to him, "How can
a man be born when he is old? Can he enter a second time into
200   his mother's womb and be born?" Jesus rebuked him and said,
"Are you a teacher of Israel, and yet you do not understand
this?" *(Jn. 3:3, 4, 10)*. He rebuked him, though as yet he did not
believe at all and knew nothing about grace. How much more
are we worthy of condemnation! We have become teachers after
grace has come, yet we do not know the mysteries of grace. We
enjoy the benefits of such great teaching and are daily taught by
apostles and prophets and doctors, as well as by the Lord Himself, and hear their testimony beforehand!
        How, tell me, can we be entrusted with guarding and car-
210   ing for the flock of the Lord if we do not know how we must
live in this life? If we do not know that we must grow in good
works and yield ourselves as slaves of righteousness *(Rom.*

6:16ff.), as those who stand before the Lord and not men *(cf. 2 Cor. 8:21; Eph. 6:7)* and have vowed to serve the living God *(1 Thess. 1:9)* without blame? If we do not know what are the character and the qualities that are required of us if we are to be leaders of others, how shall we tend that flock according to the will of Christ, the Chief Shepherd *(1 Pet. 5:4)* and lead it forth to pastures of eternal life *(cf. Jn. 10:9, 3)?* How great is our hardness of heart and our contempt for God and things divine! We are like "the adder that stops its ears" *(Ps. 58:5),* we have become as it were deaf and dumb *(cf. Mk. 9:25)* like those who are dead; our spiritual senses are disabled, we do not understand the words that are spoken. We do not even know that there is such a thing as Christianity, we are ignorant even of the mystery of the Incarnation and have no exact knowledge of the mysteries of Christians. Yet we shamelessly presume to teach the multitude about the light of knowledge, and even to show them the light of knowledge itself! Knowledge is not the light! Rather, it is the light that is knowledge, since "in it and through it and from it are all things" *(Rom. 11:36).* We refuse the vision of the light, and so make it plain that we have not been born again, and have not attained to the light that comes from above. We are still like the unborn, or, more accurately, we have been born prematurely—we who rush to the sacred places and take possession of apostolic thrones!

[§ 8. CONDEMNATION OF THOSE WHO TRAFFIC IN SACRED THINGS.]

What is worse, most of us without fear buy the priesthood for money and seek to govern the King's flock as shepherds, though we have never been sheep. We do this merely to fill our own stomachs as if we were wild beasts, and to do all other things to which we are compelled by our propensity to evil, together with our desire and inclination for things below!

Brethren, were the apostles at the beginning like this? Were the successors of the apostles such? Did our fathers and teachers [act] thus? Woe to the dreadful audacity of such men! Not only do they become traitors and sacrilegious in the matter of material possessions, when they have eyes for nothing else than their money bags. They even dare to lay hands on the riches of God when they are not ashamed to say, "It pertains to us to bind and

250

to loose *(Mt. 16:19, 18:18)*, and we have received this power from on high for the present life." What impudence, if I am not to say, what utter madness! From whom, tell me, and for what purpose have you received this power from above? Is it because you have left everything to follow Christ *(Mk. 10:28)*? Is it because you have despised earthly glory? Is it because you have become humble in spirit? Is it because you have sold all and given it to the poor *(cf. Mt. 19:21; Mk. 10:21)*? Is it because you have lost your life or become dead to the world, and have not found it in any "will of the flesh" *(Jn. 1:13)*? Or is it because you too, like Christ's disciples of old, have heard Him say as He breathed on you, "Receive the Holy Ghost. If you forgive the sins of any,

260

they are forgiven; if you retain the sins of any, they are retained" *(Jn. 20:22f.)*?

[§ 9. THE INWARD HOLINESS REQUIRED OF THE PRIEST OF THE GOSPEL.]

"But the power belongs to the priests," they say. I know it too, for it is true. But not simply to priests as such, but to those who serve in the priestly ministry of the Gospel *(Rom. 15:16)* in a spirit of humility and who live a blameless life. [Such priests] first present themselves to the Lord *(cf. Rom. 6:16)* and offer themselves as a "perfect, holy and well-pleasing sacrifice," as their own pure act of worship *(Rom. 12:1f.; Jas. 1:27)* in the temple of their own bodies *(1 Cor. 6:19)*, inwardly and spiritually. They are accepted and appear on the altar that is on high *(Heb.*

270

9:24), offered by Christ the High Priest as a perfect sacrifice, changed and transformed by the power of the Holy Spirit. They have been transformed into Christ, who died for us and rose in the glory of His Godhead. In perfect humility they repent night and day; they mourn and pray with tears not only for themselves, but also for the flock that has been entrusted to them and "for all the holy churches of God" *(cf. 1 Cor. 11:16)* in the world. In addition, they greatly bewail other men's offenses before

280

God. They consume no more than their necessary food, nor do they seek in any way the convenience or enjoyment of their bodies, but, as it is written, they "walk by the Spirit, and do not gratify the desires of the flesh" *(Gal. 5:16)*. Further, for the sake of justice and of God's commandment they show no partiality to either poor or rich, ruler or subject, not even to him who wears the imperial diadem. No pretext, whether it be of mercy or gifts received, or of fear or anything else, visible or invisible, will cause them to grow soft or move them to ignore or trangress God's commandment, who is above all *(cf. Rom. 9:5).*   290

To such it belongs to bind and to loose *(Mt. 16:19, 18:18)*, to perform priestly acts and to teach, and not to men who have received their appointment and ordination from men only. As he says, "One does not take the honor upon himself, but he is called by God" *(Heb. 5:4).* He did not say, "He who has received appointment from men," but "He who was predestined by God and foreordained for this." Those who come from men and through men are thieves and robbers, as the Lord said: "I am the door. All who have come" and who come now, "not through Me, but climb in some other way, are thieves and robbers" *(Jn.*   300
10:7, 8, 1).

[§ 10. CHRIST, THE LIGHT OF THE WORLD.]

Be not deceived *(1 Cor. 6:9)*, brethren! He who lives in the darkness is outside the door. He who thinks that he has come in, but has not entered through the light, is himself outside the sheepfold. If Christ is the Light of the world *(Jn. 8:12)* and the door *(Jn. 10:7, 9)*, then surely the door is luminous, and not simply a door, and he who finds himself in it is in the Light of the world. But He is not the Light of the world as though He were seen by the senses, but as contemplated by the mind. The visible sun gives light only to physical eyes, and not of men alone, but also of irrational beasts, quadrupeds, and birds; the intellectual   310
sun, however, that has appeared in the world, gives light to rational souls only. Those it does not enlighten indiscriminately, without their being worthy. It is not inanimate, or to speak more accurately, without life; nor is it, like this visible sun that "rises on the just and on the unjust, and alike on the good and the evil" *(Mt. 5:45)*, a slave or a creature appointed for the service of others. Even though He is called "light" and "sun" *(cf. Mal. 4:2)*, yet He is greater than every light and greater than the sun, in that He is the Maker and Master of the light and of the sun. He is life *(Jn. 11:25)* and lifegiver, truth *(Jn. 14:6)*, righteousness, and sanctification *(1 Cor. 1:30)*, simple, not com-   320
pounded, good, all goodness, and above all goodness. Since He is the truth and is so called, He becomes truth to all who truly

turn to Him. Since He is righteousness, He is righteousness for those who hate all unrighteousness. He is sanctification for those who are washed and cleansed by tears, simple to those who have no wickedness or malice *(1 Cor. 5:8)* within them. Since He is not compound, He is such to those souls that have no duplicity or double-mindedness or lack of faith. He is good to those who do not join bodily or worldly cares and concerns to

330   the spiritual works of penitence and mingle them with them as leaven, but who draw near to Him in innocence with naked conscience and resolution of soul. He accepts their simplicity and straightway fills them with all goodness. By revealing Himself and appearing to them He makes them to be partakers of blessings that surpass mind and understanding.

[§ 11. SPIRITUAL LIGHT AND DISCERNMENT.]

"And who," you say, "will recognize such men, if indeed there are such to be found even now?" He who is enlightened by the Spirit from above. But he who speaks and does not know them, why is he willing to accept testimony on the part of others? Does he not know that even though it was in ignorance that

340   he brought in a wolf to Christ's sheep he is still held responsible for the sheep? "But who knows?" you will say. "He is but a man and does not know what is in the heart." Unless he is blind he will never fail to recognize such a person. He who sees, how can he fail to distinguish between a sheep and a wolf *(cf. Mt. 7:15)*, a robber and a shepherd *(Jn. 10:1ff.)*? But if he is blind in this respect, let him seek a guide to lead him by the hand, or, better, let him cease from so doing and distinguishing. Let him not be a guide for others *(cf. Mt. 15:14; Lk. 6:39)*, nor appoint anybody as a guide for men even if the whole world bears witness in his favor. I tell you this—he who sees spiritually and hears in the same way sees the soul of him whom he sees and encounters and

350   with whom he frequently converses. Though he may not see it in essence yet he sees its condition, its qualities, and its dispositions. Accordingly, if he has been granted to partake of the Holy Spirit, he will have this knowledge from the very sight of him. But if he who sees the man is still imperfect in grace and has not yet become like God, it is rather through his words that he who sees him and converses with him will recognize him. This our Master and our God has shown when He said, "You will know

them by their fruits" *(Mt. 7:16)*. Again [He says], "As a tree is known by its fruit, so will the nature of a man be known by what he speaks" *(cf. Lk. 6:43ff.)*.   360

[§ 12. THE FALSE JUDGMENTS OF SPIRITS WITHOUT
DISCERNMENT.]

In addition, such a person is also recognized by those whose reason and spiritual senses are sound; the rest of men lack sense and discernment even in respect of his actions. They accept someone whom they see fasting with vainglory, while they condemn one who eats with humility. Another who abstains with humility they look on as a hypocrite, while they consider someone who eats gluttonously to be simple and free from artificiality. They take pleasure in frequently joining him in eating, and so encourage their own passions. Worse than that, they regard   370
those who play the fool and speak jestingly and frivolously out of season and play practical jokes and make others laugh as if they were trying to disguise their virtue and freedom from passion by such pursuits and appearances and words. So they honor them as though they were holy and free from passions. Those who live in reverence and virtue and simplicity of heart *(Acts 2:46)* and who are truly holy they overlook and pass by as if they were no more than anyone else. Again, others look on the man who is talkative and shows off as though he, on the contrary, were an able teacher and a spiritual man; but he who keeps si-   380
lence and is scrupulous about idle talk *(cf. Mt. 12:36)* is considered to be boorish and mute. Yet others reject him who speaks in the Holy Spirit as if he were haughty and proud, being wounded by his words instead of moved to compunction. He who speaks eloquently either from his inward self or his learning and lies against their salvation they praise to the skies and accept. Thus there is no one among them who is able to see aright and to discern in accordance with reality.

[§ 13. THE ABILITY OF THE BLIND EYE TO SEE AND
OF THE DEAF EAR TO HEAR.]

Once a man is blind he is blind in respect to all things, and so he who is deaf is deaf in every respect. The blind man is un-   390
able to see one without seeing the other, nor can the deaf man hear the voice of one, and not another. Both of them are entirely

305

deprived of their respective senses. Thus he who lacks perception in one matter lacks it in all, just as he who has it in one matter is capable of perceiving all things and is beyond their sensation. He is capable of perceiving all, and is not overcome by their sensation. He who is deaf to the Word is deaf to every voice, just as he who hears the Word hears them all. The latter is
400 deaf to every voice; he hears all, yet hears no one, save those alone who form [their] words in the Word, and not even those, but only the Word who speaks without voice in their voices. But he who is deaf to the One is deaf in relation to all. He who sees in the One enjoys the comtemplation of all things; whether he abstains from their contemplation or enters into the contemplation of all he stands apart from that which he contemplates. Since he is in the One he sees all things; if he is in all things he sees nothing of them. So he who sees in the One and through the One perceives both himself and all persons and all things; he
410 who is hidden in himself sees nothing of them all. He therefore who hears, sees, and perceives knows the meaning of what is being said, but he who does not know clearly shows that his senses are neither accurate nor sound. He who is in this state does not yeat realize that he is "a composite worshiper, earthly and heavenly, one who is both temporal and eternal, who rules over the things that are on the earth yet is ruled from above, a spectator of the visible creation, an initiate into the object of thought," as a celebrated theologian has said somewhere.[1] Yet "though he was in honor, yet he was compared to the beasts that have no intelligence and became like unto them" *(Ps. 49:21 LXX)*. Having once become like to them he still remains thus, as long as he has
420 not been converted, recalled, or elevated to his former dignity according to the gift of the dispensation of our Master and Lord Jesus Christ, the Son of God. Since, to use David's expression, he is still an irrational beast, perhaps an ass or an ox or a pig, to which the pearls of ineffable knowledge are not given by God *(Mt. 7:6)*, he has in no way whatever clothed his rational and intellectual self with the image of Jesus Christ our Lord, who is the heavenly man*(1 Cor. 15:49)* and God. But if he has not put on this image in perception and knowledge, then he is no more

---

1. S. Gregory of Nazianzus, Or. 38.11 (P.G. 36, 324A).

than flesh and blood *(cf. 1 Cor. 15:50)*. He is incapable of receiving through the word any perception of the heavenly glory, just as those who have been born blind cannot by word alone see the light of the sun.   430

Come then, you who have the intelligible light in yourselves, let us give glory through it to the Father, the Son, and the Holy Ghost, now and always, forever and ever. Amen.

XXIX

[THE HERESY OF PUSILLANIMITY]

How we must not say that in our day it is impossible, for him who wishes, to arrive at the summit of virtue and to emulate the Saints of old. That everyone who teaches the things that are contrary to the divine Scriptures is, to those who accept him, a teacher of a new heresy. Concerning tears—that tears belong to us by nature.

[§ 1. THE BENEFIT OF THE PHYSICAL ABSENCE OF CHRIST.]

Fathers and brethren,

There are many who say every day, and we, too, hear them as they say it: "Were we living in the days of the apostles, and like them had been found worthy of seeing Him, we too would have become holy like them." They do not know that He is the same who speaks to the whole world both then and now. For if He is not the same who was of old and is now, who is God in every respect and in the same way, whether in His operations or in the sacred rites, how is it that the Father appears in the Son, and the Son in the Father *(cf. Jn. 10:38, 14:10–11)* through the Spirit, as He tells us in these words: "My Father is working still, and I am working" *(Jn. 5:17)*?

But perhaps someone will say, "It is not the same thing to have seen Him then physically, and now merely to hear His words and be taught concerning Him and His kingdom." I too will tell you that what is now and what was then are not exactly the same thing. Rather, what is here and now is greater, and leads us more readily to faith and assurance than if we had seen and heard Him then. At that time He appeared as an insignificant man to the ignorant Jews, but now He is proclaimed to us as true God. At that time He had visible converse with publicans and sinners and ate with them *(Mt. 9:11; Mk. 2:16; Lk. 15:2)*; now He is seated at the right hand of God the Father *(cf. Mk. 16:19)*, from whom He was never separated in any way. We believe that He gives nourishment to all the world, and we say that nothing takes place apart from Him—if, at least, we believe. Then even the lowest spoke contemptuously of Him and said, "Is this not the son of Mary *(Mk. 6:3)* and of Joseph the carpenter?" *(Mt. 13:55)*. But now He is worshiped by kings and rulers as the Son of the true God and as true God. He has glorified, and still glorifies, those who "worship Him in Spirit and in truth" *(Jn. 4:24)*. Though He often chastises them when they sin, He makes them to be of iron, instead of clay *(cf. Dan. 2:33; Rev. 2:27)*, to be over all the nations that are under heaven *(Acts 2:5)*. Then He was thought to be corruptible and mortal like any other man. It was a great thing that God the formless and invisible should, without suffering change or alteration, have taken form and be seen wholly visible altogether as a man, without differing from other men to our senses. For he ate and drank *(cf. Mt. 11:19; Lk. 7:34)* and slept *(cf. Mt. 8:24; Mk. 4:38)*, perspired *(Lk. 22:44)* and was weary *(cf. Jn. 4:6)*, doing everything that pertains to man except sin *(Heb. 4:15)*. It would have been difficult to recognize and believe that He was God, who had created the very heaven and earth and all things in them *(cf. Acts. 4:24)*.

Therefore, when Peter said, "You are the Son of the living God" *(Mt. 16:16)*, the Master called him blessed, saying, "Blessed are you, Simon Bar-Jona! For flesh and blood"—that is, seeing and hearing these things—"have not revealed this to you, but My Father who is in heaven" *(Mt. 16:17)*. Thus, he who now hears Him daily calling and proclaiming the will of His blessed Father through the Holy Gospels, but does not obey Him with fear and trembling *(cf. Eph. 6:5)* nor observe the things He commands, would not then, being present to see Him in person and hear His teaching, in any way have been willing to believe Him. There is even the possibility that in his unbelief he would have thought Him an enemy of God rather than the true God, and would have blasphemed Him!

30

40

50

60

[§ 2. THE DIFFICULTIES OF THE PAST.]

This is but what the more worldly would have said. What about the more serious minded? They say: "Had we lived in the times of the holy fathers, we too would have struggled. Had we seen their good lives and their struggles, we would have emulated them. But now that we live with slack and careless people, we are led astray by them and without wanting to we perish with them." Obviously they do not know that we, rather than they, have reached port! Let them too hear this: In the days of our fathers there were many heresies, many false christs *(Mt. 24:24; Mk. 13:22)*, many profiteers in Christ, many false apostles *(2 Cor. 11:13)*, and many false teachers *(2 Pet. 2:1)*. They went about boldly and sowed the tares of the evil one *(Mt. 13:25)*, and took many captive with their words by deceiving them, and sent off their souls to perdition.

That this is true you will find from the lives of our holy father Euthymius, and also of Antony and Sabas. It is written that Antony once wore a garment more splendid than he was used to and went up to a high place to show himself conspicuously, so that he might become conspicuous and be seized by the heretics and put to death by them. Had there been no persecution he would not have done this! In the case of the birth of our holy father Euthymius, is it not recorded that God then granted the churches to celebrate with joy the cessation of persecutions and heresies? At the death of our blessed father Sabas, have you not heard how much he had striven for the churches against the heresies of that time, and how many of the monks at that time had been led astray by the heretics? What happened at the time of Saint Stephen the Younger?[1] Did not that belong to a most grievous and severe persecution? Or are you unaware of the storm that raged then? How the monks at that time were severely shaken? Why do I try to recount these things? When I recount what happened earlier, in the time of Basil the Great, as the great Gregory (of Nazianzus) relates them, and the things that happened in the time of John Chrysostom and the subsequent holy fathers, I blame myself. I feel pity for those who do not

1. Martyred in 764 under Constantine V (Copronymus) for the veneration of the holy icons.

consider these things, they do not fully realize that all the time past was more terrible than the present, and manifestly filled with the tares of the evil one *(Mt. 13:38)*.

Nevertheless, even though the past was terrible, yet life even now has many heretics; many wolves, vipers, and serpents are living among us, even though they have no power against us *(cf. Jn. 19:11)*. Such men are, as it were, hidden by the night of their wickedness. As for those who join them and come under their darkness, they seize them and devour them; but they dare not even face those who walk in the light *(1 John 1:7)* of the divine Scriptures and go in the way of God's commandments. As the heretics see them on their way they flee from their faces as though from fire *(cf. Ps. 68: 2–3)*.

[§ 3. THE HERETICS OF THE PAST.]

Whom do you think that I call heretics? Is it not those who deny the Son of God? Is it not those who blaspheme against the Holy Ghost and say that He is not God? Is it not those who say that the Father is greater than the Son? Is it not those who confuse the Trinity into a unity or divide the one God into three gods? Those who say that Christ is the son of God, but do not believe that He has taken flesh from a woman? Those who believe that He has taken flesh, but talk nonsense about it being without a soul? Is it not those who admit that the flesh had a soul, so that it was a whole man, but do not admit that the Son of God, who is also Son of Mary the Theotokos, is one God according to the hypostasis, but divide the one Christ into two sons? What of those who ascribe a beginning to the Father, who has no beginning, and say, "There was a time when He was not"? Or those who admit that the Father is without beginning, but wrongly think and teach that the Son, being begotten from Him, took His beginning after some time as were He a creature? For it is said, there was no time when the Father was without the Son's coexisting with Him, and how can one call "Father" one who has no offspring? What of those who preach that there was one who suffered, and another who rose again? Far from it! But I am not speaking of any of those ungodly men or atheists nor of any other heresy, which have appeared as darkness, but are now dispersed by the shining light of the holy fathers in the past. Through them the grace of the most Holy Spirit has shone so

100

110

120

130

brightly that it expelled the darkness of the heresies aformentioned. Even till now their writings, inspired by God, shine more brightly than the rays of the sun, so that no one dares contradict them.

[§ 4. THE NEW HERESY—BELIEVING ONESELF TO BE UNABLE TO OBEY THE GOSPEL LIKE THOSE OF OLD.]

But the men of whom I speak and whom I call heretics are those who say that there is no one in our times and in our midst
140   who is able to keep the Gospel commandments and become like the holy Fathers. That is to say, they should believe and practice, for faith is shown by deeds *(cf. Jas. 2:18)*, just as the features of the face in a mirror. Further, that they may be both great contemplatives and see God, by the illumination and reception of the Holy Ghost, through whom the Son is perceived together with the Father. Now those who say that this is impossible have not fallen into one particular heresy, but rather into all of them, if I may say so, since this one surpasses and covers them all in impiety and abundance of blasphemy. He who
150   makes this claim subverts all the divine Scriptures. I think (that by making this claim) this vain person states that the Holy Gospel is now recited in vain, that the writings of Basil the Great and of our other priests and holy fathers are irrelevant or have even been frivolously written. If, then, it is impossible for us to carry out in action and observe without fail all the things that God says, and all the saints after first practicing them have left in writing for our instruction *(cf. 1 Cor. 10:11)*, why did they at that time trouble to write them down and why do we read them in church? Those who make these claims shut up the heaven
160   that Christ opened for us, and cut off the way to it that he inaugurated for us *(cf. Heb. 10:19f)*. God who is above all *(Rom. 9:5)* stands, as it were, at the gate of heaven and peers out of it so that the faithful see Him, and through His Holy Gospel cries out and says, "Come to me, all who labor and are heavy laden, and I will give you rest" *(Mt. 11:28)*. But these opponents of God or, rather, antichrists say, "It is impossible, impossible!"

To them the Master rightly says with a loud voice, "Woe to
170   you, scribes and pharisees *(Mt. 23:13)*! Woe to you, blind guides of the blind *(Mt. 23:16)*, because you do not enter into the kingdom, and you hinder those who wish to enter" *(Mt. 23:13; Lk.*

11:52). While He proclaims the blessedness of those who mourn now *(cf. Lk. 6:21)*, they say that it is impossible for anyone to mourn every day and weep. How great an insensitivity, how unrestrained a mouth that utters defiled words against the Most High God and makes the sheep of Christ a prey for wild beasts, those sheep for whom the only-begotten Son of God shed His blood! Rightly David, the human ancestor of our God, prophesied of such men and said: "The children of men, their teeth are spears and arrows, and their tongue a sharp sword" *(Ps. 57:5)*.

[§ 5. WE MUST REFUSE NEITHER PURIFICATION NOR TEARS.]

Tell me, why is it impossible? By what other means have the saints shone on the earth and become "lights in the world" *(Phil. 2:15)*? If it were impossible, not even they would have been able to succeed in this. They too were human like ourselves, they had nothing beyond what we have, except a will for goodness, zeal, patience, humility, and love for God. Get all these for yourself, and the soul that at present is like rock *(cf. Ex. 17:6)* will become for you a fountain of tears. But if you refuse to suffer and be distressed *(cf. 2 Cor. 4:8)*, at least do not say that the thing is impossible! He who says this denies purification, for it has never been heard that without tears a soul that has sinned after baptism has been cleansed from the defilement of sin. For it is through baptism that God has taken away every tear from the face of the earth *(cf. Is. 25:8)*, having abundantly shed abroad His Holy Spirit *(cf. Tit. 3:6)*. But as I have heard from the divine Scripture, some adults at the moment of their Baptism have shed tears, having been smitten with compunction by the coming of the Spirit; yet not painful tears of suffering, but such as were sweeter than honey *(cf. Ps. 119:103)*. They came by the action and gift of the Holy Ghost, they were shed from their eyes without pain and without sound. Those who some day will have been found worthy to experience such tears will know of what I have spoken and will bear witness that it is true, as the voice of the theologian bears witness to me. For he[2] says: "Let one man offer one thing, another man another thing," and after enumer-

180

190

200

---

2. S. Gregory of Nazianzus, Or. 19, 7 P.G. 35, 1049D–1052A.

ating a great number of things he finally cries out, "Let all offer tears, let all offer purification, let all offer (their) ascent and their straining forward to that which lies ahead" *(Phil. 3:13).*

[§ 6. TEARS AS A NECESSITY IN OUR LIVES.]

210

220

230

Has he then in this matter distinguished and separated some persons from others, and told us that is was possible for some, and impossible for others? I will attack you as you deserve, you who are uncircumcised in heart and ears *(Acts 7:51)*! Has the great Gregory said, as you foolishly pretend, that some men have obtained a hard nature and are forever incapable of compunction and tears? Far from it! There is no human nature that has less aptitude for tears and weeping and mourning,[3] nor has this saint, nor any other saint, said or written to this effect. But that weeping comes naturally to all of us, let the newborn children teach you! For as soon as they come forth from the womb and fall on the ground they weep *(Wis. 7:3)*, and for their nurses and mothers this is a sign of life. For if the child does not weep, it is not said to be alive, but as it weeps it shows thereby that human nature has mourning and tears as a concomitant from birth. As our holy father Symeon the Studite used to say, it is with such weeping that man ought to spend his present life and die with it, if he wishes to be saved and enter into the blessed life *(cf. Mt. 19:17)*, since the tears of birth are expressive of the tears of this life present here (on earth). For as food and drink are necessary for the body, so are the tears for the soul; so much so that he who does not daily weep—I hesitate to say every hour, for fear of seeming to exaggerate—will destroy his soul and cause it to perish from hunger.

[§ 7. TEARS AS A GUARANTEE OF THE VISION OF GOD.]

240

If then, as we have shown, tears and weeping are concomitants of our nature, let no one renounce this benefit of nature nor let anyone by malice, wickedness *(cf. 1 Cor. 5:8)*, and pride of soul become arrogant and be changed, contrary to nature,

---

3. S. John Climacus differs somewhat on this point; see *Scala Paradisi*, P.G. 88, 805 C, in which he stresses that the effort, rather than the abundance of tears, is judged by God.

into a counterpart of stone. Rather, let him employ his uttermost zeal for the commandments of God; let him, I pray, guard
this great gift inviolate in his heart. Let him keep it by poverty
and humility, in innocence of soul and simplicity, in endurance
of temptations and constant meditation of the divine Scriptures,
as he is continually penitent at all times and mindful of his own
failures. Let no one neglect such activity; but if anyone despairs
of his own salvation and lies down on the bed of laxity, at least
let him not say that this is impossible for those who are zealous.
He who makes this claim shuts the very door of the kingdom of   250
heaven in our faces! Take away the tears, and you remove with
them purification; but apart from being purified there is no one
who is saved, no one whom the Lord calls blessed, no one who
sees God *(cf. Mt. 5:8; Heb. 12:14)*.

[§ 8. LISTENING TO HOLY WRIT.]

But if these things follow on those who do not mourn in accordance with the Lord's commandment, tell me, how is this
heresy not the worst of all heresies? It was in vain, according to
your view, that the condescension of God and His ascension
took place! It was to no avail that the apostles preached, that all
the saints gave their instructions, since they constantly call on
us to mourn! All divinely inspired Scripture *(2 Tim. 3:16)* is use-   260
less to you who are in such a state and think that way! You are
"like the deaf adder that stoppeth her ears" *(Ps. 58:5)*! It would
appear to me that you ascribe salvation solely to your cloak,
cowl, and scapular—in some cases, to a very heavy and impressive beard—and so, as you put your trust in them you take pride
in them! But be of good cheer, you who are naked and exposed
(Heb. 4:13)! Even though you refuse to hear the divine Scripture
as it daily shouts it at you with a loud voice, we shall yet stand
before the judgment seat of Christ *(Rom. 14:10)*, so that "each
one may receive good or evil, according to what he has done in   270
the body" *(2 Cor. 5:10)*.

[§ 9. THE FAULTS OF MONKS BEFORE GOD'S JUDGMENT.]

Even though this is not pressing on us yet, yet impending
for us all, where, at that time, will the robe that covers and

adorns our bodies be? Where will be the fine scapulars? Where will be the resplendent and transparent mantles? Where will be the elegant and strong sandals? Where will be the belts that are so much like the girdles of women? Where the meetings with nobles? Where the protocol of greetings? Where the striving for the first place (cf. Mt. 23:6)? Where the sumptuousness of tables? Where—if I may mention this as well—this going ahead of one's brother to take greater quantities and greater delicacies from what is being served—a fault in which I am the first, and from which vain people like myself suffer? Where will be our conceit and arrogance, our ruling and being ruled? Where our spacious cells, decorated magnificently like bridal suites? Where the precedences of offices and officials, in which we think that we have the preeminence over others? Where our unbridled and unseemly laughter? Where the sumptuous banquets and the lengthy meals, and the untimely conversations during them? Where will be the great names? Where the holiness others attribute to us, or we attribute to ourselves? Where will be those who now flatter and deceive us, who call us holy and wipe away the traces of our feet? Where the raised seats and those who because of them consider themselves more glorious than the rest? Where the courting of favor and the eagerness to attain some position or rise to a greater one? Where will be contradiction, insubordination, and unwillingness to appear inferior to someone else? Where our attachment to our relatives? Where the honor from those seculars and rulers who visit us, and from whom I think that I, wretch as I am, am the first to claim more honor? Where the pretended prudence of those who are honored for their knowledge and wisdom of the world (cf. Col. 2:3)? Where our presumption and illusion that we are something, though we are nothing? Where will then be our glib tongue and the fine phrases that flow as though from a fountain? Where will be then, or, rather, where are now, "The wise man, the scribe, the debater of this age" (1 Cor. 1:20)? Let him draw near, let him come, and let us sit down together and take counsel concerning that dread day and that hour. Let us, as is said, set in motion all that is in ourselves and in the divine Scriptures and examine them with care (cf. Jn. 5:39), and so be taught out of them and learn what it is that will benefit us then, and seek it with great zeal.

[§ 10. A FINAL ADMONITION.]

Truly, my beloved brethren, as all Scripture explicitly proclaims, in that hour, great anguish, great fear and trembling *(cf.* 310
Ps. 55:6) will seize hold of those who, like myself, are slack, careless, and slothful. But, brethren, blessed is he who, while lying lower now than every creature, mourns and weeps night and day before God, for then he will stand at His right hand *(Mt. 25:33)* in glorious apparel *(cf. Rev. 7:9)*. Blessed is he who hears these things and does not merely groan and delay from day to day, and so passes the time of his life without profit, but who, as soon as hears the Lord say "Repent" *(Mt. 4:17)* immediately sets to work. Such a man will find mercy as an obedient and grateful 320
servant *(cf. Mt. 24:45)*, and will not be condemned with those who are disobedient. Even now he will be set free from all passions and become an approved workman *(cf. 2 Tim. 2:15)*; in the world to come he will enjoy the ineffable blessings of God with all those who from the beginning have been well pleasing to Him. May we all attain to this by the grace of our Lord Jesus Christ, to whom be glory forever and ever. Amen.

XXX

ON PENITENCE

On penitence and the beginning of a life that is worthy of praise. How he who is penitent ought to behave every day. Of tears and compunction.

[§ 1. THE GOAL OF SPIRITUAL EFFORT.]

My beloved brethren,

Listen to the sense of my words, and gladly receive it as counsel given for your good, and carry it out eagerly for your common benefit and mine as well. In this way, bit by bit, by steps that appear insignificant, we shall make progress toward greater perfection, and ascend to become perfect men in Christ.

Now this is the purpose of my discourse. When you come out of the church do not begin to be distracted toward vain and useless matters, lest the devil come and find you occupied with them. It is as when a crow finds a grain of wheat on the plain before it has been covered up with earth and picks it up and flies off. So the devil removes the memory of these words of the catechesis from your hearts (cf. Mt. 13:19; Lk. 8:12) and you find yourselves empty and deprived of salutary teaching. But if someone among you has been ordered to perform some manual labor or carry out the duties of his office, let him go off with bent head and perform it. While he works or performs his task let him say within himself:

[§ 2. THE WASTED YEARS.]

"How many days and years of my life have I spent in dissipation and frivolity, wretch that I am! How I have wasted my time until now when I have heard the divine Scriptures, without knowing at all any profit from them! What good has my present life been to me? Behold, so and so many years of my life

318

have passed. Who knows whether I will be alive tomorrow (*cf.* *Jas. 4:14*)? For many years I have been eating; I have filled my stomach with meat and wine and great gluttony. I made a fair show with my clothes; I have amused myself and laughed all by myself. I have made such and such a sum of money; I have spent it and wasted it on vain things and afterwards made more. I have had a surfeit of baths and scents; I have ridden horses and mules; I have enjoyed many and sumptuous banquets. I have envied my neighbor and insulted him; I have committed fornication; I have stolen, and lied. I have moved among famous and rich men as among companions and friends and been the guest of princes. In the world I acquired fame; I have lain on soft beds, I have indulged this earthly body with rest, I have slept to excess."

[§ 3. MORTIFICATION AND POVERTY AS MEANS OF RETRIEVING THE WASTED YEARS.]

"What good have all these things done me until now? Will they be of any use if He who has authority over all that breathes should command tomorrow that I should be taken out of this world? Indeed, not at all! From now on I will make a fresh start and leave all these things behind, and like the holy fathers I too will practice the opposite things, so that I at least do not spend the rest of the days of my life here below in vain. In place of my past gluttony I will fast so much that I cannot even move my tongue for conversation. I will afflict my belly with hunger and thirst, and my ungovernable tongue (*cf. Jas. 3:8*) will be tamed. Indeed, at the same time I shall come to sadness, pallor, and sorrow; yet I shall be freed from arrogance of thoughts, and by this means I shall readily cease from dissipation, trifling, and frivolity. I shall be poorly clothed and give my fine clothes to the poor; at the same time I will distribute whatever gold I have to the needy. From now on why should I worry about these things, if I dedicate myself entirely to Him who feeds all things? I shall renounce riding on horses and mules. As for relatives and friends and companions, I shall give them all up, for he who loves anyone more than God is not worthy of Him (*Mt. 10:37*), as He Himself says. I shall not touch a bath, I will not climb up into my bed (*Ps. 132:3*), but I will gladly sleep on the hard ground, so that even if I do not want to, I will sleep but a short time because of the hardness. What if I die? Am I worthy of living?"

[§ 4. CONFIDENCE IN GOD AND ATTACHMENT TO HIM.]

"When I do this, when I rise at midnight *(cf. Ps. 119:62)* I shall fall down and weep out of the tribulation of my soul,
70 which has sinned, and I will say to God with groanings and tears: 'Master, Lord of heaven and earth, I know that I have sinned more than any human creature, more than even the brute beasts and reptiles in Thy sight. My awesome and unapproachable God, I am not at all worthy ever to obtain mercy from Thee! Therefore I would not have dared to draw near to Thee or fall before Thee, O King who lovest men, had I not heard Thy holy voice saying, "I do not at all desire the death of the sinner, but that he should turn and live" *(Ezek. 33:11)*. Again I have heard Thee say, "There is joy in heaven over one sinner
80 who repents" *(Lk. 15:7)*. I also remember the parable of the Prodigal Son, which Thou hast spoken, O Master, how, when he returned, before he had drawn near to Thee, Thou, O Compassionate One, didst come to him and fall on his neck and kiss him *(Lk. 15:20)*. So I put my trust in the ocean of Thy goodness, and have come to Thee in the pain, grief, and sadness of my heart, although I am hardened and wounded sorely and lie in misery in the depth of the hell of my misdeeds. But from now on I give Thee my word, O Lord, that as long as thou biddest
90 me remain in this life and in this body, I will not forsake Thee, nor will I turn back from Thee. I shall no longer be attached to vain and evil things! But Thou, O my God, knowest my weakness, my misery, my faintheartedness, and the old predispositions that are about to tyrannize and oppress me. Help me, as I fall before Thee, and forsake me not. Leave me not for long to suffer derision and to be mocked by the enemy, for from now on I am Thy servant, O good [God].'"

100 Brethren, he who has just fled the world out of eagerness to repent should think on these things and resolve them within himself. He has chosen to learn this art of arts, which pertains to the life of struggle and asceticism, and for this reason has entered the stadium of this contest. It is to such a person that I address my exhortation. Possibly he is standing in our very midst

and thirsts to hear of the more strenuous things from us, and feels a compulsion to enter on true penitence.

[§ 5. CONSIDERATIONS FOR THE EVENING.]

In addition to what I have said, beloved, do not eat any food till evening. In the evening go into your cell, sit on your bed, and ponder all that I have said. First give thanks that you were vouchsafed to arrive at the end of the day and the beginning of night. Then examine yourself and call to mind how much you have sinned against God, who made you, and how many years He has shown patience toward you by letting you live. He has bestowed on you all things for bodily enjoyment—that is, food and drink, clothing to cover you, and the very cell in which you sit. He has not given way to anger, nor has He turned you away because of your sins. He has not given you over to death nor to the demons to destroy you. When you have duly called these things to mind, stand up, and spread your mat on the ground, with a little stone for a pillow, and so prepare your bed on which you are about to rest.

[§ 6. A METHOD FOR REPENTANCE.]

Listen further! I will set before you another way of fervent and genuine repentance by which you will quickly attain to tears and compunction, especially if you have a heart of stone *(Ezek. 11:19)* that is slow to mourn and without compunction. But do not let that which I am about to counsel appear as something strange and unfamiliar to the faithful, without testing it!

He who has kept himself spotless for God after his Baptism and preserved himself undefiled in accordance with the image of Him who made him *(Gen. 1:27)* and formed him needs nothing further to recall him from his condition, for he is in God. But he who after Baptism has defiled himself with unsuitable actions and lawless deeds and has made the temple of his body— or, rather, the house of God—into a house of pleasures, passions, and demons *(1 Cor. 3:16f.)* by his profligacy stands in need of repentance. He needs not only the method I am about to tell you and advise you, but also many other methods and devices. By means of them he may propitiate God and recover that divine dignity which he has lost through his sinful life. Let the discourse "On Penitence" from "The Ladder" by our father, the

110

120

130

140

divine John, persuade you, for it contains many things on this subject.

[§ 7. PRIVATE EXERCISES OF PENITENTIAL PRAYER.]

But what is the method of penitence I will expound to you by way of fatherly advice? Listen, brother, with understanding and without taking offense. Once you have prepared for yourself, as I have mentioned, the mat of your bed on which you are about to lie, rise up to pray as one who is under condemnation. First recite the Trisagion, then say the "Our Father," and as you say this remember who you are and whom you call your Father.
150 When you come to say "Lord, have mercy" and wish to stretch out your hands to the height of heaven look upwards with your physical eyes and fix your sight on your hands. Concentrate your thoughts and recall your wicked actions and how much you have sinned with your hands. Remember the foul deeds they may have committed and with fear say within yourself, "Woe to me, unclean and defiled as I am! May it not be that when God sees me stretching out my hands to Him without shame He will remember my misdeeds I have committed with
160 them, and so send fire on me to consume me!" Then turn your hands behind your back and join them, as though you were being led off to death, and sigh from the depth of your soul and say with a pitiful voice, "Have mercy on me, a sinner *(Lk. 18:13)* who am not fit to live, but who am truly worthy of all punishment," together with any other words that the grace of God gives you to utter. As you call to mind your sinful acts strike yourself violently and unsparingly and say, "How, O sinful and wretched man, could you do such and such?" Again turn your hands [behind your back] and stand, imploring God. Then beat your face, pluck at your hair and pull it, as though some terrible
170 enemy had plotted against you, and say, "Why did you commit such and such a sin?" Then, when you have sufficiently beaten yourself, join your hands in front of you and stand with joyful soul. When you have recited two or three psalms with attention and made as many reverences as you think you are able, then again stand attentively and reflect on that which I have said. Perchance God may grant that tears and compunction may come on you! If that should happen, do not retire until they are over. If it does not, do not be discouraged, but say this to your-

self: "Compunction and tears belong to those who are worthy and are ready for them. But as for me, how many years have I called on God or served Him? By what deeds have I prepared myself to receive them? Is it not enough for me that I am still alive?" When you have said these words and given thanks, sign your face and your breast and your whole body with the sign of the precious Cross, and fall down on your mat and stretch yourself on it.

[§ 8. FEELINGS OF CONTRITION DURING THE OFFICE.]

When you wake from sleep, do not turn over on the other side! Rise at once and pray again in the aforesaid manner and sleep no longer, but persevere in prayer and reading until the semantron[1] sounds. Then go off with all the rest to the Office and stand in the temple as though you were in the company of angels in heaven, with trembling because you regard yourself unworthy even to stand there with your brethren. As you stand pay heed to yourself so that you do not look around you with curiosity at the brethren, how each of them stands or how he sings, but pay attention to yourself alone, to the psalmody, and to your sins. Remember also the prayer that you offered in your cell; do not at all carry on any conversation or speak any idle word to anyone during Office, nor depart from thence before the final prayer. If you are able, do not sit down even for the reading, but withdraw to a hidden spot and listen standing. Listen as though it were God Himself speaking to you through the reader, God who "is above all" *(Rom. 9:5)*. But if you yourself are told to read the lessons, do so with the attitude that you are unworthy that your mouth should read the divinely inspired Scriptures to the brethren. When you have finished the sacred reading and are about to make the usual reverence to both sides of the choir, do not perform it with contempt or indifference, but with the thought that they are all sons of God and holy. So as you fall down and bring your head near to the ground, say secretly in your heart to them all, "Pray for me and pardon me, O saints of God, who am a sinner and unworthy of heaven and earth." If you are ordered to intone the canon,[2] do not do it neg-

---

1. The office in question is evidently Orthros (matins).
2. A variety of prose hymn in the course of the Office.

ligently or carelessly, but attentively and soberly, with the thought that in the presence of Christ, the King who rules over all, you through your voice are distributing the divine oracles to your brethren as though with your hands. Be in fear, lest, by despising Him, you fail to give to anyone the life-giving bread, or, as we have said, God's word *(cf. Jn. 6:33, 63)*, and so you be cast out as a despiser, not, I tell you, from this church, but from the kingdom of heaven! When you leave after the dismissal, remem-
220   ber how you spent the previous day, and if you have failed in any way correct it today.

[§ 9. THE PENITENCE OF A CONFIDENT AND GENEROUS HEART.]

If you, therefore, persevere in these practices, the Lord will not delay to show His mercy toward you. Here, though it is rash of me to say so, I make myself a surety for the Compassionate One, I reply on His behalf who loves mankind! May I die, if He overlooks you! May I be given over to eternal fire in your stead, if He forsakes you! Only, practice these things without hesitation of heart, without double-mindedness!

But what does it mean to do this without hesitation and double-mindedness? Take heed, beloved! Hesitation of heart
230   consists in thinking or merely reflecting in oneself, "Will God have mercy on me or will He not?" The "not" belongs to unbelief! If you do not believe that, on the contrary, God is even more willing to have mercy on you than you hope for, why do you draw near to Him and call on Him? Double-mindedness consists in not giving oneself over completely, even to the point of death, for the kingdom of heaven, but being anxious, however little, for the life of one's flesh. Know well that he who strenuously repents is bound to observe no other limit than this, that he does not kill himself by any means and become a suicide, such as by casting himself down from a precipice or by hanging
240   himself or by committing some other crime. But as for the other things by which he knows that his body is fed and stays alive, let him not at all be anxious about them, in accordance with the saying, "Seek first the kingdom of God and His righteousness, and all these things"—that is, those that fulfill the needs of the body—"will be added to you" *(Mt. 6:33)*. It is possible for him who lives militantly and in accordance with the Gospel to be fed

every day with bread and water and to stay alive, and such a man is in better health than those who enjoy more luxurious fare. Therefore Paul, who knew this, said and keeps on saying, "If we have food and clothing, with these we shall be content" *(1 Tim. 6:8)*. Again he said, "We felt that we had received the sentence of death; but that is to make us rely not on ourselves, but on God who raises the dead" *(2 Cor. 1:9)*.

[§ 10. TOWARD IMPASSIBILITY.]

Behold, we have told you, dear brother, how you must come to God and what the penitence is that you must exhibit toward Him. Do not depart from it till your last breath, nor forget the good advice of a sinner such as myself. I have failed to practice this and so I have not spoken from my actions, but it is the grace of God that has granted me to say this for your sake and for your salvation. Therefore, if you do this with God's help and persevere in this work of penitence, you will gradually perceive for yourself mysteries that are even greater by being taught them by the grace that comes from above. Not only will you be granted a fountain of tears through such practices, but also liberation from all passions. The continual quest for penitence and compunction, the search for aids and means for affliction, weeping, and compunction, the zealous practice of these things without in any way preferring oneself or performing the will of the flesh, quickly bring a man to make progress and to attain purification and impassibility. They cause him to partake of the Holy Spirit, and not only that, make him the equal of our great fathers, Antony, Sabas, and Euthymius.

[§ 11. THE SEED OF THE BEGINNINGS AND THE LABOR FOR THE HARVEST.]

These things will happen if you listen to me and love penitence and compunction. But if you are unwilling to listen to me and perform what I have called your constant occupation, do not blaspheme, either you yourself or anyone else, by calling this impossible. Do not plead, "I have made my profession, I have spent so and so many years [as a monk]." Do not recount to me how much wealth and gold you have distributed and scattered among the poor, nor say, "I have spent so and so many pieces of gold of my property and have clothed the naked, fed the hungry, and given drink to the thirsty *(cf. Mt. 25:35ff.)*. I have dispersed all my possessions, I have entered such a cave, I have gone on pilgrimage to the Lord's sepulcher, I have climbed the Mount of Olives, and now I have entered this monastery and have received the tonsure." Or else, "I was tonsured a monk before and now I stay in one cell and perform such and such devotions, and by these I shall be saved and that is enough for me!" Do not deceive yourself, brother, whoever you are, nor comfort

290 yourself with vain thoughts. You are foolish if you do so! All these things are fine, very fine, but know well, dear man, they are but the seed! See, I am telling you this in a figure of speech—you have broken up the fallow land and gone over it a second and a third time; you have sown the seed. Do you know whether the seed has sprouted from the furrows of the earth? Do you know whether it has grown? Have you seen the ears of grain coming? Have you seen the crops of the earth of your soul become white and ready for harvest *(cf. Jn. 4:35)*? Have you plucked ears from the grain and rubbed them in your hands, so that you may see the naked fruit of your labors? When you have seen this, have you taken your fill thereof and gained strength?

300 If you know these things, I prostrate myself at your feet and kiss them, and kiss their footprints, for I am not fit to embrace you face to face. Be joyful and exult *(Mt. 5:12)* as you gather in your bosom that which you have sown with great labor and weariness.

[§ 12. HOW NOT TO LOSE THE KINGDOM OF HEAVEN.]

But if you are ignorant of the things I have told you, and do not even know whether you have sown in your ground—I mean the ground of your heart—any of the more excellent fruits, what good has it done you to encompass the ends of the earth and to go to the furthest parts of the sea *(Ps. 139:9)*? None whatever! Even if I show mercy to the whole world by giving what is not my own—even if it were my own—but ignore my nakedness

310 and poverty *(cf. Rev. 3:17)*, and have reached the extremity of destitution and so am about to die destitute of all goodness and to stand before the awesome judgment seat of Christ *(Rom. 14:10)*, what good is it? We must depart from this life and from the body fully clothed and equipped if we wish to go in to the wedding feast of the king and to sit at table with his friends *(cf.*

Mt. 22:11ff.). With what garment must I and indeed everybody be clothed, so that we may not be found naked on that day *(cf. 2 Cor. 5:2f.)*? Brethren, it is Christ *(cf. Rom. 13:14)* our God! Supposing I were to travel on a pilgrimage through all the earth under heaven as if it were a single house, without omitting any country or city or failing to enter any church to worship and pray there and carefully and accurately examine everything that is in them. Yet were I to lose the kingdom of heaven, would it not have been better for me never to have been born *(Mk. 14:21; Mt. 26:24)* or to have fallen on the ground *(Wis. 7:3)*, or to have breathed the air or seen the sun with my eyes? Indeed, it would have been far better for me! 320

What then shall I do, so that I may not fall out of it? If I were to practice all the things that I have mentioned, I would receive the Holy Ghost, for He is the seed of Christ, through which we poor mortals become Christ's kin. When it falls into the good soil it "bears fruit thirtyfold and sixtyfold and hundredfold" *(Mk. 4:20)*, and this very thing is the kingdom of heaven. Apart from this all other things are useless. Brethren, if we fail to take pity on ourselves and through penitence find our souls purified and filled with light, the practice of all other things will avail us nothing, as our Lord and God tells us, "What will it profit a man, if he gains the whole world and loses his soul? Or what shall a man give in return for his soul?" *(Mt. 16:26)*. Again He says, "He who loses his life for my sake will find it, but he who finds it will lose it" *(Mt. 10:39)*. If I do not lose my soul in the former way, as I have said, by giving myself to death for Christ's sake, and find it again alive with eternal life, what will I have been profited by all other things, friends and brethren? Nothing at all! Nothing will profit us at all, beloved servants of Christ; nothing will snatch us from eternal fire if we do not forsake all things and all people and take heed to ourselves alone! 330 340

[§ 13. THE SUBJECT OF THE NEXT DISCOURSE.]

But what does it mean to take heed to ourselves? We shall reserve this, brethren, for another catechesis and endeavor to give it its due proportion in our discourse. But may God Himself, the true Wisdom, who has vouchsafed to become the Teacher of us sinners, teach me to tell both myself and my fellow- 350 servants and my brethren the things that belong to the salvation of the soul.

For Thou art the Guide and Illumination of our souls, who givest us "utterance in the opening of our mouths" *(Eph. 6:19)* and "a word to those who proclaim good tidings with great power" *(Ps. 68:12 LXX)*, and to Thee do we give glory, now and always, forever and ever. Amen.

XXXI

[SELF-EXAMINATION ON THE BEATITUDES]

How every man ought to watch over himself and carefully examine that which concerns him. How one ought to compare one's conduct with the commandments of Christ.

[§ 1. EXAMINATION OF ONE'S SELF.]

Brethren and fathers,

In the preceding catechesis, when we left our subject incomplete in order that we might avoid prolonging our discourse to excess, we were discussing what it is to watch over oneself. Now we have come to pay the debt of the discourse we owe you by the present catechesis. It is for this purpose that we have been appointed to this position. We are always obliged to supply to your charity the due measure *(cf. Lk. 12:42)* of the word. 10

What is it to take heed to oneself and to watch over oneself as we have mentioned before? That everyone should take heed to himself consists in this: that he says to himself: "Is there not some passion that has control over me? For, as I hear in the divine Scriptures, he who has even one passion only does not enter into the kingdom of heaven, for it is written, 'If a man keep the whole law, but fails in one point, he has become guilty of all of it'" *(Jas. 2:10)*. Similarly, to watch over oneself consists in this, that one says to oneself, "Have I not neglected this commandment or that? Am I careless about it, do I ignore it and fail to practice it?" For Christ our God says, "Not an iota, not a dot, will pass from the law of My commandments until all is accomplished" *(Mt. 5:8)*. Again He says, "He who breaks one of the 20

329

least of these commandments and teaches men to do so shall be called least in the kingdom of heaven" *(Mt. 5:19)*.

[§ 2. HUMILITY.]

30   But we must be even more attentive to the divine Scriptures. While they are being read a man ought to look at himself, and reflect on his soul as in a mirror *(Jas. 1:23)*. In what state is it? What do I mean? A man hears the Lord say, "Repent, for the kingdom of heaven is at hand" *(Mt. 4:17)*. He must therefore call to mind how he spends his days. If he is duly penitent he will increase and prolong his work; if he is negligent he will mend his ways.

Again he hears Him say, "Blessed are the poor in spirit, for theirs is the kingdom of heaven" *(Mt. 5:3)*. He must then constantly examine and test himself *(cf. 1 Cor. 11:28)* on every occasion of humiliation—I mean, when he is insulted, dishonored,
40   treated with contempt. He must look at himself, whether or not the virtue of humility be found in him, for he who has acquired it bears all things without being pained or burdened. Nothing that happens to him wounds his heart. If he is slightly wounded thereby, yet he is not completely disturbed; on the contrary he afflicts himself and counts himself worthless because of that wound of his heart, because he was even slightly grieved instead of receiving with joy that which happened to him. He is grieved and weeps as he enters into the inner chamber *(Mt. 6:6)* of his soul or into his cell. So he falls down before God and makes
50   confession to Him, as though he had wholly lost his own life.

[§ 3. BEING AFFLICTED.]

Then again he hears. "Blessed are those who mourn" *(Mt. 5:4)*. Note that He does not say, "Those who have mourned," but "those who constantly mourn." Here too we must examine whether we mourn daily. For if we become humble from penitence, it is clear that not one day or night will pass for us without tears and mourning and compunction.

[§ 4. MEEKNESS.]

And again (he hears), "Blessed are the meek" *(Mt. 5:5)*. Is there anyone who mourns every day who can continue to live in a state of anger and not become meek? Just as a flame of fire is extinguished by water *(cf. Sir. 3:30)*, so anger of soul is quenched by mourning and tears; so much so that a man who has spent a long time being irascible sees the temper of his soul changed and transformed into total calm. Therefore a man must look at himself in this respect as well, to see whether he is truly meek. He who is this cannot in any way bear to see the transgression of God's commandment, but laments over those who commit sin as though he himself had committed it. 60

[§ 5. HUNGER FOR RIGHTEOUSNESS.]

Then likewise (he should examine himself) whether he hungers and thirsts for God's righteousness *(Mt. 5:6)*. It is admittedly possible, if one searches, to find a person who is righteous, yet does not hunger and thirst for it. It is God who is righteousness *(cf. 1 Cor. 1:30)*, just as you hear him called "the sun of righteousness" *(Mal. 4:2)*. So he who hungers and thirsts for Him counts the whole world and the things in it as refuse *(Phil. 3:8)*. As for the honors of princes, he either counts them a disgrace, or else has no regard for human honors. 70

[§ 6. MERCY.]

And again, "Blessed are the merciful" *(Mt. 5:7)*. Who, then, are the merciful? Those who give money or feed the poor? No. But who are they? Those who have become poor for the sake of Him who became poor for our sakes *(cf. 2 Cor. 8:9)*. They have nothing to give, yet they are constantly spiritually mindful of the poor, the widows, the orphans *(cf. Jas. 1:27)*, and those who are sick. As they see them frequently, they have compassion on them and weep warm tears over them. Such was Job when he said, "I wept over every one who was infirm" *(Job 30:25 LXX)*. Whenever they have anything they gladly give alms to them *(cf. Rom. 12:8)*, and also generously remind them all of the things that serve for the salvation of their souls, by obeying Him who said, "I learned without guile and I impart without grudging" *(Wis. 7:13)*. These are the ones whom the Lord calls blessed, those who are truly merciful; for it is from such mercy, as from a step, that they climb in order to reach perfect purity of the soul. 80

[§ 7. THE PURE AND PEACEFUL HEART.]

Following this, and on this basis God calls blessed those
90   whose heart is pure, in that He says, "Blessed are the pure of
heart, for they shall see God" *(Mt. 5:8)*. He, our God and Lawgiver, knows that unless our soul attains to such a disposition it
can neither constantly mourn nor become perfectly meek, nor
yet thirst for God *(Mt. 5:4–6)*, nor yet become pure as a mirror.
But if it fails to become so, it will never contemplate the
Master's face in itself. The soul, however, who has attained to
this sees God from every (side) and is reconciled to Him *(cf.
Rom. 5:10)*. Peace is established between our Maker and God on
100   the one hand and the soul that was once hostile to Him on the
other, and it is then called blessed by God for having made
peace, for He says, "Blessed are the peacemakers, for they shall
be called sons of God" *(Mt. 5:9)*. To Him who came to give
peace to those who were near and to those who were far off
(Eph. 2:17) they have consciously reconciled themselves. He
came to reconcile us, who were enemies *(Rom. 5:10)*, to His own
Father and to unite into one those who had become separated
(cf. Eph. 2:13), impart His Holy Spirit to us and our flesh on
Himself. It is clear, then, that those who see Him have been truly reconciled to Him, in that they have found the peace they had
sought and become sons of God *(cf. Mt. 5:9; Jn. 1:12)*. "It is God
110   who justifies, who is he who condemns?" *(Rom. 8:33)*. But if
you do not love your brother whom you see, how can you love
God whom you have not seen *(1 John 4:20)*? If we are not able,
or rather, not willing to love Him, it is clear that we have not
been reconciled to Him. Let us then be eager to see Him, to be
reconciled to Him, and to "love Him," brethren, "of all our
soul" *(Mk. 12:30)*, as He Himself commanded us.

[§ 8. ENDURING PERSECUTION.]

Then again he hears Him say: "Blessed are those who are
persecuted for righteousness' sake" *(Mt. 5:10)*. So he aims to examine himself whether he has been persecuted for the sake of a
commandment of God, since, as the apostle says, "all who desire
to live in Christ will be persecuted" *(2 Tim. 3:12)*. Therefore
120   Christ adds these words and says, "Blessed are you when men
revile you and persecute you and utter all kinds of evil against

you falsely on My acount. Rejoice and be glad, for your reward is great in heaven" *(Mt. 5:11–12)*. Why then did he place those who are objects of persecution and reproach at the end, and command them, as He proclaimed with authority *(cf. Mt. 7:29)*, to "Rejoice and be glad"? For he who has shown worthy penitence for his offenses and has thence become humble—I tell you the same things twice, so I repeat—he who has been found worthy of mourning each day and becomes meek, who hungers and thirsts with his soul for the "Sun of righteousness" *(Mal. 4:2)* becomes merciful and compassionate. He makes the passions of all men, their afflictions and their weaknesses, his own. As he weeps and is cleansed he sees God and is reconciled to Him and becomes in truth a peacemaker and is found worthy to be called a son of God. Such a person is able, even though he is persecuted, beaten, reproached, abused, insulted, and hears all evil spoken against him, to endure it with joy and unspeakable gladness. God, our Master, knowing this, solemnly declared, "Rejoice and be glad" *(Mt. 5:12)*. But he who has not attained to this state and is not in possession of abundant and substantial joy within himself, how will he be able to endure all these things without vengeful thoughts? Not at all!

[§ 9. THE FINAL REWARD.]

Therefore, my fathers and brethren, let us never cease from judging and examining ourselves *(1 Cor. 4:3)* with great zeal, day by day, even hour by hour if possible! Rather, as we have said, let us go through all the commandments and see ourselves as we examine and observe ourselves in each one of them. If we should find that we are fulfilling it, let us give thanks to God our Master and from henceforth observe it without fail. If, however, up till now we have forgotten it or failed to keep it, let us, I entreat you, run to embrace it and take hold of it, lest for contempt of it we should be called the least in the kingdom of heaven *(Mt. 5:19)*. Thus as we ascend the ladder by one step after another we shall arrive, as well I know, to the very city of heaven. There, as I have said above, our Master stands and peers out, saying to us all, "Come to me, all who labor and are heavy-laden, and I will give you rest" *(Mt. 11:28)*. When we have arrived there we shall see Him as far as man is able so to do, and receive at His hands the kingdom of heaven, which is the Holy Ghost, and constantly

130

140

150

160

have it within us *(cf. Lk. 17:21)*, as the Master Himself explicitly proclaims. Thus we shall live as angels on the earth, or, rather, as sons of God. We shall be holy, and in all things of God *(cf. Eph. 5:1)* our Father. That most sweet vision of Him may we all enjoy, now and always, forever and ever. Amen.

XXXII

[BLASPHEMY AGAINST THE HOLY GHOST]

On blasphemy. That he who claims that one cannot become a partaker of the Holy Ghost in the present generation, as well as he who slanders the operations of the
Spirit and attributes them to the enemy, introduces a
new heresy into the Church of God.

[§ 1. BLASPHEMY AGAINST THE SPIRIT.]

Brethren and fathers,

As the most holy oracle of the Savior says, "Every sin will
be forgiven men *(Mt. 12:31)*, but he who blasphemes against the   10
Holy Spirit will not be forgiven, either in this age or in the age
to come" *(Lk. 12:10; Mt. 12:32)*. Let us then inquire what is the
blasphemy against the Holy Ghost.

Blasphemy against the Holy Ghost is to attribute His operations to the opposite spirit, as says Basil the Great (Reg. brev.
tract. 273, P.G. 31, 1272 BC). How does one do this? Whenever
one sees miracles brought about by the Holy Ghost or any of the
other divine gifts in any of his brethren—that is, compunction,
or tears, or humility, or divine knowledge, or a word of wisdom
from on high *(cf. 1 Cor. 12:8; Jas. 3:15, 17)*, or anything else that
is bestowed by the Holy Ghost on those who love God *(cf. Rom.
8:28)*—and says that this comes from the deceit of the devil. But   20
he also blasphemes against the Holy Ghost who works in them
(cf. 1 Cor. 12:11; Eph. 2:2) who says that those who as sons of God
are led by the divine Spirit *(cf. Rom. 8:14)*, and perform the commandments of their God and Father, are being deceived by demons. This is what the Jews of old said against the Son of God.
They saw demons driven out by Christ, yet they blasphemed
against His Holy Spirit and those shameless men said the impu-

dent words, "He casts out demons by Beelzebub, the prince of demons" *(Lk. 11:15)*. But there are some who hear these things without hearing, and see them without seeing *(cf. Mt. 13:13)*.
30   They witness all the works that divine Scripture attests as coming from the Holy Spirit's divine operation taking place, yet without trembling they say that these things happen out of drunkenness and demonic activity as though they were out of their senses. They reject all divine Scripture from their souls, and expel all the knowledge derived from it out of their minds.

[§ 2. THE IMPIETY OF DENYING THE EFFECTS OF GRACE.]

Like unbelievers and those completely uninitiated into the divine mysteries when they hear anything about divine illumination, or of the enlightenment of soul and mind, or of contem-
40   plation and freedom from passion, or of humility and tears that are poured out by the working and grace of the Holy Spirit, straightway the eyes of *their* hearts *(cf. Rom. 1:21, 11:10)* are darkened rather than enlightened, as though they could not endure the exceeding great light and power of the words. They audaciously aver that these things come from the deceit of demons. They do not tremble either before the judgment of God or at the damage they inflict on those who hear them. These imprudent men shamelessly affirm to everybody that nothing like that comes from God to any of the faithful in our day. This is more of an impiety than a heresy. It is heresy when someone turns aside in any way from the dogmas that have been defined con-
50   cerning the right faith. But to deny that at this present time there are some who love God, and that they have been granted the Holy Spirit and to be baptized by Him as sons of God, that they have become gods by knowledge and experience and contemplation, that wholly subverts the Incarnation of our God and Savior Jesus Christ *(Tit. 2:13)*! It clearly denies the renewal of the image that had been corrupted and put to death, and its return to incorruption and immortality.

[§ 3. HOW TO BE SAVED IF ONE HAS SINNED AFTER BAPTISM.]

Just as it is impossible for one to be saved who has not been
60   baptized by water and the Spirit *(Jn. 3:5)*, neither is it for him

who has sinned after Baptism, unless he be baptized from on high and be born again. This the Savior confirmed when He said to Nicodemus, "Unless one is born from on high,[1] he cannot enter into the kingdom of heaven" *(Jn. 3:3, 5)*. Again He said to the apostles, "John baptized with water, but you will be baptized with the Holy Spirit" *(Acts 1:5)*. If one is ignorant of the Baptism wherewith he was baptized as a child and does not even realize that he was baptized, but only accepts it by faith and then wipes it away with thousands upon thousands of sins, and if he denies the second Baptism—I mean, that which is through the Spirit, given from above by the loving-kindness of God to those who seek it by penitence—by what other means can he ever obtain salvation? By no means!

[§ 4. PENITENCE—THE WAY OF THE HOLY GHOST.]

For this reason I bear witness before you all; I speak and will not cease to say that those of you who have defiled their first Baptism through the transgression of God's commandments must imitate the repentance of David and of the rest of the saints. Display a worthy penitence by means of all sorts of deeds and words, that you may draw on yourselves the grace of the all-holy Spirit. For this Spirit, when He descends on you, becomes like a pool of light to you, which encompasses you completely in an unutterable manner. As it regenerates you it changes you from corruptible to incorruptible, from mortal to immortal, from sons of men into sons of God and gods by adoption and grace—that is, if you desire to appear as kinsmen and fellow-heirs of the saints and enter with all of them into the kingdom of heaven. We have known such a man in our own time, our holy father the Studite, who has lived in our generation; and not him alone, but also some others who were his disciples. Through his petitions and prayers they were found worthy to partake of such a blessing as I have mentioned, by the unutterable loving-kindness of God, who is good above all. I say this, not by way of boasting in their strength, but, giving thanks to the goodness of God and proclaiming it to you all, that you too may be eager to be found worthy of so great a blessing. By this

---

1. The Greek word in the Gospel can mean equally "anew" or "from one on high." It would appear that Symeon uses it in this double sense.

is known a love that is in accordance with God, that one should not only seek to gain possession of the good for oneself, but also strive to make its riches known to one's brethren and urge them on to seek it and find it and be enriched by it.

[§ 5. HOW IT IS ALWAYS POSSIBLE TO DRAW NEAR TO GOD.]

It is for this reason, then, as you see, that I proclaim to you, as I repeat the words of the prophet, "Draw nigh unto Him and be enlightened, and the faces of your consciences will not be ashamed" *(Ps. 34:6 LXX)*. But why? Is it because you have abandoned yourselves to slackness and carelessness and the lusts and pleasures of the flesh that you say that it is impossible for you to be cleansed by penitence and to draw near to God? And do you also claim that it is impossible to receive the grace of His Spirit and to be regenerated thereby, and to receive the adoption of sons and to become like Him? This is not impossible, it is not! It was impossible before His coming to the earth; but since He was pleased to become man and "in every respect to be made like us, yet without sin" *(Heb. 2:17, 4:15)*, God, the Master of all things, has made these things possible and easy for us. He has given us "the power to become sons of God" *(Jn. 1:12)* and "fellow heirs with Him" *(Rom. 8:17)* to whom is due all glory, honor, and worship forever. Amen.

XXXIII

ON PARTAKING OF THE HOLY SPIRIT

That it is impossible for the works of virtue to assert themselves, except through the coming of the Spirit, without whom no one is able to attain to virtue, or to be able to be of use to others or receive the confidence of their thoughts. How the Godhead in Three Persons is in all respects equal and identical in Essence.

[§ 1. THE NEED FOR KINDLING THE LAMP
OF THE SOUL.]

Brethren and fathers,

God is fire *(cf. Heb. 6:4)* and He is so called by all the inspired Scripture *(cf. Heb. 12:29)*. The soul of each of us is a lamp. 10
Now a lamp is wholly in darkness, even though it be filled with oil or tow or other combustible matter, until it receives fire and is kindled. So too the soul, though it may seem to be adorned with all virtues, yet does not receive the fire—in other words, has not received the divine nature and light—and is still unkindled and dark and its works are uncertain. All things must be tested and manifested by the light *(cf. Eph. 5:13)*. The man whose soul's lamp is still in darkness, that is, untouched by the divine fire, stands the more in need of a guide with a shining torch, who will discern his actions. As he has compassion for the 20 faults he reveals in confession he will straightway straighten out whatever is crooked in his actions. Just as he who walks in the night cannot avoid stumbling, so he who has not yet seen the divine light cannot avoid falling into sin. As Christ says, "If anyone walks in the day, he does not stumble, because he sees this light. But if any one walks in the night, he stumbles, because he

has not the light in him" *(Jn. 11:9–10)*. When He said "in him,"
30 he meant the divine and immaterial light, for no one can possess
the physical light in himself.

[§ 2. TO THE LIGHT OF THE HOLY SPIRIT
AND OF CHRIST.]

Just as it is no use to him who walks in darkness to have
many and very beautiful lamps all extinguished *(cf. Mt. 25:8)*,
for they cannot help him to see either himself or any one else, so
he who appears to have all virtues in him (even if it were possible) *(cf. Lk. 8:18)*, but has not the light of the Holy Spirit in him,
can neither see his own actions properly nor have sure knowledge whether they are pleasing to God. He is unable either to
lead others or to teach them the will of God, nor is he fit to hear
40 [in confession] the thoughts of others, even were he to become
patriarch by man's appointment, until he has the light shining
in him. For Christ says, "Walk while you have the light, lest the
darkness overtake you; he who walks in the darkness does not
know where he goes" *(Jn. 12:35)*. If, then, he does not know
where he goes, how will he show the way to others? What is the
use if someone puts an extinguished lamp on another stand *(cf.
Mt. 5:15; Lk. 8:16, 11:33)* when he lacks a burning and shining
fire? This is not what he should do! Then what should he do?
That which God who is above all *(Rom. 9:5)* has determined, for
He says, "No one after lighting a lamp puts it in a cellar or un-
50 der a bushel, but on a stand, that those who enter may see the
light" *(Lk. 11:33)*. When he says this he adds also the characteristics of the lamp, which both guides and possesses the light in itself, by saying, "The lamp of the body is the eye" *(Lk. 11:34)*.
What else does He mean by "the eye" than simply the mind,
which will never become simple, unless it contemplates the simple light *(cf. Lk. 11:34ff.)*? The simple light is Christ. So he who
has His light shining in his mind is said to have the mind of
Christ *(1 Cor. 2:16)*. When your light is thus simple, then the
whole immaterial body of your soul will be full of light. But if
60 the mind be evil, that is, darkened and extinguished, then this
body of yours will be full of darkness *(cf. Lk. 11:34)*. "Therefore
be careful lest the light in you be darkness" *(Lk. 11:35)*. So He
tells us, take heed lest you think that you have what you do not
possess *(cf. Lk. 8:18)*. See how the Master Himself addresses us

in the same way as His own servants, when He tells us, "Take heed that you do not deceive yourself and think that you have light within you, when it is not light but darkness." See to it that we too utter the same words as the Master to our fellow-servants and do not say anything that is perverted or false.

So we say: See to it, brethren, that while we seem to be in God and think that we have communion with him *(1 John 1:6)* we should not be found excluded and separated from Him, since we do not now see His light. If that light had kindled our lamps, that is, our souls, it would shine brightly in us, just as our God and Lord Jesus Christ said, "If your whole body is full of light, having no part dark, it will be wholly bright, as when a lamp with its rays gives you light" *(Lk. 11:36)*. What other witness greater than this shall we adduce to make the matter clear to you? If you disbelieve the Master, how will you, tell me, believe your fellow-servant?

[§ 3. THE KEY OF KNOWLEDGE.]

But what shall I say to those who want to enjoy a reputation, and be made priests and prelates and abbots, who want to receive the confidence of others' thoughts, and who say that they are worthy of the task of binding and loosing? *(Mt. 16:19, 18:18)*? When I see that they know nothing of the necessary and divine things, nor teach these things to others nor lead them to the light of knowledge, what else is it but what Christ says to the Pharisees and lawyers: "Woe to you lawyers! For you have taken away the key of knowledge; you did not enter yourselves, and you hindered those who were entering" *(Lk. 11:52)*. But what is the key of knowledge other than the grace of the Holy Spirit given through faith? In very truth it produces knowledge and understanding through illumination and opens our closed and veiled mind *(cf. Lk. 24:45)* through many parables and symbols, as I have told you, as well as by clear proofs.

[§ 4. THE KEY, THE DOOR, AND THE HOUSE.]

I will tell you yet again, the door is the Son, for, says He, "I am the door" *(Jn. 10:7, 9)*. The key of the door is the Holy Spirit, for He says, "Receive the Holy Spirit. If you forgive the sins of any, they are forgiven; if you retain the sins of any, they are retained" *(Jn. 20:22–23)*. The house is the Father, for "in My

70

80

90

100

Father's house are many mansions" *(Jn. 14:2)*. Pay careful attention, therefore, to the spiritual sense of the passage. Unless the key opens—as He says, "To him the porter opens" *(Jn. 10:3)*—the door is not opened. But if the door is not opened, no one enters into the Father's house, for Christ says, "No one comes to the Father, but by Me" *(Jn. 14:6)*.

[§ 5. THE KEY—SYMBOL OF THE HOLY SPIRIT.]

But that the Holy Spirit first opens our minds and teaches us the things concerning the Father and Son, He Himself again
110   said, "When He, the Spirit of truth comes, who proceeds from the Father, He will bear witness to Me *(Jn. 15:25)*, and will guide you into all the truth" *(Jn. 16:13)*. Do you see how through the Spirit, or, rather, in the Spirit, the Father and the Son are made known inseparably? Again He says, "If I do not go away, the Paraclete will not come to you *(Jn. 16:7)*. But when He comes, He will bring all things to your remembrance," and again, "If you love Me, you will keep My commandments; and I will pray to the Father, and He will give you another Paraclete,
120   to be with you forever, even the Spirit of truth" *(Jn. 14:15ff.)*. A little later He says, "In that day"—that is, when the Holy Spirit comes to you—"you will know that I am in the Father, and you in Me, and I in you" *(Jn. 14:20)*, and again, "John baptized with water, but you shall be baptized with the Holy Spirit" *(Acts 1:5)*. Rightly so, for unless one is baptized with the Holy Spirit, he does not become a son of God or a fellow-heir with Christ *(cf. Rom. 8:17)*. He also says to Peter, "I will give you the keys of the kingdom of heaven" *(Mt. 16:19)*, not keys of bronze or iron, but
130   keys worthy of that house. What is the nature of that house? Listen to Paul as he speaks in the epistle to Timothy, "In the presence of God who gives life to all things, and of Christ Jesus" *(1 Tim. 6:13)* I charge you," and a little later, "The blessed and only Sovereign, the King of kings and Lord of lords, who alone has immortality and dwells in unapproachable light" *(1 Tim. 6:15–16)*. For if, as He says, the house is unapproachable, it is clear that the door of the house is light and is itself unapproachable. But if you speak of one thing as being approachable and the other as unapproachable, that which is approachable will be consumed by that which is not, nor will the key ever be able to

open it, unless it too is unapproachable and partakes of the same 140
nature, but will be burned up by the door or door by the house,
and so will become equally inaccessible to all. Or rather, it is our
faith that will be destroyed, in that the Trinity is divided into
that which is accessible and that which is not, into greater or
less.

But beware as you hear these things, that you do not take
the images of literal houses and doors and permit the physical
pattern to be imprinted on your minds, so that your soul falls
into doubt and blasphemy. You must reflect on all these images
in a proper way, in a manner that befits God, if you are able, ac- 150
cording to the rule and standard of the spiritual interpretation,
and so you will find the right interpretation of them all. But if
you are incapable of so understanding them in a manner that befits God, then receive them by mere faith and refuse all curious
inquiry.

[§ 6. THE DWELLING OF GOD.]

The Holy Ghost is spoken of as a key because through Him
and in Him we are first enlightened in mind. We are purified
and illuminated with the light of knowledge; we are baptized
from on high and born anew *(cf. Jn. 3:3, 5)* and made into children of God. As Paul says, "The Spirit Himself intercedes for us
with sighs too deep for words" *(Rom. 8:26)*, and again, "God has
given His Spirit in our hearts, crying, 'Abba!, Father!' " *(Gal.
4:6)*. This indicates to us that the door is light; the door shows us 160
that He who dwells in the house is Himself unapproachable
light *(1 Tim. 6:16)*. He who dwells therein is no other than God,
His house is nothing else but light. Likewise the light of the
Godhead and God are not two different things. He is one and
the same, the house and He who dwells in it, just as the light
and God are the same. In theological terms we use the term *house*
of the Son, even as we use it of the Father, for He says, "Thou,
O Father, art in Me, and I in them, and they in Me, and I, O Father, in Thee, that we may be One" *(cf. Jn. 17:21, 23)*. Similarly,
the Spirit says, "I will live in them and move among them" *(2
Cor. 6:16)*. "I and the Father will come and make our home with 170
him" *(Jn. 14:23)*. This He says through the Spirit, as Paul says,
"Now the Lord is the Spirit" *(2 Cor. 3:17)*. If, then, the Lord is

the Spirit, and the Father is in Him and He is in Him, and we likewise are in Him, then He is with God the Father and God is in Him.

[§ 7. THE PERSONS IN THE TRINITY.]

180

190

If there is need to state anything more precisely, that which the One is, the other Two are as well. For the Three are in the same *(cf. 1 John 5:8)* and are thought of as one Essence and Nature and Kingship. If a name is attributed to One, it is by nature applied to the others, with the exception of the terms *Father*, *Son*, and *Holy Ghost*, or the terms *beget*, *begotten*, and *proceeding*, for these alone indisputably apply to the Holy Trinity by nature and in distinctive fashion. As for an interchange of names, or their reversal, or their change, that we are forbidden to think or speak about. These terms characterize the three Persons, so that in this way we cannot place the Son before the Father nor the Holy Ghost before the Son. We must speak of them together as "Father, Son, and Holy Ghost," without the slightest difference of duration or time between them. The Son is begotten and the Spirit proceeds simultaneously with the Father's existence.

[§ 8. THE UNITY OF THE DIVINE NATURE.]

200

210

In all other cases the same name or comparison is attributed to each Person by Himself as well as to all Three together. So, if you speak of "light" *(1 John 5:8)*, then both each Person is light and the Three are one light; if you speak of "eternal life," so each of Them is likewise, the Son, the Spirit, and the Father, and the Three are one life. So God the Father is Spirit *(cf. Jn. 4:24)*, and the Spirit is the Lord *(2 Cor. 3:17)*, and the Holy Spirit is God. Each Person is God by Himself, and together the Three are one God. Each One is Lord and the Three are Lord. There is one God who is above all *(Rom. 9:5)*, Creator of all things; each One is that by Himself, and they are one God and Maker of all things. The Old Testament also says, "In the beginning God created heaven and earth. And God said, 'Let there be light,' and there was light" *(Gen. 1:1, 3)*. Thus the expression gives us to understand about the Father. When David says, "By the word of the Lord were the heavens made," we understand that this applies to the Son, "and all the host of them by the breath of His mouth" *(Ps. 32:6)*, we consider to be spoken of the Holy Ghost.

As for John, the "son of thunder" *(Mk. 3:17)*, he says in the Gospels, "In the beginning was the Word, and the Word was with God"—that is the Father, "and the Word was God"—that is, the Son. "All things were made by Him, and without Him was nothing made that was made" *(Jn. 1:1, 3)*.

[§ 9. OBTAINING THE TRUE KNOWLEDGE OF GOD.]

I beseech you therefore, you who bear the name of children of God *(1 John 3:1)* and who think that you are Christians, learn these things! You priests and monks teach others with vain words and think that you are rulers—but falsely! Ask your elders and high priests, gather yourselves together in the love of God, and first seek to learn and experience these things in fact, 220 and then have the will to see this and by experience become like God. Be anxious not merely to act a play and wear the garment thereof and so to approach apostolic dignities. Otherwise, as you in your imperfection rush to rule over others, before acquiring the knowledge of the mysteries of God, you will hear these words, "Woe to those who are wise in their own eyes, and shrewd in their own sight! Woe to those who put darkness for light and light for darkness!" *(Is. 5:21, 20)*.

So I entreat you all, brethren in Christ, first to lay a good foundation *(cf. Heb. 6:1)* of humility as you build up virtues. 230 Then through training in godliness *(1 Tim. 4:7)* raise the house *(cf. Mt. 7:24–25)* of the knowledge of the mysteries of God *(cf. Mt. 13:11; Lk. 8:10)* and so be enlightened by the divine light and see God with the purified eye of the heart *(cf. Mt. 5:8)*, as far as it is possible for us men. Then become initiated more perfectly into the mysteries of the kingdom of heaven *(cf. Mt. 13:11)*. Thus you will proceed from this knowledge, which is given from on high by the Father of lights *(Jas. 1:17)*, to the word of teaching *(cf. Rom. 12:7; 1 Tim. 4:6)* that you may instruct your neighbors "what is the will of God, what is good and acceptable and perfect" *(Rom. 12:2)*. Thus through our teaching we will bring "a people of His own" *(Tit. 2:14)* to God, who by His Holy Spirit 240 has appointed us teachers of His Church, so that we will not be cast out from Christ's wedding feast as contemptuous and without a wedding garment *(Mt. 20:10ff.)*. Rather, as wise stewards *(Lk. 12:42)* who have duly dispensed the word of teaching among our fellow-servants, and above that duly ordered our

250 own lives, may we enter in to Him without hindrance in the brightness of our lives and of heavenly knowledge. So may we be luminous and filled with the Holy Spirit and reign with Christ *(2 Tim. 2:12)*, as fellow-heirs with Him of that which belongs to the kingdom of God the Father in the Holy Ghost, the ever-living and immortal Fountain and Life. To him are due all glory, honor, and worship, now and ever, and to ages of ages. Amen.

XXXIV

[SYMEON'S APOLOGIA]

That it is dangerous for us to bury the talent God has given us, and that, on the contrary, one ought to show it openly and display it to all, and out of gratitude proclaim God's blessings that those who hear may benefit, even if some are displeased at it.

[§ 1. HOW SYMEON'S FRANKNESS HAS BEEN MISUNDERSTOOD.]

Brethren, fathers, and children in Christ our God,

Why are you suspicious of the instructions we have so often given you in different words? What judgment have you passed within yourselves against him who has so frankly spoken these   10
things?[1] Have you suspected us of saying something that is beyond the Scriptures? Have you secretly found fault with us and accused us of speaking with presumption? Have you condemned us for being boastful? If this is your attitude toward what I have spoken, may Christ pardon you! As for me, I entreat your charity that no one persist in this judgment. We have not written these things for the sake of exhibitionism—may God who has had mercy on us and led us this far not allow it! [We have written them] because we are mindful of God's gifts, which He has bestowed on our unworthy self from the beginning of life until the present moment. We give Him thanks and sing His praise as   20
a merciful Master, Benefactor, and Lord; and in gratitude we show to all of you the talent He has entrusted to us. How can we be silent before such an abundance of blessings, or out of

---

1. This would seem to have been spoken c. 995–998, when Symeon's monks were on the verge of revolt because of his strictness.

ingratitude bury the talent that has been given to us *(Mt. 25:18)*, like ungrateful and evil servants? Since we are unable to do that we proclaim His mercy, we confess His grace, we show all men His goodness toward us. By our oral teaching we encourage you too to strive that you may have part in His gifts and enjoy them, the gifts of which we, though unworthy, have been partakers through His unutterable goodness. In this we do not wrong you now, nor have we wronged you in the past *(2 Cor. 7:2)*. Rather, we long to share with you, our fellow-servants, the things we have received. You are Christ's people, a sacred flock, "a royal priesthood" *(1 Pet. 2:9)*, as you have been found worthy to hear yourselves called.

[§ 2. SYMEON SHARES GOD'S GIFTS WITH HIS BRETHREN.]

I am like a poor man who loves his brothers, who after asking for alms from a good and merciful Christian has received some coins and then runs with joy to his fellow beggars and tells them secretly, "Hurry up and run, so that you may get some too." And so he points out and shows them the man who gave him the coin, and if they are still incredulous, he opens his hand and shows it to them, so that they may hasten and quickly overtake that generous man. Even so I, the lowly, the poor, denuded of all goodness *(cf. Rev. 3:17)* and slave of the holiness of all of you, have experienced God's love for men and His compassion. I approached Him through penitence and the mediation of holy Symeon, my father and yours, and have received grace though I was unworthy of any grace. So I cannot endure to be alone and hide it in the bosom of my soul, but I tell you, all my brethren and fathers, about God's gifts and show you, as well as I am able, what is the talent that has been given to me. By speaking [about it] I lay it bare as though it were on the palm of my hand, and I tell it, not as a secret and in private, but I proclaim it with a loud voice, "Run, brethren, run!" Nor I am content with merely crying aloud, but I also show you the Master who has given it, pointing Him out to you by word of mouth instead of with my finger. For if a man gives a penny to some beggar, and the beggar then tells others so that he will have to give to them as well, he will be angry and will become the more reluctant to give. But God is not like that. He acts in a completely opposite way. For if

He gives anyone a talent, or rather some spiritual gift *(Rom. 1:11)* and he fails to proclaim this to all and publish it abroad, saying, "Come to the Master who gives generously and turns no one empty away" *(cf. Sir. 29:9)*, but on the contrary hides it and buries it when he has received it *(Mt. 25:18)*, then He is angry at him who has received the gift for being envious and unwilling to see his own brothers receive as he has received.

[§ 3. THE MOTIVES FOR HIS EXHORTATIONS.]

For this reason I cannot endure to be silent about the things I have seen, about the wonders of God I have known by fact and experience. Rather, I testify of them to all others as in God's presence, and say with a loud voice, "Run, all of you, before the door of repentance is closed to you by death. Run, that you may take hold of it before you depart this life; make haste that you may receive it, knock, that your Master may open to you *(Mt. 7:7; Lk. 11:9)* before you die, and that He may show Himself to you *(Jn. 14:21)*. Endeavor to possess the kingdom of heaven within you *(Lk. 17:21)*. Possess it consciously, and do not leave this life empty-handed, particularly you who think you have it within you unconsciously, though you have nothing because of your conceit."

Tell me then, how will he contemplate Christ's Father who has not acquired "the mind of Christ" *(1 Cor. 2:16)*? He who does not see Him speaking within himself, by what means or in what way will he say "Abba, Father" *(Rom. 8:15; Gal. 4:6)*? He who has failed consciously to acquire the kingdom of heaven within himself, how will he enter it after his death? He who does not contemplate the Son abiding in him through the Spirit *(1 John 3:24; Jn. 14:23)* together with the Father, how will he be with Them in the future? As the Lord said, "Father, I desire that they also, whom Thou hast given Me, may be with Me where I am" *(Jn. 17:24)*, and again, "I do not pray for these only, but also for all who are to believe in Me through their word, that they may all be one; even as Thou, Father, art in Me, and I in Thee, that they also may be one. The glory which Thou hast given Me I have given to them, that they may be one, even as we are one, I in them and Thou in Me, that they may be perfectly one, so that the world may know that Thou hast sent Me and hast loved them even as Thou hast loved Me" *(Jn. 17:20ff.)*.

70

80

90

Brethren, my boasting—as some regard it—consists in this, that the love of God moves me *(cf. 2 Cor. 5:14)* to reveal to you,

100 my fathers and brethren, God's ineffable goodness and love toward us. For the sake of this love He in such a way and to so great an extent glorifies those who have put their trust in Him.

[§ 4. THE UNION OF THE FATHER AND THE SON, AND OUR UNION WITH GOD.]

But please answer me as I ask you, "How so? When the Father loves the Son, is it unconsciously? Is it unconsciously and imperceptibly that the Son is with the Father?" You would certainly answer, "No!" Were we to concede this point and define that the Father and the Son do not know each other, our faith disappears and is destroyed; for if they do not know each other, then of necessity we also do not know Them. But if this is the case, then we are without God, since we have no knowledge of

110 God. But if it is true that, as He says, "the Father knows the Son, and the Son knows the Father" *(Mt. 11:27; Lk. 10:22; Jn. 10:13)* and, since He is God, is with God the Father, and similarly the Father is with the Son, as when He says, "As Thou, Father, art in Me, and I in Thee, that they also may be in Me, and I in them" *(Jn. 17:21, 23)*, He shows the equality of this mutual union. But the union of the Son with the Father is by nature and has no beginning; our union with the Son is by adoption and grace. Nevertheless we are all united together in God, and inseparably, as He again says, "I in them, and Thou in Me, that

120 they may become perfectly one" *(Jn. 17:23)*. For what purpose? "So that the world may know that Thou hast sent Me and hast loved them even as Thou hast loved Me." And Paul says, "Here there cannot be Greek and Jew, circumcised and uncircumcised, barbarian, Scythian, slave, free man, but Christ is all, and in all" *(Col. 3:11)*.

[§ 5. SYMEON IN THE SERVICE OF THE HOLY GHOST.]

You, then, who think that you are spiritual men, listen to these things and believe him who speaks. By the word of grace *(Acts 14:3, 20:32)* I tell you about the gifts that those who with fervent faith run to God and do what He has commanded receive from Him. So as I perform my ministry to the Spirit who

130 resounds from on high, spare me from all blame! Who is it that

is speaking? Listen to the Lord Himself as He says, "For it is not you who speak, but the Spirit of God speaking through you" *(Mt. 10:20)*. You see that it is not I who speak great and extraordinary things to your charity, but the Spirit of God who speaks in us. To this Peter, the chief [apostle], bears witness as he says, "No prophecy ever came by impulse of man, but holy men of God spoke, moved by the Holy Spirit" *(2 Pet. 1:21)*. But though we are insignificant and unworthy, far from all holiness and from the holy men of God, yet we cannot deny the power that has been given to us by God. We minister to you the oracles of God as those who are indebted to His grace, and display to you the talent that was given to us and the spiritual gift [bestowed on us] "through prophetic utterance with the laying on of hands" *(1 Tim. 4:14)* of the high priest who ordained us to the priesthood. He who is the very chief of the apostles commands us, saying, "As each has received a gift, employ it for one another, as good stewards of God's varied grace: whoever speaks, as one who utters oracles of God; whoever renders service, as one who renders it by the strength which God supplies" *(1 Pet. 4:10f.)*.

Therefore, brethren, it is the Spirit who speaks, not I, as the Lord and His faithful disciple assure us. But if I lie, where shall I flee from His inescapable justice, which sends into destruction those who lie, saying, "Thou shalt destroy them that speak lies" *(Ps. 5:7)*. He who fails to believe him who speaks through the Spirit commits a sin and blasphemes against the Spirit *(Mk. 3:29; Lk. 12:10)* who is speaking. Likewise if he who lacks the grace of the Spirit from on high dares to say, "I am uttering this in the Holy Spirit," like Simon Magus and his sympathizers, he will be an alien from God *(Acts 8:18ff.)* and his enemy, for he who resists the words of the Spirit *(Acts 7:51)* is in every respect an opponent of God. For God is inseparable and indivisible, for the Holy Spirit is inseparable from the eternity and the kingship of the Father and the Son.

[§ 6. SYMEON'S CONSCIOUSNESS OF HIS OWN UNWORTHINESS.]

Let us then, brethren, refuse to fight against God and become His enemies! Come, together with us "worship and fall down before Him" *(Ps. 95:6)* and do not rise from thence until

you receive God's gift, just as we who are unworthy have received it by His grace. We tell you nothing to your disadvan-
tage, brethren, but display our abundant love toward you all.
170 Had we told you that we have freely received grace from "the
Father of lights, from whom comes every perfect gift" *(Jas.
1:17)*, but that we do not want you to receive it, we should have
deserved to become an object of hatred both on the part of God
and of yourselves. But now as we present to you the truth from
divine Scripture and from experience itself and show you the
royal way, how are we wronging you? But if you look on me as
one who has no reputation, who is obscure and insignificant,
and so do not accept instruction from me, then know and learn
that "God chose what is foolish in the world to shame the wise,
180 and what is weak and despised, that He might shame the glorious and the strong" *(1 Cor. 1:27f.)*.

[§ 7. SYMEON INVOKES SCRIPTURE TO DEFEND
HIMSELF AGAINST THE ACCUSATION
OF DELUSION AND PRIDE.]

But perhaps someone will come forward and say, "The
things you are saying are great and exaggerated and beyond human power." I on my part will tell you, "They are indeed great
and above nature, for they are God's words, as I have said." He
will say, "How is it that none of the great Fathers has spoken so
explicitly about himself, or spoken such words as you speak
about yourself?" My good man, you deceive yourself! On the
contrary, the apostles and the fathers have spoken things that
are in harmony with my words, and even go beyond them. It is
190 the credibility of those who speak that makes what they say acceptable and credible. Our worthlessness, however, makes even
the things that all recognize to sound false and abhorrent.

Still, I have another reason to speak, for which I, however
unwillingly, have revealed these matters. What is it? It is the
false, unreasonable, and foolish notion of those who claim that
there does not at the present time exist such a person on the
earth and in our midst. Look how ingenious this malice is! Were
we not speaking openly, but anxious to keep our gift hidden,
they would think we were speaking the truth! But if we disclose
200 the truth by speaking of it they immediately condemn us for be-

ing proud and ignore what the holy apostles said. But what did they say? "We have the mind of Christ" *(1 Cor. 2:6)*. I would say to them, is this, in your judgment, an excess of pride? Then too [they said], "By this we know that He abides in us, by the Spirit which He has given us" *(1 John 3:24)*. How can you understand this to the discredit of the speaker? Then this [saying], "Do you desire proof that Christ is speaking in me?" *(2 Cor. 13:3)* and, "I think that I have the Spirit of God" *(1 Cor. 7:40)*. Similarly, "We did not receive the spirit of slavery to fall back into fear, but the Spirit of adoption, in which we cry, 'Abba, Father' " *(Rom. 8:15)*. And, "It is the God who said, 'Let light shine out of darkness,' who has shone in our hearts" *(2 Cor. 4:6)*. Do you consider all these things to have been uttered out of pride? How silly!

210

[§ 8. THE DESIRE FOR HOLINESS.]

But if you wish to learn how the illumination comes about in those who love the Lord, listen to Paul himself as he says, "We have this treasure in earthen vessels" *(2 Cor. 4:7)*, that is, in our bodies. But, you say, there is no such person at the present time! Tell me, why not? You may say, "Because, in my opinion, no one could become such a person at the present time, even if he wanted to, any more than one who does not want to." But if you claim that even he who wishes cannot become so, what shall we make of the passage, "But to all who received Him, He gave power to become children of God" *(Jn. 1:12)*, and, "If you will, you are all gods, and sons of the Most High" *(Ps. 82:6)*, and, "You shall be holy, for I am holy" *(1 Pet. 1:16)*? But if it is impossible for one to become such without desiring it, see that you have condemned yourself by neither wishing nor choosing to become holy; for if you want to, you are able to become that!

220

Even if you are not such a person, yet by God's will there others, very many of them, whom you do not know. For if in the days of Elijah God had seven thousand who had not bent their knees to Baal *(1 Kings 19:18)*, how much more now, when He has poured out His Holy Spirit richly upon us *(Tit. 3:5f.)*? But if one does not strip himself of everything and draw near [to Him] naked and seek to receive, the fault is not on God's part, but on the part of him who is unwilling. Just as fire eagerly (if I may

230

say so!) and naturally takes hold of the fuel, so the grace of the all-holy and adorable Spirit seeks to enkindle our souls, so that it may shine even to those who are in the world and, through those in whom it shines, direct the footsteps of the multitude *(cf. Ps. 5:9)* that they may go on the right way. Thus they too may draw near to the fire and one by one, or, if possible, all of them together, may be enkindled and shine like gods in our midst, that "the seed of the God of Jacob" *(cf. Is. 2:3)* may be blessed and may multiply *(cf. Gen. 22:17)*, and the godlike man may not fail, but shine as a light upon the earth.

[§ 9. SYMEON PROTESTS THE RIGHTNESS OF HIS INSTRUCTION.]

This, in my opinion, is the truth of the matter, and such is God's counsel toward us whom He has formed, and whom He has honored and glorified of old with the glory of His image *(Gen. 1:27)*. You, on your part, must see and test that which we say. If we have views different from those of the apostles and of the holy God-inspired fathers, if we speak contrary to what they said, if we fail to repeat what the Holy Gospels say about God, then let me be anathema from the Lord God Jesus Christ. Let it fall on me if we do not enkindle in everyone that life-giving energy and gift which is in these [writings]—yet lamentably extinguished, as far as men are able, by foolish reasonings—and fail to point to the light that already is shining, as we establish and assert all things from the Holy Scriptures themselves and clearly demonstrate them. We would be guilty of teaching other than what God's apostles taught and proclaimed as good news *(cf. Gal. 1:8)*. You on your part should not only stop your ears to prevent them from hearing it, but even stone me and kill me as an ungodly man and an atheist! Instead, however, we restore the teachings of the Master and the apostles that some have perverted. From the very divine Scriptures themselves we collect that which strengthens and corrects their thinking and that of their followers. We urge them not merely to look forward to the resurrection, to incorruption, to life [eternal] and the kingdom of heaven and to all the eternal blessings with hope, but we teach that they are present and revealed, apparent and visible, and already given as pledges to those who are elect and will be saved. If we are anxious to prove and establish the very things that others postpone till after death and the resurrection, ought we not rather be acceptable and greatly beloved by them and by all as those who perform a work of perfect love? 270

[§ 10. THE HIDDEN TREASURE BROUGHT TO LIGHT
AND SHARED.]

He who discovers a hidden treasure and keeps it for himself alone incurs blame on the part of everybody and is condemned for being avaricious; while he who does not hide it for himself, but instead shows it to everybody and shares it, allowing everyone to partake of it as much as he wants, is altogether worthy of praise and deserves to be accepted by both God and men. So I 280 too will "act foolishly" in spiritual things as I speak by God's grace *(cf. 2 Cor. 11:17, 23)*. For when a holy man in a certain place showed me the treasure hidden in the divine Scriptures, I was not slow to rise up and search for it till I saw it. When I had asked for his help and assistance and received it I left every other occupation and activity of this life and arrived at the place where that good man had told me in writing that the treasure was to be found. With much labor and toil I ceased not night and day to dig and excavate, casting the dirt aside and going 290 deeper and deeper until the treasure began to shine above the earth. So, when I had worked hard digging and throwing up the dirt I brought up all the treasure that had been lying below, cleared, I think, of all the earth, and so saw it clean from all defilement. As I look at it I constantly cry aloud to those who do not believe and refuse to work hard and dig, and exclaim, "Come, see, all who do not believe the divine Scriptures." This I do, obeying to the full what Solomon says, "I learned without guile and I impart without grudging" *(Wis. 7:13)*. I therefore proclaim this to everybody, as it is said, "Come, learn that it is 300 not merely in the future, but even now that the unutterable treasure which 'is above every rule and authority' *(Eph. 1:21)* lies open before your very eyes and hands and feet. Come, be persuaded that this treasure of which I tell you is 'the light of the world' " *(Jn. 8:12)*.

[§ 11. THE VARIEGATED BEAUTY OF THE TREASURE.]

It is not of myself that I say this. He who Himself is the treasure has said, and still says, "I am the resurrection and the life" *(Jn. 11:25)*; "I am the mustard seed" *(Mt. 13:31)* that was hidden in the ground; "I am the pearl" *(Mt. 13:46)* that is bought by the faithful; I am the kingdom of heaven that is hidden in your midst *(cf. Lk. 17:21)*. Just as I am seen by those who have sought and found Me now *(cf. Mt. 7:7)*, so I will shine not only in them, but above them all, just as I am shining even now, though hidden, above all the heavens *(Eph. 4:10)*. Though by My nature I cannot be contained, yet even here below I am contained in you by grace; though I am invisible I become visible. I do not show how great I am, though I remain entire while I am being seen, but [I show myself] only to the extent that the nature and ability of those who see Me can bear. I am the leaven that the soul receives and puts into its three faculties, and so is leavened and becomes entirely like Me *(cf. Mt. 13:33; Lk. 13:21)*, for as the leaven is, so also the flour that is kneaded with it becomes, together with the salt and water. For with Me, He says, who am the Son, is My Father who is of the same nature, and His Paraclete, who take the place of water and of salt. I am He who takes the place of the physical Paradise and become a spiritual Paradise for My servants. In it I place all those who believe in Me and are born again through the Spirit *(cf. Jn. 3:3, 5)*. They can no longer sin *(1 John 3:9)*, nor can the ruler of the world do anything against them *(Jn. 14:30)*, for I am in them and they are in Me *(Jn. 15:4)*; and they overcome the world *(1 John 5:4f.)* because they are outside the world *(Jn. 15:18)*, because they have Me with them who am stronger than all. I am the luminous source *(cf. Jn. 4:14)* of the immortal stream and river. In it those who love Me with [all their] soul are washed by the water that flows from Me, not after death but hour by hour, and are cleansed from every stain both in body and soul, so that they are completely radiant like a lamp and have the appearance of a sunbeam. I am the sun who rises in them every hour as in the morning and am seen by the mind, just as I in times past manifested Myself in the prophets. When they saw Me they sang My praise and constantly called on Me, as David says, "In the morning hear my voice, in the morning I shall stand before Thee, and

310

320

330

340

Thou wilt look upon me" *(Ps. 5:3 LXX)*. In another place [He says], "Then shall your light break forth like the dawn, and your healing shall spring up speedily" *(Is. 58:8)*, that is, "when you keep My commandments."

[§ 12. THE LIGHT THAT IS AVAILABLE TO ALL.]

Why am I thus compelled to tell your charity all that God, out of His thirst for our salvation, speaks to us? Simply, in order that through them all you may learn and be persuaded that those who sit in darkness must see the great Light shine *(Is. 9:2)*, if only they look toward it, and also that none of you may think that though it shone in the past, it is impossible for men of the present day to see it while they are still in the body. For if it were impossible, why did it shine then, and why does it still shine when they do not see it? Rather, the light always existed *(cf. Jn. 1:1ff.)* and always shone and still shines in those who have been cleansed. It shone in the darkness and the darkness did not overcome it *(Jn. 1:5)*, and it shines now and the darkness does not overcome it; it does not even touch it. But to state that "now" it has risen for the people that sits in darkness *(Is. 9:2)* means that even now it vouchsafes to reveal itself to those to whom it appears, for the others who are in the darkness do not receive it. For He who is invisible has appeared, both by means of the body through physical eyes to all who beheld Him, both believers and unbelievers, and He was also made known and the light of His Godhead was revealed, yet only to those who showed their faith by deeds. It was those who would say to Him, "Lo, we have left everything and followed you" *(Mt. 19:27)*. By the word *everything* he included lands, money, their own wills, to the point of contempt and abhorrence for this transitory life in order that they might taste that life which is substantial and eternal. It is altogether sweeter and preferable; it is nothing else but God Himself.

350

360

[§ 13. A FINAL ADMONITION.]

But I entreat you all, fathers and brethren, to endeavor to become partakers of such a life. It is the light of God, the Holy Ghost Himself, who sanctifies those who partake of Him *(Heb. 6:4)* and who makes them gods by adoption. As for those great words I have spoken to you, do not forget them! First yourselves

370

380

learn constantly to practice goodness and thus teach others to do the same *(Mt. 5:19)*, so that the words of your instruction may be efficacious, readily acceptable to those who hear. Otherwise, I am without blame with regard to any of you! I have not shrunk from declaring to you *(Acts 20:27)* the things that were told and made known to me and commanded by our Lord Jesus Christ through His adorable and Holy Spirit concerning the sublime gifts and graces of His Father, who with Him is God without beginning. To those who strenuously seek Him He grants to share in them through faith, at all times and up to the present. He is our good God and Benefactor, to whom is due all glory, honor, and adoration, now and always, forever and ever. Amen.

XXXV

[THE MYSTICAL EXPERIENCE OF GRACE IN THE FORM OF A THANKSGIVING]

By the same (Symeon). A thanksgiving to God for the gifts of which he has been found worthy. A description of the way in which God constantly manifests Himself to those whose hearts have been cleansed, and how they may be recognized.

[§ 1. A GENERAL THANKSGIVING FOR ALL GOD'S BLESSINGS.]

I give Thee thanks, I worship Thee, I fall before Thee, O Lord of all, all-holy King, for that Thou hast shown mercy on me, though I am unworthy, yet Thou hast honored and glorified me, as Thou hast willed from the beginning. For before the world came into being from Thee *(Jn. 17:5)* Thou didst have me wholly in Thyself, and glorify me by giving me reason and honor me with Thy image. For no other reason but for my sake, who Thou didst create according to Thine image and likeness *(Gen. 1:26)*, hast Thou brought forth all things out of nothing, and made me to be king of all earthly things for the glory of Thy mighty works and Thy goodness.

I give Thee thanks because Thou hast fulfilled every petition and desire of mine for my good in accordance with Thy promises made to us Thy servants. Beyond what I had hoped and desired, Thou hast granted yet more to me, though I am unworthy of heaven and earth. For Thou hast said, "Whatever you ask in My Name, you will receive if you have faith" *(Jn. 14:13;*

10

20   *Mt. 21:22).* I give Thee thanks, because when I longed to see one of Thy saints and when I came to faith through him, I found mercy from Thee. Not only hast Thou done this, O Gracious One, by showing to me Thy true servant, that is, the blessed and holy Symeon, and wast pleased that he should love me, but hast also granted me thousands upon thousands of other blessings I did not hope for.

[§ 2. FOR THE KNOWLEDGE OF SPIRITUAL BLESSINGS.]

Whence could I, a wretched one, have known that Thou, O our good Master, art such that I should so desire Thee? From whence could I have known that Thou showest Thyself to those who come to Thee while they still live in the world, that I

30   should have sought to contemplate Thee? From what source could I have realized that those who receive the light of Thy grace within themselves would be vouchsafed such a joy and consolation? From what source, or in what manner, could such a wretch as I have known that those who have believed in Thee receive Thy Holy Spirit *(Acts 19:2)?* For I thought that I had perfect faith in Thee and imagined that I possessed all that Thou grantest to those who fear Thee. But I had nothing whatever, as I later realized! Whence could I have known, O Master, that Thou, who are invisible and without limit, yet may be seen and contained within us? From whence was I able to think that Thou, the Master who hast created the universe, unitest Thyself

40   to men whom Thou has formed, making them bearers of God and Thy sons? I too came to long for this and sought to receive these benefits from Thee. Whence could I have known, O Lord, that I had such a God, such a Master, such a Protector, Father, Brother, King, as Thee who becamest poor for my sake *(2 Cor. 8:9)* and didst take the form of a servant *(Phil. 2:7)?*

[§ 3. THANKSGIVING FOR POSSESSING GOD.]

In truth, my Master who lovest mankind, I knew none of all these things at all. For even if I had looked into the divine Scriptures, which the saints edited and constantly read about these things, I would have received them as though they were about

50   other men or addressed to others. I remained insensitive to all

that was written. In fact, I was incapable even of the slightest thought about them.

When I heard Thy herald Paul proclaim and say, "What no eye has seen, nor ear heard, nor the heart of man conceived, what God has prepared for those who love Him" *(2 Cor. 2:9)*, I was sure that it was impossible for anyone who was in the flesh to enter into the contemplation of them. I thought that Thou didst show these things to him alone out of a special generosity, and I, the wretched one, did not know that Thou doest this to all those who love Thee. From what source or in what manner could I have known that everyone who believes in Thee be- comes a member of Thee *(cf. 1 Cor. 6:15)*, and by grace reflects 60 Divinity—who would believe it? And that he becomes blessed, in that he becomes a blessed member of the Blessed God? Whence could I have known that Thou takest the place of physi- cal food, becoming immortal and uncorruptible bread *(cf. Jn. 6:32ff.)* with which those who are hungry for Thee are never sated? That Thou art an immortal spring to those who thirst *(cf. Jn. 4:14)*, and a robe resplendent with light to those who for Thy sake wear shabby clothes? When I heard these things spoken by Thy messengers, I supposed that they pertained to the world to come and would happen only after the resurrection. I did not know that they take place now, when we are in greatest need of 70 them.

[§ 4. FOR HAVING FOUND A TRUE SPIRITUAL FATHER.]

These things I did not know, all-holy King, nor did I ever experience any desire for them. I did not ask any of them from Thee; instead, I remembered my sins and merely asked for their forgiveness from Thee. I wanted, O Master, to find a mediator and an ambassador, as I have said before, that through his inter- cession and my submission to him I might find forgiveness for my many offenses, if only in the world to come. When I heard all with one accord saying that there was now no such saint upon the earth, I fell into even greater sorrow. Nevertheless I 80 was not yet certain of this, and to such men I replied, As Thou knowest, O Master Christ, I said, "My Lord, have mercy! Has the devil become so much more powerful than God our Master that he has drawn all men to himself and brought them over to His side? Is there no one left on God's side?"

I think that for this reason, O King who lovest man, Thou didst cause Thy Holy light to shine on me as I sat in the darkness of this life and in the midst of the wicked (*cf. Lk. 1:79; Ps.*
90 *26:5*). In that light Thou didst show me Thy saint. Thou has treated me as Thy servant Paul, whom Thou didst call through Thy divine appearing, when he persecuted Thee. When he saw Thee, O Master, he said, "Who art Thou?" *(Acts 9:5)* and Thou didst not say, "I am He who made heaven and earth" *(Acts 4:24)*, nor "I am He who brought all things into being out of nothing." Nor didst Thou say, "I am He who is" *(Ex. 3:14 LXX)*, nor "The God of Sabaoth" *(cf. 1 Sam. 1:3)*, or "The God of your fathers" *(Gen. 46:3)*, nor any other of the names that pertain to Thy glory. This alone Thou didst say to him: "I am Jesus of Nazareth whom you persecute" *(Acts 9:5)*, that he might surely know that
100 Thou whom he persecuted art the God who wast incarnate for us. So Thou hast dealt with me, O Master, when Thou didst please to show me Symeon Thy saint.

[§ 5. FOR THE FIRST VISION.]

When Thy divine light had shone on all things, even on me in my wretchedness, and had made the night most bright like the day *(Ps. 139:12)*, Thou didst grant me to see him in the very height of Thy Godhead. What a terrifying vision! For he stood close to Thy divine glory, and Thou didst not adorn him with any crown nor resplendent garment, nor transformation of appearance. But Thou madest me see him as he lived in our midst and was daily seen upon earth; as such Thou showedst him in
110 heaven to me. For what purpose? That I should not think that he who appeared to me there was any other than he who was with us, and so in my error stray far away from the Good Shepherd *(Jn. 10:11)*—I who was the lost sheep *(cf. Lk. 15:6)*.

[§ 6. FOR HIS CONVERSION AND A SECOND VISION.]

Yet I, the miserable one, did not understand when this miracle took place. Bit by bit I was snatched away by slackness and neglect. I fell back into my former sins or worse. But Thou, O merciful and patient King, didst not even then turn away from

me, but through that same saint (i.e., Symeon) Thou didst turn
me back to Thee and didst grant me to fall at his holy feet. By
Thy mighty hand and Thine outstretched arm Thou didst lead   120
me out *(Deut. 5:15)* from the deceitful world and the affairs and
pleasures of the world, and separated me in body and soul from
them all. What a marvel! How great Thy love and compassion
toward us, O God, Lover of man! Thou didst set me in the ranks
of those who serve Thee. After this, O Master, not only didst
Thou grant me the pardon of my untold offenses, but also all the
blessings I have mentioned by the intercession of Thy saint;
rather, Thou Thyself hast become all things to me *(cf. 1 Cor.
15:28).*

Already Thou didst dwell in him and didst shine with Thy
divine glory, so I drew near to him and in penitence and faith   130
took hold of his feet. At once I perceived a divine warmth. Then
a small radiance that shone forth. Then a divine breath from his
words. Then a fire kindled in my heart, which caused constant
streams of tears to flow. After that a fine beam went through my
mind more quickly than lightning. Then there appeared to me
as it were a light in the night and a small flaming cloud resting
on his head, while I lay on my face and made supplication.
Afterwards it moved away and shortly after appeared to me as
being in heaven.

[§ 7. FOR STRENGTH IN TEMPTATION.]

Then, as I reflected on the meaning of the vision, some-   140
thing yet more extraordinary than all this took place. While I
was being tempted by evil demons in my sleep, and being drawn
by their machination to a passion of pollution, I resisted mightily and called on Thee, the Lord of light, for help. So I awak-
ened and escaped without harm from the hands of the tempters.
I was amazed at myself how I had shown firmness and courage,
and even more that I had not been moved toward passion. I
thought "How did this unaccustomed triumph happen, that I
should resist even while asleep and prevail over my adversaries
and enemies, and win an unexpected mighty victory through   150
Christ?" What a marvel! At once I realized that He whom I had
thought to be in heaven was within me; I mean Thee, O Christ,
my Creator and King! And then I knew that the victory was
Thine, which Thou gavest me to overcome the devil.

[§ 8. FOR THE ONGOING CLEANSING OF HIS SOUL.]

But I knew not yet, O Master, that Thou, who formedst me from clay *(Gen. 2:7)*, hadst bestowed these blessings on me. I knew not yet that Thou wast my God free from pride[1] and my Lord. I had not yet been found worthy to hear Thy voice that I might know Thee, nor didst Thou then mystically say to me, "I am" *(cf. Mt. 14:27; Mk. 6:20; Jn. 6:20)*. For I was unworthy and unclean; the ears of my soul were as yet stopped with the clay of sin, my eyes were held by unbelief and ignorance, and by the feeling of passion and its darkness. Thus I beheld Thee, O my God. I did not know, nor did I previously believe that God was seen by anyone as far as it is possible to see Thee. Nor did I consider that it was God or God's glory that from time to time was being shown to me sometimes in one way, sometimes in the other. The unexpected marvel struck me with amazement; it filled my whole soul and my heart with joy, so much so that it seemed to me as though my body partook of that unspeakable grace. Yet I did not clearly recognize that it was Thee whom I saw then. Hitherto I had frequently seen a light, at times within, when my soul had enjoyed calmness and peace. At times it appeared to me externally, from afar, or even it was completely hidden, and by its hiddenness caused me the unbearable pain of thinking I would not see it again. But when I lamented and wept and displayed complete solitude and obedience and humility it appeared to me again. It was like the sun as it penetrates through the thickness of the mist and gradually shows itself a gently glowing sphere. Thus Thou, the ineffable, the invisible, the impalpable, the immovable, who always art everywhere present in all things and fillest everything, at all times, or if I may say so, by day and by night, art seen and art hidden. Thou goest away and Thou comest, Thou dost vanish from sight and Thou suddenly appearest. So bit by bit Thou didst scatter the darkness that was within me; Thou didst dispel the mist and dissolve the thickness; Thou didst cleanse the dim eyes of my intellect. Thou

---

1. This unusual epithet for the Deity is so used by S. Symeon only in this place and in 36.138. It apparently is so used in only two other writings of Christian antiquity, both of them spurious "Acts" of Apostles, the Acts of John and the Acts of Xanthippa and Polyxena (professing to deal with the ministry of S. Paul in and near Ephesus. See the article by archbishop Basil Krivocheine in Studia Patristica, vol. II, pp. 485–494 (Berlin, 1957).

didst remove the barriers of my eyes and didst open them; Thou tookest away the veil of insensitivity. At the same time 190 Thou didst put to sleep all passion and every fleshly pleasure and totally expel them from me. Having thus brought me to this state Thou didst clear the heaven of every mist. By "the heaven" I mean the soul Thou hast cleansed in which Thou comest invisibly (how or from whence I know not). Thou who art everywhere present art suddenly found and manifested like another sun. O ineffable condescension!

[§ 9. FOR HAVING TAKEN HOLD OF GOD IN HIS SIMPLICITY.]

Brethren, such are the wonderful deeds of God toward us! As we ascend to that which is more perfect, He who is without form or shape comes no longer without form or without shape. Nor does He cause His light to come to us and be present with us in silence. But how? He comes in a definite form indeed, 200 though it is a divine one. Yet God does not show Himself in a particular pattern or likeness, but in simplicity, and takes the form of an incomprehensible, inaccessible, and formless light. We cannot possibly say or express more than this; still, He appears clearly and is consciously known and clearly seen, though He is invisible. He sees and hears invisibly and, just as friend speaks to friend face to face (cf. Ex. 33:11), so He who by nature is God speaks to those whom by grace He has begotten as gods. He loves like a father, and in turn He is fervently loved by His sons. Thus for them He becomes a strange thing to behold and even more awesome to hear, for though He cannot be fittingly 210 expressed in words by them, yet He cannot bear to be veiled by silence.

[§ 10. FOR THE MANIFESTATIONS OF THE SPIRIT IN THE LIVES OF THE SAINTS.]

Since the saints are constantly inflamed by longing for Him and mystically inspired by Him, they write sometimes to bewail the possessions of others, sometimes they expose their own failures, and at times they recount with gratitude the blessings bestowed on them and the workings of grace. They sing theological hymns of praise to Him who by His divine working has transformed them. At other times, if they hear anything that has been erroneously and faultily expressed concerning the salvation of our souls, they set it right in accordance with the measure of the knowledge *(cf. Rom. 12:3)* that has been given them. They put this in writing and bring in testimonies from the divine Scriptures, without being able to rest or be satisfied with that which they have expounded. How is it that they are able to do all these things? Because they are no longer their own *(cf. 1 Cor. 6:19)* but belong to the Spirit who is in them. He moves them and is Himself moved by them. In them He becomes all the things about which you hear in the divine Scriptures concerning the kingdom of heaven—a pearl *(cf. Mt. 13:46)*, a mustard seed *(Mt. 13:31; Mk. 4:31)*, leaven *(Mt. 13:33; Lk. 13:21)*, water, fire *(cf. Mt. 3:11; Lk. 12:49)*, bread *(Jn. 6:32–33)*, drink of life. He becomes a living fountain springing forth, a river flowing with spiritual words *(Jn. 4:17)*, word of divine life, a lamp *(cf. Mt. 5:15)*, bed, marriage bed, wedding chamber *(Mt. 22:10)*, bridegroom *(Mt. 25:1)*, friend, brother, and father. But why do I try with many words to expound the whole matter—the terms are without number! For how can the tongue measure what "eye has not seen, nor ear heard, nor the heart of man conceived" *(1 Cor. 2:9)* and express it in words? In no way whatever! For even if we possessed all these things within us because we carry with us God who supplies them, yet we cannot measure with our minds, nor in any way explain them by word.

[§ 11. FINAL RESUMÉ.]

These things we recorded, fathers and brethren, not for the sake of self-display—God forbid! For what we have is not ours to boast of—unless it were the sins committed from my mother's womb *(Ps. 22:11)*, the many impurities and transgressions, which I think not even the sand of the sea could equal in number *(cf. Josh. 11:4)*. It is God's marvelous deeds we declare and recount to you, though not as we ought, yet as we are able. In addition, we do this in order that we by this account may be of help to those who think that they have the Holy Spirit unconsciously since divine Baptism. For this discourse teaches us first of the total darkness and obscurity that at first prevails in us, that is, our alienation from the divine Light, when it clearly goes as far as ignorance about God. Then it describes the reproach on the part of the conscience, then the fear, then the desire for the remission of debts. It directs the man who seeks a mediator and helper for this purpose, for no one is able to approach by himself without shame; all are burdened by the shame of many sins. Then how by the intellectual illumination of the Spirit he obtains and sees a mediator and a shepherd and intercessor. The Spirit also shows him the beginning of the illumination, into which he had not previously been initiated. But even though he has received this revelation, when the contemplation of the Spirit departs from him and he is deprived of it he falls back into the darkness of many sins. After these things our discourse has told of the second call that takes place through the shepherd and then of the subsequent obedience, faith, humility, submission; how through these bit by bit a clear transformation takes place in our knowledge and contemplation. He who has not recognized that change taking place in himself in accordance with the description in this discourse cannot possibly have the Holy Spirit dwelling within him. But as this discourse went over these things in detail, as I have said above, it gave us no occasion for pride, but rather we rejoiced in the marvelous works of God. These things He works out of pure goodness in those who seek Him "with all their soul and heart" *(Ps. 119:2, 10)*, so that every (vain) pretext and disobedience may receive its just retribution *(Heb. 2:2)* on the day when God will judge the race of mankind *(cf. Rom. 2:16)*. To Him is due all glory, honor, and adoration, now and always, forever and ever. Amen.

260

270

XXXVI

[IN THE FORM OF A THANKSGIVING] [AT THE THRESHOLD OF TOTAL ILLUMINATION]

By our holy and great father Symeon the New [Theologian]. A thanksgiving to God for the blessings he has received at His hands, in which he also speaks of spiritual prayer and progress therein. Of divine illumination, and contemplation without error, and of love toward God.

[§ 1. SYMEON'S THANKSGIVING FOR HIS SUPERNATURAL DESTINY.]

I give Thee thanks, O Master, Lord of heaven and earth *(Mt. 11:25; Lk. 10:21)*, who before the foundation of the world *(Jn. 17:24; Eph. 1:4)* hast determined that I should come into being out of that which was not. I give Thee thanks, because before the hour and the day arrived *(Mt. 24:36)* when Thou hadst commanded that I should be brought into being, Thou the only immortal One *(1 Tim. 1:17)*, the only almighty One, who alone art good and loving toward mankind, camest down from Thy holy height *(Ps. 102:20)*. Thou didst not leave the Father's bosom; Thou wast incarnate from the holy Virgin Mary and wast born. So in advance Thou didst reform me and give me life and set me free from my forefather's fall and so restore to me the ascent into heaven. Afterwards, when I had been born and as I was gradually growing in size Thou renewedst me by Holy Baptism and formedst me anew *(cf. Tit. 3:5)* and didst adorn me with the Holy Spirit and appoint an angel of light to be my

10

368

guardian, and until mature age didst preserve me from the hostile attacks and the snares of the enemy.   20

[§ 2. FOR BEING SNATCHED FROM THE PERILS OF THE WORLD.]

But since Thou hast seen fit to save us, not by compulsion but by free choice, Thou didst permit me also to be honored by freedom of the will that I might freely choose to show love toward Thee by keeping Thy commandments. Yet in my ingratitude and contempt, like a horse set free from its reins, I so valued the dignity of my free will that I leaped away from Thy authority and cast myself down the precipice. As I was lying there senselessly wallowing and inflicting greater injuries on myself, Thou didst not turn away, nor didst Thou allow me to   30 be defiled in the mud, but by Thy tender mercy *(cf. Lk. 1:79)* Thou didst send for me and bring me up from thence and yet more gloriously honor me. From kings and princes who would use me as a vessel of dishonor *(Rom. 9:21; 2 Tim. 2:20)* to minister to their desires Thou didst deliver me by Thine ineffable judgments. Though I was full of avarice, yet didst Thou not permit me to receive gifts of gold and silver; as for glory and distinction in life, Thou grantedst me to regard as an abomination the price that was offered me instead of Thy holiness.

Yet, O Lord God of heaven and earth *(cf. Mt. 11:25; Lk.*   40 *10:21)*, I confess I regarded all these [benefits] as nothing. Again I, wretched one, cast myself into the pit and the mud of the abyss *(Ps. 69:3)* of shameful thoughts and deeds and once I had come there I fell into the hands of those who were concealed by the darkness. From these neither I alone, nor the whole world gathered into one, could have availed to bring me up from thence and deliver me from out of their hands.

[§ 3. FOR HAVING FOUND A SPIRITUAL GUIDE.]

Nevertheless when I was there held captive, miserably and wretchedly dragged about, strangled, and mocked by them, Thou the compassionate Master who lovest man didst not over-   50 look me, nor didst Thou bear me ill will nor turn away from my ingratitude, nor didst Thou abandon me for long to bandits, though I was willingly tyrannized by them. Even when I in my

369

senselessness rejoiced in being led astray by them Thou couldest not bear to see me led about and dragged in dishonor, but Thou didst have compassion, O Master, and show pity on me. It was not an angel or a man whom Thou didst send to me, miserable sinner, but Thou Thyself was moved by Thy tender goodness (*Is. 63:7*). Thou didst stoop into that exceeding deep pit; Thou 60 didst stretch forth Thy spotless hand to me, when I was sitting buried deep in the mud, and while I did not see Thee—for how could I have been able to do so or have any strength to look up at all when I was covered and choked by mud?—Thou didst grasp the hair of my head and forcibly drag me up from thence. I felt the pains and the sudden upward movement, and how I was going up, but I did not at all know who it was who brought me up, or held me to bring me up. But when Thou hadst brought me up and placed me on the ground, Thou gavest me over to Thy servant and disciple. I was yet wholly defiled, with my eyes, my ears, and my mouth still covered with mud, and therefore did 70 not see who Thou wast. I knew only that Thou art good and lovest men. So Thou broughtest me out of that deepest pit and mud, and when Thou hadst told me, "Hold on to this man, cleave to him and follow him, for he will lead you along and wash you," Thou didst inspire me with faith in him and didst depart. Where Thou didst go, I know not.

[§ 4. FOR HAVING FOUND THE FOUNTAINS OF
CLEANSING WATER.]

According to Thy command, most holy Master, I followed without turning aside from him whom Thou didst show me. 80 While he with much trouble led me to the fountains and the wells, he drew me in my blindness after him by the hand of faith, which Thou gavest me, and compelled me to follow him. While he could see clearly and lifted his feet and went over stones and through pits and obstacles, and leaped over them all, I was constantly stumbling and falling into them, and suffered many pains, many hurts and bruises. But while he cleansed and washed himself in every spring and fountain each successive hour, I passed most of them by because I did not see them. Had he not held me by the hand and made me stand close to the

fountain and guided the hands of my mind, I should not ever   90
have been able to find where the water was welling forth. But
while he showed me and let me wash myself, I often took into
my hands not only the pure water, but the clay and the mud beside the spring and so befouled my face. Often as I groped for
the spring in order to find the water I scratched the earth and
stirred up the dust and, since I could not see at all, I bathed my
face with mud as though it were water, and thought that I was
washing it perfectly clean.

[§ 5. FOR HAVING ESCAPED DISCOURAGEMENT.]

But how can I tell of all the violence and constraint I suffered thereby? It was not only thence, but also from those who   100
were frequently protesting and insinuating day by day as they
said, "Why do you waste your effort, and follow this fraud and
deceiver? It is vain and useless to expect to recover your sight! It
is no longer possible! Why do you follow him, and hurt your
feet so that they bleed? Why not rather approach some merciful
man, who will urge you to rest, to take food, and take good care
of yourself? It is impossible for you to rid yourself of this lepro-
sy of soul, or ever to recover your sight at this time. Where does
this fraud come from, who now claims to work miracles, and   110
promises you things that are impossible for any man of the present generation? Woe is you, not only because you lose the care
that is given you by compassionate people who love Christ and
their brethren, but because you also endure the hurts and
bruises to which you expose yourself because of false expecta-
tions! Most surely you will fail to obtain the things which this
mountebank and deceiver promises you! Can he do anything
whatever? Are you trying to arrive at conclusions without our
help, or to think on your own? How? Do we not all see? Are we
blind, as that man tells you in his error? We all indeed see; do   120
not let yourself be deceived, there is no other vision better than
ours" (cf. Jn. 9:40–41). But from all these men who were truly
mountebanks and deceivers, who offer their neighbor a drink of
speedy destruction (cf. Hab. 2:15), Thou the merciful and compassionate One didst deliver me through the faith and hope
Thou didst grant me, through which also Thou gavest me

371

strength to endure the aforesaid troubles and many others as well.

[§ 6. FOR THE FIRST MYSTIC GRACES.]

But in all these things I endured without ceasing though I fouled myself in the delusion that I was bathed day by day and thought I was washed clean, as Thy apostle and disciple taught me. Once when I was on my way and running to the fountain, Thou who hadst formerly drawn me up from the mud didst meet me on the way again. Then for the first time Thou didst flash around my feeble eyes with the undefiled splendor of Thy countenance. Even the light that I thought I had (cf. Lk. 8:18) I lost, being unable to recognize Thee. How would I have been able, without the strength to see the splendor of Thy countenance, or even to know of it or understand it, let alone see Thee, or know who Thou art? From thenceforth I stood by the fountain, and Thou who art without pride didst not disdain frequently to come down: Thou camest to me and laidest hold of my head and so didst dip it into the waters and so madest me see more clearly the light of Thy countenance (cf. Ps. 4:7, 89:16). Yet at once Thou didst fly away, without granting me to know who Thou wast, who wast doing this, or whence Thou camest or whence Thou wast going, for Thou hadst not yet granted this to me. Thus as Thou camest for a time and wentest away Thou didst gradually appear to me more fully; Thou didst pour the water on me and grantedst me to see more plainly and gavest me more light.

[§ 7. FOR THE DIVINE LUMINOSITY OF THE CLEANSING WATERS.]

For a long time Thou didst continue thus, and didst vouchsafe me to see an awesome thing and mystery. Thou hadst come to me and didst seem to me to be washing me in the waters and pouring them upon me and dipping me into them many times. I saw the lightnings that were flashing about me and the rays of Thy countenance mingled with the waters, and I was struck with amazement as I saw that I was being washed with luminous water. I knew not whence it came, or who supplied it; I merely rejoiced as I was being washed and grew in faith. My hope took wings and flew as high as heaven. But as for those deceivers, who had suggested to me the words of deceit and false-hood, I hated them exceedingly, I had pity on their error. I did not seek them at all, either for visits or conversation; rather I avoided the damage of even seeing them. As for my fellow-worker and my helper—Thy holy disciple and apostle—I rever-enced him as Thee who hast created me. I honored and loved him with my soul. Day and night I fell at his feet and asked him, "If you can do anything, help me" *(cf. Mk. 9:22)* for I had confi-dence that whatever he would, he was able to do before Thee.

[§ 8. FOR A RAPTURE INTO GLORY.]

When I had thus continued for a long time in Thy grace, I saw another awesome mystery. For as Thou didst return into heaven Thou didst take me and bring me with Thee. "Whether in the body or out of the body I do not know" *(2 Cor. 12:2).* Thou alone knowest, for this was Thy doing! But when I had spent an hour with Thee above, struck with wonder at the greatness of the glory—what it was, or whose it was, I know not—and astounded at the measureless height, I was totally awe-struck. Again Thou didst leave me alone upon the earth, on which I had stood before, and I was found lamenting and as-tounded at my wretchedness. Then when I had not been long below, Thou didst vouchsafe to show me Thy face in the heav-ens above, as if they were rent apart *(cf. Acts 7:56).* It was a light like a sun without form. And who Thou wert, still Thou didst not grant me to know. How could I have known Thee when Thou didst not speak to me? But Thou didst at once conceal Thyself, and I went about seeking Thee whom I did not know, and I longed to see Thy form and consciously to know who Thou wert. Therefore I continually wept because of the great vehemence and the fire of my love for Thee. I knew not who Thou art, who has brought me forth out of nothing into be-ing and taken me out of the mud, and done to me all the things that I had said.

[§ 9. FOR GOD'S COMING TO GLORIFY HIM.]

Though Thou thus didst often silently appear to me, hid-den so that I could not see Thee at all, yet I saw Thy lightning flashes and the brightness of Thy countenance, as aforetime in the waters. Again and again they encompassed me, but I was un-

160

170

180

190

able to seize hold of them; so I was mindful of how I had seen Thee on high. In my folly I suspected that it was another and so I sought with tears that I might see Thee again. Thus, when I was in great sorrow and affliction and distress *(cf. Rom. 2:9, 8:35)* I was overwhelmed. I forgot myself and the whole world and the things in the world *(cf. 1 John 2:15)* and thought not of a shadow nor anything else that existed or anything visible whatever. Thou who art invisible to all, beyond touch of comprehension, didst appear to me, and it seemed to me as though Thou wast cleansing my mind and increasing its vision, permitting me to see Thy glory even more. It was as if Thou Thyself didst 200 grow and shine yet more brightly. As the darkness vanished I perceived Thee swiftly drawing near as a moon rushing through the clouds. Thy coming was like as when we see the moon appearing and the clouds, as it were, walking over the sky. We see the moon and it seems to move at great speed, though it does not rush more quickly than its usual pace or change its original course. Thus, O Master, Thou who art unmoved didst seem to come, and didst appear to become greater and to take form, even though Thou are beyond all change and the limitation of form.

[§ 10. FOR THE RESPLENDENCE OF THE VISION OF GOD.]

When a blind man gradually recovers his sight and notices the appearance of a man and bit by bit ascertains what he is *(cf.* 210 *Mk. 8:24–25),* it is not the features that undergo transformation or take a new shape. Rather, as the vision of that man's eyes becomes clearer, he sees his features. It is as though they wholly imprint themselves on his vision and penetrate through it, impressing and engraving themselves, as on a tablet, on the mind and the memory of the soul. Even so Thou Thyself becamest visible when Thou, by the clear light of the Holy Ghost, hadst entirely cleansed my mind. As through Him I saw more clearly 220 and distinctly, Thou didst seem to me to come forth and shine more brightly, and didst grant me to see the outline of Thy form beyond shape. At that time Thou tookest me out of the world—I might even say, out of the body, but Thou didst not grant me to know this exactly *(cf. 2 Cor. 12:2–3).* Thou didst shine yet more brightly and it seemed that I saw Thee clearly in Thy entirety. When I said, "O Master, who art Thou?" then, for the first time

Thou didst grant me, the prodigal, to hear Thy voice. How gently didst Thou speak to me, who was beside myself, in awe and trembling, and somehow thought within myself saying, "What is that glory, and what is the meaning of the greatness of this brightness? How and whence have I been found worthy of such great blessings?" Thou saidest, "I am God who have become man for your sake. Because you have sought me with all your soul, behold, from now on you will be My brother (cf. Mt. 12:50; Mk. 3:35; Lk. 8:21), My fellow heir (cf. Rom. 8:17), and My friend (cf. Jn. 15:14–15)." Furthermore, as I was struck with amazement and my soul was all spent, and my strength completely gone, I answered, "Who am I, or what have I, wretched and miserable man, done, O Master, that Thou shouldest consider me worthy of such blessings and make me a partaker and fellow-heir of such glory?" I thought that this glory and this joy were beyond understanding; then Thou again, the Master, didst speak as a friend conversing with his friend, and didst say to me through Thy Spirit, which spoke in me (cf. Rom. 8:11; Mt. 10:20), "I have given you these things, and will continue to give them, solely for your intention, your will, and your faith. Whatever else have you ever had as your own? I brought you into the world naked (cf. Job 1:21)—for what could I have given you in exchange for these things? For unless you are released from the flesh you will not see that which is perfect, nor will you ever be able to enjoy it in full." When I had said, "What is greater or more resplendent than this? It is enough for me to be in this state even after death!" Thou didst say, "You are indeed too fainthearted to be contented with this. Compared with the blessings to come, this is like a description of heaven on paper held in the hand; for so the extent that this would be inferior to the reality, the glory that will be revealed (Rom. 8:18) is incomparably greater than that which you have now seen."

230

240

250

[§ 11. FOR A VISION BEFORE THE ICON OF THE THEOTOKOS.]

After these words Thou wast silent. Bit by bit, O sweet and good Master, Thou wast hidden from my eyes; whether I moved away from Thee or Thou didst depart from me, I know not. Again I returned wholly into myself, whence I thought I had come out, and entered into my former dwelling [i.e., the body].

260   At the memory of the beauty of Thy glory and of Thy words, as I walked about, sat down, ate, drank, and prayed, I wept and lived in an unutterable joy, because I had known Thee, the Maker of all things. How could I have failed to rejoice? Yet I again fell into sorrow and so I longed to see Thee again, I went off to reverence the spotless ikon of her who bore Thee. As I fell before it, before I rose up, Thou Thyself didst appear to me within my poor heart, as though Thou hadst transformed it into light;

270   and then I knew that I have Thee consciously within me. From then onwards I loved Thee, not by recollection of Thee and that which surrounds Thee, nor for the memory of such things, but I in very truth believed that I had Thee, substantial love, within me. For Thou, O God, truly art love *(1 John 4:8, 16)*.

[§ 12. FOR TRIALS AND FOR PROGRESS.]

    It is in faith that hope is planted, and in this soil it is watered by penitence and tears; then, as Thy light shines on it, it takes root and grows well. Then Thou Thyself, O good Craftsman and Creator, coming with the knife of trials—that is, humility—takest away the superfluous shoots of thoughts that rise high in the air. On faith alone, as on the sole root of a tree, Thou

280   didst graft Thy holy love *(cf. Jn. 15:1f.; Rom. 11:17ff.)*. As I see it growing day by day and continually instructing me Thou thereby both teachest and enlightenest me, and I live in joy, as though I have passed above all faith and hope, even as Paul proclaims and says, "Who hopes for what he sees?" *(Rom. 8:24)*. For if I possess Thee, what more do I hope for?

[§ 13. FOR THE WARNING TO PERSEVERE WITHOUT FAIL.]

    Again, O Master, Thou didst say, "Listen! As you see the sun reflected in the water, but do not see the sun itself, especially when you bend over to see it, so think of what happens in your case. Take care and endeavor constantly to see Me within you clearly and distinctly, as you see the sun in pure water.

290   Then you will be granted thus to see Me, as I have told you, even after death. If not, the whole course of your works, your toils, and your words will be of no avail to you; nay, rather, they will avail to greater condemnation and obtain for you more affliction, since, as your hear, 'mighty men will be mightily tested'

(Wis. 6:6). For him who was born poor poverty is no cause for shame, nor is its sorrow as great, as for one who has been rich and honored and exalted *(cf. Ps. 37:20)* in rank, and been a friend of the earthly monarch. For such a man has lost all these things and been brought down to complete destitution—even though the case is not the same in earthly and visible affairs as in the spiritual and invisible realities. Those who for some reason have fallen out of the favor and service of the earthly monarch may continue to own property and to enjoy it and live. But if one falls away from My love and friendship, he cannot live at all, for I am his life *(cf. Jn. 11:25, 14:6).* At once he is stripped of all things and is handed over to both his enemies and Mine as a prisoner. Once they seize him they will attack him the more savagely because of the affection and love that he once showed me and punish him as an object of derision and contempt."

[§ 14. FINAL HUMBLE PRAYER.]

Indeed, O all-holy King, I believe that it is so, and I put my trust in Thee, O my God, and fall down before Thee and implore Thee, preserve me, the unworthy sinner to whom Thou showedst mercy, and the plant of Thy love, which Thou didst graft into the tree of my hope, strengthen it by Thy power, that it be not shaken by the winds, nor broken by the tempests, nor uprooted by any enemy. Let it not be burnt up by the fire of negligence, nor be dried up by slackness and dissipation, nor be totally destroyed by vainglory. For Thou, who hast granted me this and worked this in me, knowest that for this reason I have no help from any man, since Thou hast physically taken away my fellow-worker and helper, who was Thy apostle, even as Thou hast willed it. Thou knowest my weakness; Thou understandest my misery and my complete inability to do anything. Do thou therefore have compassion on me even more from henceforth, O Lord who art rich in compassion. With my heart I fall before Thee, that Thou, who hast done me so many benefits, abandon me not to my will, but in Thy love stablish my soul and make Thy love take deep root in me, that in accordance with Thy holy, unspotted, and infallible promise Thou mayest be in me and I may be in Thee *(Jn. 14:20)* and I may be protected by Thy love and may protect and guard it in me. In that love Thou dost look on me, O Master, and grant me to see Thee

340 through it even now dimly, as in a mirror, as Thou hast said it *(1 Cor. 13:12)*. But hereafter in all love may I see Thee, who art love and hast deigned to be so called *(1 John 4:8, 16)*, for all thanksgiving, power, honor, and adoration are due to Thee, the Father, the Son, and the Holy Ghost, now and ever, and to unending ages of ages. Amen.

INDEX TO INTRODUCTION
AND NOTES

379

INDEX

INDEX

Koder, J., 26.
Krivochéine, Basil, 37, 364.

Laity, 5, 23.
Lauds, see *Orthros.*
Le Maitre, J., 22.
Le Quien, P. Michael, O.P., 12.
Lent, 167, 278.
Light, 7, 17, 20, 23, 24, 27–28, 29, 30, 35; children of, 23; Christ as, 24–25, 27–28, 29, 36; immaterial, 7; life in, 27; Trinity as, 36.
Liturgy, see also Offices, monastic; 2, 15, 200, 278; Eucharistic, 86, 200, 278.
Logos, 22, 33; created, 22.
Lot-Borodine, M., 31.
Love, see Charity.
Luke, 18:13, 7, 28.

Macarius, 16.
Macarius, Psuedo-, 4, 13.
Macedonian Dynasty, 6.
Magistri, 245.
Maloney, George A., S.J., 8, 23.
Man, 19, 20, 21, 22, 23, 30, 36, 259; creation of, 20; divinization of, 10, 17, 35, 36; known by God in Logos, 33; loved by God, 34; modern, 36; rational powers of, 1, 36; restoration of, 20.
Mark the Hermit, 4, 6, 13, 16, 244.
Mary, 38.
Matins, see *Orthros.*
Matthew, 25:18, 3; 25:42, 33.
Maximian, Emperor, 167.
Maximus the Confessor, 21, 22.
Mercy, Works of, 16.
Mersalians, 11, 12, 16.
Michael Psellos, 1.
Meyendorff, John, 38.
Miquel, P., 12.
Monasticism, Eastern, 1, 2, 94; Rules, 78.
Monks, 2, 5, 6, 8, 9, 10, 12, 15, 16, 19, 21, 33, 34, 76, 146, 275, 282, 283; authorized to absolve sins, 9, 12; categories of, 239; daily communion of, 86; presence, true apostolate of, 33–34; rebellious, 9, 347; worldly, 8.
Morbey, Andrew, 38.
Moses, 34.

Mysticism, see also Theology, mystical; 1, 2, 4, 5, 7, 9, 10, 11, 15, 16, 18, 19, 20, 22, 24, 25, 26, 27, 36, 259; Trinitarian, 35–36.

Nepsis, see Sobriety, Vigilance.
New Testament, see also Gospel; 12.
Nilus, Saint, 4.
Numbers, 14:10, 34.

Obedience, 8.
Offices, monastic, see also Compline, *Orthros,* Prime, Vespers; 1, 75, 76, 78, 200, 274–275, 276, 282, 283, 323; midnight, 75, 283.
Orders, Sacrament of, 8, 9, 10, 12, 44.
Origen, 4.
Orthodox Church, 37, 200, 223, 274.
Orthodoxy, Sunday of, 167.
Orthros, 9, 15, 274–275, 323.
Ottawa, 38.

Paloukiton, 13.
Paphlagonia, 5.
Paramelle, Joseph, S.J., 37.
Passions, 22, 32.
Paul, Saint, 20, 23, 36; spurious Acts of, 364.
Penance, 12, 17, 18, 20; sacrament of, 10, 12, 20.
Perfection, 21, 33.
Peter, Abbot of Stoudion, 8.
Peter, Saint, 17.
Philosophy, 2, 21; nominalist, 1.
Philoteus of Sinai, 4, 13.
Philoxenos of Mabboug, 16.
Photius, 1.
Pneumatomachoi, 16.
Possession, Demonic, 16.
Poverty, 2.
Praxis, see also Asceticism; 15, 21–22, 35.
Prayer, see also Compline, Liturgy, Office, monastic, *Orthros,* Vespers; 1, 2, 4, 5, 6, 7, 16, 21, 22, 25, 26, 27, 31, 34, 75, 200; constant, 2; private, 75, 200, 282, 283.
Predestination, 20.
Priests, 8, 11, 12, 44, 251; Ordination, 8, 9, 44.
Prime, 275.
Psalms, 23:5, 259; 31:5, 31; 51, passim, 93.

381

INDEX

Psalter, 37, 275; translation of, 37.
Pseudo-Marcarius, 4, 13.
Purification, 2, 22, 28, 30, 31, 35.
Purity of Heart, 2, 18, 19, 22, 32.

Quinisext Council, 223.

Reason, 1, 36.
Recollection, 34.
Renunciation, 16.
Repentance, 2, 9, 16, 17, 18, 23, 25, 30, 35.
Revelation, 1, 19.
Romanos the Melodus, Saint, 26.
Romans, 6:9, 18.
Rules, Monastic, 78.

Sacraments, see also Baptism, Eucharist, Orders, Penance; 10.
Saints, 26, 275.
Saint Mamas, Monastery of, 8, 14, 15, 19, 32, 41, 278, 282.
Saint Marina, Monastery of, 13, 14, 23.
Samaria, 17.
Scholasticism, Byzantine, 1, 19.
Scott, Enid, 38.
Scripture, see also Gospel, New Testament; 3, 4, 10, 11, 16, 17, 19, 20, 37, 38; versions used, 37.
Self-Love, 22, 33, 35.
Semantron, 281.
Septuagint, 37.
Sergios, 13.
Shadow, 27.
Sight, Spiritual, 7, 22.
Sin, see also Absolution, Penance; 12, 16, 20, 22, 30, 32, 36; acknowledgement of, 31; remission of, 31; sorrow for *(penthos)*, 16, 30.
Sisinnios, 9.
Sobriety *(Nepsis)*, 32.
Solitude, 20.
Son (God), see also Jesus Christ, Logos; 10, 17, 18, 36; conscious of Father, 17, 18.
Spiritual Father, see also Symeon the Studite; 5, 6, 7, 8, 9, 26, 27, 198, 278; obedience to, 8.
Spiritual Life, 13, 16.
Spirituality, Byzantine, 4, 16, 19, 30, 31, 177.
Spirituality, Western, 177.
Steidle, B., O.S.B., 31.

Stephen of Nicomedia, 2, 5, 9, 10, 19, 20, 24; objections to Symeon's theology, 9–11.
Stethatos, Nicetas, 5, 6, 8, 9, 13, 14, 20, 26, 198, 243.
Stoudion Monastery, 6, 7, 8, 14, 29, 198, 199, 244.
Symeon the New Theologian, abbot of St. Mamas, 5, 8–10, 14, 19, 32, 41, 44, 251; apophatic approach, 1, 11, 19, 36; appeal to own experiences, 2, 4, 9, 22; attitude to writings, 14; audience of, 10, 13, 15, 19, 23, 28, 33; birth, 5; charismatic approach, 9, 10; conflicts with hierarchy, 12; death, 5, 13, 23; doctrine on mysticism, 20; education, 6; entry into Stoudion, 7, 28, 198; exiled, 10–13, 15, 19, 21; exile lifted, 13; expelled from Stoudion, 8; "George," pseudonym, 6, 24, 29, 243; knowledge of Scripture, 4; language of, 11, 15; life, 5–13; love for Christ, 24, 26, 29; main themes, 27–36; mystical experiences, 2, 5, 7, 10, 22, 23, 24, 25, 26, 28–30, 35, 36, 198; opposition to, 9–10, 12; ordained a priest, 8, 44, 251; oral teaching, 3, 5; parentage, 6; poetics, 26; rebellion against, 9, 19, 347; reformer, 2; refuses episcopacy, 13; second conversion, 7; spirituality of, 30, 31, 34; strictness of, 347; sufferings of, 26; theology of, 10, 15, 20; times, 1; title of "New Theologian", 4–5, 37; tonsured, 8; Trinitarian doctrine, 20; visions of, 7, 18, 24–25, 26, 28–30, 198.
Symeon the New Theologian, writings of, 2, 5, 12, 13–27, 37; *De Confessione*, 12; *Discourses*, 3, 5, 6, 7, 9, 14–19, 20, 22, 23, 24, 25, 26, 27, 28, 30, 32, 33, 34, 35, 36; *Ethical Treatises*, 17, 19; *Hymns of Divine Love*, 8, 10, 11, 15, 19, 23–27, 28, 33, 36; Letters, 19, 26; Office in honor of Symeon the Studite, 26; Polemical works, 19; *Practical, Gnostic and Theological Chapters*, 21–23, 31; *Thanksgivings*, 26; *Theological Treatises*, 19–20, 24.

INDEX

Symeon the Studite, 5, 6, 7, 8, 26, 27, 29, 198, 239, 244; death of, 27, 239; Office in honor of, 26.

Synaxarion, 275.

Syria, 13, 223.

Tears, Gift of, 7, 9, 18, 29, 30–31, 34, 314; and Baptism in the Spirit, 30; necessity of, 30.

Temptation, 8.

Theodore Studite, Saint, 1, 275.

Theodore Tiron, Saint, 167.

Theology, Eastern Christian, 4, 5; Mystical, 1, 2, 9, 11, 16, 19; Positive, 11; Speculative, 1, 2, 9, 20; True, 19, 20, 22.

Theophana, Mother of Symeon, 6.

Trinity, 10, 16, 18, 19, 22, 24, 35–36; indwelling, 4, 5, 10, 11, 12, 13, 16, 18, 22, 23, 24, 35, 36; interaction of hypostases, 24; Symeon's doctrine on, 20; unity of, 19, 20, 24, 27.

Trisagion, 29, 200.

Vespers, 275, 281.

Vigilance (Nepsis), 30.

Virtues, 16, 21, 22, 23.

Visions, 18, 24–25, 26, 28–30, 198.

Wisdom, 2, 21.

Word, 22, 24, 32.

Worship, 1.

INDEX TO TEXT

INDEX

in man, 54, 55, 58, 59, 144, 164,
182, 187, 195, 263, 349, 350, 353,
356, 363, 376, 377; members of,
154, 171, 240, 361; mind of, 194,
297, 340, 349, 353; pleasing of, 51;
poverty of, 151, 152, 360; presence
of, 58, 121, 245, 365; promises of,
187; reign of, 42, 292; as Savior, 43,
58, 67, 85, 136, 158, 205, 207, 231,
232, 242, 260, 263, 295, 296, 336;
seal of, 50–51, 53, 54–55; second
coming of, 63, 90, 147; seeing of,
44, 49, 58–59, 120, 162, 185, 233,
251, 332, 333; servants of, 60, 62,
64, 162, 173, 196, 214, 234, 290, 356;
serving of, 44, 62, 105, 113, 150,
152, 153, 162, 278; sheep of, 221,
222, 225, 285, 301, 304, 313, 348;
soldiers of, 63, 68; as source, 231;
suffering of, 43, 45, 127, 128, 158,
182, 207, 291, 292, 311; as Sun, 168,
259, 303, 333; as truth, 41, 303;
union with, 144, 182, 184, 197, 205,
206, 242, 350; as way, 131, 142, 303,
342; way to, 47–59; worship of, 69.
Church, 93, 120, 163, 167, 224, 345;
and heresy, 335; of Israel, 220; and
martyrdom, 45; and monks, 62,
75–76, 275, 276; Orthodox, 167,
200, 223, 274.
Colossians, 1:5, 147; 1:17, 219; 1:18,
219; 1:24, 218; 1:26, 196, 207; 1:28,
186; 2:3, 53, 225, 316; 2:14, 182;
2:19, 219; 3:1, 134, 207; 3:2, 55; 3:3,
127; 3:5, 147, 263; 3:8, 117; 3:9, 68,
265, 274; 3:10, 274; 3:11, 350; 3:12,
148, 171.
Commandments, of Christ, 42, 45, 48,
51, 62, 69, 104, 111, 134, 135, 136,
151, 155, 160, 184, 185, 187, 196,
207, 225, 229, 230, 239, 250, 252,
262, 263, 264, 293, 294, 309, 329,
330, 332, 342, 369, 370; of God, 52,
57, 58, 63, 64, 66, 68, 79, 93, 94, 97,
100, 101, 102, 106, 123, 127, 130,
131, 136, 137, 138, 147, 156, 165,
172, 173, 174, 179, 185, 189, 197,
204, 208, 217, 224, 247, 250, 262,
265, 279, 284, 286, 291, 302, 303,
311, 315, 330, 332, 337, 350; and
Holy Spirit, 236, 244; least of,
284–294; of Lord, 83, 137, 151, 186,
219, 255, 289, 291; practice of, 54,

148, 151, 164, 165, 185, 186, 188,
189, 197, 248, 268, 288, 292, 295,
312, 333, 335.
Compassion, 53, 54, 55, 66, 139, 144,
148, 199, 200, 247, 331, 333; of God,
99, 171, 243, 249, 256, 271, 324, 348,
363, 370, 377.
Compunction, 45, 159, 267; and
monks, 73–74, 221, 223, 305; and
penitence, 70–89, 132, 282, 286,
325; and tears, 46, 47, 73, 79, 82,
87, 160, 168, 175, 188, 313, 314, 318,
321, 322, 323, 330, 335; and will,
71, 72.
Conscience, 78, 213, 244, 245, 246, 252,
282, 304, 338, 366.
Consolation, 54, 57, 177, 360.
Constantine V, 310.
Constantinople, 199, 223, 243.
Contemplation, 51, 159, 183, 192, 196,
198, 202, 204–208, 233, 262, 268,
303, 306, 336, 361, 367, 368; of
Christ, 58, 144; of God, 48, 56, 127,
146, 191, 193, 265, 312, 349, 360.
Contrition, 48, 175, 202, 323; of heart,
48, 55, 74, 79, 87, 223, 323, 324;
practice of, 85–86; of soul, 46, 73,
80–82, 86; and tears, 80–82, 86, 106.
1 Corinthians, 1:20, 316; 1:27, 50, 352;
1:30, 303, 331; 2:6, 298, 353; 2:9, 81,
162, 190, 249, 253, 366; 2:10, 273;
2:12, 125; 2:13, 261; 2:16, 194, 263,
297, 340, 349; 3:6, 232; 3:16, 321;
3:18, 300; 3:39, 143; 4:3, 216, 283,
333; 4:5, 228; 4:6, 191, 4:8, 209; 4:11,
175; 4:21, 223; 5:5, 271; 5:8, 304,
314; 6:9, 104, 289, 303; 6:15, 154,
361; 6:18, 90; 6:19, 287, 302, 366;
7:29, 110; 7:31, 94; 7:40, 353; 8:8,
176; 9:2, 45; 9:22, 233, 247; 9:24, 44;
9:25, 284; 10:7, 179; 10:10, 174;
10:11, 312; 10:31, 69; 11:1, 143;
11:16, 302; 11:28, 86, 330; 11:29, 86;
11:31, 71; 12:3, 183; 12:8, 335; 12:11,
335; 12:12, 218; 12:27, 154, 219;
13:3, 297; 13:4, 174; 13:8, 237; 13:11,
189; 13:12, 253, 378; 13:14, 174;
14:30, 71; 15:28, 363; 15:33, 47, 277;
15:44, 189; 15:45, 68; 15:47, 274;
15:48, 274; 15:49, 274, 306; 15:50,
148, 307; 15:52, 88, 128; 15:53, 266.
2 Corinthians, 1:3, 125; 1:5, 182; 1:9,
325; 1:12, 214; 1:14, 45; 2:9, 361; 3:1,

INDEX

INDEX

INDEX

Gregory of Nyssa, 107.
Gregory the Wonder Worker, 107.

Habakkuk, 2:15, 371.
Heart, and Christ, 291, 376, 377;
contrition of, 48, 55, 74, 79, 87,
223, 323, 324; desire in, 44, 111,
112, 155, 156, 160, 174, 206, 270,
286; and God, 82, 272, 282, 287,
367; and grace, 217, 336; hardness
of, 71, 72, 73, 79, 81, 96, 97, 102,
103, 122, 168, 321; and Holy Spirit,
54, 336; humility of, 48, 55, 65,
72–73, 80, 115, 122, 188, 200, 291,
305, 315; joy in, 181, 257, 258, 330,
364; and light, 43, 201, 287, 353;
and meditation, 62, 63, 75; purity
of, 53, 55, 57, 58, 83, 85, 88, 124,
148, 160, 197, 198, 202, 218, 236,
238, 332, 345, 359; and sin, 66, 85,
86, 91, 95, 106, 110, 155, 160, 169,
229, 283, 304, 323, 326; troubled,
61, 70, 84, 85, 199, 201, 215, 251,
268, 290, 320.
Heaven, 194; Kingdom of, 41, 42, 45,
48, 51, 52, 53, 55, 58, 61, 83, 87, 90,
103, 108, 118, 122, 129, 131, 135,
145, 146, 152, 158, 161, 172, 187,
197, 223, 263, 280, 285, 289, 292,
293, 294, 315, 324, 326–327, 330,
333, 337, 342, 345, 349, 354, 356,
366; path to, 42, 45, 49, 136, 142,
248–249.
Hebrews, 1:3, 50, 236; 1:14, 220; 2:2,
102, 367; 2:3, 118, 296; 2:9, 100, 182;
2:11, 154; 2:14, 101; 2:17, 338; 3:1,
145; 4:12, 66, 68, 194; 4:13, 74, 106,
155, 315; 4:15, 50, 101, 182, 249,
309, 338; 5:4, 303; 5:14, 67; 6:1, 163,
345; 6:4, 339, 357; 6:20, 178; 7:26,
182; 9:24, 302; 9:26, 128; 10:1, 297;
10:19, 312; 10:24, 172; 11:9, 123,
233; 11:13, 178; 11:38, 123, 136, 154,
248; 12:12, 114; 12:14, 91, 158, 315;
12:29, 225, 339; 13:5, 99; 13:9, 88;
13:21, 151.
Hell, 45, 47, 49, 50, 58, 64, 92, 96, 99,
100, 115, 117, 120, 130, 131, 132,
141, 174, 215, 256, 257, 320.
Heresy, 100, 232, 308–317, 335, 336.
Holiness, 162–166, 351.
Holy Spirit, 85, 154, 180, 242, 259,
307, 378; and blasphemy, 335–338;

and Christ, 59, 129, 145, 183, 187,
308, 311, 327, 332, 333, 342, 349,
353, 375; comfort of, 158, 160–161;
and enlightenment, 52, 53, 148,
217, 230, 232, 248, 261, 264, 273,
297, 304, 305, 342, 367; gifts of, 52,
54, 80, 149, 160, 163, 166, 181, 217,
252, 261, 286, 313, 335; and grace,
50, 64, 102, 122, 124, 133, 148, 150,
164, 188, 189, 217, 245, 247, 283,
311, 336, 337, 338, 341, 354;
guidance of, 69, 335; and
inspiration, 150, 247, 278; and
knowledge, 58, 336, 342, 358; and
life, 49, 121, 159, 296, 297; light of,
122, 159, 174, 184, 248, 300, 336,
337, 340–341, 374; in man, 88, 163,
201, 264, 287, 349, 366, 367, 368;
and purification, 46, 146, 249, 266,
302, 338; received (partaking of),
82, 93, 119, 122, 125, 126, 128, 143,
149, 158, 164, 184, 187, 195, 198,
218, 236, 252, 287, 302, 304, 313,
325, 327, 335, 337, 339–346, 353,
357, 360; seal of, 50, 54; speaking
of, 351, 375; and wisdom, 79, 253;
work of, 198–203, 204, 244, 313,
335, 336.
Hope, and charity, 42, 45; in Christ,
50, 228, 231, 232, 238, 240, 371, 372,
377; in God, 155, 187, 246, 286; for
heaven, 354, 372; for mercy, 324.
Humility, 52, 56–57, 123, 148, 159,
313, 345; and Christ, 292–293, 376;
and divinity, 234; of heart, 48, 55,
65, 72–73, 80, 115, 122, 188, 200,
291, 315; and Holy Spirit, 53;
lacking, 243; and monks, 65, 68, 75,
79, 80, 112, 114, 115, 126, 177, 188,
214, 217, 218, 221, 222, 223, 234,
278, 281, 305; and sin, 84, 96, 98,
105, 271; of soul, 87, 188, 200, 202,
214, 236, 239, 267, 330; of spirit, 55,
83, 104, 118, 175, 259.

Ignatius, 107.
Illumination, 198, 368–378.
Incarnation, 45, 50, 101, 134, 153, 154,
301, 336, 362, 368.
Isaac, 93.
Isaiah, 2:3, 354; 5:20, 345; 5:21, 345;
6:9, 218; 8:18, 45; 8:21, 229; 8:22,
229; 9:2, 54, 357; 13:13, 102; 14:12,

INDEX

INDEX

393

INDEX

forgiveness of, 44, 174, 181, 206, 281, 291, 299, 302, 335, 341, 361, 367; and light, 299; and monks, 61, 66, 77, 78, 80, 113–115, 175, 288–289; and pain, 254–255; pardon of, 96, 323, 347; purification of, 54, 197; repentance, 69, 84, 86, 90, 91, 96, 97, 98, 99, 105, 111, 115, 117, 118, 131, 132, 143, 169, 174, 187, 202, 252, 289, 298, 302, 320, 331.

Sion, 42.

Sirach, 1:2, 93; 3:30, 331; 15:3, 166; 29:9, 349; 30:37, 276; 51:26, 167.

Sloth, 47, 94, 102, 108, 112, 117, 126, 317.

Sodom, 93, 247.

Solomon, 355.

The Son, 72, 98, 125, 128, 133, 154, 184, 187, 188, 195, 197, 221, 242, 306, 307, 308, 309, 311, 313, 341, 342, 343, 344, 345, 349, 350, 351, 356, 378.

Soul, cf. also Light; and body (flesh), 47, 50, 58, 68, 151, 159, 168, 174, 178, 180, 181, 195, 205, 215, 229, 249, 267–273; care of, 221–222; Christ in, 182; contrition of, 46, 73, 80–82, 86; darkness of, 120, 122, 148, 248, 255, 265, 309, 339, 340, 341; and death, 50, 96, 129, 180, 250, 296; defiled, 51, 56, 88, 157, 159, 160, 174, 230, 313, 371; and ecstasy 56, 258; enemy of, 131, 132; enlightened, 86, 231; freed, 59, 191; God in, 190, 195; and grace, 150; growth of, 41, 87, 210, 218, 231; healing of, 168–169, 256–258, 357; joy in, 43, 48, 88, 120, 121, 146, 179, 200, 201, 205, 219, 236, 255, 258, 267, 272, 333, 375, 376; life of, 183; perfected, 181; and passions, 56, 91, 118, 148, 152, 159, 188, 194, 205, 222, 231, 236, 259, 270, 271, 272, 289, 365; purification of, 53, 54, 80–82, 86, 87–89, 90, 92, 124, 127, 152, 157, 159, 160, 174, 195, 205, 259, 299, 313, 327, 331, 343, 364–365; and sin, 61, 67, 80, 91, 157, 228, 229, 259, 279, 313, 320, 322; sorrow of, 52; states of, 267, 268, 271; and virtue, 219, 220.

Spirit, breaking of, 45; contrite-, 254; humility of, 55, 83, 104, 118, 175,

259; illumination of, 247–248; peace of, 173; poverty of, 51, 52, 53, 75, 330.

Spirituality, and fasting, 168–169; and guide, 231–237, 282, 283, 369–370; fullness of, 189–190; practices of, 41, 78–79, 119, 120.

Stephen the Younger, Saint, 310.

Stethatos, Nicetas, 198, 243.

Symeon the New Theologian, 41, 45, 60, 61, 91, 92, 96, 150, 173, 198, 204, 206, 207, 213, 226, 231, 238, 239, 243, 251, 259, 275, 337, 359, 364, 368; Apologia, 347–358; appointment as abbot, 41, 44–46; as "George," 243–245, 250–251.

Tarasius, 107.

Tears, 217, 308; and communion, 70, 71, 83, 85, 86, 87; and compassion, 139, 199, 200; and compunction, 46, 47, 73, 79, 82, 87, k60, 168, 175, 188, 313, 314, 318, 321, 322, 323, 330, 335; continual, 83–85, 86, 87, 103, 121, 223, 314, 317, 363; and contrition, 80–82, 86; and Holy Spirit, 336; necessity of, 314; of penitence, 58, 70–89, 91, 92, 99, 105, 108, 118, 154, 160, 174, 196–197, 200, 224, 282, 376; and purification, 53, 54, 58, 68, 70, 87, 224, 227, 252, 304, 313, 314, 315; and sin, 255, 259; and sorrow, 54, 215, 320, 331, 364.

Temptation, 136–139, 157, 158, 169, 218, 251, 315, 363.

Theodora, 105.

Theodore of Studios, Saint, 275.

Theodore Tiron, Saint, 167.

Theophylact, 227.

1 Thessalonians, 1:9, 301; 3:2, 221; 4:1, 222; 4:17, 88, 118, 189; 5:5, 298; 5:17, 83.

2 Thessalonians, 2:8, 230; 2:9, 101; 3:6, 224.

Timothy, 342.

1 Timothy, 1:9, 297; 1:14, 136; 1:17, 216, 368; 1:19, 185; 2:1, 73; 2:4, 277; 2:5, 216; 3:7, 142, 280; 3:8, 220; 3:9, 214; 3:15, 222; 4:6, 345; 4:7, 345; 4:8, 159, 290; 4:13, 171, 278; 4:14, 351; 5:8, 139; 6:7, 92, 155; 6:8, 57, 63, 325; 6:12, 62; 6:13, 184, 342; 6:15,

INDEX